EUROPEAN UNION ENVIRONMENTAL LAW

European Union Environmental Law

Law

An Introduction to Key Selected Issues

PETER G.G. DAVIES
University of Nottingham, UK

ASHGATE

Published by
Ashgate Publishing Limited
Gower House
Croft Road
Aldershot
Hants GU11 3HR
England

Ashgate Publishing Company
Suite 420
101 Cherry Street
Burlington, VT 05401-4405
USA

Ashgate website: http://www.ashgate.com

British Library Cataloguing in Publication Data
Davies, Peter G. G.
  European Union environmental law : an introduction to key
  selected issues. - (European business law library)
  1. Environmental law - European Union countries
  2. Environmental law, International
  I. Title
  341.7'62'094

Library of Congress Control Number: 2003113557

ISBN 1 85521 582 9

Printed in Great Britain by Antony Rowe Ltd, Chippenham, Wiltshire.

Contents

Preface and Acknowledgements

Environmental Law has undoubtedly become a key area of activity for the European Community. Much has been achieved over the last thirty years, but major challenges clearly lie ahead. Although no attempt has been made to offer comprehensive coverage of this rapidly growing area of the law, this book endeavours to introduce the student to some of the particularly important areas of debate and/or concern in EU Environmental Law. In this way, it is hoped that the reader will find the work to be an understandable platform from which to begin his/her appreciation of the subject. A select bibliography is provided at the end of each chapter to facilitate further research.

As all scholars of this subject are very well aware, the law is constantly changing and evolving. By the time any book is published, no doubt further developments will have already taken place. Such is the nature of legal developments in this area. It should however be noted that I have endeavoured to state the law as at 1 March 2003 when the manuscript was finalised and sent to the publishers. Accordingly, the work takes into account the coming into force of the Treaty of Nice on 1 February 2003.

Parts of the final chapter reflect work previously published in the *International and Comparative Law Quarterly* and in Cameron and Zillman (eds.), *Kyoto: From Principles to Practice*. Whilst I have had the chance to considerably update this work on climate change for this book, I would nevertheless wish to thank both the British Institute of International and Comparative Law and Kluwer Law International for their cooperation in this regard.

Many former and current colleagues provided advice and assistance throughout the writing of this book, and I am indebted to them all. Particular thanks are due to Geraint Howells, who asked me to participate in the series, and to Paolo Galizzi and Catherine Redgwell with whom I have over a number of years thoroughly enjoyed teaching the EC Environmental Law course on the LLM in Nottingham. Many thanks are also due to my family for their encouragement.

Special thanks are due to Jennie for her constant support and understanding. The book would simply not have seen the light of day without her tireless patience and encouragement. I owe a very special debt to her and our Ruddington family for their unstinting support and love.

Peter Davies
Nottingham

Abbreviations

AC	Appeal Cases
AJIL	American Journal of International Law
All ER	All England Law Reports
CLJ	Cambridge Law Journal
CMLR	Common Market Law Reports
CMLRev	Common Market Law Review
ECR	European Court Reports
EELR	European Environmental Law Review
ELJ	European Law Journal
ELRev	European Law Review
ENDS	Environmental Data Service
Env LR	Environmental Law Reports
EPL	Environmental Policy and Law
ICLQ	International and Comparative Law Quarterly
ILM	International Legal Materials
JEL	Journal of Environmental Law
LIEI	Legal Issues of European Integration
LQR	Law Quarterly Review
MLR	Modern Law Review
OJ	Official Journal
RECIEL	Review of European Community and International Environmental Law
WLR	Weekly Law Reports

| YEEL | Yearbook of European Environmental Law |
| YEL | Yearbook of European Law |

Table of Cases

Court of First Instance

Opinions

Cases Before National Courts

Chapter 1

The Community and
Environmental Competence

The development of an environmental policy must be regarded as one of the most notable achievements of the European Community. While action so far has certainly not proved adequate to halt the general decline in the state of the European environment, Community activity has contributed to certain positive developments in recent years including a significant reduction in sulphur dioxide emissions from industrial plants,[1] the phasing out of the use and production of ozone layer depleting substances, the decline in heavy metal environmental concentrations due to reductions in lead and mercury emissions, and the recovery of some of the Community's most polluted lakes and rivers as a result of improvements in water and sewage treatment.[2] Major challenges unquestionably lie ahead but significant measures have been adopted in a variety of fields, and no lawyer practising in the Community's Member States can now regard himself as competent in this field without a thorough appreciation of the intricacies of the Community's environmental legislation. The importance of the Community's environmental strategy has indeed been reflected in the fact that environmental protection has been identified by the European Court of Justice as being one of the Community's essential objectives.[3] In addition, the need to integrate environmental requirements into the definition and implementation of the Community's other policies and activities is now constitutionally recognised in the EC Treaty.[4]

Early Development of a Community Strategy on the Environment

Progress to date in developing a Community environmental policy is all the more remarkable when one bears in mind that no specific mention was made of the need to protect the environment in the treaty establishing the European Economic Community (the 1957 EEC Treaty).[5] In the aftermath of yet another war between the nations of Europe, the political priority of the original Member States was to secure

---

1   Sulphur dioxide emissions are major contributors to the acidification of lakes and forests.
2   European Environment Agency, *Environment in the European Union at the turn of the Century* (1999), and also COM (2001) 31.
3   Case 240/83 *ADBHU* [1985] ECR 531, para.13.
4   Article 6 EC.
5   Signed in March 1957; entered into force in January 1958.

peace and promote economic development by establishing a common market. Concern for the environment was certainly not a political priority, and in the period 1957-72 only a small number of Community measures could possibly be classified as environmental in nature. Examples include a directive relating to permissible sound levels and exhaust systems in motor vehicles,[6] a directive regulating the emission of pollutants from vehicles fitted with diesel engines,[7] and a directive concerning the classification, packaging and labelling of dangerous substances.[8] The primary object of such measures was to facilitate the functioning of the common market; any environmental purpose could only be regarded as incidental to this goal.[9]

The 1960s and early 1970s marked the advent of a period of raised environmental consciousness among the general public which served to fuel subsequent political developments.[10] At the Community level, the 1972 Paris Summit Meeting of the Community's Heads of State and Government undoubtedly provided the necessary impetus for the eventual development of a distinct Community policy on the environment. At this meeting the Heads of State and Government of the Member States endorsed the need to pay particular attention to the environment in the pursuit of continued economic expansion, and called on the Community to develop an environmental protection strategy.[11] Growing public concern had made Community action politically acceptable and desirable. But how could environmental aspirations be linked to the achievement of any of the Community objectives established in the 1957 EEC Treaty? The latter noted that the tasks of the Community included the promotion of *"the harmonious development of economic activities"* and *"a continuous and balanced expansion"*.[12] Recognising these objectives, the Council approved the Community's first Action Programme on the Environment in November 1973 noting that the promotion of these responsibilities

> *cannot now be imagined in the absence of an effective campaign to combat pollution and nuisances or of an improvement in the quality of life and the protection of the environment.*[13]

---

[6]   Directive 70/157 OJ 1970 L42/16.

[7]   Directive 72/306 OJ 1972 L190/1.

[8]   Directive 67/548 OJ 1967 L196/1.

[9]   These measures were adopted on the basis of Article 100 of the 1957 EEC Treaty with a view to approximating laws affecting the establishment of the common market.

[10]   Important steps were for example taken at the international level to begin to formulate a concerted strategy to prevent continued environmental deterioration; see United Nations Conference on the Human Environment 5-16 June 1972, (the 'Stockholm Conference') UN Document A/CONF.48/14/Rev.1.

[11]   Significantly, the Environment and Consumer Protection Service was established in 1973 within the European Commission and became a Directorate-General in 1981. That part of the Commission with responsibility for the environment is now known as DG Environment (issues relating to the environment and consumer protection were divided in 1989).

[12]   1957 EEC Treaty, Article 2.

[13]   Programme of Action of the European Communities on the Environment (OJ 1973 C112/1); this first programme covered the years 1973-76.

Attention therefore had to be paid not simply to the pursuit of economic growth, but also to the quality of that growth. But what of the precise legal base for environmental action? Bearing in mind the Community enjoys competence only in those areas in which it has been given treaty-based competence,[14] the lack of a specific and valid legal basis for a directive would be grounds for annulment of the measure by the Court of Justice on the premise that the measure was an illegal encroachment on the national competence of Member States. As no mention had been made of the environment in the 1957 EEC Treaty, surely any attempt to adopt measures with environmental objectives would be undermined? This proved not to be the case in reality. The Community's institutions were willing to base environmental legislation on either ex Article 100 (now Article 94 EC) or ex Article 235 (now Article 308 EC), or, more commonly, a combination of the two. This flexible application of the 1957 EEC Treaty ensured the early development of an environmental policy at the Community level.

Ex Article 100 (now Article 94 EC)

Ex Article 100 allowed for the adoption of directives to harmonise Member States' legislation and/or practice for the purposes of establishing and maintaining the common market.[15] Environmental legislation was therefore introduced utilising this article as its legal basis if it was necessary to harmonise national measures for common market purposes. A national measure prohibiting the sale of certain goods on environmental grounds, or a Member State's policy which places a financial burden on its own industry by insisting on compliance with pollution standards, necessarily impacts on free trade and competition. The adoption by the Community of a suitable harmonising environmental measure could therefore be justified on the grounds that the pursuit of an integrated market would be hindered by the continued application of diverse national environmental laws and policies. In effect, harmonising legislation was deemed necessary to ensure a level playing field throughout the Member States. Underlining its flexible approach to the interpretation of the Treaty, the Court of Justice accepted in *Commission* v *Italy* that environmental measures could indeed be adopted under ex Article 100 (now Article 94 EC) indicating that

> *[p]rovisions which are made necessary by considerations relating to the environment ... may be a burden upon the undertakings to which they apply and*

---

14 The first paragraph of Article 5 EC notes that "[t]he Community shall act within the limits of the powers conferred by it by this Treaty and of the objectives assigned to it therein".

15 Ex Article 100 (Article 94) prior to the Single European Act noted:

The Council shall, acting unanimously on a proposal from the Commission, issue directives for the approximation of such provisions laid down by law, regulation or administrative action in Member States as directly affect the establishment, or functioning of the common market.

if there is no harmonisation of national provisions on the matter, competition may be appreciably distorted.[16]

Examples of directives adopted in part under ex Article 100 include the Shellfish Waters Directive,[17] the Directive on the Combatting of Air Pollution from Industrial Plants,[18] and the original Waste Framework Directive.[19]

Ex Article 235 (now Article 308 EC)

Environmental measures were also adopted under ex Article 235 which enables legislation to be passed where it is necessary to attain one of the objectives of the Community, but where the Treaty has not provided the necessary powers.[20] Recognising the need for protection of the environment, the Court of Justice affirmed that the need to protect the environment is indeed "one of the Community's essential objectives".[21] On the whole, ex Article 100 (Article 94 EC) and ex Article 235 (Article 308 EC) were used in combination but the latter has on occasion been utilised as a sole basis for environment related legislation where, as Rehbinder and Stewart note, "different national regulations of an activity potentially harmful to the environment do not have a clear or exclusive financial impact on trade or industry".[22] In this way Community measures have been adopted which would otherwise have been impossible under ex Article 100 owing to the lack of a relationship between the measure and the functioning of the common market. For example, the Wild Birds Directive which established a system of protective management and control of birds was introduced utilising ex Article 235 (Article 308 EC) as its legal base.[23] Other examples of Community measures adopted solely on the basis of ex Article 235 include a Directive regulating the Importation of Certain Seals and Products Derived from such Seals, and the Regulation on the Importation of Whales and other Cetacean Products.[24]

---

[16]   Case 91/79 *Commission* v *Italian Republic* [1980] ECR 1099, para. 81

[17]   Directive 79/923 OJ 1979 L281/47.

[18]   Directive 84/360 OJ 1984 L188/20.

[19]   Directive 75/442 OJ 1975 L78/32.

[20]   Ex Article 235 (Article 308) notes:

   If action by the Community should prove necessary to attain, in the course of the operation of the common market, *one of the objectives of the Community* and this Treaty has not provided the necessary powers, the Council shall, acting unanimously on a proposal from the Commission and after consulting the European Parliament, take the appropriate measures.

[21]   Case 240/83 *ADBHU supra* n.3, para.13.

[22]   Rehbinder and Stewart, *Environmental Protection Policy* (1985), p.28.

[23]   OJ 1979 L103/1.

[24]   Council Directive 83/129 Concerning the Importation into Member States of Skins of Certain Seal Pups and Products derived therefrom (OJ 1983 L91/30), and Council Regulation 348/81 on Common Rules for Imports of Whales and other Cetacean Products (OJ 1981 L39/1). Similarly, see Council Directive 82/884 on a Limit Value for Lead in Air (OJ 1982 L378/15).

The lack of a specific constitutional basis in the 1957 EEC Treaty did not therefore prove a hindrance to the introduction and implementation of a Community-wide environmental policy, and, in the absence of express guidance in the Treaty, environmental action programmes expounded the principles and aims of that policy.[25] Member States and Community institutions had concluded that the adoption of certain environmental measures was politically desirable. Less desirable proposals of an environmental nature could effectively be vetoed by any Member State as both ex Article 100 and ex Article 235 required unanimity in Council. Individual Member States felt secure that Community competence in this field would not impinge on their own national competence unless they themselves had concluded that a Community effort was appropriate.[26]

The Single European Act (SEA)

This sense of security was to change with the amendment of the 1957 EEC Treaty by the SEA which came into force in 1987.[27] The establishment of the common market had not been achieved by 1986. This was due in part to the fact that necessary legislation had been delayed, or rejected having failed to gain unanimous consent in Council. The signing of the SEA in 1986 was intended to kick-start the process by facilitating the adoption of measures to establish the internal market by the end of 1992. Ex Article 100a EC (now Article 95 EC) was inserted by the SEA to provide for the passing of measures which would accelerate the completion of the internal market. Measures adopted under ex Article 100a would henceforth be introduced using the "cooperation" procedure.[28] This process increased Parliament's powers by providing it with a second reading and increased influence.[29] Where the cooperation procedure applied, a measure could be adopted by a qualified majority in Council rather than requiring the unanimous backing of all Member States. This change to the legislative procedure should not be underestimated; environmental measures critical to the internal market legislative programme could now be adopted despite the opposition of a dissenting Member State.

---

[25] The Sixth and current Action Programme covers the period 2001-2010; OJ 2002 L242/1. See also the First Programme of Action, *supra* n.13, Second Programme of Action (OJ 1977 C139/1), Third Programme of Action (OJ 1983 C46/1), Fourth Programme of Action (OJ 1987 C328/1), and the Fifth Programme of Action (OJ 1993 C138/1).

[26] See generally Scott, *EC Environmental Law* (1998), pp.5-6.

[27] The Single European Act (SEA) was signed in February 1986 and came into force on 1 July 1987.

[28] Now Article 252 EC.

[29] Under the cooperation procedure introduced by the SEA, Parliament could ultimately reject a proposed measure in which case there would need to be unanimity in Council to adopt it. If Parliament merely proposed amendments to a measure, these amendments had to be assessed by the Commission, and the Council had to act unanimously to adopt the proposed re-examined measure.

The SEA additionally and importantly introduced a specific legal basis for Community environmental policy into the Treaty, ex Articles 130r, 130s and 130t (now Articles 174, 175 and 176 EC; the "Environment Title").[30] The Community now had express competence to introduce legislation where specific action on environmental matters was required. Adoption of legislation to protect the environment would henceforth be possible without either the need to expressly assert a link to common market aspirations or the Community's constitutional objectives. The addition of the Environment Title to the Treaty represented an express acknowledgement of the existence and importance of the Community's environmental policy, as well as the opportunity to incorporate the objectives of that policy, and the principles upon which it is based, into the Treaty.[31] These environmental objectives and principles are addressed in some detail in chapter 2, but it is worth noting at this stage that the objectives seek to establish the field within which the Community may exercise its competence, while the environmental principles are recognised as providing guidance to the direction of the Community's environmental policy.

The new cooperation procedure did not however apply to legislation adopted under the Environment Title. Instead, legislation adopted under ex Article 130s had to attract the unanimous approval of all Member States.[32] Additionally, the role of Parliament – an institution which generally seeks to strengthen provisions in legislative proposals to afford greater environmental protection – was merely consultative, its opinions having no binding legal effect. The seeds of future dispute between the Community's institutions had been sown.

The "Titanium Dioxide" Case

Ultimately the choice of legal base is an issue for the Court of Justice to rule upon. In the "Titanium Dioxide" case the ECJ was obliged for the first time to assess whether the correct legal base for a particular directive was ex Article 100a (Article 95 EC) to facilitate the completion of the internal market, or ex Article 130s (Article 175 EC) specifically to pursue environmental ends.[33] The directive in question provided for the approximation of national programmes to reduce and eliminate

---

30   Articles 174, 175 and 176 make up Title XIX (ex Title XVI) of the Treaty.

31   See now Article 174(1) and (2) EC. For a detailed account of the impact of the SEA on environmental policy see Kramer, *Focus on European Environmental Law* (1992) pp.62-85, and Vandermeersch, 'The Single European Act and the Environmental Policy of the European Community' (1987) 12 ELRev 407.

32   Unanimity was therefore the norm at that time for legislation under ex Article 130s. However ex Article 130s(2) did leave open the opportunity to enact legislation under the Environment Title using qualified majority voting but only where the Council decided unanimously that matters should be agreed in this way.

33   Case C-300/89 *Commission* v *Council* [1991] ECR I-2867.

pollution caused by waste from the titanium dioxide industry.[34] The Commission's original proposal was based on ex Article 100 (Article 94 EC) and ex Article 235 (Article 308 EC). Subsequent to the entry into force of the SEA, a revised proposal was based on ex Article 100a (Article 95 EC) which would have required a qualified majority vote in Council. This proposal was eventually adopted by the Council in 1989 but having changed the legal base to ex Article 130s (Article 175 EC) under which the unanimous consent of the Member States in Council was required.

The Council had taken the view that the main purpose of the measure was to eliminate pollution caused by waste from the titanium dioxide industry, and that therefore the principal objective of the measure was to protect the environment. However, the Commission expressed concern at the precedent which would have been set by adopting such a measure under a legal base which required unanimity. If unanimity was required, the Community would only advance at the speed of that Member State least receptive to change. As such the Commission, supported by the European Parliament, made application for the annulment of the measure on the grounds that the legal base was incorrect, arguing that its principal objective was to improve conditions of competition in the titanium dioxide industry, and that therefore the legal basis should have been ex Article 100a.

In its judgment the Court of Justice indicated that

> *in the context of the organization of the powers of the Community the choice of the legal basis for a measure may not depend simply on an institution's conviction as to the objective pursued but must be based on objective factors which are amenable to review. Those factors include in particular the aim and content of the measure.*[35]

The ECJ went on to determine that the directive had two *aims*: the harmonisation of national programmes to reduce and eliminate waste in the titanium dioxide industry, an environmental objective; and the improvement of conditions of competition in the industry, an aim relevant to the successful completion of the internal market.[36] In similar fashion, the *content* of the directive was held by the ECJ to have a twofold purpose: the reduction of pollution, clearly an environmental aim; and also the creation of greater uniformity of production conditions which, due to their impact on production costs, affected conditions of competition and the internal market.[37] An analysis of the measure's aim and content had therefore underlined that the directive to an equal degree pursued the two objectives of protecting the environment and facilitating the completion and functioning of the internal market. The reaching of

---

[34] Directive 89/428, OJ 1989 L201/ 56. As a result of the judgment in this case, this measure was declared void and eventually replaced by Directive 92/112 OJ 1992 L409/11 which was adopted under ex Article 100a (now Article 95 EC).

[35] Para. 10 of the judgment.

[36] Para. 11 of the judgment.

[37] Para. 12 of the judgment.

such a conclusion would normally have meant that the measure in question should have been enacted under a dual legal base.[38] However, the ECJ had to make a decision between the two alternative provisions bearing in mind that the legislative procedures applicable under ex Article 100a and ex Article 130s were different.

In its ruling, the Court of Justice determined that a directive aimed equally at achieving environmental goals and the completion of the internal market did not *have* to be adopted under the Environment Title. After all, ex Article 130r at that time stipulated that environmental protection should be a component of the Community's other policies.[39] In addition, measures relating to the environment and health had the ability to place significant burdens on industry and, in the absence of harmonisation, could contribute to the considerable distortion of competition.[40] The ECJ also noted that ex Article 100a(3) required the Commission, in proposals intended to accelerate the completion of the internal market, to take as a base a high level of protection in matters relating to environmental protection.[41] This served to underline that a measure with environmental objectives can be effectively pursued on the basis of harmonising measures adopted under ex Article 100a (Article 95).The ECJ therefore concluded that the measure in question fell within the scope of ex Article 100a (Article 95 EC) as it intended to approximate national rules on industrial production with a view to eliminating distortions of competition. The directive was annulled, the ECJ ruling that it should have been based on ex Article 100a (Article 95 EC).

The judgment had underlined that, despite the introduction of the Environment Title by the SEA, measures with environmental objectives could be adopted under ex Article 100a. Clearly this had potentially wide-ranging implications as adoption under the internal market provision made it much easier for measures to be passed in Council as there was no need for unanimous agreement. Parliament's support for the Commission's action had stemmed from the fact that its influence would be greater under the legislative process relating to internal market provisions. Under the relevant procedures relating to the adoption of a measure under Article 100a, the cooperation procedure was to be applied, whereas Parliament needed merely to have been consulted under Article 130s. This most certainly seems to have influenced the ECJ's final decision. Forced to make a choice between potential legal bases, the

---

38   Case 165/87 *Commission* v *Council* [1988] ECR 5545.

39   Para. 22 of the judgment. The Court observed that ex Article 130r(2) at that time noted that "environmental protection requirements shall be a component of the Community's other policies" and hence that "a community measure cannot be covered by [ex] Article 130s merely because it also pursues objectives of environmental protection".

40   Para. 23 of the judgment.

41   Para. 24 of the judgment. Ex Article 100a(3) noted that proposals for internal market measures were obliged to take as a base a high level of environmental protection. As such, the ECJ indicated that "the objectives of environmental protection referred to in [ex] Article 130r may be effectively pursued by means of harmonizing measures adopted on the basis of [ex] Article 100a".

Court of Justice opted for that which offered the greater influence to Parliament.[42] Referring to Parliament's increased role under the cooperation procedure as a reflection of "a fundamental democratic principle that the peoples should take part in the exercise of power through the intermediary of a representation assembly",[43] the judgment showed awareness of the need to redress the so-called "democratic deficit" within the Community.

In principle, the "Titanium Dioxide" ruling would hasten the future adoption of environmental measures of a controversial nature, although the ECJ's subsequent decision in *Commission* v *Council* did underline that ex Article 130s was not to be regarded as an inessential legal base.[44] The Court decided that Directive 91/156 amending the Framework Directive on Waste[45] was *primarily* aimed to protect the environment, and that its accepted impact on the functioning of the internal market was only *ancillary* to this principal objective. Applying the "centre of gravity" approach, the "Titanium Dioxide" case was distinguished on this basis, the correct legal base for Directive 91/156 being ex Article 130s. From this judgment and the "Titanium Dioxide" ruling Lenaerts has correctly deduced that where a measure has the dual objectives of environmental protection and facilitating the functioning of the internal market, the Court would look to the aim and content of the measure to ascertain whether it had a primary objective. If such an objective was found and related to the need to protect the environment, the correct legal base would be ex Article 130s (even though the measure also had incidental effects on the promotion of the internal market). If the primary objective was to eliminate distortions of competition in a given area, the correct legal base would be ex Article 100a despite the measure having an ancillary objective in the environmental field. Where no division could be made as to the importance of a measure's dual objectives, the ECJ would be likely to endorse that legal base which offered the European Parliament the greatest influence in the applicable legislative procedure.[46]

---

[42] See Scott, *supra* n.26, pp.8-9, and Weatherill, *Law and Integration in the European Union* (1995), p.90 (cf. Kramer, *European Environmental Law Casebook* (1993), p.28).

[43] Para. 20 of the judgment.

[44] Case C-155/91 [1993] ECR I-939. The "centre of gravity" or "principal objective" test used in this case has also been applied in other judgments to ascertain correct legal base (see for example Case C-187/93 *Parliament* v *Council* [1994] ECR I-2857, and Case C-377/98 *Netherlands* v *Parliament and Council* [2001] ECR I-7079). The application of this approach has been criticised on the basis that it leads to the making of arbitrary judicial decisions as to a measure's principal objective when in fact the latter is by no means certain; see Kramer, *EC Environmental Law* (2000), pp.57-59.

[45] Directive 91/156 amending Directive 75/442 on Waste, OJ 1991 L78/32. See chapter 7 on waste management for discussion of the obligations under this framework directive.

[46] See Lenaerts, "The principle of subsidiarity and the environment in the European Union: keeping the balance of federalism" in Abraham, Deketelaere and Stuyck (eds.), *Recent Economic and Legal Developments in European Environmental Policy* (1995) pp.30-32 (cited in Deketelaere, Schutyser, Swinnen, Van Calster and Verhoosel, *European Environmental Law* (1998), at p.54).

The Extension of Parliament's Powers; the Treaty on European Union, the Treaty of Amsterdam and the Treaty of Nice

Since these rulings the 1992 Treaty on European Union, otherwise known as the Maastricht Treaty,[47] the 1997 Treaty of Amsterdam[48], and the 2001 Treaty of Nice have entered into force. Maastricht and Amsterdam have in particular amended the legislative procedures for adoption of legislation under ex Article 100a and ex Article 130s.[49] The Maastricht Treaty considerably increased Parliament's powers by providing it with an effective veto over legislation adopted under ex Article 100a through the "codecision" procedure.[50] Henceforth, qualified majority voting in Council and the codecision procedure now applied in relation to the adoption of internal market legislation under ex Article 100a. Additionally, the general legislative procedure to be applied for the introduction of the majority of legislative measures under the Environment Title was changed from unanimity in Council to qualified majority voting under the cooperation procedure.[51] Important distinctions between the legislative procedures applicable under ex Article 100a and ex Article 130s therefore still remained. While in the majority of cases only a qualified majority vote was now required in Council, the cooperation procedure applied to measures adopted under ex Article 130s, while measures under ex Article 100a were adopted under the codecision procedure. Parliament enjoyed the ability on two occasions to propose changes to proposals under the cooperation procedure, but its powers were not as strong as under the codecision procedure.

---

[47]   The Treaty of Maastricht was signed on 7 February 1992 and came into force on 1 November 1993.

[48]   The Treaty of Amsterdam was signed on 2 October 1997 and came into force on 1 May 1999.

[49]   See Wilkinson, "Maastricht and the Environment" (1992) 4(2) JEL 221 at pp.227-231, and Macrory, "The Amsterdam Treaty: An Environmental Perspective" in O'Keefe and Twomey (eds.), *Legal Issues of the Amsterdam Treaty* (1999), pp.177-178.

[50]   See the now Article 251 EC on the codecision procedure. In particular, Article 251(2) notes that Parliament is to be given an initial opportunity to make comments on a Commission proposal. If the Council is unwilling to accept any of Parliament's amendments, it must adopt a "common position". Parliament then may reject this common position "by an absolute majority of its component members" in which case "the proposed act shall be deemed not to have been adopted".

[51]   We will note later that in certain areas unanimity was – and still is – required. Note also that post-Maastricht, "general action programmes setting out priority objectives to be attained" (such as Environmental Action Programmes) are adopted by qualified majority vote under the codecision procedure (now Article 175(3) EC). The Sixth Environmental Action Programme was the first to be adopted under this legislative procedure (although the fifth programme was revised in this manner; OJ 1998 L275/1).

Action programmes are formulated within the Commission and have traditionally been regarded as non-binding statements of objectives. However, since Maastricht they must now be formally adopted by Parliament and Council under Article 175(3) EC rather than simply approved by the Council. As a consequence of the more legal nature of action programmes subsequent to this change, Kramer has noted that "*[w]hile, in theory, the Commission remains free to ignore a request for a proposal on a specific directive by the [European Parliament] and the Council formulated in the decision which adopts an action programme, in practice the pressure to take heed of such a request will be considerable*"; Kramer, "Thirty Years of EC Environmental Law" 2 *Yearbook of European Environmental Law* (2002), p.164.

Further changes were however importantly introduced by the Treaty of Amsterdam. Qualified majority voting in Council under the codecision procedure is now the norm for measures adopted under both Articles 95 EC (ex Article 100a) *and* 175 EC (ex Article 130s). The ability of the European Parliament to influence the content of Community environmental measures has therefore been increased under the legislative procedure applicable to the majority of measures under Article 175 EC. As a consequence, the European Parliament has undoubtedly been able to strengthen the content of certain measures such as the Water Framework Directive adopted in late 2000.[52]

The "Titanium Dioxide" case was undoubtedly of considerable importance at the time,[53] but, as the general legislative procedures under Articles 95 EC (ex Article 100a) and 175 EC (ex Article 130s) are now identical, it is less likely that a dispute, as in the "Titanium Dioxide", case will arise in the future.[54] However, such a possibility cannot be ruled out bearing in mind that important differences exist as to the ability of Member States to introduce or maintain more stringent environmental measures after the adoption of harmonising legislation, depending on whether the harmonising measure is adopted under Article 95 EC or the Environment Title.[55] The ability to adopt stricter measures will actually be addressed in chapter 2,[56] but suffice to note at this point that it is easier to apply stricter national laws after harmonisation under Article 175 EC.

It should also be stressed that legislation which impacts upon the environment has often been adopted under other provisions of the EC Treaty including Article 37 EC (to further the implementation of the Common Agricultural Policy), Article 71 EC (to establish a Common Transport Policy), and Article 166 EC (to adopt research and development programmes).[57] Whilst the legislative procedures are generally speaking the same under Article 71 EC and Article 175 EC (qualified majority voting under the "codecision" procedure),[58] codecision has not been extended to the

---

52   Directive 2000/60 OJ 2000 L327/1. See ENDS Report No. 305 (2000), pp.50-52.

53   Scott notes that Member States' willingness to accept qualified majority voting as the norm post-Maastricht under the Environment Title may have been influenced by the judgment: "retention of the veto under Article 130s would not have served to increase the power of individual Member States, given the strength of the European Court's preference for Article 100a, in a dual objective scenario", *supra* n.26, p.9.

54   See Macrory, *supra* n.49, p.178.

55   Macrory, *ibid*.

56   See discussion in chapter 2.

57   Measures have also been adopted under Article 133 EC (Common Commercial Policy) by a qualified majority vote in Council. There is no element of participation by the European Parliament. Kramer however notes that "[i]n practice ..., Article 133 is not applied to environmental measures, at least not without Article 175"; see Kramer, *supra* n.44, p.69. Pursuant to amendment by the Nice Treaty, measures based on Article 133 EC will generally continue to be passed by qualified majority voting, although certain measures relating to agreements in the fields of trade in services and the commercial aspects of intellectual property are to be adopted by unanimity. Parliament still has no participation role.

58   In relation to the Transport Title of the EC Treaty, most measures will be adopted by qualified majority vote under Article 71(1) EC. However, where "the application of provisions concerning the principles of the regulatory system for transport would be liable to have a serious effect on the standard of living and on employment in certain areas and on the operation of transport facilities", they will be adopted by unanimity after having consulted the European Parliament (Article 71(2) EC).

passing of measures under Article 37 EC or the adoption of specific programmes under Article 166(4) EC.[59] Legislation enacted under these Treaty provisions is to be adopted by a qualified majority vote in Council but only after having merely consulted Parliament.

The discrepancy in the legislative procedures under Article 175 EC and Article 37 EC has in particular caused political tensions in the past. For example, prior to the entry into force of the Amsterdam Treaty, the European Parliament questioned the legal base of measures adopted under Article 37 EC which amended existing measures on the protection of the Community's forests against air pollution,[60] and against fire.[61] As the measures had been adopted under ex Article 43 EC (now Article 37 EC), Parliament had only been consulted. Had the regulations been adopted under the Environment Title, the cooperation procedure would at that time have applied. In a bid to assert its more active participation in law-making under the Environment Title, the European Parliament brought an action to annul the measures in question.[62] In its ruling the ECJ looked to the aim and content of the measures, before concluding that the regulations should be annulled. The legislation might have had "certain positive repercussions on the functioning of agriculture", but these effects were incidental to the primary aim of the schemes introduced under the measures for the protection of forests.[63] Measures which afforded protection to forests were judged to

> *inherently form part of the environmental action for which Community competence is founded on [ex] Article 130s of the Treaty.*[64]

The Treaty of Nice was signed on 26 February 2001 and entered into force on 1 February 2003.[65] It extends the applicability of the codecision procedure generally but does not introduce the codecision requirement in agricultural policy under Article 37 EC, or for the adoption of specific research and development programmes under Article 166(4) EC. Accordingly, it remains the case that the European Parliament need only be consulted in relation to measures adopted under this provision. It would therefore be premature to assert that disputes as to the

---

59 Macrory, *supra* n.49, p.178.

60 Regulation 307/97 OJ 1997 L51/9.

61 Regulation 308/97 OJ 1997 L51/11.

62 Cases C-164/97 and C-165/97 *European Parliament* v *Council* [1999] ECR I-1139. For an overview of the judgment, see (2000) 12(1) JEL 94-95. In Case C-405/92 *Etablissement Armand Mondiet SA* v *Armement Islais SARL* [1993] ECR I-6133 the ECJ had previously been called upon to examine whether the correct legal basis for a drift net ban was ex Article 130s (now Article 175 EC) or ex Article 43 (now Article 37 EC); in this case the Court determined that the measure "primarily" had been taken under the common agricultural policy (the conservation and rational exploitation of fish stocks), and any environmental considerations were "contributory" factors only in the decision to adopt the measure; see paras. 24-28 of the judgment.

63 Para. 15 of the judgment.

64 *Ibid.*

65 Ireland became the last Member State to ratify following a second referendum in October 2002.

correctness of legal base will totally become a thing of the past when one recalls that adoption of legislation under an alternative Article 175 EC legal base will generally require the utilisation of the codecision procedure.[66]

Retaining the Need for Unanimity

Whilst it has been noted that the legislative procedure for the adoption of most measures under Article 95 EC and Article 175 EC is now the codecision procedure with qualified majority voting in Council, the adoption of certain measures under Article 175 still requires unanimity in Council. In such instances, the role of Parliament is minimised in the sense that it need only be consulted. After the entry into force of the Treaty of Nice, the following environmental measures require a unanimous vote in Council and consultation with the European Parliament prior to adoption in accordance with Article 175(2) EC:

(a) provisions primarily of a fiscal nature;

(b) measures affecting:

- *town and country planning;*

- *quantitative management of water resources or affecting, directly or indirectly, the availability of those resources;*

- *land use, with the exception of waste management;*

(c) measures significantly affecting a Member State's choice between different energy sources and the general structure of its energy supply.[67]

The Community therefore only enjoys competence to adopt secondary legislation in these areas with the unanimous consent of all Member States in Council.

The categories noted in Article 175(2) EC can be criticised for being vague in nature and require further discussion.

Provisions Primarily of a Fiscal Nature

A measure which therefore seeks to introduce an EC-wide tax on carbon dioxide emissions would require the unanimous consent of all Member States.[68] As the main

---

[66] See similar comment by Macrory (*supra* n.49, p.178) in relation to changes to the Treaty introduced by the Amsterdam Treaty.

[67] It further notes that the Council "may, under the conditions laid down in the first subparagraph, define those matters referred to in this paragraph on which decisions are to be taken by a qualified majority".

[68] See COM (92) 226.

objective of such an instrument would be to introduce an eco-tax, it would qualify as a measure which is "primarily of a fiscal nature". The concern of some Member States, so apparent in the "Titanium Dioxide" case, to retain the need for unanimity in Council voting was reflected in the debate pre-Amsterdam as to whether the introduction of an environmental Community-wide tax should require unanimous consensus in Council or a qualified majority vote. A proposal to introduce qualified majority voting for the introduction of Community environmental taxes was rejected in the Intergovernmental Conference which eventually adopted the Amsterdam Treaty.[69] This rejection must come as no surprise to those who have followed the vain attempts to adopt a Community-wide carbon energy tax.[70] Attempts to introduce qualified majority voting for certain types of environmental taxes were supported by the Commission, Austria, Belgium, Denmark and the Netherlands at the Nice Intergovernmental Conference, but failed due to the opposition of the UK (supported by Sweden and Ireland).[71] Whilst qualified majority voting with the codecision procedure is now the norm for measures adopted under the Environment Title, certain Member States remain reluctant to give up their effective veto in those areas which are regarded by them as being issues of particular sensitivity and importance both economically and politically. Taxation is one such area.

A strong case could however be made that where the fiscal element of a proposed measure is merely ancillary to its main objective, the measure can be adopted by qualified majority vote in Council.[72] Whether a proposed measure's main objective or just its ancillary purpose is to introduce an environmental tax may well be controversial, and might ultimately be an issue to be determined by the ECJ. Measures of "a fiscal nature" should nevertheless be interpreted restrictively to include provisions which seek to harmonise taxation, but not to include a measure which merely allows for the imposition of charges and fees by Member States.[73]

---

[69]   See Van Calster and Deketelaere "Amsterdam, the IGC and Greening the EU Treaty" (1998) 7 EELR 12, at p.19. By virtue of Article 95(2) unanimity is also still required for fiscal measures affecting the internal market.

[70]   See chapter 8.

[71]   ENDS Report 312 (January 2001), p.42. The declaration on Article 175 EC by the Nice Intergovernmental Conference did however further encourage the greater use of market-orientated instruments in the environmental field. Declaration 9 adopted by the Intergovernmental Conference notes:

> The High Contracting Parties are determined to see the European Union play a leading role in promoting environmental protection in the Union and in international efforts pursuing the same objective at global level. Full use should be made of all possibilities offered by the Treaty with a view to pursuing this objective, including the use of incentives and instruments which are market-oriented and intended to promote sustainable development.

[72]   See Kramer, *supra* n.44, p.64, and Jans, *European Environmental Law* (2000), p.46.

[73]   Kramer, *supra* n.44, p.64, and Jans, *supra* n.72, p.45.

Measures affecting: town and country planning; quantitative management of water resources or affecting, directly or indirectly, the availability of those resources; land use, with the exception of waste management

Whilst it is clear from this provision that waste management measures need not be adopted in Council on a unanimous vote,[74] there has traditionally been far less certainty as to which measures do actually require unanimity. Before amendment by the Treaty of Nice, this subsection had been worded in the following terms:

> *measures concerning town and country planning, land use with the exception of waste management and measures of a general nature, and management of water resources.*

Were we therefore to imply that all Community measures relating to water management should be adopted by unanimity? The ECJ provided guidance in this respect in *Spain v Council*.[75]

The Spanish government had argued that Decision 97/825[76] approving the conclusion of the Convention on cooperation for the protection and sustainable use of the River Danube (the Convention) should have been adopted by unanimity under ex Article 130s(2) (now Article 175 [2]) and the second sentence of ex Article 228(2). By contrast, the Council had adopted the measure under ex Article 130s(1) (now Article 175 [1]) together with the first sentence of ex Article 228(2).[77] Ex Article 228(2) at the time the decision was adopted noted that

> *Subject to the powers vested in the Commission in this field, the agreements shall be concluded by the Council, acting by a qualified majority on a proposal from the Commission. The Council shall act unanimously when the agreement covers a field for which unanimity is required for the adoption of internal rules...*[78]

In the light of ex Article 228(2) the ECJ determined that the issue turned on whether internal Community rules concerning the provisions of the Convention would have been adopted on the basis of ex Article 130s(1), requiring a qualified majority, or under ex Article 130s(2), which required unanimity. The Council had taken the view that the measure should be adopted by qualified majority, while Spain argued that it related to the management of the water resources of the River Danube catchment area and should have been adopted by unanimity. In interpreting the concept of "management of water resources", the ECJ compared the various language versions. The French and Dutch versions implied that the concept should be confined to the

---

74 For example, the End-of-Life Vehicles Directive is a recent example of a directive which was correctly adopted utilising Article 175(1) EC rather than Article 175(2) EC as its legal base (OJ 2000 L269/34).

75 Case C-36/98 [2001] ECR I-779.

76 Decision 97/825 OJ 1997 L342/18.

77 In addition, ex Article 228(3) first paragraph had given the European Parliament certain consultation rights.

78 Ex Article 228 has been amended and renumbered by the Treaty of Amsterdam as Article 300 EC.

quantitative aspects of water management, rather than qualitative considerations. The German, Spanish, Italian, Portuguese, Finnish, Swedish, Danish, English, Irish and Greek versions would have allowed both quantitative and qualitative aspects to be covered. Divergence between the language versions clearly therefore existed. The issue therefore had to be determined by reference to the purpose and general scheme of the rules. In making this particular assessment, the ECJ commented on the second indent of ex Article 130s(2) (now Article 175(2) EC) in the following terms:

> *[A]part from the measures concerning the management of water resources, the second indent of the first paragraph of [ex] Article 130s(2)of the Treaty refers to measures relating to town and country planning and to land use with the exception of waste management and measures of a general nature. These are measures which ... regulate the use of the territory of the Member States, such as measures relating to regional, urban or rural management plans or the planning of various projects concerning the infrastructure of a Member State.*[79]

The Court further stipulated that Member States' territory, land and their water resources were to be regarded as limited resources, and the measures which required unanimity in Council under the second indent of ex Article 130s(2) affected those resources in the sense that they regulated

> *the quantitative aspects of the use of those resources, or in other words, measures related to the management of limited resources in its quantitative aspects and not those concerning the improvement and the protection of the quality of those resources.*[80]

Accordingly, the "management of water resources" was in the view of the ECJ not to be regarded as covering

> *... every measure concerned with water, but covers only measures concerning the regulation of the use of water and the management of water in its quantitative aspects.*[81]

In relation to the issue at hand, the ECJ noted that the principal purpose of the Convention was the protection and improvement of water quality, although it incidentally referred to the quantitative aspects of the use and management of waters. Applying the "centre of gravity" test, the ECJ determined that the Council was right to adopt the measure under ex Article 130s(1) (now Article 175 [1]).

This case therefore underlined that a distinction had to be made between "quantitative" and "qualitative" aspects. The changes to this subsection of Article 175(2) EC introduced by the Treaty of Nice in relation to water resources are reflective of the ECJ's ruling in that only measures affecting "quantitative

---

[79] Para. 51 of the judgment.
[80] Para. 52 of the judgment.
[81] Para. 55 of the judgment.

management of water resources or affecting, directly or indirectly, the availability of those resources" now require unanimity. Measures which principally seek to regulate the quantitative aspects of the use of Member States' territory, land and water resources do therefore require unanimity in Council. Any future Community measure which sought to introduce regional or urban management plans in these areas would require unanimity, as would major infrastructure projects like motorways, dams and reservoirs. Such plans or major projects would affect the use of a limited resource, and Member States retain a veto over whether and where such strategically important projects are to be introduced.

On the other hand, Community measures seeking principally to regulate the qualitative aspects of these limited resources can be adopted under Article 175(1) EC. Measures regulating the quality of waters, for example, are to be adopted on a qualified majority vote in Council. Moreover, where a Community measure principally seeks to regulate the quality of water, but also incidentally regulates water quantitatively, Article 175(1) EC remains the correct legal base. The Water Framework Directive for example was appropriately adopted by qualified majority bearing in mind that its stated primary purpose was "concerned with the quality of waters ...". The directive undoubtedly also included quantitative measures but these should be regarded as ancillary to its main purpose.[82]

What are we to make of other changes to this particular subsection of Article 175(2) EC made pursuant to the Treaty of Nice? Measures "affecting" rather than "concerning" the use of a Member State's territory now require unanimous consent. This is perhaps significant in that it might be claimed that measures which merely touch upon rather than specifically concern these areas now require unanimity.[83] This is an issue which the ECJ may ultimately need to determine. Additionally, reference to "measures of a general nature" has been deleted. This may well be an important change particularly if, for example, one accepts that Community measures relating to environmental impact assessment previously fell within this category.[84] It might now be argued that any further measures of this nature or amendments to the Environmental Impact Assessment Directive or Strategic Environmental

---

[82] The preamble further notes that "[c]ontrol of quantity is an ancillary element in securing good water quality and therefore measures on quantity, serving the objective of good quality, should also be established"; para 19; OJ 2000 L327/1. Note also comment by Jans in relation to the proposal for this measure; *supra* n.72, p.48.

[83] ENDS Report 312 (January 2001), p.42.

[84] The adoption of a measure relating to EIA might have been categorised as one of the exceptional "measures of a general nature" which could have been passed by qualified majority prior to the entry into force of the Treaty of Nice. Neither the 1997 amendment to Directive 85/337 on the assessment of the effects of certain public and private projects on the environment (Environmental Impact Assessment Directive), nor Directive 2001/42 on the Assessment of the Effects of Certain Plans and Programmes on the Environment (Stategic Environmental Assessment Directive) required unanimity in Council. Both were adopted under the codecision procedure despite having implications in relation to "town and country planning" and "land use".

Assessment Directive will henceforth require the unanimous support of the Member States in so far as they affect management plans or strategic projects concerning the infrastructure of a Member State.[85]

Measures significantly affecting a Member State's choice between different energy sources and the general structure of its energy supply

Any Community measure which has a major impact as to the extent to which Member States could pursue an energy strategy based on a particular source of energy supply (such as nuclear or perhaps hydro-electric power) would require unanimous agreement in Council. This can be justified by the fact that the security of energy supply is of fundamental strategic importance to any nation.[86] A degree of discretion has been factored into the determination as to whether a proposed measure affects a Member State's choice between energy sources and general structure of energy supply. Only measures "significantly" affecting this area require unanimity in Council. The Council therefore enjoys a level of discretion in determining when a measure "significantly" so affects. No changes to this particular provision were made by the Treaty of Nice.

The Subsidiarity and Proportionality Principles

Subsidiarity

Although aspirations to protect the environment would seem to share little in common with the original purposes of the 1957 EEC Treaty, Community competence in the area of the environment is now one recognised as being shared with the Member States in accordance with the principle of subsidiarity. In the exercise of their powers, the Community's institutions must make sure that they comply with the principle of subsidiarity. This principle has been the focus of much debate in recent years.[87] Although not expressly mentioned in the 1957 EEC Treaty or the Single European Act (SEA), the latter introduced the principle as a condition

---

[85]   ENDS report 312 (January 2001), p.42.

[86]   Specifically in relation to nuclear energy, Kramer has noted that "care had been taken to provide in the EC Treaty that any such changes would be decided by unanimity"; "Differentiation in EU Environmental Policy" (2000) 9 EELR 133, at p.136.

[87]   See for example Brinkhorst, "Subsidiarity and EC Environment Policy - a Panacea or a Pandora's Box" (1993) 2 EELR 8; Cass, "The Word that Saves Maastricht? The Principle of Subsidiarity and the Division of Powers within the European Community", (1992) 29 CMLRev 1107; Freestone and Somsen, "The Impact of Subsidiarity" in Holder (ed.), *The Impact of EC Environmental Law in the United Kingdom* (1997) pp.87-99; Gonzalez, "The Principle of Subsidiarity", (1995) 20(4) ELR 355; Timmermans, "Subsidiarity and Transparency" (1999) 22 Fordham International Law Journal 5106; Toth, "A Legal Analysis of Subsidiarity" in O'Keefe and Twomey (eds.), *Legal Issues of the Maastricht Treaty* (1994), chap.3; Wils, "Subsidiarity and EC Environmental Policy: Taking People's Concerns Seriously" (1994) 6(1) JEL 85; and Wyatt, "Is Subsidiarity Justiciable?" in O'Keefe (ed.), *Liber Amicorum Gordon Slynn* (2000).

for the legality of Community environmental action. Ex Article 130r(4) post-SEA noted that the Community

> *shall take action relating to the environment to the extent to which the objectives referred to in paragraph 1 can be better attained at Community level than at the level of the individual Member States.*

Whilst this particular paragraph was deleted from the Environment Title by the Maastricht Treaty, the second paragraph of Article 5 EC (ex Article 3b) now applies the subsidiarity principle to all areas that do not fall within the Community's exclusive competence stipulating that the Community will take action

> *only if and insofar as the objectives of the proposed action cannot be sufficiently achieved by the Member States and can therefore, by reason of the scale or effects of the proposed action, be better achieved by the Community.*

In effect, two tests must therefore be satisfied: a negative one in the sense that objectives cannot be sufficiently achieved (the "necessity" criterion); and a positive test in that the objective of the action is better achieved at the EC level by reason of scale or effects of the proposed action (the "effectiveness" criterion). The principle does not apply where the Community exercises exclusive competence. In this regard, the Commission has supported the view that the free movement of goods, persons, services and capital, the Common Agricultural Policy and the Common Commercial Policy fall within the areas reserved to the Community alone.[88] If a measure affects the environment but is based on a Treaty article providing for action in any of these areas, it is arguable that the subsidiarity principle has no application.[89] However, as in other spheres, such as those relating to consumer protection, employment and transport, the competence of the Community in the area of environmental policy cannot be regarded as exclusive, and the issue of subsidiarity is certainly of relevance to action, the principal purpose of which is environmental in nature.

The subsidiarity principle seeks to identify the appropriate level for action, thereby ensuring that decisions are taken as close as possible to the citizen. It is deliberately ambiguous in nature allowing much room for political discussion as to its practical implementation. For example, how can one gauge whether the objectives of a proposed action could not be "sufficiently achieved" by the Member States? Also, how can it be assessed whether or not a measure is "better achieved" at a certain level? In a specifically environmental context, is a measure "better achieved" at a Community level because it is more cost effective than action at national level, or should it purely be assessed on whether or not action will better protect the environment?[90]

---

[88]   See Craig and de Burca, *EU Law: Text, Cases and Materials* (1998), p.125.

[89]   See Hancher, "EC Environmental Policy - a Pre-cautionary tale?" in Freestone and Hey (eds.), *The Precautionary Principle and International Law; the Challenge of Implementation* (1996), at p.194.

[90]   Kramer, *supra* n.44, p.13.

The application of the subsidiarity principle could potentially lead to the limiting of action at the Community level where it is no longer appropriate, or perhaps the extension of such activity where required. Rather than regarding the principle as prohibiting action at Community, national or regional level, the Commission has supported the combining of the principle of subsidiarity with the concept of "shared responsibility" which involves

> *not so much a choice of action at one level to the exclusion of others but, rather, a mixing of actors and instruments at the appropriate levels, without any calling into question of the division of competences between the Community, the Member States, regional and local authorities.*[91]

An example of this approach can be seen in the application of the Habitats Directive.[92] We will note in chapter 4 that the measure has been adopted at the Community level but requires action at the Member State and/or regional government level to propose a list of national sites in need of protection, and eventually to designate such sites as "Special Areas of Conservation" (SACs). In maintaining the integrity of SACs the onus is placed on Member States to take action to establish a system which avoids habitat destruction and the disturbance of species. Indeed, the form of the vast majority of EC environmental measures can in fact be said to be in line with the principles of shared responsibility and subsidiarity as most measures take the form of directives which allow legally binding objectives to be established at the Community level while allowing the manner of practical implementation to be determined at national, regional or local levels.[93]

A degree of guidance as to the application of the subsidiarity principle has been provided by the Protocol on the Application of Subsidiarity and Proportionality annexed to the Treaty of Amsterdam. Under the terms of the Protocol, reasons must be stated for any legislative proposal justifying the measure in terms of the subsidiarity and proportionality principles.[94] Both the necessity and effectiveness tests must be satisfied, and certain guidelines are specified which should be used in assessing whether these tests have been fulfilled:

---

[91]   Fifth Environmental Programme of Action, *supra* n.25, chapter 8. On the Commission's viewpoint see also 'Commission report to the European Council on the adaptation of Community legislation to the subsidiarity principle', COM (93) 545 final. On Parliament's stance that subsidiarity should not water down the Community's environmental policy, see European Parliament resolution A3-0380/92 on the application of the principle of subsidiarity to environment and consumer protection policy: OJ 1993 C42/40.

[92]   OJ 1992 L206/7. See Fifth Environmental Programme of Action, *supra* n.25, table 18.

[93]   Brinkhorst, 'Subsidiarity and EC Environment Policy – a Panacea or a Pandora's Box' (1993) 2 *EELR* 8, at p.20. The EC Treaty's Protocol on the Application of the Principles of Subsidiarity and Proportionality notes that *"[o]ther things being equal, directives should be preferred to regulations and framework directives to detailed measures"*; para. 6.

[94]   The Commission in fact endorsed this practice several years before the Amsterdam Treaty; see Commission Report on the Adaptation of Community Legislation to the Subsidiarity Principle (COM (93) 545).

- *The issue under consideration has transnational aspects which cannot be satisfactorily regulated by action by Member States.*

Community action which has endeavoured to combat a range of environmental problems with transboundary impact, such as global warming, acidification, depletion of the ozone layer, the transboundary movement of hazardous waste, pollution of international watercourses, and the protection of migratory species and their habitats, can be justified under this wide-ranging criterion. A recent example of a measure which satisfies this "transnational" criterion is the directive on national emission ceilings for certain atmospheric pollutants.[95] The measure establishes upper limits on emissions of sulphur dioxide, nitrogen oxide, volatile organic compounds and ammonia for each Member State to be complied with by 2010 at the latest. It is based on the premise that acidification, soil eutrophication and low level ozone formation are largely caused by these transboundary pollutants and that effective action requires a coordinated Community-wide response.

Pollution undoubtedly fails to respect national boundaries, and the transboundary impact of pollutants therefore calls for a coordinated response. Without coordinated, cooperative action of a Community-wide nature in relation to such issues, individual Member States may prefer to ignore the need for national action for economic or social reasons, thereby negating the effectiveness of action adopted by neighbouring states. However, certain environmental issues would not necessarily have a transboundary impact. Measures seeking to reduce noise pollution may not, for example, be introduced to relieve transnational effects and therefore could not be justified under this particular criterion.[96]

- *Actions by Member States alone or lack of Community action would conflict with the requirements of the Treaty, or would otherwise significantly damage Member States' interests.*

Unilateral action by a Member State may conflict with EC Treaty requirements where, for example, it leads to the distortion of competition or amounts to a disguised restriction on trade. The Community will therefore continue to enjoy a wide degree of competence in facilitating the functioning of the internal market by adopting measures which also have an environmental objective. The Commission's efforts to introduce emission limits for petrol fuelled equipment such as lawnmowers, chainsaws, generators and water pumps can for example be justified in this respect.[97] The measure establishes product standards in the sense that it sets limits for the emission of hydrocarbons, nitrogen oxides and carbon monoxide from certain non-road mobile machinery. This directive is intended to reduce emissions

---

[95] OJ 2001 L309/22.
[96] Van Calster and Deketelaere, *supra* n.69, p.21.
[97] Directive 2002/88EC, OJ 2003 L35/28.

which contribute to the formation of low-level ozone. Without the adoption of such a Community measure, action by one Member State alone may have conflicted with the requirements of the Treaty in relation to the free movement of goods.

Any assessment as to whether lack of Community action "would otherwise significantly damage Member States' interests" would be a difficult one to make. There are no express objective criteria to be applied in this respect, and it would not be too cynical to conclude that the issue has been left deliberately vague and may facilitate justification of a range of Community initiatives.

*   *Action at Community level would produce clear benefits by reason of its scale or effects compared with action at the level of Member States.*

This can be said to be closely connected to the justification for Community action where an issue has transboundary effects. A regional response would often be better placed "by reason of its scale or effects" to combat such a problem. Community action which effectively coordinates Member States' activities to the benefit of the environment would presumably also meet this criterion. For instance, in chapter 2 we will note that the setting up of the European Environment Agency in the early 1990s has led to the coordination of efforts to collect information on the environment throughout the Community. The making available by the Agency of comparable and consistent pan-European information on the state of the environment has proved most useful to decision-makers in the legislative process. Another example of action which produces clear benefits in line with this guideline is the Landfill Directive.[98] This measure seeks to prevent or reduce risks to public health and harmful environmental impact caused by disposing of waste by landfill, and to reduce reliance on landfill generally as a method of disposing of waste. It can therefore be said to produce clear environmental benefits "by reason of its effects" by binding all Member States thereby preventing a "race to the bottom" in which waste would otherwise be diverted away from those countries with strict landfill regulations to states with little landfill control.

Despite the guidance offered by the Protocol, considerable questions remain as to the appropriate level for action.[99] Indeed, it is unclear from the text of the Protocol as to whether all three criteria must be met for a proposed action to be justified. It is however likely that, if just one is satisfied, the proposal would be justified as being in compliance with the subsidiarity principle. The guidelines are nevertheless undoubtedly ambiguous by nature prompting one commentator quite correctly to note:

---

[98]   OJ 1999 L182/1.

[99]   Cross has aptly referred to subsidiarity as a principle which "far from deciding the issue of the appropriate level for action in relation to a particular matter, to a large extent ... merely provides the peg upon which disputants may hang their political differences"; "Subsidiarity and the Environment" 15 *YEL* 107 (1995) at p.109.

[a]n examination of Community environmental legislation in the light of the ... guidelines would reveal that probably not one environmental directive or regulation would fail to pass the test.[100]

Proportionality

The "proportionality principle" also has an important bearing on the extent to which the Community may exercise environmental competence. It is applicable to all spheres of the Community's activities whether in areas of shared competence or otherwise. The third paragraph of Article 5 EC stipulates that

[a]ny action by the Community shall not go beyond what is necessary to achieve the objectives of this Treaty.

Burdens imposed must be minimised and be proportionate to the objective to be realised leaving "as much scope for national decision as possible".[101] This demands that the form of Community action should be "as simple as possible, consistent with the satisfactory achievement of the objective of the measure".[102] The trend away from the early style of environmental legislation (which often set highly detailed rules such as specific emission limit values) to the adoption of measures establishing only frameworks for action can be said to be reflective of this requirement.[103] Framework measures typically set narrowly defined objectives but provide Member States with as much flexibility as possible in implementation taking into account regional and local conditions. The fact that environmental directives often adopt the "minimum harmonisation" technique can also be said to be in line with the proportionality principle.[104] A Community measure adopting this technique establishes minimum standards, only allowing Member States to impose more stringent national standards as long as they are compatible with primary Community law.[105]

While early Community action was typified by "command and control" regulatory instruments imposing detailed and legally binding restrictions on certain activities with a view to attaining greater environmental protection, there is now widespread acknowledgement that this approach has its limitations and needs to be supplemented by a new range of approaches.[106] Legally binding regulatory

---

[100] Jans, *supra* n.72 p.14.

[101] Protocol to the EC Treaty on the Application of the Principles of Subsidiarity and Proportionality (added by the Treaty of Amsterdam), para.7.

[102] *Ibid*, para.6.

[103] See Report of the Group of Independent Experts in Legislative and Administrative Simplification ("the Molitor Report") which recommended simplification of Community legislation; COM (95) 288.

[104] See also Jans, *supra* n.72, p.16.

[105] On Member States' ability to adopt more stringent environmental measures, see chapter 2.

[106] See, for example, Scott, *supra* n.26, pp.29-31.

instruments may not always be appropriate.[107] The Fifth Environmental Action Programme advocated the broadening of instruments to promote sustainability by changing human behaviour, activities and values. In this respect, the endorsement of market-based voluntary agreements can also be regarded as in line with the proportionality principle.[108] The use of voluntary agreements between the Community and industry has been undoubtedly limited to date, but significantly the Commission has signed agreements with European, Japanese and Korean car manufacturers with a view to reducing greenhouse gas emissions from new cars. We will return to these agreements in the context of our subsequent discussion on climate change.[109] The Community's environmental policy still for the most part consists of the traditional command and control type of legislation,[110] but these voluntary agreements have certainly fostered a new type of cooperative relationship with industry rather than the more typical confrontational approach.

Some Concluding Remarks

Community competence in the area of the environment is therefore now recognised as being shared with the Member States in accordance with the principle of subsidiarity, and has facilitated the adoption of the most wide-ranging set of legally binding environmental rules to date at the regional level. No attempt has been made in this book to cover the Community's environmental activities comprehensively,[111] but the reader should be aware that more than three hundred environmental measures have been adopted since the early 1970s addressing issues relating to air pollution, waste management, nature protection, water pollution, dangerous substances, noise pollution, and genetically modified organisms. A growing number of measures have also been adopted in the agriculture, energy, and transport sectors seeking to minimise environmental harm.

---

[107] For example, the Commission has acknowledged the need for a set of minimum criteria for environmental inspections in Member States which have to be acceptable to Member States. To achieve the desired objective of the proposed measure, the Commission considered that the most appropriate form of action was the adoption of a non-binding recommendation rather than a legally binding measure; OJ 2001 L118/41. See European Commission, "Better Lawmaking 1999" COM (1999) 562 at p.4. For an example of a Community scheme which encourages voluntary participation, see the eco-label scheme; OJ 2000 L237/1.

[108] Directive 2000/53 on End-of-Life vehicles (OJ 2000 L269/34) for example provides that Member States can transpose particular elements of the measure by means of agreements; Article 10(3). See Lee, "New Generation Regulation? The Case of End-of-Life Vehicles" (2002) 11(4) EELR 114, at pp.116-117. More generally on the use of voluntary code/agreements and the proportionality principle, see Jans, *supra* n.72, pp.14-15.

[109] See chapter 8.

[110] See Haigh, *Manual of Environmental Policy: the EC and Britain* (looseleaf), 2.4-1.

[111] See however Haigh (*supra* n.110) for an excellent overview of Community environmental measures adopted to date. Also see Jans, *supra* n.72, chapter 8.

However, the number of measures passed should not be seen as the benchmark of success. Profound challenges still need to be addressed - we will note in subsequent chapters that the mere existence of a directive will not necessarily ensure that its content is appropriate, or that it is adequately implemented or enforced. In addition, we will observe that the Community's strategy has yet to come to terms effectively with significant environmental problems such as global warming, the destruction of biodiversity, and the ever-increasing generation of waste. Indeed, in relation to the general state of the environment, the European Environment Agency has indicated that "it is clear that more needs to be done across a large front to improve environmental quality and ensure progress towards sustainability".[112]

Over the coming years the Community will expand through the enlargement process. New challenges will arise, but also exciting prospects in the environmental field. Many industrial areas in Accession countries bear the scars of the heavily-polluting industries of the Communist era, but opportunities exist to promote environmentally-friendly practice/technology in the reorganisation of industries.[113] Additionally, substantial parts of the territories of certain Central and Eastern European countries remain largely unaffected by industrial activity, and a balance must therefore be struck to accommodate continued economic expansion whilst providing effective protection for biological diversity. Indeed, the exercise of the Community's environmental competence over the next thirty years must generally endeavour to promote the sustainable development of all Member States' economies, whether those states have recently acceded to the Community or not.[114] This will necessitate the integration of environmental concerns into all areas in which the Community exercises competence. The task of achieving sustainability is a key Community objective, and the "integration principle" is of fundamental importance in this field. They will be addressed in the next chapter together with other objectives and principles relevant to the Community's environmental strategy.

---

[112] European Environment Agency, *supra* n.2.

[113] *Ibid.*

[114] *Ibid.*

Select Bibliography

Bar and Kraemer, "European Environmental Policy after Amsterdam" (1998) 10(2) JEL 315.

Brinkhorst, "Subsidiarity and EC Environment Policy - a Panacea or a Pandora's Box" (1993) 2 EELR 8.

Cross, "Subsidiarity and the Environment" 16 *Yearbook of European Law* (1996) 107.

Deketelaere, Schutyser, Swinnen, Van Calster and Verhoosel, *European Environmental Law* (1998), chapter 1.

Freestone and Somsen, "The Impact of Subsidiarity" in Holder (ed.), *The Impact of EC Environmental Law in the United Kingdom* (1997) pp. 87-99.

Hession and Macrory, "Maastricht and the Environmental Policy of the Community: Legal Issues of a New Environment Policy" in O'Keefe and Twomey (eds.), *Legal Issues of the Maastricht Treaty* (1994), chapter 10.

Jans, *European Environmental Law* (2000), chapters 1 and 2.

Kramer, *EC Environmental Law* (4th ed, 2000), chapters 1 and 2.

Macrory, "The Amsterdam Treaty: an Environmental Perspective" in O'Keefe and Twomey (eds.), *Legal Issues of the Amsterdam Treaty* (1999), chapter 11.

Scott, *EC Environmental Law* (1998), chapter 1.

Van Calster and Deketelaere, "Amsterdam, The IGC and Greening the EU Treaty" (1998) 7 EELR 12-25.

Vandermeersch, "The Single European Act and the Environmental Policy of the European Community" (1987) 12 ELRev 407.

Wilkinson, "Maastricht and the Environment: the Implications for the EC's Environment Policy of the Treaty on European Union" (1992) 4(2) JEL 221.

Wils, "Subsidiarity and EC Environmental Policy: Taking People's Concerns Seriously" (1994) 6(1) JEL 85.

Chapter 2

Environmental Objectives and Principles

The EC Treaty makes reference to a number of objectives and principles which are of relevance to the policy and law-making process, and which will provide the focus of discussion in this chapter.

The Pursuit of Sustainable Development

Following the insertion into the Treaty of an express legal basis for environmental action pursuant to the Single European Act, the importance of the Community's environmental strategy was further underlined by changes occasioned by the Maastrict Treaty. Post Maastricht the Community's activities were explicitly to include a policy in the sphere of the environment,[1] and Article 2 was amended to note that Community activity would *inter alia* now "promote ... sustainable and non-inflationary growth respecting the environment".[2] However, those whose first priority centred on the need for greater environmental protection were disappointed that the opportunity had not been taken to introduce the concept of "sustainable development" as an express objective. In their view the term "sustainable growth" could be interpreted as meaning "sustained growth", and consequently encourage the promotion of economic objectives as a priority over environmental issues.[3] "Sustainable development" on the other hand endorses the notion that in the pursuit of continued development an equitable balance has to be achieved between economic, social and environmental considerations, and was defined by the 1997 report of the Brundtland Commission as development which

> meets the needs of the present without compromising the ability of future generations to meet their own needs.[4]

Further modifications in this context were to follow pursuant to the Amsterdam Treaty. The latter amended the preamble to the Treaty on European Union (TEU) by noting the determination of the parties to promote "economic and social progress for

---

[1] Article 3(k) (post Maastricht); now Article 3(1)l EC.

[2] Article 2 (post Maastricht).

[3] Wilkinson, "Maastricht and the Environment" (1992) 4(2) JEL 221, at p.223.

[4] World Commission on Environment and Development (Report of the Brundtland Commission), *Our Common Future* (1987), p.8.

their peoples, taking into account the principle of sustainable development ...", and modified the Union's objectives by including reference to the achieving of "balanced and sustainable development" as a stated objective.[5] Achieving sustainable development is therefore now a consideration in decisions affecting the European Community and the other two pillars of the Union (common foreign and security policy, and justice and home affairs cooperation).[6] In addition, Article 2 of the EC Treaty was amended by the Treaty of Amsterdam to note the need for "balanced and sustainable development of economic activities" together with "a high level of protection and improvement of the quality of the environment".[7] Furthermore, Article 6 EC now stipulates that

> *[e]nvironmental protection requirements must be integrated into the definition and implementation of the Community policies and activities referred to in Article 3, in particular with a view to promoting sustainable development.*[8]

It is undoubtedly politically significant that the pursuit of sustainable development is now therefore a stated aim of both the European Union and the European Community.

"Sustainable development" is not further defined in the EC Treaty. The lack of such a definition certainly reduces the concept's justiciability. However, if developments in international environmental law can influence the debate, the notion of sustainable development would suggest that the pursuit of economic growth must take due account of the need to preserve the environment; although environmental considerations should not be prioritised over the need for economic growth, resources should not be diminished to the extent that the needs of future generations cannot be sustained. In June 1992 the world's Heads of State met in Brazil at the UN Conference on Environment and Development (UNCED) and *inter alia* adopted the so-called "Rio Declaration".[9] The EC proved an active participant at UNCED and is a signatory to the Rio Declaration. The latter is not legally binding in the same way that an international treaty is, but it has received wide endorsement and is an important "soft law" international instrument. As such - and in the absence of a definition in the EC Treaty - it can provide an insight into the notion of "sustainable development", although its terms should not be regarded as legally binding in the strict sense on the Community legal order.

---

5   Article 2 (ex Article B) of the Treaty on European Union.
6   Macrory, "The Amsterdam Treaty: An Environmental Perspective" in O'Keefe and Twomey (eds.) *Legal Issues of the Amsterdam Treaty* (1999), p.172.
7   Article 2 EC.
8   This is the so-called "integration principle" and will be discussed in greater depth later in this chapter.
9   See Sands, *Principles of International Environmental Law* (1995), pp.198-208, and Boyle and Freestone, *International Law and Sustainable Development* (1999), pp.8-16.

Key elements of the concept of sustainable development have been identified from the text of the Rio Declaration.[10] These include the notion of sustainable utilisation which is akin to one of the objectives of the EC's environmental policy to be addressed later, namely the "prudent and rational utilisation of natural resources". Additionally the concept of sustainable development endorses an approach in which environmental and economic developmental needs are integrated. This is reflected in the important EC principle already referred to, and to be discussed below in greater depth, that environmental protection requirements must be integrated into the definition and implementation of the Community's policies.[11]

The concept of sustainable development in the Rio Declaration additionally supports the notion of meeting needs within the present generation whilst giving due consideration to the needs of future generations. In this respect, Principle 3 of the Rio Declaration indicates that development

> *must be fulfilled so as to equitably meet developmental and environmental needs of present and future generations.*

As far as the present generation is concerned, natural resources should therefore be used in a fair and appropriate manner with a view to reducing social division and levels of poverty.

In relation to obligations owed to future generations, Brown-Weiss has championed the notion that the present generation must pass on the heritage of the earth to future generations in no worse a state than in which it has been inherited. This implies that the quality of the natural environment should not be allowed to deteriorate,[12] and that resources must not be depleted to such an extent that those who come after us have more limited options.[13] The notion that the environment must be preserved for the benefit of future generations is regarded by international environmental lawyers as an important component of sustainable development, and represents a key factor which should be taken into account by decision-makers. Importantly the Commission has acknowledged the duty owed to future generations,[14] and the consequent need to take decisions bearing in mind the need for long-term management.[15] This view has been endorsed by the Council which has referred to

---

[10] Sands, *supra* n.9, p.199.

[11] Article 6 EC.

[12] At the Community level, Article 174(1) notes that an objective of environmental policy is to contribute to the pursuit of "preserving, protecting and improving the quality of the environment". See *infra* nn.50-54 and accompanying text.

[13] Brown-Weiss, *In Fairness to Future Generations* (1989). See also Boyle and Freestone, *supra* n.9, p.12-13.

[14] See, for example, European Commission, "Europe's Environment: What Directions for the Future?" (2000); "the current generation has an obligation to future generations to leave sufficient stocks of social, environmental and economic resources for them to enjoy levels of well being at least as high as our own", p.11.

[15] European Commission, "Consultation paper for the preparation of a European Union strategy for Sustainable Development", SEC (2001) 517, p.49.

the concept of sustainable development as taking "a long-term view, looking at the welfare of both present and future generations".[16]

At UNCED a programme of action, *Agenda 21; Earth's Action Plan*, was adopted with a view to promoting sustainable development globally. Under this detailed plan, states were encouraged to develop new strategies to achieve sustainability. Influenced by Agenda 21, the Community's Fifth Environmental Action Programme endorsed the task of moving towards sustainability noting that

> *[t]he Community, as the largest economic/trading partner in a world where it is increasingly seen that growth has to be environmentally sustainable, must exercise its responsibility to both present and future generations. To this end it must put its own house in order and provide an example to developed and developing countries alike in relation to the protection of public health and the environment and the sustainable use of natural resources.*[17]

Progress in attaining sustainability has been slow, the Commission noting that the Fifth Environmental Action Programme did "not achieve its objectives",[18] and additionally that

> *the Union is far from achieving its ... objective of sustainable development. The task now facing us is how we can give substance to this commitment. In essence it requires a change in the way we define economic, social and environmental objectives so that they become complementary and jointly contribute to sustainability.*[19]

This is no easy task, but, prompted by the Community's international obligations,[20] the Commission drew up a consultation paper for the preparation of a long-term internal strategy. In this paper the Commission endeavoured to shift discussion from "abstract discussion of definitions and concepts into the area of everyday policy making".[21] Having received numerous responses to this paper, the Commission published its proposed strategy in May 2001.[22] The strategy endorses the Brundtland Commission's definition of sustainable development, and identifies priority issues which must be addressed urgently to attain sustainability. These have been selected taking into account the severity of the threat posed, the perceived irreversibility of

---

[16] Council Recommendation on the broad guidelines of the Economic Policies of the Member States and the Community, OJ 2001 L179/1, para.3.8.

[17] "Towards Sustainability: A European Community programme of policy and action in relation to the environment and sustainable development" (OJ 1993 C138/5), "Introduction" to the programme.

[18] European Commission, *supra*. 14, p.23.

[19] *Ibid*, p.26.

[20] At a meeting of the UN General Assembly in 1997 signatories to the Rio Declaration pledged to have devised strategies to achieve sustainable development by the time of the 2002 World Summit on Sustainable Development.

[21] European Commission, *supra* n.15, p.56.

[22] European Commission,"A Sustainable Europe for a Better World: A European Union Strategy for Sustainable Development" COM (2001) 264.

the problem, and the extent to which the issue is a difficulty common to all Member States. Principal objectives identified in the strategy include the limiting of climate change and the increased use of clean energy, addressing threats to public health (particularly threats to food safety), managing natural resources more responsibly, and improving the transport system and land use. Underlining that the concept of sustainability is not purely environmental in nature, the strategy for sustainable development additionally highlights that poverty and social exclusion, and the implications of an ageing society are key social and economic dangers to the promotion of sustainability and a better quality of life. The Göteborg European Council meeting held in June 2001 welcomed the Commission's communication embracing a new approach to policy-making in which economic, social and environmental impacts of all policies (including the EC's transport, fisheries and agricultural policies) should be scrutinised in a coordinated manner, and duly considered in the making of decisions.

The concept of sustainable development presents a vision for the future. Although a symbolic political acknowledgement of the importance now placed on the need to protect the environment by taking due account of the fragility of its carrying capacity, it is however difficult to see a court of law entertaining an action to nullify the legitimacy of a measure or action on the basis that it fails to comply with the notion of sustainable development. This is particularly the case when one bears in mind that, in the pursuit of the long-term objective of sustainable development, decision-makers are undoubtedly left with the ability to exercise a high degree of discretion.[23] Herein lies the weakness of the concept; whilst almost all can sign up to the general task of achieving sustainability, it has proved difficult to change behaviour and values on a more specific level. Whilst the average citizen endorses the need for greater environmental protection, are we willing to make the necessary changes in lifestyle to bring about meaningful and long-term change?[24] On the more positive side, certain legal tools can be utilised in the pursuit of sustainable development. The environmental impact assessment (EIA) process discussed later in this book should be seen for instance as an instrument which seeks to facilitate sustainability,[25] and the exercise of the right of access to environmental information can encourage the long-term advancement of sustainability by empowering the individual citizen to take steps to enforce obligations of an environmental nature or to lobby for necessary change.[26]

---

[23] Boyle and Freestone, *supra* n.9, p.16. See also European Commission, *supra* n.22, at pp.4-5 where the role of political leadership and policy-making is highlighted.

[24] See also similar point by Kramer, "Thirty Years of EC Environmental Law: Perspectives and Prospectives" 2 *Yearbook of European Environmental Law* (2002), pp.181-182.

[25] See chapter 5.

[26] Boyle and Freestone, *supra* n.9, p.16. At the Community level, see Directive 90/313 on Access to Environmental Information, OJ 1990 L158/56 now repealed by Directive 2003/4/EC, OJ 2003 L41/26.

Integrating Environmental Considerations into other Policy Areas

The EC Treaty includes a number of general principles which offer guidance to the development of policy. The significance of the general principles of subsidiarity and proportionality to the Community's environmental activities has already been noted in chapter 1. Another general principle of considerable importance is the "integration principle" which requires that environmental considerations are taken into account in the preparation and implementation of all policies which impact upon the environment. This principle has been described by distinguished international lawyers as being "fundamental to the concept of sustainable development",[27] and was first acknowledged by Community primary law on the entry into force of the SEA in 1987. The Environment Title then noted that

> *[e]nvironmental protection requirements shall be a component of the Community's other policies.*[28]

The Fifth Environmental Action Programme advocated the integration of environmental concerns into key economic sectors (particularly tourism, transport, energy, industry and agriculture), and the wording of the Environment Title following the entry into force of the Maastricht Treaty was changed to note that

> *[e]nvironmental protection requirements must be integrated into the definition and implementation of other Community policies.*[29]

This obligation was reinforced by the Amsterdam Treaty in that specific reference in the Environment Title to the duty to integrate has now been removed, and replaced by Article 6 EC which stipulates:

> *Environmental protection requirements must be integrated into the definition and implementation of the Community policies and activities referred to in Article 3, in particular with a view to promoting sustainable development.*

In effect, the integration principle is now not simply a guiding principle in the environmental sphere. Instead, it is a general principle of EC law which guides the Community's policy objectives and activities, and the implementation of those

---

[27]   Boyle and Freestone, *supra* n.9, p.10. Rio Declaration, Principle 4 notes that "*environmental protection shall constitute an integral part of the development process and cannot be considered in isolation from it*".

[28]   Ex Article 130r(2) EC post SEA.

[29]   Ex Article 130r(2) EC post Maastricht. The Community's Fifth Environmental Action Programme acknowledged the need to take due account of the fragility of the environment in the pursuit of continued economic expansion in the following terms:

> *Within the Community, the long-term success of the more important initiatives such as the Internal market and economic and monetary union will be dependent upon the sustainability of the policies pursued in the fields of industry, energy, transport, agriculture and regional development; but each of these policies, whether viewed separately or as it interfaces with others, is dependent on the carrying capacity of the environment.*

policies.[30] This is reflected in the fact that the integration principle has been used by the ECJ to justify the adoption of Community measures under legal bases other than the Environment Title,[31] in justifying a Community-wide agricultural ban on the export of live cows from Britain during the BSE crisis,[32] and as a justification for national measures promoting renewable energy sources.[33] The principle seeks to ensure the correct balance is struck between potentially competing interests with a view to minimising or eradicating the most harmful impacts upon the environment, a process which has been endorsed by the Sixth Environmental Action Programme with a view to reducing "pressures in the environment from various sources".[34]

There is however uncertainty as to what "environmental protection requirements" actually are, and the extent to which they should be taken into account. The environmental principles in Article 174(2) EC must form part of the environmental protection requirements which are to be integrated into the definition and implementation of the Community's policies and activities.[35] These environmental principles are discussed below and include the principles of prevention, precaution, rectification at source and polluter pays. In appropriate circumstances, other policy areas (such as those relating to transport, energy or agriculture) should therefore endorse preventive measures or a precautionary approach minimising environmental impact. However, the Community's legislators possess a wide discretion in determining the content of specific legislative measures, and it would be very difficult to seek the annulment of a piece of legislation for failure to take an environmental principle into account.[36] Due consideration should nonetheless be given to the environmental impact of Community activities. In this context, it is noteworthy that Declaration 12 to the Final Act of the Amsterdam Treaty stipulates that

---

[30] Grimeaud, "The Integration of Environmental Concerns into EC Policies: A Genuine Policy Development?" (2000) 9 EELR 207, at p.216. See also Wasmeier, "The Integration of Environmental Protection as a General Rule for Interpreting Community Law" (2001) 38 CMLRev 159, at p.161.

[31] See, for example, that in the "Titanium Dioxide" case (Case C-300/89 *Commission* v *Council* [1991] ECR I-2867) the ECJ noted that the wording of ex Article 130r post SEA declared that "environmental protection requirements shall be a component of the Community's other policies". From this the ECJ deduced that the mere fact that a measure has an environmental objective did not infer that its legal base must necessarily be under the Environment Title. See also Case 62/88 *Parliament* v *Council* [1990] ECR I-1527.

[32] Case C-180/96 *UK* v *Commission* [1998] ECR I-2265, paras. 99-100: "*Where there is uncertainty as to the existence or extent of risks to human health, the institutions may take protective measures without having to wait until the reality and seriousness of those risks become fully apparent. That approach is borne out by Article 130r(1) of the EC Treaty, according to which Community policy on the environment is to pursue the objective inter alia of protecting human health. Article 130r(2) provides that policy is to aim at a high level of protection and is to be based in particular on the principles that preventive action should be taken and that environmental protection requirements must be integrated into the definition and implementation of other Community policies.*"

[33] Case C-379/98 *PreussenElektra AG* v *Schleswag AG* [2001] ECR I-2099, para. 76.

[34] Preamble, at para. 13 (OJ 2002 L242/1).

[35] Kramer, *EC Environmental Law* (2000), p.15.

[36] Kramer notes that "only in extreme cases could it be argued that Community policies do not take into account environmental protection requirements in their definition and implementation. Normally, the wide discretion which is available under Article 6 would not make such an action successful"; *ibid*, p.16.

> *the Conference notes that the Commission undertakes to prepare environmental assessment studies when making proposals which may have significant environmental implications.*

Any such impact assessment would, however, involve a decision-making process in which environmental concerns represent just one of the competing interests to be taken into consideration. It is highly unlikely that environmental interests should be given priority over other competing concerns.[37] For example, the Community's transport policy must take due account of potential environmental impacts, but the fact that a particular proposal in that field might have negative environmental effects could be outweighed by economic and social considerations. If this proved to be the case, negative environmental impact should be assessed and kept to a minimum, but environmental harm may well still be inflicted even if due account is taken of the integration principle.

In the early 1990s, independent research had concluded that integration of environmental protection requirements into other policy sectors had been of limited practical importance, and supported calls for a more effective approach.[38] The Commission agreed on measures with a view to ensuring more effective integration of environmental considerations into its policy-making in 1993.[39] A Commission report published in 1997 noted that a degree of progress had been made in that, for example, so-called "integration correspondents" had been identified in all relevant Directorates General. These individuals have responsibility for ensuring that policy is developed in the particular directorate in question in such a way that due account is taken of the environment and the need to achieve sustainable development.[40] In addition, a Directors General Environment network, chaired by the Director General of DG Environment, was established to facilitate discussion of environmental issues in all policy areas.[41] Nevertheless, it remained at best uncertain as to the impact of these innovations on the policy process, and indeed the Commission acknowledged that there was a clear lack of commitment to its overall strategy.[42] Specifically there was evidence that Directorates General saw little benefit in examining their activities to assess environmental impact.[43]

The Heads of State at the Luxembourg European Council in December 1997 requested that the Commission develop a strategy to fulfil the requirements of the

---

[37]   Wasmeier, *supra* n.30, p.163.

[38]   Baldock, Beaufort, Haigh, Hewett, Wilkinson, Wenning, *The Integration of Environmental Protection Requirements into the Definition and Implementation of Other EC Policies* (1992).

[39]   SEC (93) 785 final.

[40]   "Communication to the Commission on Integration of Environmental Considerations in Commission Policy-Making and Management", Communication C (97) 1844, p.9 [available at http://europa.eu.int/comm/environment/enveco/integration/com_en_971844.pdf].

[41]   *Ibid.*

[42]   *Ibid*, p.10.

[43]   *Ibid*, p.8.

new Article 6 EC. In response, the Commission noted that continued environmental regulation and the use of clean technologies can certainly assist in resolving environmental problems, but that important policy changes in all sectors as well as important behavioural changes would be required to meet the objectives of Article 6 EC.[44] The issue of tackling climate change, one of the most pressing environmental problems, provides a classic example of the need to integrate environmental protection requirements into other policies, and can be used to highlight this assertion.[45] We will note in our subsequent discussion on global warming in chapter 8 that the Community has introduced important environmental legislation to reduce greenhouse gases. These measures include the Integrated Pollution Prevention and Control Directive which *inter alia* obliges Member States to adopt the necessary measures to ensure that industrial plants operate in such a manner that energy is used efficiently.[46] Environmental regulation can therefore play a very useful role, but the problem can only be effectively addressed if policy and patterns of behaviour within other sectors (such as the transport, energy and agriculture sectors) are changed by taking environmental considerations fully into account. For example, greater use must be made of renewable energy rather than of energy from the more traditional coal-fired power stations, and transport policy must take into account the need to promote alternative methods of transit rather than fostering the current dependence on road transportation.

In June 1998 the Cardiff European Council gave support to the Commission's suggestion that key Commission policy proposals should be accompanied by an environmental impact assessment. The European Council also called on the Transport, Energy and Agriculture Councils to devise their own approaches to achieving effective integration of environmental considerations into policy definition (the "Cardiff process"). Other sectoral Councils including Development, Internal Market, Economic and Financial (ECOFIN), Industry, General Affairs and Fisheries have subsequently been engaged in the devising of their own strategies.[47] It is too soon to assess the specific impact of any such strategy.[48] However, general progress towards integration over the last ten years has undoubtedly proved difficult, the Commission having indicated that

---

[44] European Commission, "Partnership for Integration - A Strategy for Integrating Environment into European Union Policies" COM (98) 333, p.5.

[45] See also *ibid*, pp.9-10.

[46] Council Directive 96/61/EC OJ 1996 L257/26.

[47] On the sectoral strategies see generally European Commission, *supra* n.14, pp.30-32, and pp.34-39. Also Haigh, *Manual of Environmental Policy* (looseleaf), chapter 3.

[48] To facilitate progress, the Sixth Environmental Action Programme *inter alia* requires the *"establishing [of] appropriate regular internal mechanisms in the Community institutions, taking full account of the need to promote transparency and access to information, to ensure that environmental considerations are fully reflected in Commission policy initiatives, including relevant decisions and legislative proposals";* Article 3(3) (OJ 2002 L242/1).

> *[w]hile there is growing awareness of the importance of integrating environmental objectives into other policies, ... this approach ... is poorly developed in many sectors. The underlying trends in many economic sectors and their continuing link with environmental impacts gives cause for concern.*[49]

Some progress has however been made. We will for instance note in subsequent discussion that the obligation to carry out environmental impact assessment of projects likely to cause significant harm has allowed environmental concerns to be taken into account in certain decision-making processes, and that adherence in the future to a process of strategic environmental assessment of plans and programmes will assist in ensuring that environmental considerations are considered at an even earlier stage. Another positive example is the work of the European Environment Agency which has embarked on a process of collecting and making available environmental information, a necessary operation if environmental concerns are to be meaningfully taken into account in general policy direction. However, general progress is slow and real political commitment to implement the obligation to integrate would appear at present to be lacking within the Community and its Member States. It is therefore of crucial importance that integration strategies are made the subject of transparent regular reviews, and that the positive aspects of integration – including the potential to improve human health and enhance job opportunities – are brought to the attention of those decision-makers who would otherwise not share a natural propensity towards the safeguarding of environmental protection requirements.

Specific Objectives of the Community's Environmental Policy

Whilst the pursuit of sustainable development can be regarded as a general objective of the Community, the specific objectives of the Community's environmental policy are to be found in Article 174(1) EC of the Environment Title:

Community policy shall contribute to pursuit of the following objectives:

- *preserving, protecting and improving the quality of the environment;*
- *protecting human health;*
- *prudent and rational utilisation of natural resources;*
- *promoting measures at international level to deal with regional or worldwide environmental problems.*

These objectives provide assistance in defining the realm within which the Community can exercise its environmental competence.

---

[49] Commission, *supra* n.14, p.23. See also European Commission, "The Cologne Report on Environmental Integration: Mainstreaming of Environmental Policy" SEC (99) 777.

Preserving, Protecting and Improving the Quality of the Environment

Defining what we mean by the "environment" is certainly not an easy task. The EC Treaty itself makes no attempt at all to provide a definition of the term. The absence of a definition in primary Community law has in fact facilitated the adoption of a wide variety of measures as the objective of "preserving, protecting and improving the quality of the environment" has been interpreted broadly by the Community's institutions.[50] Action has been taken designed to reduce or prevent the deleterious impact of a wide range of environmental hazards or potential risks ranging, for instance, from the control of genetically-modified organisms to the use of leghold traps.[51] Numerous pieces of legislation have been adopted which provide sectoral pollution control by imposing regulatory standards to reduce environmental impact on a single environmental medium. More recently, the Community has moved towards greater use of integrated environmental protection controls which take account of impacts on all three environmental media.[52]

Community environmental action has not solely aspired to afford a level of protection to that part of the "environment" forming part of Member States' sovereign territory. We will note subsequently that the Community enjoys shared competence with the Member States to promote measures at the international level to deal with regional or worldwide environmental problems (such as climate change, ozone layer depletion and acidification). In relation to the scope of a specific piece of Community secondary legislation, it is also of interest to note that the English High Court in *R* v *Secretary of State for Trade and Industry ex parte Greenpeace Ltd*[53] has ruled that the Habitats Directive applied not only to UK sovereign territory (including its territorial sea), but also to the UK's Continental Shelf and to the superjacent waters up to a 200-mile limit beyond the baseline from which the UK's 12-mile territorial sea is measured. This expansive approach to the sphere of application of a directive has been mirrored in a more recent example of Community secondary legislation. Whilst the Habitats Directive did not specifically indicate that it applied to an area beyond the sovereign territory of a Member State, a directive adopted in 2001 concerning national emissions for certain atmospheric pollutants expressly stipulates that it applies not only to sources of pollutants in the territory of Member States and their 12-mile territorial seas, but also in Member States' Exclusive Economic Zones (EEZs) which can stretch a further 200 miles from sovereign territorial waters.[54]

---

[50] Jans, *European Environmental Law* (2000), p.25.

[51] Directive 2001/18 on the Deliberate Release into the Environment of GMOs, OJ 2001 L106/1, and Regulation 3254/91 on the Use of Leghold Traps in the Community, OJ 1991 L308/1.

[52] Directive 96/61, *supra* n. 46.

[53] [2000] Env. L.R. 221.

[54] Directive 2001/81 on National Emissions for certain Atmospheric Pollutants OJ 2001 L309/22, Article 2.

Protecting Human Health

A variety of pollutants are known to have a deleterious impact on the quality of our environment, and can have a direct impact on human health. For example, there is growing evidence that dangerous chemicals can accumulate in the environment and facilitate the promotion of risks to health (such as food poisoning, immunity suppression, asthma, allergies, infertility, and some forms of cancer).[55] Considerable efforts have been made at the Community level to reduce the level of contaminants over the last thirty or so years. In relation to hazardous chemicals, these include measures to assess the potential risk of substances and to classify dangerous substances,[56] and to regulate the marketing and use of dangerous substances.[57] Other measures which have been introduced to regulate dangerous substances produced by industry include the "Seveso Directive" which seeks to prevent major accidents from industrial activities,[58] and also the Directive on Integrated Pollution Prevention and Control (IPPC Directive).[59] In the pursuit of greater protection of human health the Community has also seen fit to regulate the authorisation and use of pesticides,[60] and noise levels from certain vehicles and in the workplace.[61] Numerous other directives have additionally aimed to protect human health by seeking to improve the quality of water,[62] to manage waste more effectively,[63] and to improve air quality.[64]

---

[55]   See generally the European Commission's proposal for a Sixth Environmental Action Programme COM (2001) 3.

[56]   Directive 67/548 on the Approximation of Laws, Regulations and Administrative Provisions Relating to the Classification, Packaging and Labelling of Dangerous Substances (OJ 1967 L196/1) as amended most recently by Directive 2001/59 (OJ 2001 L225/1).

[57]   Directive 76/769 on the Approximation of the Laws, Regulations and Administrative Provisions Relating to Restrictions on the Marketing and Use of Hazardous Substances and Preparations (OJ 1976 L262/201) as most recently amended by Directives 2002/61 (OJ 2002 L243/15) and 2002/62 (OJ 2002 L183/58).

[58]   Directive 82/501 on Major-accident Hazards of Certain Industrial Activities (OJ 1982 L230/1) now repealed by Directive 96/82 on the Control of Major-accident Hazards Involving Dangerous Substances (OJ 1997 L10/13).

[59]   Directive 96/61, *supra* n. 46.

[60]   Directive 91/414 Concerning the Placing of Plant Protection Products on the Market (OJ 1991 L230/1) as most recently amended by Directive 2003/31 (OJ 2003 L101/3).

[61]   For example, Directive 70/157 on the Approximation of Laws Relating to the Permissible Sound Level and the Exhaust System of Motor Vehicles (OJ 1970 L42/16) as most recently amended by Directive 1999/101 (OJ 1999 L334/41). Examples of other measures include a directive regulating noise from tractors (Directive 74/151 OJ 1974 L84/10) and a measure relating to aircraft noise levels (Regulation 1592/2002 OJ 2002 L240/1). In relation to the workplace, see Directive 86/188 on the Protection of Workers from the Risks Related to Exposure to Noise at Work (OJ 1986 L137/28) as most recently amended by Directive 98/24 (OJ 1998 L131/11). Note also the Community's more recent efforts in this sphere; Directive 2002/49 Relating to the Assessment and Management of Environmental Noise, OJ 2002 L189/12.

[62]   See in particular the Water Framework Directive (Directive 2000/60 Establishing a Framework for Community action in the Field of Water Policy, OJ 2000 L327/1).

[63]   See chapter 7.

[64]   Such as Directive 96/62 on Ambient Air Quality Assessment and Management (OJ 1996 L296/55).

There is little doubt that such action at the Community level has played a significant part in reducing some risks to health. Reductions in sulphur dioxide levels and the concentration of lead in ambient air, as well as improvements in the quality of drinking water offer examples of real improvements in this regard. However, much still needs to be done. For example, dust concentrations as well as levels of nitrogen dioxide and ozone continue to contribute to increased mortality rates and decreased life expectancy.[65] In addition, risks to human health continue from nitrate and pesticide residues, and from increased exposure to noise pollution.[66] Whilst we are beginning to appreciate more about the effects of pollutants on human health, the Sixth Environmental Action Programme acknowledges that a better understanding is required if effective preventive action is to be taken.[67] Taking action to improve or protect the environment and health is one of four priority areas for action under this programme which promotes a more integrated approach in tackling risks to human health.[68]

Prudent and Rational Utilisation of Natural Resources

This objective of the Community's environmental policy is recognised by the Commission as a condition for sustainable development.[69] The current significance of this goal is underlined by the fact that the Sixth Environmental Action programme identifies action on the "sustainable use and management of natural resources and waste" as another of its four priority areas for action. To facilitate the prudent and rational use of natural resources, it is imperative that consumers and producers modify their practices to ensure that resources are "used within their capacity for renewal".[70] Moderating consumption and production patterns in this way will reduce pressures on the natural environment and its resources.

The Sixth Environmental Action Programme seeks to "decouple" the utilisation of resources and waste generation from the pace of economic growth. The Community's waste management strategy is addressed later in this book,[71] but a

---

65   European Environment Agency, *Environment in the EU at the Turn of the Century* (1999).

66   *Ibid.*

67   *Supra* n.48, Article 7(1).

68   The others being the tackling of climate change, protection of nature and biodiversity and promoting the sustainable use and management of natural resources and waste.

69   European Commission's proposal for a Sixth Environmental Action Programme COM (2001) 3, p.11. At the international level, while the Rio Declaration stipulated that States have the sovereign right to exploit their own natural resources to assist in improving the lives of their people, it further notes that "*to achieve sustainable development and a higher quality of life for all people, States should reduce and eliminate unsustainable patterns of production and consumption*" (Principle 8).

70   As noted in World Conservation Union, United Nations Environment Programme, World Wide Fund for Nature, *Caring for the Earth: A Strategy for Sustainable Living* (1991), p.10. This report highlights the action which needs to be taken to promote sustainable living.

71   See chapter 7.

variety of other measures are also designed to promote the more efficient use of resources and assist in this "decoupling". These include horizontal measures promoting environmental impact assessment,[72] eco-labelling,[73] and eco-auditing.[74] Measures promoting greater use of renewable sources of energy also facilitate the prudent and sustainable use of resources.[75] Additionally, the Commission's plans to introduce a regime on environmental liability should be seen as another example of a way in which further depletion of natural resources can be minimised by imposing liability on those who by their actions damage the environment and harm human health.[76]

Promotion of Measures at the International Level to Deal with Regional or Worldwide Environmental Problems

Many environmental issues of their very nature require an international coordinated response, and in recent years the Community has become a party to a variety of international legal instruments.[77] Examples include the UN Convention on Biological Diversity,[78] the UN Convention on Climate Change,[79] the Geneva Convention on Long-Range Transboundary Air Pollution,[80] the Vienna Convention for the Protection of the Ozone Layer and its Montreal Protocol on substances which deplete the Ozone Layer,[81] the Basel Convention on the Transboundary Movement of Hazardous Waste,[82] and the Barcelona Convention for the Protection of the Mediterranean Sea against Pollution.[83] Bearing in mind the Commission's assertion that "approximately one third of Community environmental policy aims to implement legally binding international agreements",[84] the influence of

---

[72] See chapter 5.

[73] The original eco-label scheme was established by Regulation 880/92 on a Community Eco-Label Award Scheme (OJ 1992 L99/1). This measure was replaced by Regulation 1980/2000 on a Revised Community Eco-Label Award Scheme (OJ 2000 L237/1). On the eco-label award scheme see *infra* n.146 and accompanying text.

[74] Regulation 761/2001 Allowing Voluntary Participation by Organisations in a Community Eco-management and Audit Scheme (EMAS), OJ 2001 L114/1.

[75] See chapter 8.

[76] COM (2002) 17.

[77] See Macleod, Hendry and Hyatt, *The External Relations of the European Communities* (1996), pp.325-326, and Haigh, *Manual of Environmental Policy: the EC and Britain* (looseleaf), chapter 13.

[78] See Decision concerning the conclusion of the Convention on Biological Diversity, OJ 1993 L309/1.

[79] See Decision concerning the conclusion of the Convention on Climate Change, OJ 1994 L33/11.

[80] See Decision concerning the conclusion of the Geneva Convention on Long-Range Transboundary Air Pollution, OJ 1981 L171/11.

[81] See Decision concerning the conclusion of the Vienna Convention for the Protection of the Ozone Layer and the Montreal Protocol on Substances which Deplete the Ozone Layer, OJ 1988 L297/8.

[82] See Decision concerning the conclusion of the Basel Convention on the Transboundary Movement of Hazardous Waste, OJ 1993 L39/1.

[83] See Decision concerning the conclusion of the Barcelona Convention for the Protection of the Mediterranean Sea against Pollution, OJ 1977 L240/77.

[84] European Commission, *supra* n.14, p.21.

international agreements upon the Community's environmental strategy should not be underestimated.

Since the adoption of the SEA, the Community has enjoyed express competence to cooperate with international actors in the environmental sphere.[85] Article 174(4) EC notes that

> *Within their respective spheres of competence, the Community and the Member States shall cooperate with third countries and with the competent international organisations. The arrangements for Community cooperation may be the subject of agreements between the Community and the third parties concerned, which shall be negotiated and concluded in accordance with Article 300.*
>
> *The previous subparagraph shall be without prejudice to Member States' competence to negotiate in international bodies and to conclude international agreements.*

Prior to the SEA and the provision of external environmental competence, the Community had also entered into international environmental agreements by virtue of the "doctrine of parallelism" which has been referred to by McGoldrick as an acknowledgement that "as the internal competence [of the Community] develops, so the external competence automatically develops".[86] Article 281 EC bestows the Community with legal personality, and in the *ERTA* case the Court of Justice interpreted this provision as meaning that

> *in its external relations the Community enjoys the capacity to establish contractual links with third countries over the whole field of objectives defined in Part One of the Treaty ....*[87]

In effect, the ECJ had ruled that the Community enjoyed implied treaty-making powers where it possessed internal legislative competence. Implied competence was therefore enjoyed by the Community in a given subject matter where it possessed power to legislate internally and had exercised that power.[88] In practice, it has been very rare that the Community has entered into an international environmental agreement without having first adopted specific internal rules addressing the subject matter.[89] However, it is worthy of note that the Community can additionally enter

---

[85] Ex Article 130r(5) which became Article 130r(4) post Maastricht. After the coming into force of the Amsterdam Treaty, this article was renamed Article 174(4) EC.

[86] McGoldrick, *International Relations Law of the European Union* (1997), p.48.

[87] Case 22/70 *Commission* v *Council (ERTA)* [1971] ECR 263, para. 14 of the judgment.

[88] *Ibid*, paras 17-19. On extent of external competence, see generally Macleod, Hendry and Hyatt, *supra* n.77, pp.47-53.

[89] Macleod, Hendry and Hyatt, *supra* n.77, pp.325-326. Note however that the Community became a party to the 1974 Paris Convention for the Prevention of Marine Pollution from Land-based Sources before adopting internal rules covering the subject matter of the agreement; Nollkaemper, "The EC and International Environmental Cooperation - Legal Aspects of External Community Powers" (1987) 2 Legal Issues in European Integration 55, p.73-74. Also that the Community concluded the 1992 Climate Change Treaty even though no corresponding legally binding internal measures had yet been adopted at that time; Jans, *European Environmental Law* (2000), p.81.

into international treaties where it enjoys internal competence but has not yet adopted internal measures. In such a situation, the Community's participation at the international level would need to be necessary to achieve a specific objective of the EC Treaty which could not have been realised by the adoption of internal legislation alone.[90]

External environmental competence allows the EC to play an important and influential role at the international level. Environmental agreements have taken the form of "mixed agreements" under which joint action by the EC and its Member States is required in negotiation, participation and application.[91] The Court of Justice has underlined the need for "close cooperation" between Member States and the Community institutions in negotiations for and the conclusion of such mixed agreements, as well as in the fulfilment of relevant obligations.[92] The need for such close association has been referred to by the ECJ as a "requirement of unity in the international representation of the Community."[93]

The power to act in mixed agreements is shared in the sense that power to legislate rests in part with the EC and in part with the Member States.[94] Such shared competence is acknowledged in the second paragraph of Article 174(4) EC which notes that the Community's ability to cooperate and make agreements with third countries is without prejudice to Member States' powers to negotiate and conclude agreements. The precise boundaries of respective competences are often difficult to identify, a fact which has proved to be a source of frustration to some third parties.[95] It is now usual for an international agreement to require a declaration of competence from the Community on the issue,[96] but these declarations are often vague and fail

---

90   See Opinion 1/94 (re the WTO agreement) [1994] ECR I-5267.

91   On "mixed agreements" generally see Macleod, Hendry and Hyatt, *supra* n.77, chapter 6.

92   Opinion 1/94 (*Re WTO Agreement*), *supra* n.90.

93   *Ibid.*

94   In principle, the EC could enjoy exclusive competence in an agreement which impacted upon the environment in accordance with the *ERTA* judgment – if the Community has adopted internal rules which exhaustively regulate the field, the EC possesses exclusive competence. However, if the internal rules in question are adopted under Article 175 EC, they cannot be said to regulate exhaustively as they are to be regarded as minimum standards only as Member States have the ability to maintain or introduce more stringent protective measures (see Article 176 EC). Accordingly, Member States can participate with the EC in a mixed agreement covering the subject area concerned. Key environmental agreements concluded on the basis of ex Article 130s (now Article 175) include the 1989 Basel Convention on the Control of Transport of Hazardous Wastes, the 1992 Climate Change Convention, the 1992 Biodiversity Convention and the 1985 Convention for the Protection of the Ozone Layer. See generally Macleod, Hendry and Hyatt, *supra* n.77, p.327.

95   See Nollkaemper, *supra* n.89, pp. 81-82.

96   See, for instance, Article 13 of the 1985 Ozone Layer Convention which stipulates that the treaty is open to ratification by "regional economic integration organisations" (para.1), but that any such organisation "and its Member States shall decide on their respective responsibilities for the performance of their obligation under the convention..." (para.2). Para. 3 notes that the extent of cooperation will be made in a declaration on ratification. Similar requirements are made in Article 22 of the Climate Change Convention, and Article 34 of the Biodiversity Convention. On EC participation in the Ozone Layer Convention, see Temple Lang, "The Ozone Layer Convention: A New Solution to the Question of Community Participation in Mixed International Agreements" (1986) 23 CMLRev 157-176.

to add clarity. The Community's declaration on acceding to the Convention on Biological Diversity, for example, merely noted that "the Community alongside its Member States has competence to take actions aiming at the protection of the environment", before proceeding to note those measures already adopted at Community level of relevance to matters covered by the convention.[97]

The Community's ability to participate in international environmental agreements assists in raising the profile of the organisation internationally. Representing a bloc of influential industrialised states, its involvement can also offer it the opportunity to take on a leadership role. For example, it is highly unlikely that specific targets on greenhouse emission reductions would have been agreed under the Kyoto Protocol without the influence and lobbying of the Community.[98] In addition, the EC insisted in the negotiations for a Protocol to the 1985 Ozone Layer Convention that any proposed measures should place generally applicable limits on production capacity of depleting substances, rather than seek simply to regulate the use of such substances as aerosol propellants only. The Community's stance had initially angered the USA which felt that a ban on the use of CFCs in aerosol propellants would provide the quickest way to reduce CFC emissions.[99] However, the Community criticised this "uses" approach as it provided no limit on other uses of CFCs, and eventually successfully insisted that measures must indeed seek to limit the general production of CFCs. Haigh correctly indicates that the Montreal Protocol on Substances which Deplete the Ozone Layer would have been "less satisfactory" requiring "complete revision after the ozone hole discovery" had the Community's approach not eventually been adopted.[100]

Another example of the Community's influence at the international level can be seen in the negotiations for the 1998 United Nations/ Economic Commission for Europe Convention on Access to Information, Public Participation in Decision-Making and Access to Justice in Environmental Matters (the "Aarhus Convention").[101] The Aarhus Convention seeks to guarantee certain public participation rights for citizens in environmental decision-making with a view to assisting in the tackling of environmental concerns, and achieving sustainability in the long term. It endeavours to empower citizens allowing them to take steps to ensure that environmental obligations are recognised and effectively enforced. In negotiations on Pillar I of the Aarhus Convention,[102] the Community's 1990 Directive on Freedom of Access to

---

[97] Jans, *supra* n.89, p.89. See Decision concerning the conclusion of the Convention on Biological Diversity OJ 1993 L309/1, pp.18-19.

[98] See further chapter 8.

[99] Haigh, *supra* n.77, 6.12-3.

[100] See Haigh, *ibid*, at 6.12-4, and generally 6.12-2 - 6.12-5.

[101] 38 ILM (1999) 517.

[102] Pillar I concentrates on freedom of access to environmental information, Pillar II on citizens' rights to participate in decision-making, and Pillar III on access to justice in environmental matters. On the Aarhus Convention generally, see Brady, "The New Convention on Access to Information and Public Participation in Environmental Matters" (1998) 28/2 Environmental Policy and Law 69.

Information on the Environment ("Access to Information Directive")[103] provided an important initial basis for discussion between participating states.[104] Furthermore, it soon became clear to the Community and its Member States that lessons had to be learnt from experience gained at the Community level in the implementation of the Access to Information Directive, and that these lessons had to be incorporated into the final text of the Aarhus Convention. The Access to Information Directive places an obligation on Member States to ensure that public authorities with responsibilities for and possessing information on the environment make this information available to individuals as soon as possible, or within two months of their request at the latest. However, failings in implementation had become all too apparent. For example, the definition of "environmental information" proved imprecise allowing some public authorities to refuse access to certain information which clearly had implications for the environment.[105] In addition, public authorities whose primary responsibilities did not directly relate to the environment but which nevertheless had an important impact on the environment had occasionally taken the view that the Access to Information Directive did not apply to information it held.[106] The sharing of this experience by the Community and its Member States with all 38 state participants in the negotiations for the Aarhus Convention ensured that the text of the final treaty minimised the risk of these failings being repeated at the international level.[107]

Guiding Environmental Principles

Whilst the principles of subsidiarity and integration are examples of general EC Treaty principles which are of particular relevance to policy impacting upon the environment, Article 174(2) EC [ex Article 130r] sets out a specific set of principles which afford guidance to the Community's environmental policy in that it

shall be based on the precautionary principle and on the principles that preventive action should be taken, that environmental damage should as a priority be rectified at source and that the polluter should pay.

---

[103] Directive 90/313 OJ 1990 L158/56. In the light of experience since the entry into force of this measure, the Commission proposed a new directive to repeal the original measure; see now Directive 2003/4/EC OJ 2003 L41/26.

[104] See European Commission, "Report on the Experience Gained in the Application of Directive 90/313 on Freedom of Access to Information on the Environment" COM (2000) 400, p.8.

[105] For example, access to information concerning the economic case for the operation of the THORP nuclear fuel reprocessing plant was refused; see ENDS Report 255, p.30 and ENDS Report 307, p.41.

[106] See COM (2000) 402.

[107] The definitions of "environmental information" (Article 2(3)) and of "public authority" (Article 2(2)) in the Aarhus Convention significantly improve on the definitions of these terms in the Access to Information Directive by providing less room for discussion as to whether the obligation to provide access to environmental information applies.

The ECJ in the *Peralta* case ruled that these principles provide only guidance to the direction of the Community's environmental policy noting that "[ex] Article 130r is confined to defining the general objectives of the Community in the matter of the environment".[108] It would therefore be difficult to contemplate the success of an action questioning the validity of a measure on the basis that it fails to take due account of one or more of these principles. This should not however be completely ruled out, the Court of Justice noting in *Safety Hi-Tech* and in *Bettati* that a measure would be subject to review but only on the limited question as to whether the legislature had "committed a manifest error of appraisal regarding the conditions for the application of [ex] Article 130r".[109] The possibility therefore exists for the ECJ to at least consider such an issue in the future, but the broad discretion afforded to the Community institutions in pursuing environmental objectives would seem to restrict significantly the likelihood of a successful review application.

Precautionary Principle

The SEA had noted that the Community's environmental policy shall be based on the preventive, polluter pays and rectification at source principles.[110] In the mid to late 1980s, the precautionary principle was of growing importance, but had yet to gain the level of acceptance of these other environmental principles. It was not until the entry into force of the Maastricht Treaty that reference to the precautionary principle was incorporated into the Environment Title.

Although there is no definition of the principle in the EC Treaty, the precautionary principle has been widely thought to endorse the taking of action to prevent environmental harm from a perceived risk in situations where a causal link between an activity and consequent damage to the environment has yet to be scientifically established beyond any doubt. In view of the potentially serious or irreversible deleterious effects on the environment from potentially damaging activities, immediate action should nevertheless be taken to eradicate or minimise environmental harm.[111]

Despite action to date, damage to the environment clearly continues at an alarming rate. Bearing this in mind, the application of the precautionary principle should be seen as an acknowledgement that a new approach to environmental regulation is

---

[108] C-379/92 *Criminal proceedings against Matteo Peralta* [1994] ECR I-3453, para. 57. Some lawyers nevertheless do take the view that these principles are binding in nature and must therefore be taken into account in every piece of legislation; see discussion in Kramer, *supra* n.35, p.10.

[109] Case C-284/95 *Safety Hi-Tech Srl* v *S and T Srl* [1998] ECR I-4301, para. 37, and Case C-341/95 *Gianni Bettati* v *Safety Hi-Tech Srl* [1998] ECR I-4355, para.35. For discussion as to the implications of these cases, see Doherty (1999) 11 JEL 378.

[110] See Douma, "The Precautionary Principle in the EU" (2000) 9(2) RECIEL 132-143, at p.133.

[111] See for example Rio Declaration, Principle 15:
Where there are threats of serious or irreversible damage, lack of full scientific certainty shall not be used as a reason for postponing cost-effective measures to prevent environmental degradation.

required which endorses the precautionary principle.[112] There is clearly a close link between sustainable development and the precautionary principle as highlighted as far back as 1990 in the Bergen Economic Commission for Europe Ministerial Declaration on Sustainable Development: "[i]n order to achieve sustainable development, policies must be based on the precautionary principle."[113] Evidently, for example, there may well be a need to take a precautionary approach to an issue bearing in mind the potential long-term impact of certain polluting activities, and the need to take action to safeguard the interests of present and future generations.

Mindful of the lack of definition in the EC Treaty and concerned that the taking of precautionary action may be used as a disguised restriction on trade, the Commission, in early 2000, adopted guidance as to when and how to use the principle.[114] This guidance is not intended to be "set in stone" but rather to provide input into the debate on the principle's application.[115] A resolution adopted by the Nice European Council on the precautionary principle supported the "broad lines" of the Commission's approach.[116] The Commission takes the following view in relation to the application of the precautionary principle:

> *[w]hether or not to invoke the precautionary principle is a decision exercised where scientific information is insufficient, inconclusive, or uncertain and where there are indications that the possible effects on the environment, or human, animal or plant health may be potentially dangerous and inconsistent with the chosen level of protection.*[117]

The Commission is therefore of the view that the application of the principle is not to be confined to environmental concerns, but also to issues which potentially affect health issues relating to humans,[118] other animals and plants.[119]

---

[112] See paper by Douma entitled "The Precautionary Principle" available at http://www.asser.nl/EEL/index5.htm.

[113] *Bergen Ministerial Declaration on Sustainable Development in the ECE Region*, Article 7 (15 May 1990); signed by 34 countries and the EC's Environment Commissioner.

[114] European Commission, "Communication on the Precautionary Principle" COM (2000) 1.

[115] *Ibid*, p.9.

[116] Nice European Council meeting (7, 8 and 9 December 2000), Resolution on the Precautionary Principle (Annex III to the Presidency conclusions), para.1.

[117] European Commission, *supra* n.114, p.8.

[118] ECJ case law confirms this belief. See Case C-157/96 *R* v *MAFF, Commissions of Customs and Excise ex parte National Farmers' Union et al* [1998] ECR I-2211 on the validity of Commission measures to ban the export of British meat to third countries following the establishment of a probable link between BSE in cows and new variant Creutzfeldt-Jakob disease in humans. The Court upheld the Commission's action noting that "[a]t the time when the contested decision was adopted, there was great uncertainty as to the risks posed by live animals, bovine meat and derived products. Where there is uncertainty as to the existence or extent of risks to human health, the institutions may take protective measures without having to wait until the reality and seriousness of those risks become fully apparent"; paras. 62-63 of the judgment. See also the BSE judgment; Case C-180/96 *UK* v *Commission* [1998] ECR I-2265, para. 99.

[119] European Commission, *supra* n.114, p.9.

The Commission's communication advocates due consideration of the application of the precautionary principle after identification of a potential problem and a scientific risk evaluation

> *which because of the insufficiency of the data, their inconclusive or imprecise nature, makes it impossible to determine with sufficient certainty the risk in question.*[120]

The scientific evaluation of risk should however be as complete as is possible in the circumstances.[121] A political decision may then be made as to whether to take precautionary action. In making this determination, decision-makers will need to be made aware of the extent to which there is scientific uncertainty. They must also bear the level of uncertainty in mind as well as public concerns regarding the potential risk, and the unacceptableness or otherwise of the risk involved.

The Commission's communication underlines that the Community's institutions have a broad discretion in determining whether or not to apply a precautionary approach. The decision may even be made not to take any action at all, but rather to wait for new scientific evidence.[122] The Court of First Instance has seen fit to underline the broad discretion of the Community's institutions in applying the precautionary principle.[123] Where precautionary action is necessary, the Commission's communication stipulates that any measure must be proportional to the level of protection chosen, be non-discriminatory in application, and ensure consistency with any previous measures. In addition, action should be based on an examination of the potential costs and benefits of action or inaction, and be subject to review in the light of new scientific evidence.[124]

Some interpretations of the principle have contentiously gone so far as to support a reversal of the burden of proof in the sense that responsibility is placed on those who wish to use a method or substance to prove that it is safe. On this issue, the Commission has accepted that the application of the principle of prior approval may be the most appropriate approach to adopt. In this way, the onus can be placed on industrialists to prove that drugs, pesticides or food additives are safe where risk to

---

[120] *Ibid*, p.15.

[121] See also Case T-70/99 *Alpharma Inc* v *Council* [2002] ECR II-3495, paras. 155-157.

[122] European Commission, *supra* n.114, pp.16-17.

[123] The Court of First Instance has indicated that "the Community institutions are entitled, in the interests of human health to adopt, on the basis of as yet incomplete scientific knowledge, protective measures which may seriously harm legally protected positions, and they enjoy a broad discretion in that regard"; Case T-13/99 *Pfizer Animal Health SA* v *Council* [2002] ECR II-3305, para. 170.

[124] See European Commission, *supra* n.114, pp.18-21.

human health cannot be determined with sufficient certainty.[125] In similar vein, the proposal for the Sixth Environmental Action Programme encouraged the broader application of the reversal of the burden of proof approach

> *making producers responsible to prove that any hazardous substances they currently use and any that they create and plan to use do not present unnecessary or unacceptable risks for the environment and human health.*[126]

In situations where a prior approval system does not exist or is not anticipated, the Commission's guidance on the precautionary principle advocates that determination of the issue as to the burden of proof should be made on a case-by-case basis.

The precautionary principle already plays an important part in regimes established by secondary EC legislation. For example, the directive on water intended for human consumption expressly notes that minimum quality standards have been established taking into account the precautionary principle.[127] Also, in seeking to harmonise national laws and practices when deliberately releasing genetically modified organisms (GMOs) into the environment and placing GMOs on the market, the provisions of Directive 2001/18 note that Member States must ensure that "*in accordance with the precautionary principle* ... all appropriate measures are taken to avoid adverse effects on human health and the environment which might arise from deliberate release or placing on the market of GMOs".[128] In addition, the eco-label regulation specifically notes the importance of ensuring that implementation of the eco-label scheme complies with the precautionary principle.[129]

Importantly, Member States under the Directive on Integrated Pollution Prevention and Control (IPPC Directive) are also legally obliged to give due consideration to the precautionary principle when determining the basic obligations of operators controlling the most polluting industrial operations. The IPPC Directive seeks to guarantee that any authorisation for the operation of such plants takes into account

---

125 *Ibid*, p.21. See for example Council Regulation 2821/98 which banned the use of specific antibiotics in animal feed (OJ 1998 L351/4). Article 2 notes that the banning of the substances will be re-examined in the light *inter alia* of results from "the surveillance programme of microbial resistance in animals which have received antibiotics, to be carried out by the persons responsible for putting the additives concerned into circulation".

126 COM (2001) 31, para. 8.3.

127 Directive 98/83 on the Quality of Water Intended for Human Consumption OJ 1998 L330/32, recital 13 (preamble).

128 OJ 2001 L106/1, Article 4(1) (emphasis added). The preamble notes that the precautionary principle was taken into account at the drafting stage and that it must also be taken into account by Member States in implementation. This directive repeals Directive 90/220 (OJ 1990 L117/15) with effect from 17/10/2002. On Directive 90/220, see Case C-6/99 *Association Greenpeace et al* [2000] ECR I-1651. In this judgment, the ECJ acknowledged the role of the precautionary principle in the system established by the measure (see, for example, para. 44 of the judgment). Additionally, the ECJ held that a Member State is not obliged to give its consent to the placing of GMOs on the market where it has new information "which leads it to consider that the product for which notification has been received *may* constitute a risk to human health and the environment"; para. 45 (emphasis added).

129 Regulation 1980/2000, *supra* n.73, Article 1(4).

its impact on all three environmental media by obliging Member States to ensure installations are run in such a manner that "all the appropriate preventive measures are taken against pollution, in particular through the application of the best available techniques".[130] Certain special considerations to be taken into account in determining "best available techniques" (BAT) are listed in Annex IV of the IPPC Directive, and include the nature of emissions and the use of less hazardous substances. Due regard should be given to these Annex IV considerations in determining BAT "bearing in mind the likely costs and benefits of a measure and the principles of precaution and prevention".[131] The legality of any national legislation transposing the IPPC Directive could therefore be challenged if it fails expressly to note that the precautionary principle must at least be given due consideration by competent national authorities when determining BAT.[132]

The potential significance of the precautionary principle on the Community's environmental policy can perhaps best be shown by the fact that Member States should no longer be able legitimately to argue that an element of scientific uncertainty negates the need for protective action at the Community level. Although Article 174(3) EC notes that in preparing environmental policy account must *inter alia* be taken of "available scientific and technical data", the lack of conclusive scientific data should not necessarily preclude the adoption of protective measures when one bears in mind that the Community's environmental policy shall take account of the precautionary principle.[133]

Preventive Principle

It has long been established that early action which seeks to prevent environmental damage is preferable to measures which counteract the impact of pollution once it has taken place.[134] The preventive principle has been a central feature of all the Community's Action Programmes on the Environment, the third programme noting for example that "prevention rather than cure should be the rule".[135] In this way environmental harm can be minimised in a cost-effective manner. Community action which has, for instance, sought to introduce environmental impact assessment,[136] to combat air and water pollution,[137] to facilitate access to

---

130 Directive 96/61, *supra* n.46, Article 3(a).

131 Annex IV.

132 Douma, *supra* n.110, pp.134-135.

133 See generally Jans, *supra* n.89, at p.33 and p.41.

134 For example, see the Community's First Programme of Action on the Environment at Title II, para.1 (OJ 1973 C112/1).

135 OJ 1983 C46/1, para. 9.

136 Directive 85/337 on the Assessment of the Effects of Certain Public and Private Projects on the Environment (as amended), OJ 1985 L175/40. See generally, chapter 5.

137 For example, Directive 96/62 on Ambient Air Quality Assessment and Management (OJ 1996 L296/55), and Directive 75/440 Concerning the Quality Required of Surface Water Intended for the Abstraction of Drinking Water (OJ 1975 L194/26).

environmental information for decision-makers and members of the public,[138] to limit industrial accidents,[139] or to afford protection to habitats of wild fauna and flora, can be seen to adopt a preventive approach.[140]

Waste management policy also provides a good example of the endorsement of the preventive principle in that the primary importance of waste prevention has been constantly underlined with a view to reducing detrimental environmental impact.[141] The preventive principle has been endorsed in measures which, for example, regulate the shipment of waste,[142] and the manner in which waste is disposed of.[143] In recent years, the onus placed on the producers of products to take into account the waste management implications of a product through its life cycle should also be seen as preventive in nature. The End-of-life Vehicles Directive, for example, seeks to avoid the generation of waste by reducing the use of hazardous substances (such as lead, mercury and cadmium) in vehicles in such a way that recycling is facilitated and the disposal of hazardous waste is reduced. As such, producers are obliged to take into account the need for the recycling of vehicles in design and production.[144]

Community legislation promoting the voluntary "eco-label" and "eco-management and audit schemes" (EMAS) also provide good examples of the endorsement of a preventive approach.[145] Both measures are good examples of the alternative approaches to traditional "command and control" strategies particularly encouraged in the Fifth Environmental Action Programme. Under the current eco-label scheme, products (goods or services) which have a reduced impact on the environment in their life-cycle are promoted by the awarding of an eco-label.[146] The eco-label logo on products is designed to make the consumer fully aware of those goods which have reduced environmental impact compared to other similar products. In this way, it is expected that purchasing behaviour might be modified to prevent future environmental damage, and encourage efficient use of natural resources. Under the EMAS scheme,[147] participating organisations can apply for the registration of any of their sites with a view to evaluating and improving environmental performance. Registration would be likely to improve an organisation's public image, but

---

[138] Directive 90/313, supra n. 26.

[139] Directive 96/82 on the Control of Major Accident Hazards Involving Dangerous Substances, OJ 1997 L10/13.

[140] See generally, chapter 4.

[141] See Council Resolution on a Community Strategy for Waste Management OJ 1997 C76/1, para. 16.

[142] Council Regulation on the Supervision and Control of Shipments of Waste within, into and out of the European Community OJ 1993 L30/1.

[143] See Directive 1999/31 on the Landfill of Waste OJ 1999 L182/1, and Directive 2000/76 on the Incineration of Waste OJ 2000 L332/91.

[144] Directive 2000/53 on End-of-Life Vehicles OJ 2000 L269/34.

[145] See generally Ost, "A Game without Rules? The Ecological Self-Organisation of Firms" in Teubner, Farmer and Murphy (eds.), *Environmental Law and Ecological Responsibility* (1994), at p. 352.

[146] Regulation 1980/2000, *supra* n.73.

[147] Regulation 761/2001, *supra* n.74.

participants must abide by certain rules including the requirement that it carries out an environmental review of its activities, and subsequently sets up an audited environmental management system. In this way the EMAS scheme seeks to promote good practice in industry in a bid to prevent or minimise environmental impacts. It is also an example of a market-mechanism which seeks to commit organisations to act positively to protect the environment over and above their obligations imposed by regulatory controls.

Environmental Damage Should as a Priority be Rectified at Source

The rectification at source principle would seem to encourage the adoption of controls at the point of emission rather than controls further down the pollution pathway.[148] Clearly however any supposed preference for emission standards has not prevented the Community from more often endorsing the setting of quality standards which focus on the results of a polluting act rather than the actual source of pollution.[149] In its jurisprudence, the ECJ has had cause to make reference to the rectification at source principle. For example, in the *Kobenhavns Kommune* judgment,[150] the ECJ ruled that a system for the collection of non-hazardous building waste intended for recovery constituted an obstacle to exports if it prevented producers of such waste from exporting it. It further noted that such an obstacle to exports could not be justified for environmental protection reasons by application of the rectification at source principle where there is no danger to the environment.[151] By necessary implication, it might be presumed that a restriction on the export of waste could be justified by the application of the rectification principle where the export of waste constitutes an environmental danger.[152] The *Walloon Waste* case provides another example of a judgment in which the ECJ also had reason to refer to the rectification at source principle.[153] The Court ruled that the principle required that each region, municipality or other local authority must take measures to make sure that the waste it produces is collected, treated and disposed of, and that disposal should consequently take place as close as possible to the place

---

[148] See Jans, *supra* n.89, p.36.

[149] Kramer notes astutely that "Community practice, certainly as regards air and water pollution, prefers quality standards"; *supra* n.35, p.18.

[150] Case C-209/98 [2000] ECR I-3743.

[151] Para. 51 of the judgment.

[152] Jans, *supra* n.89, p.37.

[153] Case 2/90 *Commission v Belgium* [1992] ECR I-4431. See also Case C-422/92 *Commission v Germany* [1995] ECR I-1097 where a German rule which in general required the disposal of waste to take place within its national borders was said to be in conformity with the rectification at source principle; see para. 34 of the judgment. In addition, see Case C-155/91 *Commission v Council* [1993] ECR I-939 where the ECJ concluded that Directive 91/156 was intended to implement the rectification at source principle as endorsed in the Environment Title. For this reason, *inter alia*, the ECJ concluded that the measure was properly based on ex Article 130s.

where it is produced so that the transport of waste is limited as far as possible.[154] By making reference to the rectifiation at source principle, the ECJ was therefore able to justify action taken at the national level which imposed important restrictions on the dumping in Belgium of hazardous waste originating in another Member State.

Polluter Pays Principle

The "Polluter Pays" principle endorses the concept that those who are responsible for pollution should pay for the costs of dealing with the pollution (reduction, prevention or elimination). The concept raises certain critical questions which have hampered its application.[155] What exactly is "pollution"? Which entity in the "pollution chain" should be responsible for the costs to the environment? Is the "polluter" to be regarded as the producer of the product sold to the consumer? Should not the consumer of the product bear responsibility in some way? If someone is to pay, should there be a ceiling on the level of payment to be made? Although some guidance has been given,[156] these issues have presented difficulties for policy-makers, and prior to the adoption of the Fifth Environmental Action Programme in late 1992, the polluter pays principle had been referred to only in the text of Community waste legislation such as the framework Directive on Waste as amended,[157] the Directive on the Disposal of Waste Oils,[158] and the Directive on Toxic and Dangerous Waste.[159]

We have mentioned earlier that the Fifth Environmental Action Programme endorsed the broadening of the range of policy instruments utilised to protect the environment.

---

[154] Para. 34 of the judgment. For further discussion of this controversial case, see chapter 6 on environmental protection and the free movement of goods.

[155] European Commission, Consultation Paper for the Preparation of a EU Strategy for Sustainable Development SEC (2001) 517, p.50.

[156] See Council Recommendation regarding Cost Allocation and Action by Public Authorities on Environmental Matters OJ 1975 L194/1.

[157] Council Directive 75/442 on Waste (OJ 1975 L194/39) as amended by Council Directive 91/156 (OJ 1991 L78/32): *in accordance with the "polluter pays" principle, the cost of disposing of waste must be born by the holder who has waste handled by a waste collector or by an undertaking as referred to in article 9, and/or the previous holder or the producer of the product from which the waste came*; Article 15.

[158] Council Directive 75/439 on the Disposal of Waste Oils OJ 1975 L194/23 as amended by Council Directive 87/101 OJ 1987 L42/43: *indemnities [to collection or disposal undertakings] may be financed, among other methods, by a charge imposed on products which after use are transformed into waste oils, or on waste oils. The financing of indemnities must be in accordance with the "polluter pays" principle*; Article 15.

[159] Council Directive 78/319 on Toxic and Dangerous Waste OJ 1978 L84/43; *in accordance with the "polluter pays" principle, the cost of disposing of toxic and dangerous waste, less any proceeds from treating the waste, shall be born by the holder who has waste handled by a waste collector ... and/or the previous holders or the producer of the product from which the waste came*; Article 11. This directive has been repealed by Council Directive 91/689 on Hazardous Waste OJ 1991 L377/20.

Complementing the more traditional regulatory approach to environmental protection, the programme highlighted opportunities presented by the adoption of economic instruments, such as eco-taxes and charges for polluting activities. These market-based instruments have the ability to internalise environmental costs in the price of finished products and services. In this way, scope for the application of the polluter pays principle is widened. In addition, companies are encouraged to research into environmentally friendly technology and a contribution is made to the integration of environmental considerations into economic policy. Economic instruments are increasingly being adopted at the national level. Denmark, Finland, the Netherlands and Sweden have, for example, led the way in adopting national carbon/energy taxes on motor fuel and other energy products. Typically these taxes have fixed higher levels of taxation on commodities deemed to be more harmful to the environment (leaded petrol, non-renewable fossil energy sources) than on more environmentally friendly products (unleaded petrol, and wind, wave and solar energy).[160] However, while the introduction of such economic instruments by Member States has attracted the express endorsement of the Council as a way in which to implement the polluter pays principle in practice,[161] efforts to introduce Community-wide environmental taxes, such as the carbon tax and the taxation of energy products, have been thwarted by the need for unanimity in Council.[162]

Whilst it is still widely acknowledged that to date neither the Community nor its Member States have implemented the polluter pays principle to a sufficient degree,[163] the Sixth Environmental Action Programme underlines its significance, and there are now clear signs that Community policy-makers are moving towards a wider application of the principle:

• Endorsement of the principle in the Community's waste management policy strategy continues as a way in which "all economic actors, including producers, importers, distributors, and consumers bear their specific share of responsibility as regards the prevention, recovery and disposal of waste".[164] Mindful of the

---

[160] Tax reductions and exemptions to promote environmental protection at the national level are increasingly being provided in the energy sector to promote renewables. These are a form of State Aid which in principle may have a negative impact on the internal market. The Commission has recently adopted guidelines in this respect; see European Commission, "Community Guidelines on State Aid for Environmental Protection" OJ 2001 C37/3.

[161] Recommendation on the Broad Guidelines of the Economic Policies of the Member States and the Community OJ L 2001 179/1, para.3.8: "*Government action is often delayed by concerns about possible short-term consequences of policies to protect the environment on economic growth, employment and on the competitiveness of individual firms, sectors and Member States. In this context, Member States should make increased use of market-based instruments in pursuit of economic objectives, as they provide flexibility to industry to reduce pollution in a cost-effective way, as well as encourage technological innovation. Furthermore, they are often the most efficient way to curb pollution since they lead to the internalisation of external costs in prices. They are therefore a way to implement more consistently the polluter-pays-principle.*"

[162] See chapter 8 for further discussion.

[163] European Commission, *Consultation Paper for the Preparation of a EU Strategy for Sustainable Development* SEC (2001) 517, pp.50-51.

[164] Council Resolution on a Community Strategy for Waste Management OJ 1997 C76/1, para.13.

environmental damage caused by the operation of a landfill site, the Landfill Directive, for example, obliges Member States to ensure that the cost of setting up, operating and closing a sites are passed on in the price imposed by the operator to those who use the landfill as a way to dispose of their waste.[165] Users of site are therefore regarded as polluters who should pay for the costs incurred in minimising detrimental environmental impact.

• The Sixth Environmental Action Programme envisages the adoption of an Integrated Product Policy (IPP) to minimise the environmental impacts of products throughout their entire life cycle. The Commission's Green Paper on IPP underlines that a key element in this process is the internalising of environmental costs in the price of products.[166] Renewed efforts are therefore expected and could include differentiated taxation to favour environmentally friendly products such as those goods which have been awarded an eco-label.[167] The Commission also proposes to "investigate the main price elements which are not in conformity with the polluter pays principle" with a view to encouraging debate as to how best to internalise environmental costs.[168]

• There are clear moves toward greater "producer responsibility". This concept seeks to emphasise the role of producers in the pollution chain and is linked to the polluter pays principle. The Directive on End-of-Life Vehicles, for example, obliges Member States to ensure that the last owner of a car can deliver it to an authorised treatment facility free of charge and that car manufacturers meet all, or a significant part, of the cost involved.[169] As the manufacturers of cars, producers can be regarded as "polluters" who have responsibility for the environmental impact of their product.

• The Water Framework Directive obliges Member States to take account of the principle that costs of water services, including environmental costs, should be recovered.[170] Water-pricing policies must, if necessary, be adjusted in this respect in accordance with the polluter pays principle.

• Member States are obliged to bring into force laws ensuring that adequate port reception facilities are made available for ship-generated waste. In line with the polluter pays concept, the costs incurred in running these treatment and disposal facilities will be recovered from fees imposed on ships visiting Member States' ports.[171]

---

[165] Directive 1999/31, *supra* n.143, Article 10.

[166] COM (2001) 68.

[167] *Ibid*, p.11.

[168] *Ibid*.

[169] See Directive 2000/53, *supra* n.144, Article 5(4).

[170] Directive 2000/60, *supra* n.62, Article 9.

[171] Directive on Port Reception Facilities for Ship-generated Waste and Cargo Residues (OJ 2000 L332/81), Article 8.

Most importantly, the Commission has put forward a proposal for a directive on environmental liability.[172] This seeks to establish a framework within which environmental damage to protected biodiversity, to waters covered by the Water Framework Directive, and to human health (due to land contamination) is prevented or remedied. The proposed measure seeks to lay down rules on restoration objectives, and as to the choice of the most appropriate measures of restoration. A critically significant aspect of the proposal is that the operator who has caused damage to the environment or who is facing an imminent threat of damage taking place must, whenever possible, pay for the cost of restorative measures. Where such restorative measures have already been taken by relevant authorities, steps must be taken to recover costs. The adoption in the future of a directive based on this proposal would certainly amount to the most far-reaching application to date of the polluter pays principle at the Community level.

The Principle of a High Level of Protection and the "Environmental Guarantee"

In addition to the four principles specific to environmental policy already addressed, Article 174(2) EC notes that the Community's environmental policy

shall aim at a high level of protection taking into account the diversity of situations in the various regions of the Community.

The need to aim at a high level of protection undoubtedly provides an important starting point in deliberations as to the extent to which policy should offer protection to the environment. Indeed, Article 2 EC notes that one of the Community's tasks is to promote "a high level of protection and improvement of the quality of the environment". However, much discretion is still left to the decision-makers as to the appropriate level of protection which should be afforded. The concept of a "high level of protection" is ambiguous in itself, and the ECJ has confirmed that, to be compatible with Article 174(2) EC, the level of protection "does not necessarily have to be the highest that is technically possible".[173] The high level of protection principle can also be seen to be further watered down by the fact that Article 174(2) EC stipulates that due account should be taken of "the diversity of situations in the various regions of the Community". Environmental diversity throughout the Member States must therefore also be taken into account as is stressed by a similar stipulation in Article 174(3) EC that the Community, in preparing its policy in this

---

[172] Proposal on environmental liability with regard to the prevention and remedying of environmental damage, COM(2002) 17. Prior to the putting forward of this proposal, the Commission had issued a white paper; see European Commission, "White Paper on Environmental Liability" COM (2000) 66 final. On the white paper, see Wilde, "The EC Commission's White Paper on Environmental Liability: Issues and Implications" (2001) 13(1) JEL 21, and Bergkamp, "The Commission's White Paper on Environmental Liability: A Weak Case for an EC Strict Liability regime" (2000) 9 EELR 105.

[173] Case C-284/95 *Safety Hi-Tech Srl* v *S & T Srl, supra* n.109, para.49.

field, must take account of the "environmental conditions in the various regions of the Community".

The need to aim at a high level of protection is therefore a highly important consideration in determining policy, but other considerations must also be considered. This is underlined by the fact that Article 174(3) EC further notes that in preparing environmental policy the Community shall also take into account "available scientific and technical data", "the potential benefits and costs of action or lack of action", and "the economic and social development of the Community as a whole and the balanced development of its regions". Although the ECJ has been prepared to confirm that a measure indeed aims to establish a high level of protection,[174] it would be a brave step to conclude that any given measure is invalid on the basis that it fails to establish a "high level of protection" when one bears in mind the vague nature of this concept, and the wide degree of discretion given to decision-makers in determining environmental policy.

In relation to proposals for internal market legislation, Article 95(3) EC establishes a corresponding stipulation in relation to the level of protection to be provided. Where legislation concerning the environment is to be adopted under Article 95 EC, specific Commission proposals

> *will take as a base a high level of protection, taking account in particular of any new development based on scientific facts. Within their respective powers, the European Parliament and the Council will also seek to achieve this objective.*

Under Article 174(2) EC the Community's environmental *policy* will aim at a high level of protection, while specific *proposals* for legislation will take a high level of protection as a base under Article 100a. It is therefore arguable that the judicial review of a specific piece of Community legislation as to whether it sets a high level of protection may be easier if the measure is adopted under Article 100a. However, the fact that the European Parliament and the Council within their respective powers need only "seek to achieve this objective" would appear to make the high level of protection principle difficult to enforce legally in the context of Community legislation which is actually adopted by these Community institutions.[175]

Charter of Fundamental Rights

The "Charter of Fundamental Rights of the European Union" was solemnly proclaimed by the Council, Commission and European Parliament in December 2000.[176] Designed to strengthen the protection of fundamental rights, it is also intended to ensure that citizens become more involved in European matters and that

---

[174] See C-341/95 *Gianni Bettati* v *Safety Hi-Tech, supra* n.109, para.46.
[175] Van Calster and Deketelaere, "Amsterdam, the IGC and the EU Treaty" (1998) 1 EELR 12, at p.15.
[176] OJ 2000 C364/1.

their rights are made more visible. The Charter is addressed to the institutions and bodies of the European Union, as well as the Member States when they are implementing Community Law. It fails to establish a right to a clean environment as had been proposed by environmental NGOs,[177] but Article 37 of the Charter notes that

[a] *high level of environmental protection and the improvement of the quality of the environment must be integrated into the policies of the Union and ensured in accordance with the principle of sustainable development.*

The wording is mandatory in nature but it remains as yet unclear as to the legal nature of the Charter and its provisions. When in June 1999 the Cologne European Council agreed that a draft Charter should be prepared, it noted that the Charter should first be solemnly proclaimed. Next, due consideration would need to be given as to "whether, and, if so, how the Charter should be integrated into the treaties".[178] Both the Commission and European Parliament support incorporation into the Treaty on European Union,[179] and the view that the provisions of the Charter should be regarded as legally binding rather than a mere political declaration.[180] According to the Declaration on the future of the Union annexed to the Treaty of Nice,[181] the status of the Charter is a topic which must be discussed and settled, and following the Laeken European Council in December 2001, a European Convention was created to propose a new framework for the European Union.[182] One of the issues under discussion within this Convention is the legal status of the Charter which ultimately will have to be determined by the governments of the Member States. A decision is likely to be taken at the Inter-Governmental Conference in 2004.

Whether or not it is given formally binding status in the future, the Commission has suggested that the text of the Charter is drafted in such a way that the ECJ may well refer to it in judgments, and see fit to interpret it in a manner which affords it legal force.[183] Certainly the Court of First Instance has already seen fit to make reference to the provisions of the Charter in its jurisprudence.[184] Let us assume for the sake of argument that Article 37 is indeed attributed legally binding status. The provision

---

177 ENDS Report 312 (January 2001), pp.42-43.

178 Cologne European Council; 3-4 June 1999 (Conclusions of the Presidency), Annex IV.

179 See European Commission, "Communication on the Legal Nature of the Charter of Fundamental Rights of the European Union" COM (2000) 644.

180 *Ibid.*

181 OJ 2001 C80/85.

182 See http://european-convention.eu.int/.

183 This is the view of the Commission with regard to the Charter generally; see European Commission, "Communication on the Legal Nature of the Charter of Fundamental Rights of the European Union" COM (2000) 644, p.6.

184 See Case T-177/01 *Jégo-Quéré & Cie SA* v *Commission* [2002] ECR II-2365, para.42 [reference to the right to an effective remedy, Article 47 of the Charter], and Case T-211/02 *Tideland Signal Ltd* v *Commission* [2002] II-3781, para 37 [reference to the right to have affairs handled impartially and fairly, Article 41 of the Charter].

could be said to add much needed definition to the integration principle in the sense that not only must environmental protection requirements be integrated into the definition and implementation of all Community policies in accordance with Article 6 EC, but the level of integration must additionally afford a high level of environmental protection.[185] It might also be said to place an onus on the ECJ to assess whether relevant policies afford this level of protection.[186] However, it would still be highly unlikely that a policy approach could be made the subject of a successful judicial review on the basis it fails to provide a high level of protection when one bears in mind the broad discretion of Community institutions in adopting policy, and the ambiguous nature of the concept of a high level of protection.

Higher National Standards after Harmonisation?

We have noted that the aim of policy in this field is not necessarily to aspire to the *highest* level of protection possible.[187] However, the application of the minimum harmonisation technique and the "environmental guarantee" underlines that there is still room for the exercise of national competence after harmonisation to apply more stringent national measures in certain circumstances. In this way, those Member States which wish to maintain their own higher national environmental standards, or introduce stricter environmental measures, can do so. Other Member States less keen to apply similar standards for economic, social, political or geographical reasons need only abide by the common standard established by the harmonising measure.[188]

The Minimum Harmonisation Technique and Article 176 EC   Some directives introduce a system of "total harmonisation" by fixing common uniform standards, whilst others apply the "minimum harmonisation" technique. If the directive is an example of total harmonisation, the power of Member States to introduce a separate national system of regulation by way of derogation is annulled apart from in those defined situations stipulated by the harmonising measure.[189] Rather than adopting the total harmonisation approach, environmental directives routinely allow for differentiated integration by adopting "minimum harmonisation" in which measures seek to establish minimum standards only.[190] Where the minimum harmonisation

---

[185] ENDS Report 312 (January 2001) at pp.42-43.

[186] *Ibid.*

[187] See *supra* n.172 and accompanying text. See also *Gianni Bettati* v *Safety Hi-Tech* where the ECJ notes that "whilst it is undisputed that [ex] Article 130r(2) of the Treaty requires Community policy in environmental matters to aim for a high level of protection, such a level of protection, to be compatible with that provision, does not necessarily have to be the highest that is technically possible"; C-341/95 *supra* n.109, para. 47

[188] On differentiation generally, see Kramer, "Differentiation in EU Environmental Policy" (2000) 9 EELR 133.

[189] For example, Directive 84/631 established a comprehensive system of regulation with regard to the transfrontier shipment of hazardous waste. Member States had lost the ability to regulate other than in the manner established by the Community's comprehensive system of regulation; see Case C-2/90 *Commission* v *Belgium* [1992] ECR I-4431.

[190] See generally on minimum harmonisation, Weatherill, *Law and Integration in the European Union* (1995), pp.151-157.

technique has been adopted, the Community has indeed entered the field but harmonisation is to be regarded as a minimum allowing Member States to impose more stringent national standards. In effect, stricter national rules are not pre-empted and uniformity of standards is not necessarily envisaged even after harmonisation. It is however important to stress that any national measures imposing more stringent standards must be compatible with primary Community law. In particular they must be compatible with Articles 28-30 EC.[191]

Some of the earlier Community measures enacted under ex Article 100 and ex Article 235 expressly stipulated that they allowed for stricter national standards than those established in the directive itself. For example, the Surface Water for Drinking Directive includes the following safeguard clause:

Member States may at any time fix more stringent values for surface water than those laid down in this directive.[192]

A similar clause can be found in the Bathing Water Directive,[193] and a variety of other measures.[194] Later legislation adopted under the internal market provision of ex Article 100a (now Article 95) has often adopted exhaustive measures, but some measures contain clauses which endorse minimum harmonisation by explicitly allowing for the adoption of stricter measures by Member States. Council Directive 94/62 on Packaging and Packaging Waste for example allows Member States in defined circumstances to set higher recycling and recovery target rates than are established in the directive "in the interest of a high level of environmental protection".[195]

Measures enacted under the Environment Title are to be regarded as minimum standards only, and differentiation in environmental standards is accepted in principle. Article 176 EC notes:

The protective measures adopted pursuant to Article 175 shall not prevent any Member State from maintaining or introducing more stringent protective measures. They shall be notified to the Commission.

---

[191] See further chapter 6. See also Case C-389/96 *Aher-Waggon GmbH* v *Germany* [1998] ECR I-4483 in which a German national measure imposing stricter regulation on levels of aircraft noise than in the applicable harmonising directive was justified. Directive 80/51 on the Limitation of Noise Emissions as amended only established minimum standards and allowed Member States to introduce stricter rules compatible with the Treaty.

[192] Directive 75/440 Concerning the Quality Required of Surface Water Intended for the Abstraction of Drinking Water in the Member States, Article 6 (OJ 1975 L194/26).

[193] Directive 76/160 Concerning the Quality of Bathing Water, Article 7(2) (OJ 1976 L31/1).

[194] See, for example, Directive 84/360 on the Combatting of Air Pollution from Industrial Plants, Article 14 (OJ 1984 L188/20), and Directive 76/464 on Pollution Caused by Certain Dangerous Substances Discharged into the Aquatic Environment, Article 10 (OJ 1976 L129/23).

[195] Council Directive 94/62 on Packaging and Packaging Waste OJ 1994 L365/10, Article 6(6). See also Directive 98/70 Relating to the Quality of Petrol and Diesel Fuels, Article 6 (OJ 1998 L350/58).

The ECJ confirmed in *Criminal Proceedings against Fornasar et al* that "[i]t must be observed that the Community rules do not seek to effect complete harmonisation in the area of the environment",[196] before underlining that ex Article 130t (now Article 176 EC) allows Member States "to introduce more stringent protective measures".[197] Member States are therefore free to adopt or maintain more stringent protective measures where a measure is adopted under Article 175 EC even if the relevant Community measure fails specifically to indicate that they may do so.[198]

Application of the "environmental guarantee" The ability to apply stricter national laws can also be facilitated by the so-called "environmental guarantee" applicable in relation to internal market legislation. It will be recalled that, although the Commission's proposals concerning the environment "will take as a base a high level of protection, taking account in particular of any new development based on scientific facts", Article 95(3) EC notes that the European Parliament and the Council within their respective powers need only "seek to achieve this objective". However, Articles 95(4) and 95(5) now note:

> *If, after adoption by the Council or by the Commission of a harmonisation measure, a Member State deemed it necessary to maintain national provisions on grounds of major needs referred to in Article 30, or relating to the protection of the environment or the working environment, it shall notify the Commission of these provisions as well as the grounds for maintaining them.*

> *Moreover, without prejudice to paragraph 4, if after the adoption by the Council or by the Commission of a harmonisation measure, a Member State deems it necessary to introduce national provisions based on new scientific evidence relating to the protection of the environment or the working environment on grounds of a problem specific to that Member State arising after the adoption of the harmonisation measure, it shall notify the Commission of the envisaged provisions as well as the grounds for introducing them.*

A "guarantee" is therefore provided that Member States need not necessarily reduce their own existing national level of environmental protection following the adoption of a harmonising Community measure. Nor will they be denied the opportunity to introduce national environmental law applying higher environmental standards after the Community has entered the field by adopting harmonising legislation.[199]

---

[196] [2000] ECR I-4785, para. 46.

[197] *Ibid.*

[198] See, for example, Case C-510/99 *Criminal proceedings against Xavier Tridon* [2001] ECR I-7777, para. 45.

[199] It is important to stress that there would be no need to rely on obtaining the approval of the Commission under the "environmental guarantee" of stricter national provisions where the harmonising measure itself adopts the minimum harmonisation technique, or specifically permits the possibility of adopting more stringent national rules; Sevenster, "The Environmental Guarantee After Amsterdam: Does the Emperor Have New Clothes?" 1 *Yearbook of European Environmental Law* (2000), p.291 at n.1, and Jans, *supra* n.89, p.122.

The original "guarantee" had been introduced into the Treaty by the 1987 Single European Act. Ex Article 100a(4) stipulated the following:

> *If, after the adoption of a harmonisation measure by the Council acting by qualified majority, a Member State deems it necessary to apply national provisions on grounds of major needs referred to in [ex] Article 36 [now Article 30 EC], or relating to protection of the environment or the working environment, it shall notify the Commission of these provisions.*

Did this mean that only existing national measures could be justified, or could the environmental guarantee also be utilised with regard to the introduction of new national laws? The ECJ never clarified this point which has now been rendered purely academic since the changes brought in by Amsterdam which represent the current wording of the guarantee. Both existing and new measures can in principle now be justified. A second issue of debate relating to the original wording of the guarantee centred on the fact that ex Article 100a(4) would only be applicable where the harmonising measure had been adopted by qualified majority. Might it therefore have been correct to imply that any Member State wishing to utilise the guarantee under ex Article 100a(4) had to have voted against the adoption of the relevant harmonising measure in question? All but one of the Commission's decisions on the application of Article 100a(4) related to notifications made by Member States which had indeed voted against the harmonising measure in question.[200] The exception related to a notification by Sweden in relation to a measure adopted prior to Sweden's accession.[201] It could therefore be implied from these decisions that the Commission took the view that it was a necessary precondition for a Member State to have voted against the harmonising measure in question to utilise ex Article 100a(4).[202] The ECJ did not however determine conclusively on the matter.[203] No reference is now made however in the current wording of the guarantee to the need for the measure to have been adopted by QMV in Council. As such, it is suggested that a Member State now need not necessarily have voted against the harmonising measure in Council to be in a position to utilise the guarantee.[204]

---

[200] Commission Decision 96/211 Concerning the Notification by Denmark of PCP (OJ 1996 L68/32); and Commission Decision 94/783 Concerning the Prohibition of PCP Notified by Germany (OJ 1994 L316/43) [this decision replaced an original 1992 Decision quashed on procedural grounds in Case C-41/93 *France* v *Commission* [1994] ECR I-1829].

[201] Commission Decision 1999/5 Concerning the Notification by Sweden Concerning the Use of Certain Colours and Sweeteners in Foodstuffs (OJ 1999 L3/13). The Commission decision stresses however that Sweden had declared that it would have voted against the text of the measure adopted.

[202] Sevenster, *supra* n.199, pp.295-296.

[203] In *Criminal proceedings against Antoine Kortas* (Case C-319/97 [1999] ECR I-3143) the French government cast doubt as to whether Sweden could rely on ex Article 100a(4) as it had not engaged in the adoption procedure for the harmonising directive in question. Sweden had yet to become a Member State. The ECJ indicated that there was nothing in the wording of ex Article 100a(4) to indicate that a country which joins the Community after a particular measure has been adopted could not rely on the provision. This did not conclusively answer the question however as to whether a country that was a Member State had to vote against the harmonising measure in question to utilise ex Article 100a(4); see Sevenster, *supra* n.199, p.298.

[204] Verheyen, "The Environmental Guarantee in Practice - a Critique", (2000) 9 RECIEL 178 at p.180, and Jans, *supra* n.89 p.124.

The new wording of the environmental guarantee makes a distinction between the maintenance of stricter national measures and the introduction of new measures after internal market legislation has been adopted.

- *Maintenance of national measures after harmonisation*

A Member State would need to show that its existing national provisions were necessary on grounds of the major needs noted in Article 30 EC, or relating to the protection of the environment or the working environment. Additionally, it must notify the Commission of the provisions in question and the grounds for maintaining them. The major needs referred to in Article 30 include the grounds of public morality, policy and security, as well as the protection of health and life of humans, animals or plants. The burden of proving that national measures are justified by such major needs rests with the requesting Member State.[205]

- *Introduction of national measures*

Member States again have to notify the Commission of the envisaged national provisions and the grounds for their introduction. In addition, the national provisions must be based on new scientific evidence relating to the protection of the environment or the working environment, and that evidence must have arisen after the adoption of the harmonising directive in question.[206] In relation to the nature of the scientific evidence submitted, it is likely that the Commission will take a precautionary approach where there is a lack of conclusive scientific certainty.[207] It is important to stress that the scientific evidence relied on by a Member State must relate to a problem specific to that Member State which has arisen after the harmonisation measure has been adopted. A mere desire to introduce stricter national laws which is not founded on a problem specific to a Member State would not be sufficient grounds for the introduction of a national measure.

Whether or not Member States deem it necessary to maintain national measures (under Article 95(4) EC) or to introduce new measures (under Article 95(5) EC), the Commission must approve or reject any such national provisions within six months

---

[205] In Commission Decision 2001/571 (OJ 2001 L202/46) Germany failed to prove that maintaining national laws in the field of pharmacovigilance (the supervision of medicinal products once authorised) was justified in order "to protect the health and life of humans".

[206] See, for instance, Commission Decision 2000/509 Concerning Draft Laws Notified by Belgium Concerning Limitations on the Marketing and Use of Organostannic Compounds (OJ 2000 L205/7). The request by Belgium in relation to its draft national laws was rejected by the Commission on the basis that the scientific evidence relied on by Belgium was already known and taken into account when the Community harmonising measure in question was adopted.

[207] In relation to Article 95(4) EC, the Commission in its Decision 1999/835 (OJ 1999 L329/82) noted that there were uncertainties as to the level of harm exposure to creosote would occasion. Nevertheless, existing Danish measures placing limitations on the marketing and use of creosote were "justified in the light of the precautionary principle"; para. 110. See also Douma, *supra* n.110.

of notification by the Member State concerned.[208] In the absence of any decision by the Commission within the six months' time period, the national measures in question will be deemed to have been approved.[209] The six months' time period can however be extended for a further period of up to six months "[w]hen justified by the complexity of the matter and in the absence of danger for human health."[210] In determining the validity of the national measures, the Commission under Article 95(6) must verify the following:

- *Whether or not they are a means of arbitrary discrimination;*

The application of national measures would be deemed to fail this test if they allowed differences in treatment between like products to be applied. National provisions must apply to all products whether they are manufactured at home or imported from other Member States. For example, the Commission in 2002 approved a request from Finland as to national laws prohibiting the marketing of phosphorous mineral fertiliser with a cadmium content over a certain level, taking *inter alia* into account the fact that the national provisions applied to national and imported fertilisers in a like manner.[211]

- *Or, a disguised restriction on trade between Member States;*

A national measure which gives a preference to domestic production by impeding the import of products from other Member States would not be allowed. The Commission has seen fit to make reference in its deliberations in this respect to the results of investigations into the relevant market.[212]

---

[208] Article 95(6) EC.

[209] *Ibid.* This is in contrast to the ex Article 100a(4) process where no time limit was mentioned. The ECJ in Case C-319/97 *Criminal proceedings against Kortas* (supra n.203) ruled that, even in a situation where the Commission had not reached a determination within a reasonable period, Member States were not allowed to apply national measures notified under ex Article 100a(4) until the Commission had come to a decision as to their legitimacy.

Interestingly, Article 95(7) notes that when *"pursuant to paragraph 6, a Member State is authorised to maintain or introduce national provisions derogating from a harmonisation measure, the Commission shall immediately examine whether to propose an adaptation to that measure"*. Furthermore, Article 95(8) stipulates that *"when a Member State raises a specific problem in a field which has been the subject of prior harmonisation measures, it shall bring it to the attention of the Commission which shall immediately examine whether to propose appropriate measures to the Council"*.

[210] The Commission made use of such an extension in relation to draft Dutch laws limiting the marketing and use of creosote; Commission Decision 2001/599 (OJ 2001 L210/46).

[211] Commission Decision 2002/398 (OJ 2002 L138/15). See also the approval of similar Swedish (Commission Decision 2002/399, OJ 2002 L138/24) and Austrian rules (Commission Decision 2002/366, OJ 2002 L132/65).

[212] See, for example, Commission Decision 1999/831 on Dutch Laws Limiting the Marketing and Use of PCPs (OJ 1999 L329/15).

- *And whether or not they shall constitute an obstacle to the functioning of the internal market.*[213]

This is a new requirement when compared to the provisions of ex Article 100a(4). It has been interpreted by the Commission as reflecting the proportionality test in that the question must be asked as to whether the national measure presents a disproportionate effect in relation to the objective being pursued. If so, the Commission will not give its approval to the national measure in question.

It will be recalled that the ECJ never determined whether the original wording of the environmental guarantee allowed only existing national measures to be justified, or whether the legitimacy of national laws introduced after harmonisation could additionally be confirmed. If the view is taken that the introduction (as opposed to the maintenance) of national measures could never have been approved under ex Article 100a(4), Article 95(5) EC now offers an opportunity for Member States to seek such approval. However, if one takes the view that ex Article 100a(4) would indeed have allowed Member States to introduce new laws as well as to justify existing national measures, it is now certainly more difficult to gain approval of new national measures introduced since harmonisation under the provisions of the current version of the environmental guarantee.[214] After all, national measures could have been justified on the grounds of major needs referred to in Article 30 (which *inter alia* include public policy and public security), or relating to the protection of the environment or the working environment under ex Article 100a(4). This is still the situation in relation to maintaining national provisions under Article 95(4). However and by comparison, the introduction of new national rules can now only be justified in relation to the protection of the environment or the working environment under Article 95(5).[215]

The fact that national provisions must now be based on new scientific evidence that has arisen after the adoption of a harmonising measure also presents a new hurdle in relation to the introduction of more stringent national measures after harmonisation. The Commission's decision relating to the introduction of German measures concerning mineral wool has underlined that the scientific proof put forward by a Member State must have arisen since the date of adoption of the harmonising directive in question.[216] If the scientific proof relied on was known at the time the directive was adopted, it would not constitute "new" scientific proof.

---

[213] Article 95(6) EC. The Commission issued a number of decisions relating to Article 95(4) to (6) in October 1999; for an insight into these decisions (including the manner in which Article 95(6) has been interpreted by the Commission), see Van Calster, "Green Unilateralism: the European Commission and the Environmental Guarantee in Article 95 EC" (2000) 9 EELR 232.

[214] Sevenster, *supra* n.199, p 309.

[215] *Ibid*.

[216] Commission Decision 1999/836 (OJ 1999 L329/100). At the time of writing, Germany awaits a determination from the ECJ as to the legitimacy of the Commission's decision; Case C-512/99 *Germany v Commission*. Advocate General Tizzano delivered his opinion on 30 May 2002 (not yet reported) and took the view that Germany's request should be rejected.

Some Concluding Remarks

Since the entry into force of the Single European Act, the EC Treaty has undoubtedly undergone a "greening" process. The integration principle is now to be regarded as applicable to all the Community's policies, and the pursuit of sustainable development has been endorsed. Moreover, the EC Treaty now has an express legal basis for environmental action in the Environment Title, and stipulates both the objectives of the Community's environmental strategy as well as the environmental principles which offer guidance to decision-makers. Governments have consequently seen fit to vocalise their endorsement of the Community's general environmental objectives. However, mere expressions of support must be backed up by meaningful action if the environment is to be protected adequately. This requires the adoption, implementation and enforcement of effective environmental legislation. The need for cooperation throughout the "regulatory chain" with this in mind will provide the focus of discussion in the next chapter.

Select Bibliography

Baldock, Beaufort, Haigh, Hewett, Wilkinson, Wenning, *The Integration of Environmental Protection Requirements into the Definition and Implementation of Other EC Policies* (1992).

Boyle and Freestone, *International Law and Sustainable Development* (1999).

Douma, "The Precautionary Principle in the EU" (2000) 9(2) RECIEL 132-143.

European Commission, "Communication on the Precautionary Principle" COM (2000) 1.

European Commission, "A Sustainable Europe for a Better World: A European Union Strategy for Sustainable Development" COM (2001) 264.

Grimeaud, "The Integration of Environmental Concerns into EC Policies: A Genuine Policy Development?" (2000) 9 EELR 207-218.

Jans, *European Environmental Law* (2000), chapters 1 and 2.

Kramer, "Differentiation in EU Environmental Policy" (2000) 9 EELR 133.

Kramer, *EC Environmental Law* (4th ed, 2000), chapters 1 and 2.

Lee, "(Pre)cautionary Tales: Risk, Regulation and the Precautionary Principle" in Boswall and Lee (eds.) *Economics, Ethics and the Environment* (2002), chapter 9.

Loibl, "The Role of the EU in the Formation of International Environmental Law" 2 *Yearbook of European Environmental Law* (2002), pp 223-240.

Macleod, Hendry and Hyatt, *The External Relations of the European Communities* (1996).

Macrory, "The Amsterdam Treaty: an Environmental Perspective" in O'Keefe and Twomey (eds.), *Legal Issues of the Amsterdam Treaty* (1999), chapter 11.

McGoldrick, *International Relations of the EU* (1997).

Nollkaemper, "The EC and International Environmental Cooperation - Legal Aspects of External Community Powers" (1987) 2 Legal Issues in European Integration 55.

Sevenster, "The Environmental Guarantee After Amsterdam: Does the Emperor Have New Clothes?" 1 *Yearbook of European Environmental Law* (2000), pp 291-310.

Thieme, "EC External Relations in the Field of the Environment" (2001) 10(8/9) EELR 252.

Van Calster, "Green Unilateralism: the European Commission and the Environmental Guarantee in Article 95 EC" (2000) 9 EELR 232.

Van Calster and Deketelaere, "Amsterdam, The IGC and Greening the EU Treaty" (1998) 7 EELR 12-25.

Verheyen, "The Environmental Guarantee in Practice - a Critique" (2000) 9 RECIEL 178.

Wasmeier, "The Integration of Environmental Protection as a General Rule for Interpreting Community Law" (2001) 38 CMLRev 159.

Wilkinson, "Maastricht and the Environment" (1992) 4(2) JEL 221.

Chapter 3

Implementation and Enforcement: the Importance of Coordination through the "Regulatory Chain"

The Community's environmental policy has developed apace since the early 1970s with the adoption of more than 300 pieces of legislation, and yet, despite this activity, it is clear that the state of the environment continues to decline.[1] Too often both lawyers and politicians appear satisfied to see legislation adopted without having considered either the difficulties involved in practical application, or whether there are suitable mechanisms in place at a Community or national level to ensure effective enforcement. The 1992 House of Lords report on implementation and enforcement of EC environmental legislation for example concluded that

[i]mplementation and enforcement of environmental legislation go to the heart of the Community's policy. But Community environmental legislation is being widely disregarded, and the Community has paid insufficient attention to how its policies can be given effect, enforced or evaluated ... substantial changes in attitude are required.[2]

Responsibility for implementation and enforcement of environmental legislation primarily rests with the Member States, a responsibility spelt out in the fidelity/solidarity clause of Article 10 EC:

Member States shall take all appropriate measures, whether general or particular, to ensure fulfilment of the obligations arising out of this Treaty or resulting from action taken by the institutions of the Community. They shall facilitate achievement of the Community's tasks. They shall abstain from any measure which could jeopardize the attainment of the objectives of this Treaty.

---

[1]   The Commission in the Fifth Environmental Action Programme noted that there had been a "slow but relentless deterioration of the general state of the environment of the Community notwithstanding the measures taken over the past two decades"; OJ 1993 C138/1. The European Environment Agency noted in 1999 that "the state of the European Union's environment remains a serious concern ... it is clear that more needs to be done across a large front to improve environmental quality and ensure progress towards sustainability", *Environment in the EU at the Turn of the Century* (1999).
[2]   House of Lords Select Committee on the European Communities, 9th Report, 1991-92, *Implementation and Enforcement of Environmental Legislation*, H L Paper 27, Volume I, p.47 ("House of Lords 1992 Report").

In addition to the role of national governments, it is also important to appreciate that the Commission has a responsibility under Article 211 EC to "ensure that the provisions of this Treaty and the measures taken by the institutions pursuant thereto are applied". Therefore whilst Member States are obliged to transpose Community legislation into their national legal systems, facilitate its practical application, monitor such application and take enforcement action when necessary, the Commission is obliged to evaluate Member States' implementation and be prepared to bring infringement proceedings under Article 226 EC when appropriate.

Implementation and enforcement of environmental legislation are often not seen as priorities by Member States. In other fields of law, such as competition law, firms will monitor their rivals' activities to minimise any competitive advantage gained by them through non-compliance with legislation; competent regulatory authorities are lobbied to take enforcement action when necessary. In the field of the environment this is unlikely to happen; there is minimal economic incentive in drawing attention to, for instance, the acidification of a lake or the pollution of a wetland site.[3] Environmental non-governmental organisations (NGOs) like Greenpeace, Friends of the Earth, and the Council for the Protection of Rural England seek to redress this imbalance but have often lacked funding and political influence to do so.[4]

In the 1970s and early 1980s Member States came under little pressure from the Commission to improve compliance. Too much attention was given by DG XI (now known as DG Environment) to the adoption of new legislation rather than the effective implementation and enforcement of existing measures. It was only when severely criticised in 1984 by the European Parliament that the Commission began to take its enforcement role more seriously by utilising its enforcement powers against those Member States which had failed to implement Community legislation.[5] The European Council added emphasis to the move towards greater awareness of the need to enforce legislation by noting in 1990 that

---

[3]   See Kramer, *Focus on European Environmental Law* (1997), p.1, and pp.19-20.

[4]   *Ibid.*, p.20. See *R v Secretary of State for the Environment, ex parte Royal Society for the Protection of Birds* [1997] Env LR 431 in which an application for interim relief by the RSPB was denied by the House of Lords as the RSPB was not in a position to give a cross undertaking in damages in relation to the large commercial loss which may have resulted from any delay in the development of a port caused by the granting of interim measures. Interim relief had been sought whilst a preliminary reference was made by the House of Lords to the Court of Justice on various issues. The action for interim relief sought a declaration that the Secretary of State would have acted unlawfully if he failed to act to avoid deterioration of habitats by taking steps as outlined in the Habitats Directive. See also (1995) 7(2) JEL 245.

[5]   The Commission was criticised for "having failed to perform fully and properly its role of guardian of the Treaties"; European Parliament Resolution on the Treatment of Waste in the EC, OJ 1984 C127/67. Parliament's investigation had looked generally at implementation problems and in particular at implementation of Directive 78/319 on toxic and dangerous waste (OJ 1978 L84/43); toxic waste had disappeared in 1982 whilst in transit from Seveso. See Kramer, *EC Environmental Law* (2000), p.236, and Macrory and Purdy, "The Enforcement of EC Environmental Law against Member States" in Holder (ed.), *The Impact of EC Environmental Law in the UK* (1997), p.34.

Community environmental legislation will only be effective if it is fully implemented and enforced by Member States. We therefore renew our commitment in this respect.[6]

The Community has been increasingly preoccupied post-Maastricht with ensuring "better lawmaking" and the Commission's current strategy to improve the implementation and enforcement of Community environmental law stresses the importance of coordination through the "regulatory chain". This regulatory chain is defined as "the whole process through which legislation is designed, conceived, drafted, adopted, implemented and enforced",[7] and necessarily involves actors at a national and regional level as well as Community institutions. This chapter will focus on the following stages in the regulatory chain:[8]

- formulation of legislation

- transposition of legislation into national legal orders

- practical application of Community obligations at a national level

- enforcement

- evaluation and review of legislation.

Roles, procedures and principles relevant to the overall effectiveness of the regulatory chain will be assessed bearing in mind the need to improve implementation and enforcement of Community legislation in this field. In doing so, it is of importance to note that the majority of EC environmental measures are directives which, in accordance with Article 249 EC, are legally binding as to the result to be achieved, but also afford discretion to Member States as to the form and method of implementation.

Formulation of Legislation

In the Community's decision-making process the Commission has responsibility for proposing and drafting legislation. In fulfilling this role it is aware that environmental legislation is often of a technical and scientific nature:

---

6 European Council "Declaration on the Environmental Imperative" (Dublin), Bull. EC 1990 Vol 23 No 6, p. 18.

7 European Commission, "Implementing Community Environmental Law" COM (96) 500 final, Annex I. In response to this 1996 Communication, the Council adopted a Resolution on the drafting, implementation and enforcement of Community environmental law; see OJ 1997 C321/1.

8 The chapter draws in particular from the Commission's deliberation published in 1996 on improving implementation (see *supra* n.7), and the two reports by the House of Lords Select Committee on the European Communities on this issue: see House of Lords 1992 Report *supra* n.2, and its 2nd Report, 1997-98, *Community Environmental Law: Making it Work*, H L Paper 12 ("House of Lords 1997 Report").

> *Environmental protection has to take account of complex inter-dependencies and inter-relationships between the environmental media (air, water, soil) and biodiversity: unless care is taken, action to protect one medium can adversely affect another. It has to bear in mind climatic, seasonal and geographical variations in environmental conditions. It has to reflect a constantly changing state of knowledge.*[9]

It is therefore of importance that the views of relevant experts and interested parties are taken into account by the Commission when adapting provisions to technical and scientific progress. Individuals with recognised expertise in the area are appointed to committees which give advice to the Commission in the drafting process.[10] These committees have been generally criticised for lacking transparency in their deliberations; access to data upon which these committees give advice has been denied, and there has been criticism of the manner in which scientific advisors are appointed.[11] A lack of transparency specifically in an environmental context has proved especially frustrating bearing in mind that the "credibility of advances in scientific knowledge and the development of new hypotheses rely heavily on the open process of peer review".[12] In relation to the drafting of new environmental legislation, the Commission has indicated its awareness "of the need ... for an open and consultative process in the pre-proposal and drafting stages",[13] but there have been clear instances when proposals for Community action have been outdated from a scientific viewpoint.[14] The need for greater scrutiny of committee proceedings was endorsed in Council Decision 1999/468 which obliges the Commission to inform

---

[9]   European Commission, *supra* n.7, p.3.

[10]   See generally on committees established by the Commission to develop and formulate policy and legislation Schaefer, "Committees in the EC Policy Process: A First Step Towards Developing a Conceptual Framework" in Plender and Schaefer (eds.), *Shaping European Law and Policy: the Role of Committees and Comitology in the Political Process* (1996) pp. 3-10, and Kapteyn and Ver Loren van Themaat, *Introduction to the Law of the European Communities* (1998) pp.390-399. Also Bradley, "The European Parliament and Comitology: On the Road to Nowhere?" (1997) 3 ELJ 230, Vos, "The Rise of Committees" (1997) 3 ELJ 210, and Joerges and Neyer, "From Intergovernmental Bargaining to Deliberative Political Processes: The Constitutionalisation of Comitology" (1997) 3 ELJ 273. See also Kramer on the 1996 agreement between the Council and the Parliament which allows members of the European Parliament to obtain the agendas of comitology committees, and to ask whether they can attend meetings of such committees; *supra* n.5, p.33.

[11]   House of Lords 1997 Report, *supra* n.8, p. 18. For comment on environmental comitology committees, see Tufet-Opi, "Life after End of Life: The Replacement of End of Life Product Legislation by an European Integrated Product Policy in the EC" (2002) 14(1) JEL 33 at pp.45-46.

[12]   House of Lords 1997 Report, *supra* n.8, p.18.

[13]   European Commission, *supra* n.7, p.16.

[14]   See comments by the UK's Environment Agency on the Commission's 1994 proposal (COM (94) 36) to amend the Bathing Water Directive which it criticised for not reflecting "the latest scientific evidence available at that time"; House of Lords 1997 Report, *supra* n.8, p.38. After the proposal was put forward by the Commission, subsequent debate highlighted this shortcoming. The Commission has since acknowledged that the 1994 proposal had indeed been "outdated"; European Commission, "Developing a New Bathing Water Policy" COM (2000) 860.

the European Parliament about the work of these committees and to forward to it all draft implementing measures.[15]

The Commission has also acknowledged the need in recent years to take steps to widen its other general pre-legislative consultation procedures. The EC Treaty's Protocol on the Application of the Principles of Subsidiarity and Proportionality (added by the Amsterdam Treaty) notes that the Commission "should consult widely before proposing legislation and, where appropriate, publish consultation documents". In recent times greater use has indeed been made of Green Papers, White Papers, seminars and round-table discussions which seek the views of interested parties on policy strategies,[16] and there has been a growing willingness on the part of the Commission to consult fully with industry on research programmes (such as the Auto Oil Programme which the Commission began in 1992 in an attempt to develop a strategy to control vehicle emissions). Similar cooperation and consultation with industry over the eco-audit proposal[17] proved effective in selling the process to the UK's Confederation of British Industry.[18] It is encouraging to note that the latter has indicated that

[i]n the past the Commission has consulted on a formal basis ... [h]owever, the Commission did not listen. The Commission is now listening and taking note, taking into account the fact that some of the comments made can help it to improve what it is seeking to do.[19]

---

[15] Article 7(3) of Council Decision 1999/468 laying down the procedures for the exercise of implementing powers conferred on the Commission (OJ 1999 L184/23). Article 7(5) notes that the "references of all documents sent to the European Parliament ... shall be made public in a register to be set up by the Commission in 2001". See also Agreement between the European Parliament and the Commission on procedures for implementing Council Decision 1999/468 (OJ 2000 L256/19); this agreement acknowledged the impact of Case T-188/97 *Rothmans International BV* v *Commission* [1999] ECR 2463 by underlining the European Parliament's ability to request access to the minutes of committee meetings. On the wider debate of opening up the Community's policy-making to allow greater involvement of the public and organisations, see the White Paper on European Governance (COM 2001 428; OJ 2001 C287/1) in which *inter alia* the Commission proposes publishing guidelines on collection and use of expert advice which clarifies what advice has been given, by whom and the alternative views available.

[16] See for example the Green Papers on EU Energy Policy [COM (94) 659], Renewable Energy [COM (96) 576], on Future Noise Policy [COM (96) 540]. See also the Green Paper on Remedying Environmental Damage [COM (93) 47] and the subsequent White Paper on Environmental Liability [COM (2000) 66]. Some evidence points to the fact that consultation seems to be reasonably wide-ranging, the Commission in its White Paper for a Community Strategy and Action Plan on Renewable Energy [COM (97) 599] noting that in response to the Green Paper on Renewables " ... a broad public debate took place during the early part of 1997 focusing on the type and nature of priority measures that could be undertaken at Community and Member States' levels. The Green Paper has elicited many reactions from the Community institutions, Member States' governments and agencies, and numerous companies and associations interested in renewables. The Commission organised two conferences during this consultation period where the issues were extensively discussed". For another example of the Commission's willingness to consult, see the "Four stage process: Communication, Consultation, Conference and Proposal" adopted in the Commission's strategy to develop a new bathing water policy COM (2000) 860.

[17] COM (91) 459.

[18] House of Lords 1992 Report, *supra* n.2, p.10

[19] Dr D Taylor, representative of the CBI, House of Lords 1997 Report, *supra* n. 8, p.19 of the Minutes of Evidence.

The establishment of the European Environment Agency in 1993 has also assisted in providing advice which can be used in the formulation of policy. Based in Copenhagen, its primary objective is to

> *provide the Community and the Member States with ... objective, reliable and comparable information at European level enabling them to take the requisite measures to protect the environment, to assess the results of such measures and to ensure that the public is properly informed about the state of the environment.*[20]

The Agency's role therefore is basically that of an information gatherer and provider.[21] The Commission has acknowledged that its environmental policy will rely "heavily on the flow and quality of information ... in relation to the environment"[22] and has a close working relationship with the Agency. The collection and analysis of environmental information which informs the decision-maker can only facilitate better law-making, and, more specifically, the provision of comprehensive environmental data by the Agency to the Commission can only assist the latter in its legislative capacity. The Agency's existence reflects the growing awareness that the provision of accurate and relevant environmental information is of significance not only in the formulation of legislation but also in the subsequent analysis of its effectiveness.[23]

---

[20] Council Regulation on the European Environment Agency and the European Environment Information and Observation Network ("The Agency Regulation") OJ 1990 L120/1.The regulation was amended by Council Regulation 933/99 (OJ 1999 L117/1). Each Member State has one representative on the Agency's Management Board. Norway, Iceland and Liechtenstein, although not members of the Community, are also full members of the Agency and each also have a Board representative. From 1 August 2001 these countries were joined as members by the following countries: Bulgaria, Cyprus, Latvia, Malta, Slovenia and the Slovak Republic. These have since been joined on the Board by representatives from other potential Accession states, namely Czech Republic, Estonia, Hungary, Lithuania, and Romania. Poland joined in 2003, and Turkey will also join the Agency once it has ratified its Agency membership agreement. Commission delegates and representatives designated by the European Parliament complete the Board's make-up.

[21] The EEA is *inter alia* obliged to produce periodic state of the environment reports; see *Europe's 21 Environment: The Dobris Assessment* (1995), and *Europe's Environment: The Second Assessment* (1998).

[22] European Commission, *supra* n.1, p.39.

[23] With the intention of supporting policy action, the Agency's work concentrates on three main "instrumental pillars": the operation of a *networking* system which exploits existing Member States' and international organisations' capacities to produce quality information; the establishment of a *European monitoring and reporting system*; and the development of the *European Environmental Reference Centre* for the use of Community institutions, Member States and the public which gives access through the Internet to environmental data and information. The networking system provides the focus of our discussion on the role of the Agency in the formulation of policy and/or legislation. The Agency's monitoring role will be discussed later in this chapter when considering the evaluation and monitoring of legislation. The Reference Centre provides an Internet-accessed public information system which allows for the downloading of information held by EIONET and other national and international sources. Access is, for instance, given to state of the environment reports on most European countries (http://www.eea.eu.int/frdb.htm), and data and information can be accessed from the Agency's latest pan-European state of the environment report. A "Catalogue of Data Sources" has also been developed facilitating access further, as well as a "Sustainability Targets and Reference database" (STAR) which *inter alia* notes international policy targets applicable to Europe, and national policy targets and initiatives of an innovative nature.

The European Environment Information and Observation Network (EIONET) plays a central part in much of the Agency's work, assisting the latter in collecting and disseminating information, and contributing to a coordinated approach with a view to improving the comparability and consistency of environmental data for policy makers. EIONET enables information and data to be moved around the various players in the network to facilitate the monitoring process. It is coordinated by the Agency at Community level but comprises various types of national participants: National Focal Points which are designated by each Member State and are responsible for the transfer of information to the Agency from those elements of EIONET located in its country; Main Component Elements of Existing National Information Networks comprising "any institution which ... could contribute to the work of the Agency, taking into account the need to ensure the fullest possible geographical coverage of their territory";[24] and Topic Centres which have the necessary expertise and facilities to carry out particular tasks identified in the Agency's work programme.[25] EIONET is therefore a network made up of national information gathering and monitoring institutions, with the Agency as its overall coordinator. Access to EIONET via the Web has effectively connected all National Focal Points, Topic Centres, Main Component Elements and National Reference Centres[26] in a collaborative information network system allowing exchange of data and document sharing which minimises unnecessary duplication, and facilitates reporting on issues such as air and water quality, and the conservation status of biological diversity. The network is importantly linked to the Commission, providing invaluable environmental information to Community policy-makers.[27]

The European Consultative Forum on the Environment and Sustainable Development ("European Green Forum") was established on 5 June 1997 but did not enjoy the level of success experienced by the Agency.[28] Made up of individuals

---

[24] Agency Regulation, Art. 4(2). These organisations are therefore those national institutions which collect and supply environmental information, or have expert knowledge on environmental monitoring or science.

[25] A variety of partner institutions across the Community contribute to the work of these Centres.

[26] Certain institutions may be nominated by Member States as "National Reference Points" to offer assistance in technical coordination in their respective countries.

[27] In addition to cooperating actively with other bodies, including the Organisation for Economic Co-operation and Development (OECD), the United Nations Economic Commission for Europe (UNECE), the United Nations Environment Programme (UNEP), the United States Environmental Protection Agency (EPA) and the World Health Organization (WHO), the Agency additionally has for some time worked closely with Central and Eastern European states with economies in transition to build information gathering capacities. Even before widening its membership to include non-EC states, National Focal Points had been established in all thirteen Central and Eastern European countries in the EC's PHARE programme. The PHARE programme seeks to foster closer economic integration.

[28] Commission Decision 97/150 OJ 1997 L58/48. The European Green Forum replaced the previous Consultative Forum on the Environment which operated between 1993-1996, and differed from its predecessor in that its Chair was independent of the Commission, and it advised not only on environmental issues but also on wider matters relating to sustainable development. On the work of the earlier forum, see Falke "Comitology and other Committees: a Preliminary Empirical Assessment" in Plender and Schaefer (eds.), *supra* n.10, pp. 159-160.

with a range of expertise, the Forum's task was to generate ideas which the Commission could use in policy formation relating to the environment and the issue of sustainable development. The Forum deliberated on issues such as the integration of environmental issues in other policies, climate change, employment and the environment, trade and globalisation, and environmental matters relating to the Community's enlargement. Doubt has however been cast on the extent to which the Forum's views were indeed taken into account by the Commission, and the Forum was closed in September 2001 to make way for a proposed sustainable development round table.[29]

On a more positive note, the Commission has shown a degree of willingness to involve environmental NGOs in the consultation process in recent years. Participation of NGOs in this process can certainly still be improved,[30] but they are now more likely to be recognised as effective information gatherers with an important role to play in the development, implementation and enforcement of environmental policy, rather than as a hindrance to the process.[31] The Fifth Environmental Action Programme noted that the involvement of such organisations is "crucial to the general process of awareness building, to the representation of public interest and concern, and to the motivation and engagement of the members of the general public".[32] The Community has provided financial support to environmental NGOs since the mid 1970s, and, in a bid to make that process more transparent and accountable, now adopts formal programmes of assistance. The current programme was adopted in 2002 and establishes a five-year action programme to promote environmental NGOs.[33]

Drafting Environmental Legislation

Too little attention at times seems to have been paid in the drafting of directives to

---

[29]   Kramer has noted that in practice "the impact of the opinions given by the Forum seems to have been rather limited"; Kramer, *supra* n.5, p.31.

[30]   See Newell and Grant, "Environmental NGOs and EU Environmental Law" 1 *Yearbook of European Environmental Law* (2000), pp.231-237.

[31]   *Ibid.*, pp.237-244. See for instance the consultation process prior to the adoption of the proposal for a new directive on public access to environmental information (COM (2000) 402) in which *inter alia* NGOs played an active role; see page 8 of the proposal.

[32]   European Commission, *supra* n.1, chap 3.

[33]   Decision 466/2002 Laying Down a Community Action Programme Promoting NGOs Primarily Active in the Field of Environmental Protection, OJ 2002 L75/1. Note also the previous programme as outlined in Council Decision 97/872 Establishing a Community Action Programme Promoting NGOs Primarily Active in the Field of Environmental Protection, OJ 1997 L354/25 (on experience gained under Council Decision 97/872 see the Commission's 2001 report COM (2001) 337). The type of financial assistance offered by these programmes is essential to the existence of certain NGOs: Birdlife International, for instance, is an organisation which has closely monitored the implementation of the Community's measures as they relate to the conservation of nature, and its Brussels office received approximately 30 per cent of its operational costs in 1995 from Community funds. In addition, the European Environmental Bureau, the umbrella organisation for environmental NGOs based in Brussels, has received Community funding since 1974. For criticism of NGO dependency on Commission funding, see Newell and Grant, *supra* n.30, p.230.

the manner in which legislation is to be implemented.[34] The UK's Environment Agency for instance has drawn attention to the lack of guidance on the criteria for the designation of sites and areas by Member States under the Shellfish Water Directive[35] and the Freshwater Fish Directive[36] with the result that

> *[o]nly two Shellfish waters were designated in Ireland whereas France designated 88 sites. Italy designated 403 km of waters under the Freshwater Fish Directive whereas the UK designated over 55,000 km.*[37]

Certainly ambiguity and vagueness in directives has limited the effectiveness of legislation,[38] particularly when exploited by a Member State attempting to avoid the practical implications of implementation. The UK's implementation of the 1975 Bathing Water Directive is a case in point.[39] Article 1(2) of the Bathing Water Directive notes *inter alia* that "bathing water" is fresh or sea waters where "bathing is not prohibited and is traditionally practised by a large number of bathers". No further guidance on the designation of bathing beaches was forthcoming from the Commission; much therefore depended on Member States exercising their discretion as to designation in good faith. In 1979 the UK's Department of the Environment issued a circular offering guidance to competent designating authorities in the UK which noted that unless at some time during the bathing season there were at least 500 people in the water, it would not expect the designating authority to deem it a bathing water for the purposes of the directive.[40] On the other hand, any stretch of beach with over 1500 bathers per mile would be designated, and if between 750 and 1500 bathers per mile were sighted, the relevant water and local authorities would need to discuss "whether the water in question was sufficiently well used to be classified". Pursuant to this guidance just 27 bathing waters were initially designated by the UK.[41] This list did not include the well-known tourist beaches of Blackpool or Southport. In making this determination it is believed that reliance had been placed upon aerial photographs taken on an occasion when the number of bathers on the beaches was less than the guideline numbers.[42] Even the

---

[34] House of Lords 1992 Report, *supra* n.2, p. 35.

[35] Directive 79/923 OJ 1979 L281/47. On failure to designate appropriate shellfish waters, see Case C-225/96 *Commission* v *Italy* [1997] ECR I-6887.

[36] Directive 78/659 OJ 1978 L222/1. On failure to designate appropriate waters, see Case C-291/93 *Commission* v *Italy* [1994] ECR I-859.

[37] Evidence by the Environment Agency in House of Lords 1997 Report, *supra* n.8, p.35 of the Minutes of Evidence.

[38] See Wyatt, "Litigating Community Environmental Law - Thoughts on the Direct Effect Doctrine" (1998) 10(1) JEL 9.

[39] OJ 1976 L31/1.

[40] See comment on Case C-56/90 *Commission* v *UK* [1993] ECR I-4109 by Geddes (1994) 6(1) JEL 131.

[41] *Ibid.*

[42] *Ibid.*

land-locked country of Luxembourg designated more "bathing waters" than the UK.[43] In 1987 the UK increased the number of waters designated by 362 following criticism by the Commission.[44] The UK's reluctance to designate more beaches can be put down to the capital expenditure which water and local authorities would necessarily incur in bringing designated waters up to the standards required in the Bathing Water Directive.

The EC Treaty's Protocol on the Application of the Principles of Subsidiarity and Proportionality stipulates that "the form of Community action shall be as simple as possible, consistent with satisfactory achievement of the objective of the measure and the need for effective enforcement". However, the substance of directives finally adopted by the Council has often been very different from the Commission's initial draft proposal following amendment in the legislative process to take account of Parliament's deliberations, and those of the individual Member States expressed in the Council. Compromises are often made, particularly in the Council, leading to the adoption of legislation which at times contains imprecise wording capable of wide and differing interpretation.[45] The 1984 Directive on Air Emissions from Industrial Plants[46] provides an example.[47] In a bid to reduce the threat of acid deposition, the Commission's proposal had noted that an authorisation was only to be given to the operation of an industrial plant if the relevant national authorities were satisfied that every measure had been taken to reduce emissions "in accordance with the state of the art".[48] In the version finally adopted by the Council the phrase "state of the art" was omitted and replaced by the need to ensure "all appropriate preventive measures against air pollution have been taken, including the application of best available technology, provided that the application of such measures does not entail excessive costs" (so-called "BATNEEC").[49] It is to be regretted that the first of the "Technical Notes" providing guidance on the concept of BATNEEC were not issued by the Commission until December 1990 even though all Member States were obliged to comply with the directive by 30 June 1987. These "Technical Notes" certainly seem to have had minimal influence on the UK's guidance to local authorities and inspectors on the BATNEEC concept.[50] Inevitably vagueness of key

---

43   Haigh, *Manual of Environmental Policy: the EC and Britain* (looseleaf), 4.5-5; Luxembourg identified 39 areas.

44   Geddes, *supra* n.40, p.132.

45   Macrory, "Environmental Citizenship and the Law: Repairing the European Road" (1996) 8(2) JEL 219, at p. 226.

46   Directive 84/360 on Combatting of Air Pollution from Industrial Plants OJ 1984 L188/20.

47   See Haigh, *supra* n. 43, 6.9-4 - 6.9-5.

48   COM (83) 173.

49   See Haigh, *supra* n. 43, 6.9-3.

50   See generally on this issue Haigh, *supra* n. 43 at 6.9-3, and Kramer, *Focus on European Environmental Law* (1992) pp. 149-150. On the concept of BATNEEC Kramer notes that the "inclusion of the cost element ('excessive costs') into the notion has made the whole concept, seen from the Community perspective, a flop, since everybody introduces his own concept of what excessive costs are. As a consequence the notion has not led to any Community-wide pressure for gradually introducing clean technologies for air or water emissions" although he further notes that "such innovation has ... been achieved where national regulators specified in detail what the notion meant in their own eyes"; *ibid*, p.215.

words in directives coupled with this type of lack of guidance as to their meaning can lead to inconsistencies and difficulties in enforcement.[51]

In addition, the Council has on occasion qualified an already ambiguous term in its unpublished minutes giving rise to even more difficulties in implementing and assessing compliance with Community measures. In 1976, for example, the Directive on Pollution Caused by Certain Dangerous Polluting Substances Discharged into the Aquatic Environment noted that emission limits values were to be established by the Council "taking into account the best technical means available".[52] Haigh notes that Council minutes, which were not made public, qualified the term in stipulating that "best technical means available is to take into account the economic availability of these means".[53] Following criticism that such an approach adds to a general lack of transparency in the legislative process, it now appears less likely that such qualifications will be made by the Council.[54]

Ambiguity in directives might in fact be included to lure Member States into agreeing to their adoption in the first place but, although the drive for clarity may well deprive those concerned of certain agreements, this may well be acceptable if the overall quality of Community legislation improves. Acknowledging drafting problems, the Commission indicated in 1996 that it would

> *ensure that all proposals for new Community environmental measures or amendments of existing measures are drafted in accordance with the principles of achieving maximum clarity, transparency and certainty in order to make the implementation process simpler and quicker.*[55]

---

[51] Article 4(1); see Haigh, *supra* n. 43 at 6.9-5.

[52] Directive 76/464 OJ 1976 L129/23, Article 6(1).

[53] See Haigh, "Background paper for invited experts and participants to the Joint Public Hearing (European Parliament and Commission) on Effective Environment Protection (30 May 1996)" reproduced in House of Lords 1997 Report, *supra* n.8, at p.63.

[54] Under the Council's "Code of Conduct on Public Access to the Minutes and Statements in the Minutes of the Council acting as a Legislator", Haigh notes that "there is an agreement that (a) this practice should be used much more sparingly and (b) that when it is used, the results of it should be published"; *ibid*, p.145. See also Council Decision 2002/682 adopting the Council's Rules of Procedure (OJ 2002 L230/7); Article 9(1) notes that, when acting in its legislative capacity, "the results of votes and explanation of votes by Council members, as well as the statements in the Council minutes and the items in those minutes relating to the adoption of legislative acts, shall be made public".

[55] European Commission, *supra* n.7, para. 47. On Community activity relating to the quality of legislation since 1992, see Xanthaki, "The Problem of Quality of EU Legislation: What on Earth is Really Wrong?" (2001) 38 CMLRev 651, at pp.653-659. See in particular the inter-institutional agreement on the quality of drafting adopted in December 1998 ((OJ 1999 C73/1). In the White Paper on European Governance (*supra* n.15) the Commission notes it has "committed itself to withdraw proposals where inter-institutional bargaining undermines the Treaty principles of subsidiarity and proportionality or the proposal's objectives. The Council and European Parliament must instead stick to the essential elements of legislation ... and avoid overloading or over-complicating proposals". With reference to the aforementioned Bathing Water Directive, the Commission has acknowledged that the definition of bathing water "left too much room for interpretation" and that any new directive "would correct this by introducing clear and unambiguous definitions"; COM (2000) 860, p.7.

This commitment is laudable but must also be coupled with a willingness on the part of Member States to implement within the spirit of the Community legislation in question. Legislation adopted by the Community will almost invariably leave some measure of discretion to the Member States on the manner of implementation especially bearing in mind the prevalence of directives in this area. Whilst the Commission must ensure the eradication of unnecessary ambiguity, Member States must be seen to implement in such a way which ensures the purpose of the legislation is achieved.

Transposition of Community Legislation into National Legal Systems

Reference has already been made to the fact that the majority of EC environmental measures take the form of directives[56] which are legally binding "as to the result to be achieved, upon each Member State" but afford discretion as to the form and method of implementation by national authorities.[57] All Member States have at some time or other been guilty of failing to comply with their Community obligations by implementing environmental measures too late and/or incorrectly transposing directives.

Late Implementation

Directives establish a time period within which the Member States must transpose the measure into national legislation. Within two months of the adoption of a directive, Member States are placed on notice by the Commission of the need to notify the national measures which transpose or implement the relevant EC measure. Towards the end of the transposition period the Commission will warn a Member State which has failed to notify of the need to do so before the deadline. Throughout the transposition period Member States are regularly reminded of the need to notify national measures in "package meetings" in which outstanding matters, which may eventually lead to infringement proceedings before the European Court under Article 226 EC, are discussed.

---

[56]   Use is also made of regulations, though less frequently. Regulations have been adopted when giving legal effect in the Community to international legal obligations; see for instance Regulation 338/97 implementing the 1973 Convention on International Trade in Endangered Species (CITES), OJ 1997 L61/1. In implementing international obligations there is a perceived benefit in uniform application throughout the Community. Regulations have also been used when legislation establishes EC financial funds for environmental projects, and administrative bodies such as the European Environment Agency. See generally Kramer, *supra* n.3, pp. 3-4, and Macrory and Purdy, "The Enforcement of EC Environmental Law against Member States" in Holder (ed.) *The Impact of EC Environmental Law in the United Kingdom* (1997), pp.28-30. On the discussion as to whether directives or regulations are the most appropriate form of legislation in this area, see Macrory, *supra* n. 45, pp.226-227.

[57]   Article 249 EC.

If the transposition deadline expires without the necessary notification, the legal unit within DG Environment commences the non-compliance procedure by sending a formal letter of notice under Article 226 EC to the Member State in question requesting it to fulfil its obligations under EC law. No excuse will be entertained that a delay in transposition is due to domestic problems of a constitutional or political nature,[58] even though, for instance, in Germany the federal government's powers to force the Länder to implement certain Community environmental law are restricted.[59] Despite the reminders to the Member States before the date by which implementation must take place, timely implementation is unusual. Kramer has noted that "rarely have more than three Member States notified their implementation measures ... by the time the transposition period has expired",[60] and the Commission has indicated that "Member States are finding it difficult to comply with the deadlines for the transposal of Community directives on the environment".[61]

Incorrect Implementation

Once national implementing measures have been notified, the Commission's next priority is to ensure that such measures comply with the relevant directive. Has the directive been implemented completely and accurately? The legal unit within DG Environment has the task of assessing compliance and it is clear there is an under-staffing problem.[62] Their task of checking correct implementation is made even more onerous by the sharing of competence by central government with the regions or provinces in several Member States: Kramer has noted that the Commission "do not have to deal with one national piece of legislation but as regards Spain, for instance, 17 pieces of legislation, as regards Italy more than 20, as regards Germany 16 and so on".[63] Even in states in which central government is responsible for the adoption of implementing measures, it may well be that a directive is not transposed by a single national measure. An extreme example is the implementation of the Environmental Impact Assessment Directive in the UK; over forty separate implementing regulations have been adopted to implement its provisions.[64]

---

[58] See for example Case 1/86 *Commission* v *Belgium* [1987] ECR 2797.

[59] See House of Lords 1992 Report *supra* n.2, p.15. In both Germany and Austria nature conservation falls within the competence of the Länder.

[60] Kramer, *supra* n.3, p.7.

[61] European Commission, "Fifteenth Annual Report on Monitoring the Application of Community Law (1997)" OJ 1998 C250/1, p.51.

[62] For example, Macrory and Purdy have noted that there were "less than 20 individuals" in the legal unit; *supra* n.5, p.37. George Kremlis (Head of DG Environment's Legal Unit) has indicated that just 18 lawyers are responsible for dealing with 46% of all complaints received each year by the entire Commission; ENDS Environment Daily issue 1221 (Friday 24 May 2002).

[63] Evidence by Kramer in House of Lords 1992 Report, *supra* n.2, vol.II p.3

[64] See Haigh, *supra* n.43, 11.2-7 - 11.2-8.

DG Environment's task of assessing correct implementation would be made easier if all Member States were to adopt the method first adopted by Denmark of submitting a "table of compliance" indicating the particular piece of national implementing legislation which is intended to implement individual obligations in a given Community directive.[65] The table directs the legal unit to the relevant national measure. Unfortunately, only Germany, Finland, Sweden, the Netherlands, France and sometimes Denmark and Ireland, provide these tables.[66] More usually DG Environment's legal unit will be sent pages of national measures and asked to sift through the material to establish correct application of relevant Community law throughout the territory of the Member States in question, Macrory noting that "some Member States seem to take an almost perverse pleasure in leaving it to Commission officials to puzzle out the intricacies of what are often complex national laws themselves and relate them to the Directive in question".[67]

Particular problems may be faced in implementing Community measures effectively by those Member States with the most advanced national environmental programmes. The Institute for European Environmental Policy has indicated that

> *a comprehensive body of environmental protection legislation may prove to be an impediment to speedy compliance with a directive since existing national control arrangements may need to be adapted. Bureaucratic inertia may then hinder the reordering of administrative competences, structures and procedures and the legal measures necessary to adapt equivalent national control arrangements to the requirements of the directive might be given a low political priority when the existing arrangements are regarded as perfectly adequate.*[68]

Over-reliance on existing national legislation can be a hindrance to effective implementation of the detailed obligations of Community measures. In its implementation of Directive 80/68 on the Protection of Ground Water Against Pollution by Certain Dangerous Substances,[69] Germany relied on its existing measures and was found by the Court of Justice to have failed adequately to implement.[70]

---

65   Macrory, *supra* n.45, p.225.

66   European Commission, "Eighteenth Annual Report on Monitoring the Application of Community Law" COM (2001) 309.

67   Macrory, *supra* n.45, p.225. It is likely that an obligation to include a "concordance table" will now be included in future proposals for directives; COM(2002) 725, para.2.2.3.

68   Memorandum by the Institute for European Environmental Policy, London dated 21 January 1992 reproduced in the House of Lords 1992 Report *supra* n.8, vol. II, p. 168.

69   OJ 1980 L 20/43.

70   Case C-131/88 *Commission* v *Germany* [1991] ECR I-825. See generally Macrory, "The Enforcement of Community Environmental Laws: Some Critical Issues" (1992) 29 CMLRev 347, at 354-355.

In addition, the ECJ has indicated that implementation of Community measures by administrative practice or non-binding circular amounts to inadequate implementation when the measures in question creates rights for individuals. In these circumstances, for reasons of legal certainty, Member States must introduce legislation or a legal framework which clearly indicates the full extent of the rights and obligations created and should not rely on "mere administrative practices which are alterable at the will of the administration and are not given adequate publicity".[71] In reducing the number of instances of incorrect transposition generally, the introduction of a process which encourages effective consultation between Member State and the Commission before national implementing legislation is finally adopted would certainly be beneficial. At present, the Commission usually sees implementing legislation only after it has been finalised; prior consultation would allow errors and omissions to be eradicated in a cooperative rather than an adversarial manner.[72]

Practical Application of Community Obligations at National Level

Where a Member State has transposed on-time and correctly, attention then focuses on assessing whether the aims of the directive are being met in practice. A variety of competent bodies at national, regional and local level are responsible for the practical application of national measures which implement Community obligations. Practical application in this sense refers to action taken by a Member State to fulfil or implement the specific requirements of directives on the ground. These requirements could be the achieving of a defined product standard, compliance with a stated procedure, or adherence to quality standards.

Difficulties involved in practical application can be exemplified by assessing implementation of EC measures in the water sector. Approximately 10% of complaints made in 2000 related to water pollution.[73] The Commission has indicated that

> *[i]n relation to the improvement of water quality, the size and the complexity of the obligation imposed by the traditional approach of the Community legislation in this area, which relies principally on fixing quality objectives, establishing clean up programmes and systems of prior authorisation and the compilation of reports, still creates considerable problems for the administrations of the Member States. Some of the Member States have major difficulties in satisfactorily applying the Community directives in this area.*[74]

---

71 Case C-131/88 *Commission* v *Germany* [1991] ECR I-825, para.61. For a detailed analysis of the requirements of transposition, see Jans, *European Environmental Law* (2000) pp.135-159.

72 See House of Lords 1997 Report, *supra* n.8, pp. 20-21. See also Macrory who suggests a "general requirement that draft legislation ... is sent to the Commission at least six months before the date for compliance"; *supra* n.45, p.225.

73 European Commission, *supra* n.66.

74 European Commission, *supra* n.7, Annex II.

Indeed, compliance with the Drinking Water Directive[75] has been conspicuous by its absence,[76] and during 1999 infringement proceedings were being pursued against approximately half of the Member States in relation to non-implementation of the Bathing Water Directive.[77] Reasons for non-compliance include the fact that often implementation of environmental directives is not seen as a political priority. This is especially the case when practical implementation would incur large capital investment.[78]

Directives also invariably require Member States to monitor compliance but those national inspectorates in existence are often under-resourced. In this context it is important to draw attention to the encouraging and useful work of the "European Union Network for the Implementation and Enforcement of Environmental Law" (IMPEL). IMPEL, formerly known as the Chester Network, is a network of the environmental authorities of the Member States and was established in late 1992.[79] The IMPEL Network is informal although the Commission is also a member and shares the chairmanship of management meetings. IMPEL acts as a forum for the exchange of expertise and best practice among national environmental agencies. As such, it endeavours to foster greater cooperation between Member States in the application of environmental legislation by facilitating exchange of information and experience between national environmental inspectors and enforcement officers. IMPEL's primary focus has been on the practical application of environmental legislation regulating pollution, and has *inter alia* facilitated exchange of information and experience on the authorising of industrial plant operations, and on best practice in compliance monitoring at industrial installations. In addition, it has carried out a comparison of enforcement procedures in the Member States, and organised exchanges of national inspectors intended to help develop contacts

---

[75] Council Directive 80/778 Relating to the Quality of Water Intended for Human Consumption, OJ 1980 L229/11.

[76] Kramer writing in 1997 noted that "there is not one Member State which fully complies with the requirements of the directive", *supra* n.3, p. 17.

[77] European Commission, "Seventeenth Annual Report on Monitoring the Application of Community Law" COM (2000) 92, p.68.

[78] The Water Services Association (WSA) have estimated that in the period 1990-1996 the cost of implementing EC legislation, particularly concerning bathing water, urban waste water and drinking water, amounted to at least £8.5 billion in capital expenditure; evidence by Mr J Green, Chairman Environmental Committee WSA, in House of Lords 1997 Report, *supra* n.8, p.27 of the Minutes of Evidence. See generally Kramer, *supra* n.3, pp. 19-24, and Macrory, *supra* n.70, pp.356-362 for discussion on reasons for non-compliance.

[79] The Network has a small secretariat based in DG Environment, and its activities are determined in its two plenary meetings held each year. These meetings are co-chaired by the Commission and the Member State which holds the Presidency of the European Union. For further details on IMPEL see its website: http//europa.eu.int/comm/environment/impel/index.htm.

between inspectors throughout the Community.[80] In this way national inspectors can learn from each other on issues of common concern ensuring a greater consistency in approach to implementation, application and enforcement.

Enforcement

If a Member State fails to fulfil its Community obligations, the notion of "dual vigilance" allows Community law to be enforced at two different levels. The Commission may bring proceedings under Article 226 EC before the Court of Justice against a defaulting State at the Community level, whilst an individual may seek to protect rights granted by Community law before national courts in the absence of implementation by a Member State.

Role of the Commission

The Commission has a discretion to bring infringement proceedings under Article 226 EC against a Member State for alleged failure to fulfil obligations under Community law.[81] In matters such as non-transposition, the Commission's own investigations do uncover infringements, but it is important to stress that the Commission has no environmental inspectorate as such, and therefore relies to a large extent on individuals and NGOs bringing alleged infringements to its notice in the form of a complaint.[82] The complaint must be in writing but need not be

---

[80] It is also encouraging to note that the Commission, when drafting legislation, now consults IMPEL on practical implementation issues.

[81] Article 226 EC

If the Commission considers that a Member State has failed to fulfil an obligation under this Treaty, it shall deliver a reasoned opinion on the matter after giving the State concerned the opportunity to submit its observations.

If the State concerned does not comply with the opinion within that period laid down by the Commission, the latter may bring the matter before the Court of Justice.

In 1997, 37 environmental cases were referred to the Court of Justice by the Commission and 69 reasoned opinions were sent to Member States; European Commission *supra* n.61, p.49. In 1998, 15 environment cases were referred and 118 reasoned opinions sent; European Commission, "Sixteenth Annual Report on Monitoring the Application of Community Law" COM 1999 301. In 1999, 43 cases were referred and 63 reasoned opinions delivered; European Commission, *supra* n.77. In 2000, the Commission brought 39 cases before the ECJ and delivered 122 reasoned opinions; European Commission, *supra* n.66.

The Treaty also provides for an infringement action to be brought by a Member State against another Member State. Such action would be regarded as controversial in a political sense and is very rarely taken (see however Case 141/78 *France* v *United Kingdom* [1979] ECR 2923 in which the Court of Justice concluded that the UK national measures on fishing net mesh sizes were incompatible with EC law).

[82] Alternatively the Commission may act on petitions made available by the European Parliament, or following questions raised by the European Parliament. There has been a rising trend in the number of environmental complaints in recent years: in 1998, 432; 1999, 453; 2000, 543 [see European Commission, *supra* n.66]. Commission officials on rare occasions have been known to carry out inspection missions; see for example that officials made visits in 1998 and 1999 to Zakinthos to assess the level of protection afforded to sea turtles. As a result of these fact-finding missions, the Commission brought a successful claim against Greece for failing to abide by its obligations under the Habitats Directive (Case C-103/00 *Commission* v *Hellenic Republic* [2002] ECR I-1179).

technical in nature. A simple postcard to the Commission initiated the action concerning the quality of bathing water at Blackpool and Southport against the UK.[83] The complainant need not demonstrate a formal legal interest and may file a complaint free of charge. Some complaints are discarded due to lack of substance. Having received and registered a legitimate complaint, the Commission has recently stipulated that its Secretariat General will send the complainant an acknowledgement which also provides the case number which must be given by the complainant in any future correspondence.[84] In most cases an informal letter will then be sent to the Member State's permanent representative to the Community asking for a response and further information within a two-month period.[85] If the Member State does not respond or responds inadequately, the Commission will send a letter of formal notice to the Member State's foreign secretary. This letter importantly defines the subject matter of the alleged infringement.[86] At this stage the complainant would be informed that the Commission was formally commencing the Article 226 EC procedure.

The Commission has an internal rule that the issue will be investigated and a decision made whether to open proceedings or close the case within one year of the date of registration of the complaint by the Secretariat General. If insufficient evidence is obtained in this period, the case may be closed; this rule is frequently applied flexibly. During the evidence-gathering stage, discussions will be held with officials of the Member State and most cases will be settled to the Commission's satisfaction. The Member State may for instance offer clarification on points of issue which satisfies the Commission, or may adopt implementing legislation. If the Commission remains unsatisfied, it will give a reasoned opinion which details the legal arguments against the Member State. Discussions between the Commission and the Member State usually continue for at least two months after the issuing of the reasoned opinion. If the Commission remains unconvinced by the Member State's response, it registers its application before the Court of Justice.

In the event that the Court of Justice finds against the Member State, the latter is obliged under Article 228 EC to take the appropriate measures to comply with the judgment. The Maastricht Treaty amended Article 228 EC (ex Article 171 EC) by

---

83   Case C-56/90 *Commission* v *United Kingdom* [1993] ECR I-4109.

84   Commission Communication to the European Parliament and the European Ombudsman on Relations between the Complainant in respect of Infringements of Community law (OJ 2002 C166/3: COM 2002 141).

85   In cases of blatant infringement the Commission has dispensed with the informal letter to the permanent representative and proceeded immediately to send a formal letter alleging non-compliance to the foreign secretary.

86   This subject matter cannot subsequently be extended; Case 51/83 *Commission* v *Italy* [1984] ECR 2793.

allowing the Commission to ask the ECJ to impose either a specific lump sum as a penalty or fines against those Member States which fail to comply with the ECJ's findings. In January 1997 the Commission made its first requests relating to infractions of environmental law. It asked the Court to impose financial penalties ranging from sums of ECU 26,000 to ECU 30,000 for each day the Member States in question continued to ignore the ECJ's judgment.[87] In four of these five cases the issues were settled to the Commission's satisfaction by the end of 1997.[88] The threat of fines therefore seems to encourage compliance with judgments, and the Commission appears prepared to use its powers.[89] The mere threat of a fine is clearly however not always successful in ensuring compliance, and in July 2000 Greece became the first Member State to be actually fined under the procedure for its failure to fulfil its waste management obligations in the Chania area of Crete. Greece was fined the sum of EUR 20,000 for each day it failed to fulfil its obligations, such sum being based on "the duration of the infringement, its degree of seriousness and the ability of the Member State to pay".[90] Any daily penalty under this process runs from delivery of the Article 228 EC judgment until the day the Member State in question complies with the original judgment it had failed to comply with. Action under Article 228 EC can act as a means to deter, but it should be noted that any fines would be paid into the Commission's EC Own Resources account and are not therefore directly invested to alleviate environmental pressures.

The use of the Article 226 EC procedure in an environmental context has a number of drawbacks.

Time period   The process is a lengthy one averaging over four years from registration of a complaint to ECJ judgment. The first case of an environmental nature brought successfully against the UK took over 60 months to draw to a conclusion once the formal letter had been issued.[91] Whilst a conciliatory or cooperative approach is acceptable to a degree in dispute settlement, such a long

---

[87]   European Commission, *supra* n.61, p.50.

[88]   *Ibid.* Principles to be taken into account in determining the level of fines are established in two documents; Memorandum on applying Article 171 (OJ 1996 C242/6), and Memorandum on the method of calculating the penalty payments pursuant to Article 171 (OJ 1997 C63/2).

[89]   In 1997 either Article 228 letters were sent or Article 228 reasoned opinions notified in fifteen cases; *ibid.* In 2000 eight reasoned opinions were sent under Article 228; European Commission, *supra* n.66.

[90]   Case C-387/97 *Commission* v *Hellenic Republic* [2000] ECR I-5047, para. 92. Greece had failed to implement measures necessary to comply with the ECJ's judgment in Case C-45/91 *Commission* v *Hellenic Republic* [1992] ECR I-2509. The Commission has since noted that Greece paid EUR 1,760,000 in December 2000 representing the sum due for the period from the judgment in July to the end of September; European Commission, *supra* n.66. The penalty came to an end on 26 February 2001 by which time the total fine had risen to EUR 4.8M (this sum was paid in full by Greece during the course of 2001); ENDS Environment Daily issue 1038 (Monday 30 July 2001).

[91]   Case C-337/89 *Commission* v *United Kingdom* [1992] ECR I-6103 (infringement of Directive 80/778 Relating to Quality of Water Intended for Human Consumption OJ 1980 L229/11).

process is not perceived by individuals or NGOs as an efficient mechanism to halt environmental decline brought about by Member States' blatant infringement of Community obligations. There is little doubt that the already substantial workload of the ECJ will rise as the number of Member States increases thereby occasioning further delays in the process.

Interim relief The Article 226 EC process is a reactive process in the sense that an infringement has already taken place before the procedure is initiated. This may mean that harm to the environment has already been inflicted before the Commission takes action. However, the Court of Justice in cases before it, such as Article 226 proceedings, may on the Commission's application grant interim relief under Article 243 EC. If the application is successful, an environmentally harmful project may be halted before construction takes place. However it is clear that the ECJ will only grant such relief if two conditions are met: circumstances must give rise to urgency, in that to delay would cause serious and irreparable harm; and the Commission must establish on the facts and on legal grounds a *prima facie* case for interim relief against the Member State concerned.[92] Bearing in mind that there is no environmental inspectorate within the Commission, it may be difficult for the under-resourced DG Environment to ascertain the time at which development works begin. Without this knowledge, any application for interim relief may come too late to prevent serious and irreparable harm, and the granting of interim relief would be rendered inappropriate.[93]

Communicating with the complainant The Commission has often been criticised for failing to keep the complainant informed in any meaningful way during the process. Unless the Commission feels the complainant could provide further information to assist in its investigations, the best the complainant can expect is a letter indicating that the matter has been closed or has proceeded to the next stage of the procedure (formal notice, reasoned opinion, referral to ECJ or closure of the case). A further criticism is that the Commission's explanations for the closure of a case are often vague adding to the sense of frustration in the process. In a communication issued in 2002 on relations with complainants, the Commission has however undertaken to give prior notice in writing to the complainant where it intends to close the case.[94] The grounds for the proposed closure will be made available, and then the complainant will be given a four-week period in which to submit further comments.[95] The complainant therefore has an opportunity to convince the

---

[92] See Case 352/88R *Commission v Italy* [1989] ECR 267.

[93] See Case C-57/89R *Commission v Germany* [1989] ECR I-2849, and Kramer, *European Environmental Law Casebook* (1993), pp.404-405.

[94] Commission Communication to the European Parliament and the European Ombudsman on Relations Between the Complainant in Respect of Infringements of Community Law (OJ 2002 C166/3: COM 2002 141).

[95] *Ibid.*

Commission otherwise, but, of course, the latter ultimately retains discretion to close the case.

The European Ombudsman's inquiries into the Commission's handling of an alleged infringement concerning the construction of a sewage plant in Parga, Greece, make revealing reading.[96] The complaint to the Commission was lodged by inhabitants of Parga in July 1995 and alleged that the project failed to comply with the Community's environmental impact assessment requirements. As a result of the initial complaint by Parga residents, Community funding for the project was initially suspended and the Commission indicated that it would bring legal proceedings against Greece. Three years later, however, in July 1998, the Commission took the decision to proceed with funding for the project under the Cohesion Fund, and in effect to cease the infringement proceedings. This decision was not however revealed to the complainant.[97] Indeed, in December 1998 the Commission actually informed the complainant that a decision was in fact still pending as to whether infringement proceedings would begin, and only in April 1999 did it indicate that the case would be closed unless new information was sent by the complainant within one month. The Commission failed to give the Ombudsman an acceptable explanation as to why it had given the impression that the case was still open when it had already approved project funding in July 1998, and the Ombudsman considered that the Commission had failed to provide adequate information to the complainant seeing as the latter believed the case was still being investigated when it was clear that the issue had been dropped in July 1998. A finding of maladministration on the Commission's part was reached. In a particularly critical decision, two further instances of maladministration were also found by the Ombudsman in relation to the Commission's handling of the case.[98]

Access to Commission documents It has proved extremely difficult to obtain access to documents relating to investigations which may lead to an infringement

---

[96] Decision of the European Ombudsman on complaint 1288/99/OV against the European Commission. The decision can be downloaded from the Ombudsman's website: http://www.euro-ombudsman.eu.int

[97] Nor to the Ombudsman at the time the latter was making his initial investigations.

[98] The Commission was found to be incorrect in coming to the conclusion that the project predated the entry into force of the EIA Directive (Directive 85/337/EEC). Earlier notes on the Commission's file underlined that it had been Commission officials' view that the EIA Directive was indeed applicable, and even the relevant Greek authorities had taken the view that the measure applied. The Commission's incorrect conclusion as to the applicability of the EIA Directive amounted to an instance of maladministration. Furthermore, the Commission had failed to ensure that the matter was dealt with impartially and properly which amounted to the third instance of maladministration in relation to the handling of the case.

procedure. In *WWF (UK)* v *Commission*,[99] the World Wide Fund for Nature applied for the annulment of the Commission's decision to refuse access to Commission documents relating to an investigation into a possible breach of Community law concerning a project in Mullaghmore, Ireland. The Court of First Instance decided that the 1994 Code of Conduct on public access to Commission documents[100] was capable of creating legal rights for third parties and that, in this case, the Commission's decision was illegal due to insufficient reasoning. However, the 1994 rules on access to Commission documentation noted that access could be refused where disclosure could *inter alia* undermine "the protection of the public interest (public security, international relations, monetary stability, court proceedings, inspections and investigations)". Having duly deliberated on the issue, the Court of First Instance concluded:

> *[T]he confidentiality which the Member States are entitled to expect of the Commission in such circumstances warrants, under the heading of protection of the public interest, a refusal of access to documents relating to investigations which may lead to an infringement procedure, even where a period of time has elapsed since the closure of the investigation.*[101]

In *Bavarian Lager Co. Ltd* v *Commission*,[102] the Court of First Instance reiterated the WWF judgment with regard to preparatory documents in infringement proceedings, stating that documents relating to the investigative stage of an infringement action should be kept confidential as to do otherwise "could undermine the proper conduct of an infringement procedure inasmuch as its purpose, which is to enable the Member States to comply of its own accord with the requirements of the Treaty or, if appropriate, to justify its position could be jeopardised".[103] In *Petrie et al* v *Commission*,[104] the documents at issue were letters of formal notice and reasoned opinions. The judgment underlined that the confidentiality requirement remains applicable even after the matter has been brought before the Court of Justice. In such circumstances, "it cannot be ruled out that discussions between the Commission and the Member States in question regarding the latter's voluntary compliance with Treaty requirements may continue during the court proceedings and up to delivery of the judgment of the Court of Justice".[105] The Court of First Instance therefore denied access noting that, prior to the Court of Justice delivering

---

99   Case T-105/95 [1997] ECR II-313.

100 Decision 94/90 on Public Access to Commission Documents OJ 1994 L46/58 as amended by Decision 96/567 OJ 1996 L247/45. On access to Council and Commission documents, see generally Dryberg, "Current Issues in the Debate on Public Access to Documents" (1999) 24 ELRev 157, and O'Neill, "The Right of Access to Community-Held Documentation as a General Principle of EC Law" (1998) 4(3) European Public Law 403.

101 Para. 63 of the judgment.

102 Case T-309/97 [1999] ECR II-3217.

103 Para. 46 of the judgment.

104 Case T-191/99 [2001] ECR II-3677.

105 Para. 68 of the judgment.

its judgment, the possibility of reaching an amicable solution between the Commission and the particular Member State concerned should be protected.

All these cases involved interpretation of the 1994 Commission decision on access to documentation. Since December 2001 these rules have been repealed, and Regulation 1049/2001 of the European Parliament and of the Council regarding public access to European Parliament, Council and Commission documents is now applicable.[106] Under this regulation exceptions *inter alia* include refusal to disclose "where disclosure would undermine the protection of ... court proceedings and legal advice ... the purpose of inspections, investigations and audits ... unless there is an overriding public interest in disclosure".[107] The provision is written in mandatory terms ("the institutions shall refuse access where disclosure would undermine ..."), but the Commission will have to assess whether the need for confidentiality is overridden by the public interest in disclosure. Now imagine a scenario where the Commission has come to the conclusion that a particular Member State is acting in a belligerent manner refusing to make efforts towards an amicable solution. In such circumstances, the Commission might take the view that the need to maintain confidentiality is superseded by the overriding public interest in disclosure. Such disclosure would undoubtedly incur the political wrath of the Member State concerned, but may raise much needed public awareness of the environmental sensitivities involved in the matter. This would seem to be an extreme scenario however. More usually, the need to maintain confidentiality in investigations seems likely to continue to place severe limitations on the documentation that can be disclosed to the public.

Political considerations Lack of transparency as to the progress of a case has added to the perception that political considerations are taken into account by the Commission in exercising its discretion as to whether to litigate. Academics in particular have raised questions as to whether political rather than legal considerations have influenced the Commission in these matters.[108] Williams, who at one time worked within DG Environment, has indicated that "[t]he perception alone

---

[106] OJ 2001 L145/43.

[107] Article 4(2).

[108] On the Commission's reasons for abandoning infringement actions against the UK over the compatibility of several UK highway projects with the Environmental Impact Assessment Directive in the early 1990s, Kunzlik notes that "[t]he Commission's incomplete and inconsistent explanations and the fact that its disposal of the discontinued cases is hard to reconcile with public statements made by [Commissioner] di Meana, shortly before he left office, left room for the suspicion (voiced in the European Parliament) that termination of the procedures was a matter of policy prompted by the UK's hostile reaction, and did not simply follow from objective scrutiny of the UK's formal response"; Kunzlik, "Environmental Impact Assessment: The British Cases" (1995)4 EELR, p.344. Scott has noted that "since his resignation, Ripa de Meana has spoken out about the political pressure exerted to dissuade the Commission from taking an action against the United Kingdom, just at the time that Maastricht negotiations were at a critical stage"; *EC Environmental Law* (1998) at p.151.

that inappropriate considerations appear to influence the outcome of legal proceedings (whether or not they do so) brings the system into disrepute and distrust".[109] All decisions on whether to proceed with an Article 226 action are taken by the Commissioners as a whole, and not simply by the Commissioner responsible for the environment. The Commission denies any political blocking in the making of these decisions, but has acknowledged that the postponing of actions sometimes takes place, but purely for legal reasons.[110]

Who can bring an action? Only the Commission can bring an action under Article 226 EC. The Commission has total discretion as to whether to proceed with infringement proceedings. Individuals, companies and NGOs may make a complaint to the Commission but cannot force the Commission to take the matter further.[111] If the Commission is unwilling to instigate Article 226 proceedings, the individual's alternative course of action would be to bring an action before the domestic courts of the Member State in issue. However, the cost of such litigation may prove prohibitive and, in addition, national procedural rules (particularly with regard to *locus standi* issues) may hinder the taking of such action.

The Commission itself has recognised that Article 226 EC has its limitations as an effective enforcement mechanism in an environmental context:

> *The Commission simply cannot monitor the thousands of individual decisions taken each year in accordance with the transposed or directly applicable environmental legislation in the different parts and levels of authority within the Member States. The daily application and enforcement of those laws in specific cases must be fully ensured by the authorities in the Member States through mechanisms which will strengthen enforcement and, at the same time, ease the control of Member States by the Commission.[112]*

---

[109] Williams, "The European Commission and the Enforcement of Environmental Law: an Invidious Position", 14 *YEL* (1994), p.354.

[110] See evidence of Head of DG Environment's legal unit, George Kremlis, to House Of Lords Select Committee on European Communities, House of Lords 1997 Report, *supra* n.8, pp. 151-152 of the Minutes of Evidence.

[111] A suggestion may be that NGOs satisfying certain criteria could be given the right to bring an Article 226 action where the Commission has considered action but has failed to take the matter further after a period of time; Kramer, *supra* n.3, pp.312-313.

[112] European Commission, *supra* n.7, para. 25. For a critical analysis of the Commission's role in enforcement, see Rawlings, "Engaged Elites, Citizens Actions and Institutional Attitudes in Commission Enforcement" (2000) 6(1) ELJ 4.

The Commission has in the past indicated that it requires its own personnel to assess complaints in such a way that late and incorrect transposition, being "infringements which cause the greatest damage to the Community legal order",[113] are given a degree of priority. Individual cases alleging failings in the practical application of directives will on the whole be a matter for national enforcement procedures, although cases alleging general mispractice by competent national authorities, or entailing serious consequences for the environment will be pursued by the Commission. The Commission therefore will be selective in pursuing matters involving practical application of environmental measures by giving preference to cases which it regards as of major concern. As such, the Commission has acknowledged its own limitations and placed a high degree of responsibility for practical enforcement on Member States. It could be argued that such an approach is in accordance with the principle of subsidiarity bearing in mind both the lack of resources available to DG Environment, and the local knowledge and experience enjoyed by national environmental agencies. However the success of this approach is dependent on the effectiveness of enforcement procedures at the national level.

Enforcement Action at National Level

Public Enforcement Authorities

Practical enforcement at national level is primarily the responsibility of public regulatory bodies such as national environment agencies or local authorities. The IMPEL Network is fostering greater coordination between these national regulatory bodies and has in particular established training schemes, and minimum criteria for inspections aiming to promote common principles for inspection of industrial installations.[114] Despite such activity it is clear that the capacities of Member States to undertake inspections still vary throughout the Community to a large extent. Although some diversity is not necessarily undesirable, there were calls in the early

---

[113] European Commission's internal guidelines on enforcement and use of Article 226 EC; reproduced in House of Lords 1997 Report, *supra* n. 8, pp.96-97. See also The White Paper on European Governance (*supra* n.15) in which the Commission indicated that infringement proceedings will as a priority focus on: the effectiveness and quality of transposition of directives; situations involving the compatibility of national law with fundamental Community principles; cases that seriously affect the Community interest (i.e. cross border implications) or the interests that the legislation intended to protect; cases where a particular piece of legislation creates repeated implementation problems; and cases involving Community financing.

[114] IMPEL, "Minimum Criteria for Inspections" (November 1997). The work of IMPEL in this respect was in large part endorsed by the Commission: COM (1998) 772. This proposal in relation to the establishing of minimum criteria led to the adoption of a non-binding instrument; Recommendation of the European Parliament and of the Council providing for Minimum Criteria for Environmental Inspections in the Member States (OJ 2001 L118/41). See generally European Commission, "Second Annual Survey on the Implementation and Enforcement of Community Environmental Law" (2000), pp.9-10.

to mid 1990s to establish an audit inspectorate within the European Environment Agency to monitor the policies and performance of Member States' national inspectors.[115] Such an "audit" inspectorate would not have impinged directly on either the Member States' or the Commission's enforcement roles, but would have been in a position to provide analysis of the adequacy or otherwise of national regulatory authorities' approaches to the enforcement of Community environmental policy. It was envisaged that the making available of such an inspectorate's deliberations to all Community institutions and Member States would have proved a catalyst for constructive debate with a view to improving the application of environmental law generally.

The review of the Agency's tasks envisaged under Article 20 of the Agency Regulation led to the adoption of the amendments to the Agency Regulation in April 1999 and the assuming of new tasks.[116] The Agency will monitor environmental measures by supporting Member States' reporting requirements and will become involved in processing Member States' reports and disseminating results. Importantly the Agency is also to carry out work to assess efficiency of measures. At the request of Member States, it will advise them on the development of their monitoring systems. This new monitoring role given to the Agency is therefore to be welcomed as it gives it the opportunity to make recommendations to Member States on the manner in which they can improve their monitoring techniques. However it falls short of the "audit" inspectorate role; the Agency will only be able to make recommendations on national monitoring when requested to do so by a Member State, and, even more significantly, the Agency has no expert role in reviewing national inspectorate performance and policies. There is no doubt that prior to the review of its tasks, there was some support within the Agency and its Management Board for the setting up of an audit or some type of inspectorate within its remit.[117] This view proved unacceptable to the Commission which seemingly continues to

---

[115] Collins and Earnshaw, "The Implementation and Enforcement of EC Environmental Law" in Judge (ed.), *A Green Dimension for the EC* (1993), pp.238-242, and House of Lords Select Committee on the European Communities, *supra* n.2, pp.21-22, and pp.40-41. The Select Committee considered that the establishment of such an inspectorate within the Agency rather than the Commission would allow it "to scrutinise the Commission's own role, notably in providing financial assistance to Member States through the Structural Funds ... through the Cohesion Fund and LIFE", *ibid*, p.41. The European Parliament was a particular advocate of the new Agency taking on a wider role.

[116] See Council Regulation 933/1999, *supra*, n.20.

[117] See for instance paper by the then Agency's Director, Domingo Jimenez-Beltran, "Role and Activities of the European Environment Agency" made available at a conference on the "Role of the EEA and Current Developments in European Environmental Law" (Copenhagen 25/26 November 1996) in which it was noted that the Agency "could ... develop into an Auditing body of the Member States' Inspectorates by the time the Millennium comes around" (p.4). At the same conference, Professor Michael Scoullos, a member of the Agency's Management Board noted that his vision of the Agency's future included being "[h]ost or close collaborator of a well thought and well equipped Inspectorate, perhaps to be in place in the beginning of the new century. Such an inspectorate could start as a small international body of experts able to 'peer review' and provide advice on the proper implementation *in situ* of measuring and controlling performance" (abstract on file with the author).

guard its own general enforcement role. The notion has also been put forward that the setting up of an European Environment Agency audit inspectorate would endanger the organisation's information-collecting role.

National Courts

We have seen that enforcement action under Article 226 EC is particularly cumbersome and slow to bring about results. Such infringement proceedings can be useful in making an example of a Member State which has failed to implement Community law or done so inadequately, but compliance with the judgment of the Court of Justice may be slow and the whole process may mean that an offending state only introduces adequate national legislation several years after infringement proceedings were begun. The role of national courts as actors in the overall regulatory chain is therefore vital to provide effective judicial protection.

Issues Relating to Standing

Bearing this in mind, there has been concern that domestic rules on standing and remedies act as obstacles which may in fact prevent individuals or groups from taking action to enforce the Community's environmental measures at a national level.[118] An applicant in a judicial review action may for instance lack *locus standi*. Results of a study on access to justice undertaken by the Oko-Institute (Freiburg) and the Foundation for International Environmental Law and Development (FIELD, London) concluded that

> *persons or groups working in favour of environmental protection face great difficulties in some Member States when they want to represent ... common interest in administrative or judicial proceedings. In certain types of cases, where an administrative decision with adverse effects on the environment does not affect the property or health of individual neighbours directly, no administrative or judicial review will take place at all. This ... is likely to distort the authority's exercise of discretion to the disadvantage of the environment. In other cases, where the administrative authorities fail to take action against contraventions of environmental law which do not affect individual rights directly, a third party often has no legal remedy in the matter, and the illegal practices may continue for some considerable period of time.[119]*

---

[118] See Geddes "Locus Standi and EEC Environmental Measures" (1992) 4(1) JEL 29. See also Gerard "Access to Justice in Environmental Matters - a case of Double Standards?"(1996) 8(1) JEL 139.

[119] Fuhr, Gebers, Ormond and Roller, "Access to Justice: Legal Standing for Environmental Associations in the EU" in Robinson and Dunkley (eds.) *Public Interest Perspectives in Environmental Law* (1995), p.75. See also generally Rehbinder "Locus Standi, Community Law and the Case for Harmonization" in Somsen (ed.), *Protecting The European Environment: Enforcing EC Environmental Law* (1996), pp.151-166.

Often a special interest, such as a property right, may need to be shown in order to bring a case to court. Many concerned individuals or non-governmental organisations will lack such a proprietary interest. Even if such a special interest can be shown, the cost of litigating may be prohibitive. The Commission has acknowledged problems relating to access to the courts noting that

> *the ability of the public ... to take part in legal actions regarding application and enforcement of Community environmental laws differs widely throughout the Community. It can however be stated that the public and public interest groups do not as a general rule have sufficient access to the national courts of the Member States in environmental matters.*[120]

In *Stichting Greenpeace Council (Greenpeace International) and Others* v *Commission*,[121] this lack of standing was mirrored at the Community level. The Court of Justice upheld the order of the Court of First Instance denying the applicants *locus standi* to seek annulment of a Community act under Article 230 EC Treaty (ex Article 173) despite Advocate General Cosmas expressing support for existing case-law on standing to be eased in situations where Community decisions impact on environmental protection issues.[122] There have been clear signs that the Court of First Instance is aware that ensuring effective legal protection is of critical importance, and, in *Jégo-Quéré & Cie SA* v *Commission* saw fit to relax the hitherto

---

[120] European Commission, *supra* n.7, para 39. For discussion on *locus standi* before national courts, see IMPEL Network, "Complaint Procedures and Access to Justice for Citizens and NGOs in the Field of the Environment within the European Union" pp.13-29 and pp.40-129 (this report can be downloaded from IMPEL's website; http://europa.eu.int/comm/environment/impel).

There is a case for specialist environmental courts to be established like the Land and Environment Court in New South Wales, Australia, with generous rules on standing – Stein interestingly notes that "[r]eading articles on European Environmental Law – particularly British - which bemoan the problems of establishing *locus standi* to seek to enforce breaches of environmental law, is like *deja vu*. 'Any person' may bring proceedings in the Land and Environment Court to remedy or restrain a breach of law. No 'special' interest in the subject matter is required. An applicant for relief does not have to be a 'person aggrieved'. No leave of the Court is required except in the case of civil or criminal enforcement of pollution legislation. Yet no 'floodgates' of litigation have been opened"; "A Unique Experiment in Environment Dispute Resolution" (1993) 23/6 Environmental Law and Policy 277-280, at p.279.

[121] Case C-321/95P [1998] ECR I-1651.

[122] See Gerard, "Access to Justice in Environmental Matters - a Case of Double Standards?" (1996) 8(1) JEL 139, Gerard, "Access to the European Court of Justice - a Lost Opportunity" (1998) 10(2) JEL 331, and Ward, "Judicial Review of Environmental Misconduct in the European Community: Problems, Prospects, and Strategies" 1 *Yearbook of European Environmental Law* (2000) 137, at pp.150-157. The Treaty of Nice will make no change to the EC Treaty in relation to private parties' standing under Article 230 EC; see Johnston, "Judicial Reform and the Treaty of Nice" (2001) 38 CMLRev 499, at p.506. On the standing of private applicants generally, see Arnull, "Private Applicants and the Action for Annulment Since *Codorniu*" (2001) 38 CMLRev 7.

strict interpretation of standing requirements under Article 230(4) to do so.[123] Yet the Court of Justice has subsequently firmly rejected this approach and reasserted the traditionally strict approach to the question of standing.[124] There have however been some encouraging signs at the national level in relation to access to justice. A refreshing degree of flexibility on standing issues has at times facilitated public interest litigation. For instance, rules in England and Wales on *locus standi* in judicial review actions are now less likely to obstruct NGOs from pursuing the litigation option. Whilst issues of standing must still be decided on a case-by-case basis, judges have been more inclined to be generous in affording *locus standi* to such organisations.[125] Indeed after the Court of Justice's judgment in *R v Secretary of State for Transport, ex parte Factortame Ltd*,[126] in which the ECJ underlined the importance of ensuring the effectiveness of the Community's legal order by ruling that national procedures which impede the protection of Community rights should be set aside, it is arguable that national rules on standing which potentially inhibit the upholding of an individual's EC rights should not be allowed to do so.[127]

The Commission has indicated that "further action on the issue of standing may be required".[128] The fact that the Community and all 15 Member States have signed the UN/ECE Convention on Access to Information, Public Participation in Decision-

---

[123] Case T-177/01 [2002] ECR II-2365. Article 230(4) EC notes that "[a]ny natural or legal person may ... institute proceedings against a decision addressed to that person or against a decision which, although in the form of a regulation or a decision addressed to another person, is of direct and *individual concern* to the former" [emphasis added]. Bearing in mind that the applicants in *Jégo-Quéré & Cie SA v Commission* had no other means of seeking an effective remedy enabling them to contest the legality of a Community measure, the Court of First Instance saw fit to reconsider its interpretation of "individual concern"; the requirement that an individual applicant seeking to challenge a general Community measure had to be differentiated from all others affected by it in the same way as an addressee was no longer appropriate. If a Community measure affects his legal position in a way which is "both definite and immediate, by restricting his rights or by imposing obligations on him", then "[t]he number and position of other persons who are likewise affected by the measure, or who may be so, are of no relevance in that regard" (para.51).

[124] Case C-50/00P *UPA v Council* [2002] ECR I-6677.

[125] See for instance Mr Justice Otton's judgment in *R v Inspectorate of Pollution, ex parte Greenpeace Ltd* (No.2) [1994] 4 All ER 329. See also the *"Pergau Dam"* case; *R v Secretary of State for Foreign and Commonwealth Affairs, ex parte World Development Movement Ltd* [1995] 1 WLR 386. On NGOs and standing see Faulks and Rose, "Common Interest Groups and the Enforcement of European Environmental Law" in Somsen (ed.), *supra* n.119, pp.202-203. To bring an action for judicial review in England and Wales the applicant must show "sufficient interest" in the matter to which the application relates under s.31(3) Supreme Court Act 1981.

[126] Case C-213/89 [1990] ECR I-2433.

[127] See Geddes, *supra* n.118, at p.39, and Ward, *supra* n.122, pp.140-141.

[128] European Commission, "Second Annual Survey", *supra* n.114, p.11. In the area of consumer law, see Directive 98/27 on Injunctions for the Protection of Consumers' Interests which gives public interest groups *inter alia* the right to enforce consumer protection law and therefore protect consumers' collective interests by approximating national laws relating to actions for injunctions (OJ 1998 L166/51). The Commission noted in 1996 that it was considering the issuing of guidelines on access to national courts for representative organisations in a bid to strengthen the enforcement of EC environmental law and policy at a national level; European Commission, *supra* n.7, para 43.

Making and Access to Justice in Environmental Matters ("Aarhus Convention")[129] may have some significance, but the provisions pertaining to access to justice are in fact somewhat disappointing.[130] The Commission is giving consideration to a proposal for a directive specifically relating to access to justice.[131] Proposals for directives adopted by the Commission relating to access to environmental information and to public participation in the environmental impact assessment procedure already do contain access to justice provisions.[132] In addition, the Commission's proposal on environmental liability is of interest. It would allow affected individuals and environmental NGOs to request relevant competent authorities to take action to prevent or remedy environmental damage.[133] Importantly, any such person or entity lodging a request must have access to a court or other independent body competent to review the procedural and substantive legality of the relevant competent authority's decision, action or failure to take action in this regard.[134]

Direct and Indirect Effect, and State Liability in Damages

Let us assume an individual or organisation has sufficient standing. Recognising the limitations of Article 226 proceedings, the Court of Justice has developed key principles of Community law designed to protect the individual's Community rights in proceedings before national courts in situations where Member States have failed to implement Community obligations adequately:[135] the principles of direct and

---

[129] 38 ILM (1999) 517. The Aarhus Convention came into force in October 2001. The EC plans to ratify the treaty during the course of 2003.

[130] The provision in the Aarhus Convention relating generally to the need for greater access to justice notes that

Each Party shall ensure that, *where they meet the criteria, if any, laid down in its national law,* members of the public have access to administrative or judicial procedures to challenge acts and omissions by private persons and public authorities which contravene provisions of its national law relating to the environment (emphasis added); Article 9(3) Aarhus Convention.

This obligation may not in fact achieve much in providing greater access to national courts - the highlighted wording would seem to allow state parties to restrict access to justice by means of their existing criteria on standing.

[131] Communication on file between the author and DG Environment. It is likely to be adopted in the course of 2003.

[132] See Common Position 24/2002 (OJ 2002 C113/1) with a view to adopting a Directive on Public Access to Environmental Information and repealing Council Directive 90/313/EEC, and Common Position 41/2002 (OJ 2002 C170/22) with a View to Adopting a Directive Providing for Public Participation in Respect of the Drawing up of Certain Plans and Programmes Relating to the Environment and Amending with Regard to Public Participation and Access to Justice Council Directive 85/337/EEC and 96/61/EC. The former makes provision for access to justice when a request for information has *inter alia* been refused, and the latter to challenge the legality of decisions, acts or omissions subject to the public participation provisions of the EIA Directive and IPPC Directive. Pursuant to the adoption of Common Position 24/2002, Directive 2003/4 on Public Access to Environmental Information has been adopted (OJ 2003 L41/26).

[133] Proposal for a Directive on Environmental Liability with Regard to the Prevention and Remedying of Environmental Damage COM (2002) 17.

[134] Article 15 of the proposal.

[135] For an analysis of the importance of these principles in enforcing Community law, see Szyszczak, "Making Europe More Relevant to its Citizens: Effective Judicial Process" (1996) 21 ELRev 351.

indirect effect, and state liability in damages pursuant to the *Francovich* ruling.[136] Each of the principles of direct effect, sympathetic interpretation or indirect effect, and *Francovich* liability, are closely linked with the principle of supremacy of Community law over conflicting national law, and have been introduced by the Court of Justice to improve the enforceability of Community law.[137] It is also important to note however that there are limits to the applicability of all three principles in practice as set out below. Each will now be briefly discussed in turn.

Doctrine of Direct Effect

If a provision of Community law is directly effective, it confers rights on individuals which are to be protected by national courts. These rights must be protected despite the absence of national implementation. In this way, if a Member State has failed to transpose the provisions of a directive, the individual is not solely dependent on action being taken on his/her behalf by the Commission under Article 226 EC or by a Member State bringing a rare action against a fellow state under Article 227 EC. An individual can rely on directly effective measures to challenge national measures incompatible with such provisions in actions before their national courts. If Community provisions are directly effective, national courts must apply these measures and ignore any national provision which is contradictory.

The rationale behind the concept of direct effect was outlined in Van Gend en Loos:

> [T]he Community constitutes a new legal order of international law for the benefit of which the states have limited their sovereign rights, albeit within limited fields, and the subjects of which comprise not only Member States but also their nationals. Independently of the legislation of Member States, Community law therefore not only imposes obligations on individuals but is also intended to confer on them rights which become part of their legal heritage. These rights arise not only where they are expressly granted by the Treaty, but also by reason of obligations which the Treaty imposes in a clearly defined way upon individuals as well as upon the Member States and upon the institutions of the Community.[138]

---

[136] Case C-6 and 9/90 *Francovich v Italy* [1991] ECR I-5357.

[137] Van Gerven notes that the Court of Justice "considers the requirements of interpretation of national laws in conformity with a directive and the principle of State liability for failure to transpose a directive within the period prescribed therefore, as complementary to its doctrine of direct effect of clear and unconditional directive provisions. Rightly so, as all these doctrines have been developed by the Court to secure for the individuals effective protection for their rights which they derive from Community law"; "Bridging the Gap between Community and National Law: Towards a Principle of Homogeneity in the Field of Legal Remedies" (1995) 3 CMLRev at p.682. See also Szyszczak, "Making Europe More Relevant To Its Citizens: Effective Judicial Process" (1996) 21 ELRev 351. For an interesting account of the Court's role in developing Community law generally, see Tridimas, "The Court of Justice and Judicial Activism" (1996) ELRev 199. On the role of national courts in a Community law context, see Maher, "National Courts as European Community Courts" (1994) 14 Legal Studies 226.

[138] Case 26/62 *Van Gend en Loos v Nederlandse Administratie der Belastingen* [1963] ECR 1 (emphasis added). On *inter alia* the general impact of this decision, see Mancini "The Making of a Constitution for Europe" (1989) 26 CMLRev 595.

The doctrine of direct effect improves the enforceability of the Community's legal order by enabling individuals to enforce rights conferred by Community measures that are "unconditional and sufficiently precise". In this way the ECJ is of the view that the "vigilance of individuals concerned to protect their rights amounts to an effective supervision in addition to the supervision entrusted by Articles 169 [now 226] and 170 [now 227] to the diligence of the Commission and of the Member States".[139] Weatherill underlines the importance of the concept:

> *Direct effect is a constitutional device that shapes a system within which Community law and national law are not distinct layers, but instead part of the same mixture. Community law becomes national law and is enforced through the national system. National courts become Community courts and enforce Community rules.*[140]

Both Treaty provisions[141] and regulations[142] are capable of direct effect. Importantly directives are also capable of satisfying the conditions for direct effect despite obligations therein being addressed to States, and giving the latter some discretion as to the form or method of implementation.[143] The ECJ has justified the potential for the direct effectiveness of directives in the following terms:

> *[I]n cases in which the Community authorities have, by means of directive, placed Member States under a duty to adopt a certain course of action, the effectiveness of such an act would be weakened if persons were prevented from relying on it in legal proceedings and national courts prevented from taking it into consideration as an element of Community law.*
>
> *Consequently a Member State which has not adopted the implementing measures required by the directive in the prescribed periods may not rely, as against individuals, on its own failure to perform the obligations which the directive entails.*[144]

However, whilst individuals can invoke directly effective provisions against a Member State ("vertical direct effect"), the argument that a Member State "may not rely on its own failure" to implement the terms of a directive offers no support whatsoever to the direct imposition of obligations on an individual ("horizontal direct effect") in such circumstances. The Court of Justice in *Marshall* confirmed the inability of directives to be horizontally directly effective noting that

---

[139] Case 26/62 *supra* n.138.

[140] Weatherill, *Law and Integration in the European Union* (1995), p.99.

[141] It is unlikely that any of the provisions of Articles 174, 175 or 176 EC are directly effective; see Kramer, "Direct Effect of EC Environmental Law", in Somsen (ed.) *supra* n.119, pp.113-115.

[142] Case 148/78 *Pubblico Ministero v Ratti* [1979] ECR 1629, para.19.

[143] See Case 41/74 *Van Duyn v Home Office* [1974] ECR 1337 and Case 148/78 *Pubblico Ministero v Ratti*, *supra* n.142.

[144] Case 148/78 *Pubblico Ministero v Ratti*, *supra* n.142, paras 21 and 22 of the judgment.

With regard to the argument that a directive may not be relied upon against an individual, it must be emphasised that according to [Ex] Article 189 of the EEC Treaty the binding nature of a directive, which constitutes the basis for the possibility of relying on the directive before a national court, exists only in relation to 'each Member State to which it is addressed.' It follows that a directive may not of itself impose obligations on an individual and that a provision may not be relied upon as such against such a person.[145]

The ECJ underlined this limitation to the doctrine in *Arcaro*[146] when asked to give a preliminary ruling under Article 234 EC as to the possible direct effect of a provision in a Community directive which introduced a system of prior authorisation for the discharge of cadmium into the aquatic environment.[147] The Court of Justice found it unnecessary to deliberate as to whether the provision in question was unconditional or sufficiently precise to be directly effective against the individual concerned, Luciano Arcaro. The latter was the proprietor of an Italian firm involved in the working of precious metals which had allegedly discharged cadmium into surface water without authorisation. The Court of Justice indicated that it had

made it clear that the possibility of relying, before a national court, on an unconditional and sufficiently precise provision of a directive which has not been transposed exists only for individuals and only in relation to 'each Member State to which it has been addressed'. It follows that a directive may not by itself create obligations for an individual and that a provision of a directive may not, therefore, be relied upon as such against such a person.[148]

---

[145] Case 152/84 *Marshall* v *Southampton and South-West Hampshire Health Authority* [1986] ECR 723, para 48; see Prechal, "Remedies after *Marshall*" (1990) 27 CMLRev 451. See also the ECJ's rejection of the notion of horizontal direct effect in Case C-91/92 *Paola Faccini Dori* v *Recreb Srl.* [1994] ECR I-3325 in spite of A-G Lenz's request that the ECJ reconsider its position in this respect.

[146] Case C-168/95 [1996] ECR I - 4705.

[147] Article 3 of Directive 76/464 on Pollution Caused by Certain Dangerous Substances Discharged into the Aquatic Environment of the Community (OJ 1976 L129/23). Any authorisation issued by competent national authorities had to comply with limit values and quality objectives provided for in the 1976 directive and specified in a daughter directive; Directive 83/513 on Limit Values and Quality Objectives for Cadmium Discharges (OJ 1983 L291/1). Italian national legislation failed to transpose either of these directives adequately. The Italian Court made a preliminary reference to the Court of Justice in criminal proceedings against an individual, Arcaro, who allegedly had discharged cadmium into surface waters in contravention of national legislation which purported to implement the prior authorisation procedure provided for under Community law.

[148] Para 36 of the judgment (emphasis added). On this limitation to direct effect, see Coppel, "Rights, Duties and the End of *Marshall*" (1994) 57 MLR 859, and Mastroianni, "On the Distinction between Vertical and Horizontal Direct Effect of Directives: What Role for the Principle of Equality?" (1999) 5 European Public Law 417. Also Timmermans, "Community Directives Revisited" (1997) 17 *YEL* 1 at pp. 15-24. Careful note should be made that a successful action brought by an individual against a Member State (vertical direct effect) can in fact have a horizontal impact by adversely affecting a third party; see Jans, *supra* n.71, pp.200-202. Note also that certain ECJ judgments have seemingly reduced the significance of the ban on horizontal direct effect by allowing the use of unimplemented directives, in particular proceedings between private parties; for example Case C-194/94 *CIA Security International SA* v *Signalson SA and Securitel SPRL* [1996] ECR I-2201, and Case C-443/98 *Unilever Italia SpA* v *Central Food SpA* [2000] ECR I-7535. On this line of authority, see Dougan, "The 'Disguised' Vertical Direct Effect of Directives" (2000) 59 CLJ 586, and Weatherill, "Breach of Directives and Breach of Contract" (2001) 26 ELRev 177.

Having acknowledged that direct effect of directives is confined to vertical direct effect, what or who is the "State" against whom an individual can enforce rights conferred by directly effective measures? In *Foster* v *British Gas*[149] the Court of Justice gave a broad interpretation noting that

> ... *a body, whatever its legal form, which has been made responsible, pursuant to a measure adopted by the State, for providing a public service under the control of the State and has for that purpose special powers beyond those which result from the normal rules applicable in relations between individuals, is included in any event among the bodies against which the provisions of a directive capable of having direct effect may be relied upon.*[150]

All authorities of the State, including decentralised authorities, fall within this definition of the "State". It includes local authorities,[151] tax authorities,[152] and a Chief Constable acting as a public authority carrying out responsibilities for the maintenance of public safety.[153] The ECJ's phrasing in *Foster* would also arguably include in this definition private companies which were at one stage within the public sector as long as they retained "powers beyond those which result from the normal rules applicable to relations between individuals". This is of particular importance when one bears in mind the privatisation programmes in the UK in the 1980s and early 1990s which witnessed *inter alia* British Coal, and water and electricity authorities entering the private sector having previously been under public ownership. British Gas, now in the private sector, has, for example, been deemed by the Court of Appeal in *Foster* v *British Gas* to fall within the definition of "emanation of the State",[154] and in *Griffin* v *South West Water Services Ltd*, a privatised water company was also so regarded.[155]

Conditions for Direct Effect

The Court of Justice in *Comitato di Coordinamento per la Difesa della Cava* v *Regione Lombardia* summarised the potential applicability of the direct effect doctrine to provisions of directives in the following terms:

> *The Court has consistently held that wherever the provisions of a directive appear, as far as their subject-matter is concerned, to be unconditional and sufficiently precise, those provisions may be relied upon by an individual against the State where the State fails to implement the directive in national law by the end of the period prescribed or where it fails to implement the directive correctly.*

---

149 Case C-188/89 [1990] ECR I-3313.

150 Para. 20 of the judgment (emphasis added). For comment on this case, see Szyszczak (1990) 27 CMLRev 859, and Grief (1991) 16 ELRev 136.

151 Case 103/88 *Fratelli Costanzo* v *Comune di Milano* [1989] ECR 1839.

152 Case 8/81 *Becker* v *Hauptzollamt Munster-Innenstadt* [1982] ECR 53.

153 Case 222/84 *Johnston* v *Chief Constable of the Royal Ulster Constabulatory* [1986] ECR 1651.

154 [1991] AC 306.

155 [1995] IRLR 15.

A Community provision is unconditional where it is not subject, in its implementation or effects, to the taking of any measure either by the institutions of the Community or by the Member States.

Moreover, a provision is sufficiently precise to be relied on by an individual and applied by the Court where the obligation which it imposes is set out in unequivocal terms.[156]

If a directive has been correctly transposed, the individual's rights emanate from the national measure. If this is not the case, the individual can enforce rights conferred on him/her by provisions of the directive which satisfy the conditions of direct effect. In assessing the direct effect of a Community measure it is important to stress that it is the specific provision in question which is required to be "sufficiently precise and unconditional", not the directive as a whole. Therefore an article or part of an article in a directive may be directly effective even though the rest of the directive clearly does not satisfy the direct effect test.

The specific provision of Community law in question must however be capable of being relied upon by individuals to be directly effective. For example, in *Cinisello Balsamo* a provision in a directive which obliged Member States to inform the Commission of draft national rules in a particular area of legislative activity may well have been precise and unconditional but only concerned "relations between the Member States and the Commission".[157] The provision did not give an individual a right capable of being enforced before national courts to seek the annulment of national laws which had not previously been communicated to the Commission. It only dealt with matters between the Commission and the Member States, and the individual had no interest. As such, the provision was therefore incapable of direct effect.

The question as to whether a provision can only be directly effective if it confers substantive rights on individuals rather than some kind of interest is a controversial one. If one is required to point to the presence of such a substantive right in this way as well as to the sufficiently precise and unconditional nature of the provision, one commentator has commented in such a manner that it should sound as a word of caution on the applicability of the direct effect concept in an environmental context:

when compared to individual financial and employment rights ... environmental or "general interest" rights ... tend to be less well articulated in Community law. This is because, by definition, environmental directives have as their primary purpose the protection or enhancement of the environment, although this might

---

[156] Case C-236/92 [1994] ECR I-483.

[157] Case 380/87 *Enichem Base et al v Comune di Cinisello Balsamo* [1989] ECR 2491, para. 23.

be combined with a secondary purpose of protection of human health. In the
absence of the secondary purpose, it might be argued that an environmental
directive does not confer rights on individuals. In short the language of individual
rights does not translate well into environmental law.[158]

Some academics however have argued perfectly plausibly that, as long as a provision is "unconditional and sufficiently precise", an individual need not additionally have to point to the existence of a particular right denied to him or her before that provision can be regarded as directly effective.[159] If one accepts this position, a provision which is unconditional and sufficiently precise is directly effective. Individual rights flow as a consequence of that determination and should not be seen as a necessary pre-condition for direct effect.[160] ECJ case law is inconclusive on this issue and the matter remains a source of disagreement amongst academics.[161]

In summary therefore, the provisions of a directive are incapable of horizontal direct effect and can therefore only be relied upon against a Member State.[162] The provision must be "unconditional and sufficiently precise" to be directly effective, and be capable of being relied upon as a source of interests for individuals. In addition it is also important to stress that the time limit for transposition of the directive must have expired before an individual can seek to enforce rights conferred by directly effective provisions as to do otherwise would be to penalise a state which is not in default of its obligations.[163]

---

[158] Holder, "A Dead End for Direct Effect?: Prospects for Enforcement of European Community Environmental Law by Individuals" (1996) 8(2) JEL 313, at 325. Judge Edward, a distinguished judge of the European Court of Justice, has indicated that "the Court's jurisprudence on direct effect is not readily transposable to the general and sometimes vague concepts used in environmental legislation. So direct effect has not, to date, been the formidable weapon to litigants in the implementation of environmental legislation that it has in other fields such as competition and social law"; "Foreword" in Holder (ed.) *supra* n.56, at *xiii*.

On rights in an environmental context, see Hilson, "Community Rights in Environmental Law: Rhetoric or Reality" in Holder (ed.), *supra* n.56, pp. 51-68.

[159] "[T]he direct effect of a directive provision is not dependent on the existence of an individual right that should be enshrined in the protective content or intent of the provision. Apart from the expiry of the deadline for implementation, the only test for direct effect is whether the provision is sufficiently precise and unconditional": Ruffert, "Rights and Remedies in EC Law: A Comparative View" (1997) 34 CMLRev 307 at p.321.

[160] *Ibid.*

[161] See Jans, *supra* n.71, p.189. Jans himself takes the view that "individuals who want to rely on an environmental directive do not have to show, as a condition of Community law, that their substantive rights under the directive have been affected"; *ibid.* See also Prechal and Hancher, "Individual Environmental Rights: Conceptual Pollution in EU Environmental Law?" (2001) 2 *Yearbook of European Environmental Law 89,* at pp.94-100. See generally on this issue Hilson and Downes, "Making Sense of Rights: Community Rights in EC Law" (1999) 24 ELRev 121, at pp.131-138.

[162] For another example see Case C-91/92 *Paola Faccini Dori* v *Recreb Srl* [1994] ECR I-3325.

[163] *Pubblico Ministero* v *Ratti, supra* n.142, para 43.

Community Environmental Measures and Direct Effect

The Court of Justice has sent strong indications to national courts that the terms of certain directives are capable of direct effect. For instance the ECJ has stipulated that Community measures on drinking water[164] establish rights for individuals,[165] and that a Member State is obliged to implement a measure establishing limit values for concentrations of sulphur dioxide in the atmosphere[166] in such a way that "individuals are in a position to know with certainty the full extent of their rights in order to rely on them ... before the national courts".[167] It would therefore seem that an individual would have a strong case in claiming the direct effect of these and similar provisions intended to protect public health before their national courts.

On the other hand, provisions which define mere frameworks for action by Member States do not seem to be directly effective. In a reference for a preliminary ruling under Article 234 EC the Court of Justice in *Comitato di Coordinamento per la Difesa della Cava* v *Regione Lombardia*[168] was asked whether Article 4 of Directive 75/442 on waste[169] was directly effective. Article 4 states:

Member States shall take the necessary measures to ensure that waste is disposed of without endangering human health and without harming the environment, and in particular:

- without risk to water, air, soil, and plants and animals,

- without causing a nuisance through noise or odours,

- without adversely affecting the countryside or places of special interest.

The ECJ held that the provision merely defined a framework for action to be taken by Member States. It did not oblige Member States to adopt specific measures or a particular method of waste disposal. As such, Article 4 was not directly effective in itself as it was neither unconditional nor sufficiently precise to confer rights on individuals which could be upheld before national courts against a Member State.

---

164 Directive 75/440 Concerning the Quality Required of Surface Water Intended for the Abstraction of Drinking Water in the Member States (OJ 1975 L 194/26), and Directive 79/869 Concerning the Methods of Measurement and Frequencies of Sampling and Analysis of Surface Water Intended for the Abstraction of Drinking Water (OJ 1979 L 271/44). Both measures will be repealed by Directive 2000/60 Establishing a Framework for Community Action in the Field of Water Policy (OJ 2000 L327/1) with effect from 22/12/2007.

165 Case C-58/89 *Commission* v *Germany* [1991] ECR I-4983, para. 14.

166 Directive 80/779 on Air Quality Limit Values and Guide Values for Sulphur Dioxide and Suspended Particulates, OJ 1980 L 229/30 [repealed in large part by Council Directive 1999/30 Relating to Limit Values for Sulphur Dioxide, Nitrogen Dioxide and Oxides of Nitrogen, Particulate Matter and Lead in Ambient Air (OJ 1999 L163/41) with effect from 19/7/2001].

167 Case C-361/88 *Commission* v *Germany* [1991] ECR I-2567, para. 20.

168 Case C-236/92 [1994] ECR I-483.

169 OJ 1975 L194/39.

The vagueness of the directive's provision denied it direct effect; a point of more general importance when one bears in mind earlier discussion in this chapter on the preponderance of ambiguous provisions in environmental directives.

Certain directives establish numeric standards such as limit values, emission standards, quality objectives and maximum concentrations. There is a strong argument that such provisions are directly effective in that they are precise and unconditional in placing an obligation on Member States to meet standards which have been established to protect human health.[170] However, in *Criminal Proceedings against Arcaro* Advocate General Elmer appeared controversially to cast some doubt on this submission.[171] Authorisations issued by a national competent authority to discharge cadmium were obliged to contain provisions at least as stringent as the emission limits stipulated in the 1983 cadmium directive. However Advocate General Elmer noted that these emissions standards were only a minimum and that the "competent authority is thus allowed substantial discretion in issuing discharge authorisations".[172] In consequence, the provisions in question were "not unconditional or sufficiently precise to be capable of being recognised as having direct effect." If Elmer's viewpoint is accepted, one could argue that environmental directives enacted under the Environmental Title are incapable of being directly effective bearing in mind that Member States may maintain or introduce more stringent measures than those adopted in a directive or regulation enacted under Article 175 EC.[173] It should be stressed that the Court of Justice made no comment on Advocate General Elmer's assertion at all, and it must be misleading to suggest that a directive establishing minimum standards is incapable of direct effect. The *Francovich* case may be of relevance in that the ECJ held that the right of a Member State to establish a ceiling for payment of outstanding wage claims by employees in the event of their employer's insolvency did not in itself undermine the direct effectiveness of a minimum guarantee for payment of unpaid remuneration established by an EC directive.[174] Italy had totally failed to transpose the directive in question within the time period for national implementation and had therefore failed to set a ceiling for payment of outstanding remuneration. However the flexible content of the guarantee was not in itself regarded as fatal to direct effect.[175]

---

170 Kramer, in Somsen (ed.), *supra* n. 119, pp.115-116. In *R* v *Secretary of State for* the *Environment, ex parte Friends of the Earth* [1995] Env LR 11 the standards set in Directive 80/778 on drinking water were held to be directly effective by the Court of Appeal.

171 Case C-168/95 [1996] ECR I - 4705.

172 Para. 29 of the Advocate General's opinion. See generally Macrory in ENDS Report No. 262, November 1996, pp.43-44.

173 Article 176 EC; see Macrory, *supra* n.172, p.43. See discussion in chapter 2 on ability to adopt more stringent measures.

174 Cases C-6/90 and C-9/90, *supra* n.136, paras. 15-22.

175 See Szyszczak, "European Community Law: New Remedies, New Directions" (1992) 55 MLR 690, at p.693. What did prove fatal was the absence of an identifiable person under the directive to provide the guarantee (see *Francovich and others, supra* n.136, paras. 23-27 of the judgment).

Those Community measures which impose bans on the production or use of certain substances are also arguably unconditional and precise in their nature in providing protection to the interests of the individual, and as such are directly effective.[176] In addition, provisions of directives which establish procedures to be followed by competent authorities should be capable of direct effect.[177] As long ago as the early 1990s, in the English case of *Twyford Parish Council* v *Secretary of State for the Environment and Secretary of State for Transport*,[178] McCullough J indicated in *obiter* comments that the requirement that an environmental impact assessment had to be carried out before approval was given to an Annex I project listed under the Environmental Impact Assessment Directive was "unconditional and sufficiently precise". As Annex I projects are deemed to have a significant impact on the environment under the terms of the directive, impact assessment is obligatory. In this instance, although not referred to in the judgment, the individual's interests which required protection by the national court in question are surely the right to be consulted about a proposed project, and to lobby for modification or abandonment under the impact assessment procedure.[179]

National courts' application of the concept of direct effect in certain environmental cases can at times be criticised however. In an English legal context we can for instance look at the ruling in *Wychavon District Council* v *Secretary of State for the Environment and Velcourt Ltd.*[180] Turner J, ruling as to whether the provisions of the Environmental Impact Assessment Directive were directly effective, noted that none of the provisions in the directive would be capable of direct effect. He reached this conclusion having found that several of the directive's articles were incapable of direct effect, and that none of its other provisions could therefore be directly effective. On this reasoning a Court need only find a single provision in a directive incapable of direct effect to render the entire measure similarly incapable of conferring rights on individuals. This reasoning is seriously flawed and contradicts the *Twyford* judgment which had suggested that certain provisions of the Environmental Impact Assessment Directive were directly effective. At first instance Mr Justice Turner's reasoning in *Wychavon* was followed in *R* v *North Yorkshire County Council ex parte Brown* by Mr Justice Hidden,[181] but on appeal the

---

176 Kramer in Somsen (ed.), *supra* n.119, p.116.
177 Kramer, *ibid.*, pp.117-119.
178 [1993] Env LR 37, at 46.
179 Kramer in Somsen (ed.), *supra* n.119, p.117.
180 [1994] Env LR.239.
181 [1997] Env LR 391.

English Court of Appeal concluded that the directive was capable of direct effect although without identifying the specific provisions within it which satisfied the conditions of direct effect.[182]

Undoubtedly aware of the crucial role domestic courts can play in ensuring effective implementation of the Environmental Impact Assessment Directive, the ECJ's ruling in *Aannemersberdrijf PK Kraaijeveld BV and Others* v *Gedeputeerde Staten van Zuid-Holland*[183] urged national courts generally to take a more positive role. Although not specifically confirming that provisions in the directive had direct effect, the ECJ advocated that national courts in enforcing the provisions of the directive must consider whether national authorities had exceeded their discretion under the directive, even if not specifically raised by the parties. If discretion had been exceeded, the national provisions must be set aside and then competent national authorities must "take all ... measures necessary to ensure that projects are examined in order to determine whether they are likely to have significant effects on the environment and, if so, to ensure that they are subject to an impact assessment".[184] We will return to the issue of direct effect and the EIA Directive later.[185]

The practical application of the doctrine of direct effect in an environmental context has been limited to date but it remains an important tool which potentially improves the enforceability of environmental directives by empowering individuals to enforce Community rights before national courts despite non-implementation of environmental measures by Member States.

Doctrine of Indirect Effect or "Sympathetic Interpretation"

Some measures will simply not satisfy the conditions of direct effect. Other measures may be unconditional and sufficiently precise but cannot be deemed directly effective in a particular context due to the limitation of the doctrine to "vertical" rather than "horizontal" direct effect. However in such circumstances national courts are nevertheless obliged to interpret national law in the light of the wording and purpose of Community directives.[186] Article 10 of the EC Treaty

---

182 *R* v *North Yorkshire County Council ex parte Brown* [1998] Env LR 385. The judgments in *Twyford* and *Wychavon* are difficult to reconcile in so far as they relate to the application of direct effect. It is interesting to note however that the Courts did not refer the issue to the Court of Justice for a preliminary ruling under the Article 234 EC (ex Article 177) procedure, and the cases underline the unfortunate reluctance on the part of UK courts to refer questions relating to the direct effect of environmental measures to the Court of Justice in this way; see Bell and McGillivray, *Environmental Law* (2000), p.350. On the importance of the Article 234 EC procedure in an environmental law context, see Somsen, "The Private Enforcement of Member State Compliance with EC Environmental Law: an Unfulfilled Promise" 1 *Yearbook of European Environmental Law* 311.

183 Case C-72/95 [1996] ECR I-5403.

184 Para. 61 of the judgment.

185 Chapter 5.

186 Case 14/83 *Von Colson and Kamann* v *Land Nordrhein-Westfalen* [1984] ECR 1891. For comment on the judgment, see Steiner, "EEC Directives: A New Route to Enforcement" (1985) 101 LQR 491. For more recent examples of indirect effect, see Case C-456/98 *Centrosteel* v *Adipol* [2000] ECR I-6007, and Cases C-240-244/98 *Oceano Grupo Editorial* v *Rocio Murciano Qunitero* [2000] ECR I-4491.

imposes an obligation on Member States to take all appropriate measures to ensure the fulfilment of obligations resulting from action taken by Community institutions. This duty is placed on all authorities in Member States including national courts. Therefore, in applying national law, national courts are obliged to do so in the light of the letter and purpose of relevant EC measures.[187] This obligation on national courts applies whether the national law in question pre-dates or post-dates the relevant EC measure.[188] In this way "[i]f national courts act in the manner envisaged then the absence of horizontal direct effect of directives will lose its practical significance. Community directives will be absorbed into the national legal order even in the absence of implementation".[189]

This duty to apply EC directives indirectly is of importance when Member States have inadequately implemented directives. The national court is placed under an obligation to ensure that the purpose and wording of the directive is nevertheless applied. In *R v Secretary of State for the Environment, ex parte Greenpeace* for example the High Court concluded that a Minister of State was obliged to justify the grant of an authorisation to British Nuclear Fuels for its operation of the THORP reprocessing plant as the Radioactive Substances Act 1993 had to be interpreted in the light of Euratom Directive 80/836 as amended.[190] Although the 1993 Act did not place the Minister under a duty to justify an authorisation, he/she was obliged to do so under the terms of the relevant Community measure. In this way the doctrine of indirect effect, or "sympathetic interpretation", places an onus on national courts to interpret national law in such a way as to greatly improve the efficacy and enforceability of the Community's legal order.

In *Arcaro* the Court of Justice underlined the doctrine of "indirect effect" in noting that

> The Member States' obligation, arising under a directive, to achieve the result envisaged by the directive and their duty, under [ex] Article 5 of the Treaty, to take all appropriate measures, whether general or particular, to ensure fulfilment of that obligation, are binding on all the authorities of Member States including, for matters within their jurisdiction, the courts. It follows that, in applying national law, the national court called upon to interpret a directive is required to

---

[187] In this way the Court of Justice has sought to mitigate the limitation of the doctrine of direct effect to vertical direct effect.

[188] Case C-106/89 *Marleasing SA* v La *Commercial Internacional de Alimentacion SA* [1990] ECR I-4135, para. 8. This is subject to the exception that a directive "cannot, of itself and independently of a national law adopted by a Member State for its implementation, have the effect of determining or aggravating the liability in criminal law of persons who act in contravention of the provisions of that directive"; Case 80/86 *Officier van Justitie* v *Kolpinghuis Nijmegen* [1987] ECR 3969. This exception is necessary to protect legal certainty and legitimate expectations.

[189] Weatherill, *supra* n.140, p.126.

[190] [1994] Env LR 401.

do so, as far as possible, in the light of the wording and purpose of the directive.[191]

Application of indirect effect is however limited by the fact that national courts must only "as far as possible" interpret national law in the light of the wording and purpose of an EC directive.[192] Interpretation of national law in this way will not be possible if to do so would conflict with the intent and wording of the national provision.[193] In such a situation the individual may instead rely on the possibility of bringing an action for damages against the Member State in question under the principles in *Francovich*.

State Liability in Damages

Bearing in mind the above mentioned limitations to application of the principles of direct and indirect effect, the Court of Justice in its *Francovich* ruling sought to develop the enforceabilty of Community measures by establishing the principle that Member States may in particular circumstances be required to pay damages to individuals who have suffered loss due to non-implementation of a directive:

> *[t]he full effectiveness of Community rules would be impaired and the protection of the rights which they grant would be weakened if individuals were unable to obtain redress when their rights are infringed by a breach of Community law for which a Member State can be held responsible.*[194]

The ECJ went on to establish three conditions for the award of damages.[195]

- *The result prescribed by the directive should entail the grant of rights to individuals.*

Even if the measures in question did not satisfy the conditions of direct effect, a strong argument can be made that those directives which establish limit values or quality objectives would grant rights to individuals as they are intended to protect

---

[191] Case C-168/95, *supra* n.146, para 41. For detailed comment on the application of indirect effect in the light of the *Arcaro* case, see Craig, "Directives: Direct Effect, Indirect Effect and the Construction of National Legislation" (1997) 22 EL Rev 519.

[192] See, for example, Case C-334/92 *Wagner Miret* v *Fondo de Garantia Salarial* [1993] ECR I-6911 at para. 20.

[193] *Ibid.*

[194] Cases C-6/90 and C-9/90 [1991] ECR I-5357, para. 33. See generally, Caranta, "Government Liability after *Francovich*" (1993) 52 Cambridge Law Journal 272, Craig, "*Francovich*, Remedies and the Scope of Damages Liability" (1993) 109 LQR 595, Harlow, "*Francovich* and the Problem of the Disobedient State" (1996) 2 ELJ 199, Ross, "Beyond *Francovich*" (1993) 56 MLR 55, and Szyszczak, "European Community Law: New Remedies, New Directions?" (1992) 55 MLR 690. For a more recent analysis of the law relating to state liability, see Tridimas, "Liability for Breach of Community Law: Growing Up and Mellowing Down?" (2001) 38 CMLRev 301.

[195] *Ibid*, para 40. See generally Steiner, "The Limits of State Liability for breach of EC Law" (1998) 4(1) European Public Law 69.

human health.[196] So too would measures providing a right to access to information.[197] On the other hand, it might be argued that environmental measures which afford protection to endangered species or to habitats could not be regarded as capable of granting rights to individuals.

• *It should be possible to identify the content of those rights on the basis of the provisions of the directive.*

National courts will need to make this assessment in respect of the provision in question. Evidently, certain provisions, such as those which give citizens the right to be consulted before decisions are made, do indeed satisfy this requirement.[198]

• *The existence of a causal link between the breach of the State's obligation and the loss and damage suffered by the injured parties.*

This issue of proving causation is the most problematic condition to satisfy in an environmental context. If, for example, a bather, having become ill after swimming at a bathing beach, brought an action for damages against a Member State for its non-implementation of the Bathing Water Directive, he/she would need to prove the existence of a causal link between the injury suffered and the poor quality of bathing water in which he/she took a swim. The action would be costly, and may be difficult to prove medically and scientifically.[199] National courts must determine whether such a link exists.

The Court of Justice has clarified certain issues as to the liability of the State in its law-making capacity in *Brasserie du Pecheur*[200] and *Dillenkofer*.[201] Liability does not only flow from non-implementation of Community measures. Member States are obliged to make good loss suffered by individuals as a result of any breach of Community law. In addition, although not specifically mentioned in its *Francovich* ruling, the ECJ has since concluded that, in addition to the three conditions established in *Francovich*, the breach in question must be "sufficiently serious" if liability is to be incurred. A breach is sufficiently serious where in the exercise of its legislative powers a Member State has manifestly and gravely disregarded the limits on the exercise of its powers. Also, re-emphasising the key importance of the role and jurisprudence of the ECJ, a breach is sufficiently serious where a Member State has failed to comply with a Court of Justice ruling.

---

[196] See Case C-131/88 *Commission* v *Germany, supra* n.71, and Case 361/88 *Commission* v *Germany, supra* n.167. See also Hilson, "Community Rights in Environmental Law: Rhetoric or Reality?" in Holder (ed.) *The Impact of EC Environmental Law in the UK* (1997) p.65.

[197] Directive 90/313 on Freedom of Access to Information on the Environment OJ 1990 L158/56.

[198] For example Article 6(2) of Directive 85/337 on Environmental Impact Assessment OJ 1985 L175/40.

[199] See generally Hilson, *supra* n.196, pp. 65-68, and Scott, *supra* n.108, p.161.

[200] Joined Cases C-46/93 and C-48/93 *Brasserie du Pecheur SA* v *Germany* and *R* v *Secretary of State for Transport, ex parte Factortame Ltd and others* [1996] ECR I-1029. For comment, see Craig, "Once More unto the Breach: The Community, the State and Damages Liability" (1997) 113 LQR 67.

[201] Cases C-178, 179, 188, 189 and 190/94 *Dillenkofer* v *Germany* [1996] ECR I-4845.

In assessing whether a breach is "sufficiently serious", account can be taken of the clarity and precision of the rule breached, the ECJ noting that the fact that the provision in question is imprecisely worded, and therefore capable of different interpretations, can be taken into consideration by national courts.[202] This places an added incentive on the Commission to ensure that adopted environmental measures lack some of the vagueness noted earlier in the chapter. Additionally, national courts may also take into account other considerations including whether the damage caused was intentional or involuntary, or whether any error of law was excusable or not. Where a Member State has considerably reduced or no discretion in exercising its obligations, the mere infringement of Community law amounts to a "sufficiently serious" breach;[203] for instance if a Member State has failed to transpose a directive on time, a sufficiently serious breach has occurred.

It is important to appreciate that state liability under *Francovich* can flow not only from the breach of directly effective measures, but also from provisions which do not satisfy the conditions of direct effect. In the absence of Community provisions, Member States' national legal systems must set the criteria for determining the amount of damages payable. These criteria must not be less favourable than those applicable to similar claims in domestic law.

It is of interest to note that in an appeal against a decision of the English High Court to strike out certain claims, the Court of Appeal in *Bowden v Southwest-Services Ltd*[204] found that there was at least an arguable case that the protection afforded by Directive 79/923 on the quality required of shellfish waters entailed a grant of rights to mollusc fisherman.[205] This case was one of the first to address the issue of state liability pursuant to the *Francovich* ruling in an environmental context. Lord Justice Beldam indicated that the directive's recitals

> *make clear that the purpose of the Directive is to safeguard shellfish populations from various harmful consequences. The Directive had in mind that the failure to protect the shellfish population could result in unequal conditions of competition which suggest that those who collect and market shellfish may have been intended to have a right of reparation if there was a failure to implement the Directive's requirement.*[206]

---

[202] See Case C-392/93 *R v HM Treasury ex parte British Telecommunications* [1996] ECR I-1631, para. 43.

[203] See Case C-5/94 *Hedley Lomas* [1996] ECR I-2553 para.28, Case C-127/95 *Norbrook Laboratories* [1998] ECR I-1531 para. 109, and Case C-424/97 *Haim* [2000] ECR I-5123 para. 38.

[204] [1999] 3 CMLR 180.

[205] OJ 1979 L281/47.

[206] Para. 20 of the judgment. His Lordship went on to add that although the plaintiff's claim for compensation was arguable, it was a matter which "will be for the court which finally hears the case to decide".

Although its application in an environmental context remains largely unfulfilled at present and may remain limited due to problems of proving causation, the English Court of Appeal's ruling is a reminder that the potential liability of the State in its law-making capacity remains of importance in an environmental context. At the very least it will serve as a powerful incentive to Member States to ensure timely implementation of directives, and to ensure the appropriate practical implementation of Community measures.[207]

Evaluation and Review of Legislation

The effectiveness of legislation can only be evaluated if reliable environmental data is available on a European level. The provision of accurate information will ensure that the public is more aware of the sensitivity of the environment and place added pressure on legislators to take effective action to protect the environment by adopting new or amending legislation. Most environmental directives place an obligation on Member States to report at regular intervals to the Commission on implementation. These compliance reports are potentially an important source of information, the Commission often being obliged to publish a pan-European report covering information supplied to it in this way. Generally speaking Member States' fulfilment of their reporting requirements has been very poor and of variable quality. The House of Lords Select Committee on the European Communities reporting in 1992 indicated that

> *Without information it is impossible to assess whether compliance takes place, the effectiveness of the legislation, or to gauge what further action may be called for ... [t]he Commission reports that only a minority, led by Denmark and the United Kingdom, fully met their obligations in transmitting reports to the Commission.*[208]

At the end of 1993 the Institute for European Environmental Policy carried out an investigation into the state of reporting concluding that

> *Of 64 items of environmental legislation requiring the Commission to produce reports on implementation, in the case of some 24 the Commission produced no report at all, and for a further 16, reports had either been delayed (sometimes by years) or had been published at very infrequent intervals. The reasons for this included failures by the Member States to provide information – or information of the right sort – to the Commission, and cumbersome procedures and a lack of*

---

[207] See Abboud, "EC Environmental Law and Member State Liability - Towards a Fourth Generation of Community Remedies" (1998) 7(1) RECIEL 85-92 generally on state liability under the principles in Francovich. Also Somsen, "Francovich and its Application to EC Environmental Law" in Somsen (ed.), *Protecting The European Environment* (1996) pp.135-150.

[208] House of Lords 1992 Report, *supra* n.2, pp.17-18.

resources within the Commission itself. A further reason was the lack of pressure from the Council that has given a higher priority to the adoption of new legislation.[209]

In a bid to improve this state of affairs the Standard Reporting Directive amended existing directives by requiring Member States to submit sectoral reports to the Commission covering the implementation of various related directives every three years.[210] Attempting to standardise content, these reports will respond to specific questionnaires issued by the Commission. The Commission will publish its own report within nine months of receiving Member States' reports.[211] The usefulness of this directive has however been questioned as it only requires Member States to provide information on administrative and technical measures in place, rather than the detail of practical application.[212] Additionally, it covers air, water and waste directives but not other environmental directives such as those relating to nature conservation or noise control.[213] Noting the poor past performance by Member States in fulfilling their reporting requirements and that a large number of the questionnaires were sent out late by the Commission to the Member States,[214] it is perhaps not surprising, but nonetheless disappointing, to note that not all Member States are complying with their obligations under the directive;[215] in October 1998 for example the Commission sent reasoned opinions under Article 226 EC to Luxembourg and Ireland for failure to submit reports on implementation of water directives by the due date of September 1996. The Commission has found it necessary to continue to take such action to force Member States to take their responsibilities seriously;[216] in 1999 the Commission for instance began

---

[209] Haigh, *supra* n.43, p.71. See Institute for European Environmental Policy, "The State of Reporting by the EC Commission in Fulfilment of Obligations Contained in EC Environmental Legislation" (1993).

[210] Council Directive 91/692 Standardizing and Rationalizing Reports on the Implementation of Certain Directives Relating to the Environment OJ 1991 L377/48.

[211] Under the provisions of the directive the Commission was obliged to publish a report on implementation of water directives by 1 June 1997, of air quality and major accident hazards by 1 June 1998, and of waste by 1 June 1999.

[212] See criticism voiced in evidence by Wilkinson to House of Lords Select Committee in House of Lords 1997 Report, *supra* n.8, p.144 of the Minutes of Evidence.

[213] *Ibid.*

[214] *Ibid.*

[215] See for example the Commission's report on the implementation of certain Community waste legislation for the period 1995-97 [COM 1999 752] which was a consolidated report prepared by the Commission to assess progress in implementing specific directives including the "Framework" Directive on Waste (OJ 1995 L194/47) as amended by Directive 91/156 (OJ 1991 L78/32). Member States' reports were to be submitted by 30/10/98 but none were received on time. Austria, Denmark and Finland did submit in October 1998 and eight other countries after a period of some delay. Neither Greece, Italy or Spain submitted reports at all, and Portugal's report was far from comprehensive.

[216] Additionally, France's failure to provide reports concerning Directive 78/659 on the Quality of Fresh Waters Requiring Protection or Improvement to Support Fish Life (OJ 1978 L22/1) and Directive 79/923 on the Quality Required of Shellfish Waters (OJ 1979 L281/47) led to the Commission issuing a reasoned opinion in 1999; see EU Focus Issue 39, p.12 (12 August 1999).

infringement proceedings against Spain, Denmark, Portugal, France, Italy, the Netherlands, Greece and Ireland for seemingly failing to deliver reports on measures relating to waste.[217] The Sixth Environmental Action Programme has underlined the importance of providing accurate environmental information to the overall policy process but acknowledges that current reporting systems are insufficient to assess the implementation of EC environmental legislation.

A more encouraging development has been the establishment of the European Environment Agency which has not only made accurate environmental data accessible to the Commission and national legislators, thereby assisting in the development of environmental policy, but has also endeavoured to provide more effective monitoring of environmental change in the Community. It has additionally strived to provide accurate environmental data to allow more effective evaluation of legislation and its implementation. One of its tasks, for instance, has been to endeavour to harmonise national state of the environment reporting and to assist in providing analysis of data and information. In this way and by generally developing methodology to ensure the provision of consistent and comparable information, the Agency is providing for a more efficient evaluation of the state of the environment and, importantly, of the effectiveness of existing policy and legislation.[218] Its work also seeks to establish uniformity of monitoring in areas such as water and air pollution.[219] Moreover, it has made a positive start in improving the availability of environmental data highlighting areas in which improvements have been made in recent years, but also drawing attention to those areas of the environment that continue to decline.[220] This type of information, being of vital importance to the legislator in determining the need for further legislation, is precisely the type of data which has been so sorely lacking in recent years.

The Agency's EIONET network provides the foundation for the Agency's work on the development of an effective monitoring and reporting process. Topic Centres are involved in programmes to develop monitoring activities within the Member States.[221] In the area of water resources for instance, an evaluation of inland water quality monitoring was completed in 1995, and a subsequent project has recommended the introduction of an improved national monitoring system.[222] In addition, a European water monitoring network known as "EuroWaterNet" is being

---

[217] European Commission, *supra* n.77, p.62. As to ECJ rulings, see for example Case C-435/99 *Commission* v *Portugal* [2000] ECR I-11179 in which it was held that Portugal was in breach of its obligations to submit reports on nine directives relating to waste.

[218] See also Agency, *Environment in the EU - Report for the Review of the Fifth Environmental Action Programme* (1995).

[219] Evidence by Derek Osborn, Chairman of the European Environment Agency, to the House of Lords Select Committee in House of Lords 1997 Report, *supra* n.8, pp.111-112 of the Minutes of Evidence.

[220] See, for instance, its report entitled *Europe's Environment: the Second Assessment* (1998).

[221] Monitoring reports from the Agency's Topic Centres include publications on "Surface Water Quality Monitoring" (Topic Report 2/1996), and "Air Pollution Monitoring in Europe" (Topic Report R26/1996).

[222] EEA Annual Report 1995.

designed to improve the comparability and consistency of water quality information. With regard to nature conservation, the Agency continues to assist the Commission by developing a monitoring method to analyse the current state and trends of biodiversity in the Community. Databases on areas, populations of species, and priority habitats protected under the Habitats Directive are being established to assist in the formation of the NATURA 2000 conservation network. The development of a map on ecological regions has contributed to these efforts. Furthermore, in respect of air quality issues, national monitoring is being improved by the establishment of a network covering information on a larger number of pollutants and producing data of more consistent quality to update existing databases.

In addition to these types of monitoring activities, a key Agency task is to both analyse and report on information. The Agency is obliged to produce a report on the state of the environment in Europe every five years and published the "Dobris Assessment" in 1995.[223] This state of the environment report covered 45 countries and took into account data to 1992. It was presented to a conference of all European environment ministers in Sofia in 1995, and underpinned discussion to improve environmental policies and programmes. The report has been widely welcomed and praised for accurately stressing a number of serious threats, including ozone layer depletion and climate change, and highlighting Europe's contribution to the sources of these threats. More recently a second pan-European assessment has been published and concentrates on the manner in which the environmental situation has changed since the early 1990s.[224] Analysis of those socio-economic factors which have occasioned continued environmental damage is given together with an indication of what must be done to halt further decline. Both of these detailed reports have served to document continuing problems and the effectiveness of current policy.

The Agency has also published a report on the current state of and outlook to 2010 for the Community's environment, placing an onus on policy-makers to anticipate further decline in the future by introducing clearly defined targets and preventative policies.[225] It is in this type of report that the real benefit of providing accurate and comprehensive information can be seen by giving decision-makers a window of opportunity to arrest the inevitability of environmental decline by adopting policy change. A lack of political will at the executive level to introduce effective

---

[223] Agency, *Europe's Environment: the Dobris Assessment* (1995).

[224] Agency, *Europe's Environment: the Second Assessment* (1998).

[225] Agency, *Environment in the European Union At the Turn of the Century* (1999). See also by the Agency, *Environmental Agreements: Are They Effective?* (1997) which calls for the establishment of clear targets, monitoring and reporting obligations, and transparency in negotiation and implementation of environmental agreements.

environmental programmes can hardly be reinforced by the provision of this type of information to not only policy-makers themselves, but also to the general public who are in a position to place pressure on their elected representatives.[226]

Some Concluding Remarks

The Commission's approach of fostering greater coordination within the regulatory chain is a worthy one which stresses the importance of the various players involved in the entire chain. Steps such as the establishing of IMPEL and the European Environment Agency have undoubtedly been taken in recent years to improve the overall efficiency of the chain.[227] It is to be hoped that both the work of IMPEL and the Agency continue to expand and develop as their efforts to date have shown the value of efficiently-run expert bodies in policy formulation, practical application and enforcement. However, despite these undoubted improvements, a change in political attitude is required of Member States towards protection of the environment if effective long-term action is to be forthcoming. Sufficient resources must be made available to national regulatory authorities to either improve or introduce inspectorates, and to ensure practical application. Too many Member States give the impression that they will grudgingly pass national legislation to implement Community environmental measures, but do little to ensure effective application. By making available more environmental data to the general public and NGOs, it is to be hoped that individuals and pressure groups will both apply political pressure and, if necessary, take judicial action to enforce Community rights and obligations.

The enlargement of the Community to include states in Central and Eastern Europe will present new demands particularly bearing in mind the low priority given in these countries to environmental protection in the Cold War era. The Commission has underlined the importance of the adoption and implementation of "realistic, national ... strategies for gradual effective alignment" in applicant states for eventual compliance with the Community's environmental *acquis*, and has stressed that alignment with the latter will more than likely only be achieved in the long term.[228] Improving the administrative and legislative capacity of national actors in applicant countries has been identified as a priority. In particular, the implementation and enforcement of environmental legislation in candidate countries is often the responsibility of regional or local bodies where there is an evident need for "more efficient management and additional staff training".[229] The path to accession has

---

[226] The Agency and other component parts of the EIONET are also engaged in a variety of other reporting activities. See generally the Agency's website at http://www.eea.eu.

[227] Mention should also be made of the "Environmental Policy Review Group" which provides Commission officials with the opportunity to meet with their national administrative counterparts active in the environmental field to deliberate upon the direction of policy. Its deliberations are not placed in the public domain; see Kramer, *supra* n.5, p. 32.

[228] COM (98) 294, p.1.

[229] *Ibid*, p.3.

already placed burdens on the legislative capacity of applicant countries in transposing existing Community law, and will undoubtedly continue to do so.[230] Moreover, the need for improved monitoring facilities and inspection capacity is clear, and much capital investment will be necessary particularly in the areas of air pollution reduction, water and waste management.[231] Whilst the road ahead may at times seem daunting, the enlargement of the Community eastwards will undoubtedly have a positive environmental impact. The opportunity to reduce water and air pollution in applicant countries will in particular present a chance to improve the overall state of the environment not only at the national level in candidate countries, but also throughout Europe as pollution with transboundary impact is prevented or minimised.[232]

---

[230] *Ibid.*

[231] *Ibid*, Annex I which notes that the "total investment costs of meeting the environmental *acquis* are likely to be up to ECU 120 billion for all the ten associated countries in Central and Eastern Europe". The Community's PHARE programme has to date provided financial assistance pre-accession although it is acknowledged by the Community that the bulk of the necessary funds will need to be raised by the candidate countries themselves; *ibid*, p.15.

[232] *Ibid*, p.8.

Select Bibliography

Clinton-Davies, "Enforcing EC Environmental Law: A Personal Perspective" in Somsen (ed.) *Protecting the European Environment: Enforcing EC Environmental Law* (1996) pp.1-7.

European Commission, "Implementing Community Environmental Law", COM (96) 500 final, Annex I.

European Environment Agency's Annual Reports, and Multiannual Work Programmes.

Fuhr, Gebers, Ormond and Roller, "Access to Justice: Legal Standing for Environmental Associations in the EU" in Robinson and Dunkley (eds.) *Public Interest Perspectives in Environmental Law* (1995), pp.71-108.

Geddes, "Locus Standi and EEC Environmental Measures" (1992) 4(1) JEL 29.

Hilson, "Community Rights in Environmental Law: Rhetoric or Reality?" in Holder (ed) *The Impact of EC Environmental Law in the UK* (1997) pp.51-68.

Holder, "A Dead End for Direct Effect?: Prospects for Enforcement of European Community Environmental Law by Individuals" (1996) 8(2) JEL 313.

House of Lords Select Committee on the European Communities, 9th Report, 1991-92, *Implementation and Enforcement of Environmental Legislation*, H L Paper 27, Volume I & II.

House of Lords Select Committee on the European Communities, 2nd Report, 1997-98, *Community Environmental Law: Making it Work*, H L Paper 12.

Jans, *European Environmental Law* (2000), chapters 4 and 5.

Kramer, *Focus on European Environmental Law*, 2nd ed., (1997), pp.1-25 (on implementation), 78-112 (on direct effect), pp.298-318 (on public interest litigation).

Macrory, "The Enforcement of Community Environmental Laws: Some Critical Issues" (1992) 29 CMLRev 347.

Macrory, "Community Supervision in the Field of the Environment" in Somsen (ed.) *Protecting the European Environment: Enforcing EC Environmental Law* (1996) pp.9-22.

Macrory and Purdy, "The Enforcement of EC Environmental Law against Member States" in Holder (ed.) *The Impact of EC Environmental Law in the UK* (1997) pp.27-50.

Sands, "The European Court of Justice: An Environmental Tribunal?" in Somsen (ed.), *Protecting The European Environment* (1996) pp.23-36.

Scott, *EC Environmental Law* (1998), pp.148-168.

Somsen, "Francovich and its Application to EC Environmental Law" in Somsen (ed.), *Protecting The European Environment* (1996) pp.135-150.

Williams, "The European Commission and the Enforcement of Environmental Law: an Invidious Position", 14 *YEL* (1994) 351.

Williams, "Enforcing European Environmental Law: Can the European Commission be Held to Account?", 2 *Yearbook of European Environmental Law* (2001) 271.

Winter, "On the Effectiveness of the EC Administration: the Case of Environmental

Protection" (1996) 33 CMLRev 689.

Wyatt, "Litigating Community Environmental Law – Thoughts on the Direct Effect Doctrine" (1998) 10(1) JEL 9.

Xanthaki, "The Problem of Quality of EU Legislation: What on Earth is Really Wrong?" (2001) 38 CMLRev 651.

Chapter 4

The Protection of European Habitats and Species

Pressures on the environment have in recent years had a profound bearing on European habitats to the extent that

> [r]iver ecosystems and estuaries, of vital importance to many species, have been severely damaged throughout Europe ... [and] other habitats of great biological value are now a fraction of their original size.[1]

Extensive destruction of habitats has in turn led to a marked decline in species populations with the result that half of Europe's mammal species and a third of reptile, fish and bird species are currently endangered.[2] With a view to preserving the range of remaining species and ecosystems, the international community at the 1992 Rio Earth Summit adopted the Convention on Biological Diversity.[3] "Biological diversity" is defined in this international treaty as

> the variability among living organisms from all sources including, inter alia, terrestrial, marine and other aquatic ecosystems and the ecological complexes of which they are part; this includes diversity within species, between species and of ecosystems.[4]

The Community is a party to the Biodiversity Convention[5] and is bound by its provisions which note that "as far as possible and as appropriate" State Parties are obliged to "establish a system of protected areas or areas where special measures need to be taken to conserve biological diversity" and also to "promote the protection of ecosystems, natural habitats and the maintenance of viable populations of species in natural surroundings".[6] The two key Community measures designed to

---

[1] European Commission, *Natura 2000 - Managing Our Heritage* (1997), p.4. "Heathland, steppes and peat bogs have shrunk by 60-90% ... [and since 1900] 75% of the dunes in France, Italy and Spain have disappeared"; *ibid*. Note also that "64 endemic plants of Europe have become extinct in nature and 45% of butterflies, 38% of birds species, 24% of the species and subspecies of certain groups of plants, and some 5% of mollusc species are already considered as threatened"; European Commission, *Biodiversity Action Plan for the Conservation of Natural Resources* COM (2001) 162, vol. I.
[2] *Ibid.*
[3] 31 ILM (1992) 822.
[4] Article 2 of the Biodiversity Convention. On the Community's approach to protection of biodiversity generally, see European Commission, *Biodiversity Action Plan for the Conservation of Natural Resources* COM (2001) 162, vol. II.
[5] Decision 93/626 OJ 1993 L309/1. See COM (1998) 42 as to the Community's overall strategy for implementation of the Biodiversity Convention.
[6] Article 8(a) and (d) of the Biodiversity Convention.

conserve remaining biological diversity within the territory of Member States, and therefore fulfil these international obligations, provide the focus of discussion in this chapter. The combined impact of these measures, the Wild Birds Directive[7] and the Habitats Directive,[8] is intended to offer effective protection to habitats and also of wild fauna and flora by, most importantly, establishing a Europe-wide interrelated network of protected habitat sites imposing obligations of maintenance and restoration of habitat.

The regimes established by the two measures can be regarded as contributing to the pursuit of sustainable development and the integration of environmental concerns into planning and land-use. Underlining the important influence of international law on policy in this area, these directives seek also to implement obligations under other important environmental treaties to which the EC is party, the Berne Convention on the Conservation of European Wildlife and Natural Habitats,[9] and the Bonn Convention on the Conservation of Migratory Species of Wild Animals.[10]

Action by Member States to designate suitable habitats for protection under the two directives has often been disappointing. This reluctance is due in large part to the realisation by Member States that limitations are imposed on activities within such protected areas and responsibilities assumed. For example, existing development plans may need to be modified or replaced, and the required conservation measures will be costly to implement. However it will be seen that the Court of Justice has on the whole taken a typically strident role in seeking to ensure that Member States do not lose sight of the conservation objectives of these two directives.

Protection of Wild Birds and their Habitats under the Wild Birds Directive

Widespread public unease as to the traditional mass killings in Southern Europe and North Africa of migratory birds led in the early 1970s to questions being raised in the European Parliament as to the need for Community legislation to protect wild birds.[11] Supported by a variety of non-governmental groups keen to see more protection introduced for wild birds throughout Europe, the Commission in December 1976 began the legislative process which eventually led to the adoption

---

7   Council Directive 79/409/EEC on the Conservation of Wild Birds OJ 1979 L103/1. The directive has been amended by Commission Directive 85/411 OJ 1985 L233/33, Council Directive 81/854 OJ 1981 L319/3, Commission Directive 91/244 OJ 1991 L115/41, Council Directive 94/24 OJ 1994 L164/9, and Commission Directive 97/49 OJ 1997 L223/9.

8   Council Directive 92/43/EEC on the Conservation of Natural Habitats and of Wild Fauna and Flora OJ 1992 L206/7. Member States were obliged to have transposed the directive by 5 June 1994; see Case C-329/96 *Commission* v *Hellenic Republic* [1997] ECR I-3749, and Case C-83/97 *Commission* v *Germany* [1997] ECR I-7191. The directive has been amended by Council Directive 97/62 adapting the directive to technical progress OJ 1997 L305/42.

9   Decision 82/72 OJ 1982 L38/1.

10 Decision 82/461 OJ 1982 L210/10.

11 Haigh, *Manual of Environmental Policy* (looseleaf), 9.2-4.

of the Wild Birds Directive in April 1979. It will be recalled that not until the adoption of the Single European Act was the Environment Title added to the Treaty, and the legal basis therefore chosen for the measure was ex-Article 235 (now Article 308 EC), the directive's preamble creatively noting that

> the conservation of the species of wild birds ... is necessary to attain, within the operation of the common market, the Community's objectives regarding the improvement of living conditions, a harmonious development of economic activities throughout the Community and a continuous and balanced expansion, but the necessary specific powers to act have not been provided for in the Treaty ...

The migratory range of many birds does not respect national boundaries and there is an obvious need to introduce a uniform Europe-wide system of protection. As such the directive clearly complies with one of the Treaty's guiding principles, the principle of subsidiarity, in the sense that the Community would certainly appear better placed than individual Member States to establish comprehensive transfrontier protection for wild birds, imposing common legally binding obligations. This is particularly so bearing in mind that, prior to the introduction of the Wild Birds Directive, national action in this area had been patchy and insufficient.

The preamble to the measure refers to migratory birds as the Community's "common heritage" and acknowledges that most wild birds in the Community are in fact migratory in nature. The directive however introduces measures to protect not only migratory but all wild birds, Article 2 noting that

> Member States shall take the requisite measures to maintain the population of [all species of naturally occurring birds in the wild state in the European territory of the Member States to which the Treaty applies] at a level which corresponds in particular to ecological, scientific and cultural requirements, while taking account of economic and recreational requirements, or to adapt the population of these species to that level.

Member States are obliged both to afford effective species protection,[12] and also to preserve and maintain sufficient diversity and area of wild birds' habitats.

Species Protection

Subject to certain exceptions and derogations to be discussed later, Article 5 of the Wild Birds Directive places an obligation on Member States to establish a system of protection for all species of naturally occurring wild birds, whether they be

---

[12] The obligation placed on Member States to protect wild birds that occur in the Community continues to apply to each Member State even if the natural habitat of the species in question does not occur in the territory of the Member State concerned; Case C-149/94 *Criminal Proceedings against Didier Vergy* [1996] ECR I-299.

migratory or non-migratory in nature, which ensures that the following are prohibited:

- *deliberate killing or capture by any method;*

- *deliberate destruction of, or damage to, their nests and eggs, or removal of nests;*

- *taking their eggs in the wild and keeping them even if empty;*

- *deliberate disturbance of these birds particularly during the period of breeding, in so far as disturbance would be significant having regard to the objectives of this Directive;*

- *keeping birds of species the hunting and capture of which is prohibited.*

The directive's starting point is therefore to conserve every species of wild bird. Specimens living in captivity and domestic bird species are excluded from the system of protection afforded by the measure.

By virtue of Article 6(1), Member States are obliged to adopt national legislation to ban not only the sale of live or dead wild birds but also their transportation for sale, keeping for sale and offering for sale.[13] These measures are intended to "prevent commercial interests from exerting a possible harmful pressure on exploitation levels".[14] However, the directive establishes certain important exceptions to the general obligation to afford protection. The marketing ban is relaxed for instance in respect of certain birds such as the pheasant, wood pigeon, red grouse and partridge, as long as the birds have been legally killed or captured, or otherwise legally acquired.[15] In addition, Article 7 introduces exceptions to accommodate the traditional hunting of particular types of birds.[16] Birds that may be hunted throughout the Community include the greylag and bean goose, red grouse, mallard, ptarmigan, partridge, pheasant and woodcock.[17] Other species can only be hunted in particular Member States,[18] and include the starling and various members of the crow family which were added to the list of birds that could be hunted following assertions from some Member States that the directive should allow more birds which interfere with agriculture to be legally killed within their territories.[19] This 1994 amendment to the directive was passed by a qualified majority vote despite

---

13   Article 6(1).

14   Preamble.

15   Article 6(2). The other more specific exception can be found in Article 6(3) which stipulates that, in consultation with the Commission, Member States can allow the activities noted in Article 6(1) within its own territory in respect of birds noted in Annex III/2 provided they have been "legally killed or captured or otherwise legally acquired". Birds noted in Annex III/2 include the UK's population of black grouse.

16   For a recent example of a case where a Member State had failed to comply with the combined provisions of Article 5 and 7 see Case C-159/99 *Commission v Italy* [2001] ECR I-4007.

17   Those birds that can be hunted throughout the Community are noted in Annex II/1.

18   Noted in Annex II/2.

19   See Haigh, *supra* n.11, 9.2-6.

protests from Denmark which viewed the measure relating to the starling as a backward step bearing in mind the conservation objectives of the directive.[20]

Hunting is prohibited in the rearing season and during the various stages of reproduction.[21] Migratory birds in particular must not be hunted during their periods of reproduction or during their return to their rearing grounds. It is also noteworthy that the hunting of birds must certainly not jeopardise their conservation status seeing as Article 7(4) also notes *inter alia* that the practice must comply "with the principles of wise use and ecologically balanced control of the species of birds concerned". The ECJ has interpreted Article 7(4) as meaning that a complete system of protection must be established during these periods when the survival of these birds is particularly threatened.[22] The mere protection of the majority of birds of a species is insufficient.[23]

The preamble to the directive refers to the hunting exception as "acceptable exploitation" and would seem to take account not only of ecological factors, but also economic and recreational requirements in the sense that the hunting industry is regarded by many as a sport which generates wealth and provides employment in various regions of the Community. The preamble of the measure however further notes that the use of various means and devices of killing must be prohibited due to the "excessive pressure which they exert or may exert on the numbers of the species concerned". Article 8 provides that aircraft and cars as modes of transport cannot be used, and methods of killing such as the use of nets, poisoned bait, semi – and automatic weaponry capable of holding more than two bullets, and live birds – either blind or mutilated – as decoys must be banned.[24]

In certain express circumstances, the directive allows Member States to derogate from the provisions of Article 5, 6, 7 and 8. Member States' ability to derogate in this way is intended to provide some balance to the directive's environmental objectives by allowing other interests, such as economic, agricultural and recreational concerns, to be taken into account but only in exhaustive situations where three conditions are satisfied. The first and second conditions are noted in Article 9(1) of the directive. First, there must be "no other satisfactory solution" to

---

20   Council Directive 94/24/EC, OJ 1994 L164/9. See Haigh, ibid.

21   Article 7(4).

22   See, for example, Case C-157/89 *Commission* v *Italy* [1991] ECR I-57, para.14. See also Case C-38/99 *Commission* v *France* [2000] ECR I-10941 in which the French system of opening and closing dates for hunting was held to be incompatible with Article 7(4). On the political controversy in France as to dates for the hunting season, see "French Defy EU over Hunting Season" in *The Independent* (UK), 22 June 1998, p.11.

23   Case C-435/92 *Association pour La Protection des Animaux Savages et al* v *Préfet de Maine-et-Loire et al* [1994] ECR I-67.

24   Article 8 notes that the use of means of killing noted in Annex IV(a) and the modes of transport mentioned in Annex IV(b) must be prohibited by Member States.

derogation.[25] The second condition is that the derogation must be for one of the following reasons:

(A) - *in the interests of public health and safety*

   - *in the interests of air safety*

   - *to prevent serious damage to crops, livestock, forests, fisheries and water*

   - *for the protection of flora and fauna*

(B) *for the purposes of research and teaching, of re-population, of re-introduction and for the breeding necessary for these purposes*

(C) *to permit, under strictly supervised conditions and on a selective basis, the capture, keeping or other judicious use of certain birds in small numbers.*

This last provision (sub-paragraph (C)) can in particular be regarded as vague in nature and therefore capable of broad interpretation. Indeed the ECJ itself has noted that "the capture and sale of birds, even outside the hunting season, with a view to keeping them for use as live decoys or for recreational purposes in fairs and markets may constitute judicious use authorised by Article 9(1)(c)"[26] and that the capture of a protected species to allow bird fanciers the chance to stock their aviaries may additionally constitute such judicious use.[27] Also the traditional use in France of horizontal nets known as "pantes" or "matoles" to capture skylarks has been held to be compatible with its requirements bearing in mind the number of birds captured amounted to a small proportion of the overall population concerned.[28]

If a State chooses to derogate, by virtue of Article 9(2) it must in addition comply with the third condition – namely to report to the Commission as to the extent and nature of the derogation, enabling the Commission to keep the derogation under review to assess its compatibility with the directive.[29]

---

[25]   In January 2000 the Commission made an application to the ECJ against Spain under Article 226 alleging that the regional authorities in Guipozcoa had authorised the hunting of migratory birds during their flight back to rearing areas. In this respect the Commission has argued that "*other possibilities exist for hunting the species ... such as authorising hunting in autumn, outside the prenuptial migration season*"; see Commission press release IP/00/68, 21/1/00.

[26]   Case 262/85 *Commission* v *Italy* [1987] ECR 3073, para.38. See Kramer, *European Environmental Law Casebook* (1993) at p.196 and p.203.

[27]   Case C-10/96 *Ligue Royale Belge pour la Protection des Oiseaux ASBL* v *Region Wallon*ne [1996] ECR I-6775, para.16.

[28]   Case 252/85 *Commission* v *France* [1988] ECR 2243. This was despite the fact that the use of nets falls within the prohibition in Article 8(1) read in conjunction with Annex IVa.

[29]   Article 9(2) stipulates

   The derogations must specify: the species which are subject to the derogation; the means, arrangements or methods authorized for capture or killing; the conditions of risk and the circumstances of time and place under which such derogations may be granted; the authority empowered to declare that the required conditions obtain and to decide what means, arrangements or methods may be used, within what limits and by whom; the controls which will be carried out.

For an example of a case in which a Member State was held to be in breach of its obligations under Article 9(2) (in respect particularly of the obligation to provide information on the circumstances of time and place under which such derogations may be granted), see Case 252/85 *supra* n.28.

By analysing that part of the *Commission* v *Italy*[30] case which related to derogations, an insight can be gained into the ECJ's strict interpretation of the derogation provisions. Italian national law allowed eleven wild birds to be hunted even though these birds were not included in the list of huntable birds under the terms of the directive. Italy accepted that the Commission's complaint in this respect was accurate, but asserted that the hunting of two of the eleven species, the jay and magpie, was legitimate under Article 9(1)(a) as these species were potentially harmful in character. The ECJ acknowledged that derogations from the general scheme of protection under the directive were of course acceptable, but only if made in accordance with the three conditions noted above. In this respect the ECJ *inter alia* noted the lack of proof supplied by Italy "that it was necessary to include the jay and magpie on the Italian list of birds which may be hunted in order to prevent serious damage to crops, livestock, forests, fisheries or water and that no other satisfactory solution existed".[31]

In *Commission* v *Netherlands*[32] the ECJ again underlined that derogations are allowed but only when strictly necessary in accordance with the terms of the directive – the Netherlands had infringed the directive in allowing the hunting of protected species (the carrion crow, jackdaw, jay and magpie) without satisfying the terms for legitimate derogation. It is therefore clear that where exceptions to the directive's overall scheme of protection are claimed by means of national derogations, the ECJ will not entertain the legitimacy of such derogations unless they comply in full with the provisions of Article 9(1) and the reporting requirements in Article 9(2),[33] the ECJ seeing fit to strike down most "derogations" claimed by Member States.[34]

Wild Birds' Habitats

In addition to affording specific species protection, the directive importantly establishes a two-tier structure of habitat protection. A general obligation is placed on Member States by Article 3 to act "to preserve, maintain or re-establish a sufficient diversity and area of habitats" for *all* species of wild birds within Member States' territories in the light of the requirements noted in Article 2. Requisite measures include the creation of national protected reserves, and the upkeep and management of habitats both within and outside protected areas. The re-establishment of biotopes is also envisaged as in Denmark where, since the late 1980s, successive governments have endeavoured to offset the impact of widespread

---

[30] Case 262/85 *supra* n.26.

[31] Para.14 of the judgment.

[32] Case 339/87 [1990] ECR I-851, paras.14-15. See however para.16 of the judgment which notes that the hunting of the rook did comply with the requirements of Article 9.

[33] See also Case 412/85 *Commission* v *Germany* [1987] ECR 3503 para.19, and Case 118/94 *Associazione Italiana per il WWF et al* v *Regione Veneto* [1996] ECR I-1223.

[34] See Kramer, *supra* n.26 at p.201 where numerous specific instances are provided.

national wetland reclamation schemes by restoring certain wetland areas along its west coast (such as at Vest Stadil Fjord) in an attempt to restore suitable habitats for a variety of migratory birds like the barnacle goose.[35]

On the other hand, Article 4(1) and (2) provide a more specific obligation to establish a regime to ensure the survival and reproduction of rare or vulnerable species (Annex I species) and regularly occurring migratory birds not listed in Annex I. Article 4(1) envisages the setting up of Special Protection Areas (SPAs) in stipulating that

The species mentioned in Annex I shall be the subject of special conservation measures concerning their habitat in order to ensure their survival and reproduction in their area of distribution. In this connection, account shall be taken of:

A.   *Species in danger of extinction;*

B.   *Species vulnerable to specific changes in their habitat;*

C.   *Species considered rare because of small populations or restricted local distribution;*

D.   *Other species requiring particular attention for reasons of the specific nature of their habitat.*

Trends and variations in population levels shall be taken into account as a background for evaluations.

Member States shall classify in particular the most suitable territories in number and size as special protection areas for the conservation of these species, taking into account their protection requirements in the geographical sea and land areas where this directive applies.

Article 4(2) provides that Member States should adopt

similar measures for regularly occurring migratory species not listed in Annex I, bearing in mind their need for protection in the geographical sea and land area where this directive applies, as regards their breeding, moulting and wintering areas and staging posts along their migration routes. To this end, Member States shall pay particular attention to the protection of wetlands and particularly to wetlands of international importance.

Member States must also ensure that all habitats within SPAs are protected, Article 4(4) *inter alia* originally noting that

---

[35] *Natura 2000* (European Commission DG Environment's Nature Newsletter) Issue 10 (November 1999), pp.8-10.

Member States shall take appropriate steps to avoid pollution or deterioration of habitats or any disturbances affecting the birds, in so far as these would be significant having regard to the objectives of this Article.[36]

The Commission has shown a willingness to enforce the obligation to afford protection by, for example, making an application to the ECJ against Ireland due to the Irish Government's failure to eradicate sheep overgrazing in the largest SPA in Ireland (the Owenduff-Nephin Beg Complex in County Mayo). The Commission alleged that overgrazing led to the erosion of peat soils and a consequent threat to rare bird species including the golden plover and the greenland white-fronted goose.[37]

The process of designating SPAs throughout the Community is intended to result in the formation of a coherent interrelated system of protection for Annex I rare, endangered or vulnerable species, such as the golden eagle, arctic tern, snowy owl, kingfisher, and stone curlew, and also for regularly occurring migratory wild birds in general. Member States are obliged to provide the Commission with "all relevant information" to enable it to ensure the areas of protection "form a coherent whole which meets the protection requirements of these species".[38] This information is placed into a database of SPAs held by the Environment Agency's Topic Centre for Nature Conservation. Germany has been particularly disappointing in its reluctance to share data on its protected areas with the Commission and the Agency, as have Belgium, Ireland and Spain.[39] In the absence of full cooperation from all Member States in this respect, the Commission has found it hard to coordinate the system in such a way that ensures that an effective transfrontier system of protection for wild birds is provided which takes into account stop-off points along migratory routes.

Failure to Designate an Area as a Special Protection Area

The establishing of SPAs is evidently of fundamental importance to the success or otherwise of the directive, and in *Commission* v *Spain* (*Santona Marshes* case)[40] Spain's failure to classify the Santona Marshes as a SPA provided an example of the Commission's willingness to take infringement proceedings against Member States which fail to designate suitable areas.[41] There was little room to doubt the site satisfied the ornithological criteria for special protection under Article 4(1) and (2)

---

36 Article 7 of the Habitats Directive has amended this first sentence of Article 4(4); nevertheless a system of protection is still required of Member States; see later discussion at n.121 and accompanying text.
37 Commission press release IP/OO/4, 1/6/00. See the subsequent ECJ ruling; Case 117/00 *Commission v Ireland* [2002] ECR I-5335.
38 Article 4(3).
39 *Natura 2000* (European Commission DG Environment's Nature Newsletter) Issue 10 (November 1999), p.3.
40 C-355/90 *Commission* v *Spain* [1993] ECR I-4221.
41 For another example, see also Case C-96/98 *Commission* v *France* [1999] ECR I-8531 in which France was *inter alia* held to have failed to designate a sufficient area in the ornithologically important Poitevin Marshes as SPAs. Also see Case C-374/98 *Commission* v *France* [2000] ECR I-10799 concerning the Basses Corbières area.

of the directive. Described by the ECJ as "one of the most important ecosystems in the Iberian peninsula for many aquatic birds",[42] the Santona Marshes were regularly visited by nineteen Annex I species and at least fourteen species of migratory birds.[43] It also constituted wetlands area of international importance within the meaning of Article 4(2). The Spanish measures in place excluded 40,000 square metres of the marshes which were accordingly left unprotected and susceptible to the deterioration clearly suffered by other marshland areas along the sea coast. Even within the area afforded protection by national measures, Spain had evidently failed to adopt the management measures necessary to provide protection as required by the directive.

Spain argued that, in deciding whether or not to designate an area as a SPA, ecological requirements were subordinate to other interests, in particular social and economic interests. If not subordinate, at the very least social and economic interests should be balanced against ecological requirements. In support of its argument, it made reference to the provisions of Article 2.[44] The ECJ disagreed with this argument underlining that the economic and recreational interests referred to in this provision "do not enter into consideration"[45] in the process of classifying SPAs under Article 4, and cannot be used to undermine the ecological objectives of the directive. Spain had therefore failed to fulfil its obligations by not designating the Santona Marshes as a SPA.

Wils has subsequently noted that while Article 2 underlines the directive's "general philosophy", it "should not be used to give restrictive interpretations of articles which are sufficiently clear on their own".[46] Indeed the ECJ's judgment has served to underline that, although Member States have a degree of discretion in classifying areas as SPAs, if a particular individual site evidently meets the ornithological criteria in Article 4 by, for instance, being an important habitat for rare wild birds or a wetland of essential importance to migratory birds, it *must* be designated as a SPA.[47] Importantly, the ECJ also ruled that Member States are obliged to take

---

[42]   Para.27 of the judgment.

[43]   *Ibid.*

[44]   It will be recalled that Article 2 notes "Member States shall take the requisite measures to maintain the population of [wild birds] at a level which corresponds in particular to ecological, scientific and cultural requirements, *while taking account of economic and recreational requirements*, or to adapt the population of these species to that level". [Emphasis added].

[45]   Case C-355/90 *Commission v Spain supra* n.40, para.19.

[46]   Wils, "The Birds Directive 15 Years Later: a Survey of the Case Law and a Comparison with the Habitats Directive" (1994) 6(2) JEL 218, at p.227. The ECJ in the *Santona Marshes* case noted that the economic and recreational requirements referred to in Article 2 did not "constitute an autonomous derogation from the general system of protection established by the directive"; para.19 of the judgment.

[47]   Freestone describes this ruling as one which "radically reduces the margin of appreciation left to Member States in the establishment of SPAs in that failure to establish a site which meets these criteria as a SPA is a breach of the directive"; see Freestone, "The Enforcement of the Wild Birds Directive: a Case Study" in Somsen (ed.), *Protecting the European Environment: Enforcing EC Environmental Law* (1996), p.246. Note that it has been argued that the duty to classify the site as a SPA under Article 4(1) is directly effective; see Freestone, *ibid.* at p.247, and Wils, *supra* n.46, pp.229-230. See also Jans' viewpoint noted *infra* in n.55.

appropriate steps to avoid deterioration of those habitats most suited to conservation of wild birds even when the area in question had not been classified, but should have been by the Member State in question.[48]

In *R v Secretary of State for the Environment, ex parte Royal Society for the Protection of Birds*,[49] the *"Lappel Bank"* case, the ECJ reiterated its approach in the *Santona Marshes* case in once again dismissing the notion that economic requirements could be taken into account by Member States in designating SPAs to protect vulnerable Annex I species and/or migratory birds. The RSPB had argued that the inter-tidal mudflats known as Lappel Bank should have been included in the Medway Estuary and Marshes SPA. The Medway Estuary and Marshes had been recognised as a wetland area of international importance and designated by the UK as a SPA in December 1993. However, the Lappel Bank area was to be reclaimed and developed as part of an extension to the Port of Sheerness, a flourishing cargo port which employed significant numbers of workers in an area of high unemployment. The Lappel Bank area was clearly the only area into which the Port could expand and it was for this economic reason that the UK's Secretary of State for the Environment had excluded it from the designated SPA. The area was also one which satisfied the ecological criteria of the directive in that it was an important component of the estuarine ecosystem and host to migratory species of birds. The ECJ's judgment stipulated that, whilst Member States can take into account economic and recreational requirements mentioned in Article 2 in introducing national protection measures for non-Annex I birds or non-migratory species,[50] a Member State is not authorised to take into account economic requirements when designating and defining the boundaries of a SPA for the protection of Annex I species and regularly occurring migratory species pursuant to Articles 4(1) and (2).

More recently, the ECJ in *Commission v Netherlands*[51] turned its mind to the general obligation on Member States to designate a sufficient number and size of classified areas as SPAs for Annex I species, rather than the specific obligation to designate a particular site as in the *Santona Marshes* and *Lappel Bank* cases. The ECJ ruled that

> *Member States are obliged to classify as SPAs all the sites which, applying ornithological criteria, appear to be the most suitable for conservation of the species in question.*

> *Thus where it appears that a Member State has classified as SPAs sites the number and total area of which are manifestly less than the number and total area of the sites considered to be the most suitable for conservation of the species*

---

[48] Paras.20-22 of the judgment. See also Case C-96/98 *Commission v France, supra* n.41, para.41.

[49] Case C-44/95 *R v Secretary of State for the Environment, ex parte Royal Society for the Protection of Birds* [1996] ECR I-3843. See case note by Harte, "Nature Conservation: The Rule of Law in European Community Environmental Protection" (1997) 9(1) JEL 139.

[50] *Ibid.*, para.24.

[51] Case C-3/96 ECR [1998] I-3031. See also Haigh, *supra* n.11, 9.2-12/13.

in question, it will be possible to find that that Member State has failed to fulfil its obligations under Article 4(1) of the directive.[52]

In addressing the specific situation in the Netherlands, the ECJ went on to cast doubt on the assertion that purely ornithological criteria had been applied in the Dutch national designation process noting that in its defence the Dutch Government had incorrectly indicated that it was quite appropriate in such a process to take into account economic and recreational requirements. The Dutch Government in fact failed to inform the ECJ as to the exact criteria which it used to designate SPAs, and in the absence of such documentary evidence, the ECJ was satisfied that the "Inventory of Important Bird Areas in the European Community",[53] put forward in evidence by the Commission, was the only document before it containing scientific evidence allowing it to come to a decision as to whether the Netherlands had classified the most appropriate areas of its territory in number and area as SPAs. The Commission had argued that this document supported the conclusion that the 23 SPAs designated by the Netherlands represented less than half the number of appropriate sites, and just over 40 per cent of the total area suitable for designation. Though not legally binding, this inventory was of "acknowledged scientific value"[54] in the case and led the ECJ to conclude that the Netherlands had failed to fulfil its general obligations under the directive by classifying an insufficient number and total area of its territory as SPAs.

The *Commission* v *Netherlands* case has therefore further underlined the ECJ's determination to interpret the directive's obligations strictly and in a manner which seeks to ensure effective protection for wild birds and their habitats. It is refreshing to note that, in the absence of alternative scientific evidence, the ECJ endorsed the Commission's approach of assessing the suitability of sites by making reference to the "Inventory of Important Bird Areas in the European Community" prepared by independent experts in association with the Commission and Birdlife International.[55] Bearing in mind the Commission's admission that "[t]he vast majority of the Member States have failed to respect their collective commitment ... to create a coherent network of Special Protection Areas for birds"[56] and that "[s]everal important sites known to be of interest are still not protected under Community

---

[52]   Paras.62 and 63 of the judgment.

[53]   International Council for Bird Preservation, *Inventory of Important Bird Areas in the European Community* (1989; Technical Publication No. 9).

[54]   Para.70 of the judgment.

[55]   See also the ECJ's willingness to accept this document as evidence in subsequent cases: Case C-166/97 *Commission* v *France* [1999] ECR I-1719, para.11, and Case C-96/98 *Commission* v *France supra* n.41, para.13. Jans interestingly submits that, in the light of the ECJ's judgment in Case C-3/96 *Commission* v *Netherlands* (*supra* n.51), Article 4(1) may be directly effective bearing in mind the restrictions placed by the Court on a Member State's discretion to designate SPAs; Jans, *European Environmental Law* (2000), p.181.

[56]   *Natura 2000* (European Commission DG Environment's Nature Newsletter) Issue 10 (November 1999), p.1.

legislation",[57] the judgment sends a clear message to Member States that a general failure to designate a sufficient number of suitable sites covering an appropriate area of territory will not be tolerated by the ECJ.

As at April 2002, more than 22 years after the adoption of the directive, over 2,800 SPAs covering almost 230,000 square kilometres had been designated throughout the Community. However, only a small minority of Member States had satisfied the Commission that they had fulfilled their obligations in designating SPAs.[58] France has for some time particularly disappointed as far as designation of SPAs is concerned.[59] However, on a more positive note the Commission accepts that in recent years "substantial progress" has been made in Austria, Finland and Sweden since their accession to the Community, and that "significant progress" has also been forthcoming in countries such as Ireland, Italy and Luxembourg.[60]

Modifications to Sites Designated as Special Protection Areas

Imagine that a site has indeed been designated as a SPA under the directive. In what circumstances, if any, can works be carried out which would reduce the size of that SPA? The ECJ considered this issue in *Commission v Germany* ("*Leybucht Dykes*" case).[61] Leybucht forms part of a recognised wetland of international importance, the Ostfriesische Wattenmeer, well known as a nesting, breeding and staging point for a variety of wild birds including the Annex I listed avocet. In the mid 1980s the decision was made to strengthen the dyke works as part of a coastal defence project. Work began in 1986, and, by the end of 1987, the Commission had formed the opinion that the operations were incompatible with Germany's obligations under the directive bearing in mind the Leybucht formed part of an existing SPA and the new line of the dyke would effectively reduce the size of the protected habitat area.

The ECJ's ruling provided an interpretation of the first sentence of Article 4(4) of the directive which, it will be recalled, noted that in SPAs

> *Member States shall take appropriate steps to avoid pollution or deterioration of habitats or any disturbances affecting the birds, in so far as these would be significant having regard to the objectives of this Article.*

---

[57] *Ibid.*

[58] The Commission updates its "barometer" on compliance which can be found at http://europa.eu.int/comm/environment/nature/barometer/barometer.htm.

[59] *Natura 2000* (European Commission DG Environment's Nature Newsletter) Issue 13 (December 2000), p.6. There have also been problems in Germany; in explaining its decision to make an application to the ECJ under Article 226, the Commission in July 1999 stipulated that just under 40 per cent of sites recognised by the *Inventory of Important Bird Areas in the European Community* had yet to be designated by Germany as SPAs; Commission press release IP/99/514, 15/7/99.

[60] *Ibid.* It is noteworthy however that, despite such progress, the Commission made an application to the ECJ under Article 226 against Italy in 1999 claiming that more than half of the areas identified in the *Inventory of Important Bird Areas in the European Community* had yet to be designated as SPAs; Commission press release IP/99/514, 15/7/99.

[61] Case C-57/89 [1991] ECR I-883.

Bearing these obligations in mind, could a Member State legitimately reduce the size of a SPA? The ECJ concluded that Member States were certainly not able to exercise a general discretion as to whether modifications or reductions of SPAs could take place, as, if they were to possess such a discretion, Member States would be in a position unilaterally to undermine the system of protection afforded by designating an area as a SPA. This was not however to say that a reduction in the size of a SPA could *never* be justified, but such a reduction in the view of the ECJ would only be justified on exceptional grounds corresponding "to a general interest which is superior to the general interest represented by the ecological objective of the directive".[62]

Germany, supported by the UK Government, had argued that the economic and recreational considerations noted in Article 2 should be taken into account in defining "exceptional ground", but this submission was flatly rejected by the ECJ noting in its judgment that Article 2 "does not constitute an autonomous derogation from the general system of protection" established by the directive.[63] A reduction in the size of the Leybucht SPA could not therefore be justified on economic or recreational grounds, and it is this crucial part of the judgment which served to highlight the degree of protection afforded to SPAs.

The ECJ however went on to emphasise that the type of interest it did regard as superior to the general interest represented by the directive's ecological aims included works designed to protect human life. As such, action to prevent the danger of flooding and provide coastal protection was acceptable "as long as those measures are confined to a strict minimum and involve only the smallest possible reduction of the special protection area".[64] In essence, the ECJ underlined the special degree of protection attributed to species and habitats within SPAs – only in very limited circumstances related to public health or safety could a reduction in the size of a SPA be contemplated, and even then the measures must comply with the principle of proportionality. It is of more general interest to note that such judicial clarification had proved necessary in this case due to the lack of clarity in the wording of the directive. Indeed, uncertainty as to the implications of designating an area as a SPA in part explains the general reluctance of Member States to designate sufficient sites under the directive.[65]

The apparent success of the *Leybucht Dykes* case in reinforcing the rigorous protection of SPAs proved short lived as Member States took the first legislative opportunity to modify the implications of the judgment, Baldock correctly noting that

---

62   *Ibid.*, paras.21-22.

63   *Ibid.*, para.22. See earlier judgments in Case 247/85 *Commission* v *Belgium* [1987] ECR 3029 at para.8, and Case 262/85 *Commission* v *Italy supra* n.26, at para.8.

64   Para.23.

65   Nollkaemper, "Habitat Protection in European Community Law: Evolving Conceptions of a Balance of Interests" (1997) 9(2) JEL 271, at p.276.

the decision "fuelled political pressures to amend the directive so as to allow more scope for developments within SPAs".[66] In May 1992 the Habitats Directive was adopted. Article 7 of the Habitats Directive amended the first sentence of Article 4(4) of the Wild Birds Directive[67] by *inter alia* allowing social or economic factors to be taken into account in defining imperative reasons of overriding public interest which would be capable of justifying a project despite its negative environmental impact on the protected site in question.[68] The amendment effectively negated the significance of the *Leybucht Dykes* case with effect from June 1994.[69] It is however important to stress that these amendments made by the Habitats Directive to the Wild Birds Directive do not impact on the initial classification of an area as a SPA – in this respect the ruling in the *Santona Marshes* case remains good law, and economic requirements cannot be taken into account by Member States in designating SPAs to protect vulnerable Annex I species and/or migratory birds. If a particular individual site evidently meets the ornothological criteria in Article 4 of the Wild Birds Directive, it must be designated as a SPA and economic considerations must not be taken into account in such classification or the determination of its boundaries.[70]

Habitat and Species Protection under the Habitats Directive

The provisions of the Habitats Directive are intended to complement those of the Wild Birds Directive by establishing a system of protection for other species and also for naturally occurring habitats. The most important feature of the Habitats Directive is the establishing of a network of special areas of conservation known as "Natura 2000", referred to by the Commission as "the cornerstone of Community nature conservation policy".[71] In establishing this interlinked coherent European ecological network, the aim is to ensure that both the distribution and profusion of certain types of natural habitats and species' habitats, both marine and terrestrial, are either maintained or, if need be, restored at a "favourable conservation status".[72] The measure encourages the designation of sites to conserve biodiversity but not to the total exclusion of all other interests, Article 2(3) noting that

---

66   Baldock, "The Status of SPAs for the Protection of Wild Birds" (1992) 4(1) JEL 139, at p.143.

67   See Article 7 of the Habitats Directive.

68   See Article 6(4) of the Habitats Directive.

69   See however discussion (*infra* n.120) and accompanying text on case C-374/98 *Commission v France* (*supra* n.41) where the Court of Justice indicated that "the areas which have not been classified as SPAs but should have been so classified continue to fall under the regime governed by the first sentence of Article 4(4) of the birds directive"; para.47 of the judgment.

70   Case C-44/95 *R v Secretary of State for the Environment, ex parte Royal Society for the Protection of Birds supra* n.49, para.42.

71   European Commission, *supra* n.1, p.10. The Habitats Directive enshrines into EC environmental law the basic obligations of the 1979 Berne Convention on the Conservation of European Wildlife and Natural Habitats. The Community became a signatory in late 1981.

72   Article 3(1).

> *Measures taken pursuant to this Directive shall take account of economic, social and cultural requirements and regional and local characteristics.*

In this sense the directive seeks to contribute to the overall aim of sustainable development,[73] and obliges measures to be taken to conserve both species and habitats.

Species Protection

A system of protection must be established by Member States for animal species listed in Annex IV(a). By virtue of Article 12(1), the following actions must be prohibited:

- *all forms of deliberate capture or killing of specimens of these species in the wild;*

- *deliberate disturbance of these species, particularly during the period of breeding, rearing, hibernation and migration;*

- *deliberate destruction or taking of eggs from the wild;*

- *deterioration or destruction of breeding sites or resting places.*

The case of *Commission* v *Greece* provides a good example of an action brought against a Member State for its failure to establish and implement an effective system of protection for a species noted in Annex IV(a).[74] On a rare investigative trip from Brussels, Commission officials visited Zakinthos to assess whether appropriate measures had been established to protect the sea turtle *Caretta caretta*. The latter produce offspring only every two or thre years. Between the end of May and the end of August the turtles crawl on to the beach and lay approximately 120 eggs. Two months later the baby turtles are born and are at their most vulnerable. The Commission's officials had nevertheless noted the presence of mopeds on the beach and small boats near the breeding beaches. In finding against Greece, the ECJ held that the use of these modes of transport constituted deliberate disturbance during the turtles' breeding period. Moreover, the presence of buildings on the breeding beaches was deemed liable to lead to the deterioration or destruction of the turtles' breeding sites.

---

[73]   See European Commission, *supra* n.1, p.12. The UK's Minister for the Environment, Michael Meacher, noted in 1998 that the reason for designating a site under the directive was "to put a flag on the site which says 'take notice', not 'keep out'"; *Natura 2000 and People - a Partnership* (proceedings of a conference held in Bath, UK 28-30 June 1998 at p.8).

[74]   Case C-103/00 *Commission* v *Hellenic Republic* [2002] ECR I-1147.

In addition to bringing in a system of effective protection, Member States are also obliged to bring in national legislation to ban the keeping, transport, and sale or exchange of Annex IV(a) species by virtue of Article 12(2). Annex IV(a) includes members of the lynx family and all cetaceans; there is often an overlap between those animal species noted in Annex IV(a) and those animal species in Annex II concerning which, as we will note later, the directive envisages the setting up of a system of protection for their habitats. Article 13 notes that a protection system must also be introduced for plant species listed in Annex IV(b), many of which indeed also appear in Annex II.

The framework for species protection resembles in part that provided for species of naturally occurring wild birds under the Wild Birds Directive in the sense that there are similarities between the prohibitions on activities that impact on protected species. However, the Wild Birds Directive started from the premise that all wild birds are to be protected whereas under the Habitats Directive, unless a species is specifically noted in an Annex as one that should be protected, or one that may require protection,[75] there is no obligation placed on Member States to introduce conservation measures.[76]

Provided that there is no satisfactory alternative and the derogation is not detrimental to the maintenance of a favourable conservation status of the species in question, Member States can derogate from the provisions establishing a system of species protection.[77] Any national derogations are subject to a system of monitoring by the Commission as to their compatibility with the directive, and must be made for one of the reasons specifically noted in the directive. Those reasons include grounds of a research or educative nature, in the interests of protecting wild fauna, flora and habitats, to facilitate the re-population or re-introduction of a species, and to prevent serious damage to crops, livestock, forests, fisheries and water and other types of property. Also the taking or keeping of specimens of Annex IV species "under strictly supervised conditions ... in limited numbers specified by the competent national authorities" may be appropriate. Additionally, a Member State may deem it necessary to grant exemptions "in the interests of public health and public safety, or for other reasons of overriding public interest, including those of a social or economic nature and beneficial consequences of primary importance for the environment".[78]

Just as under the provisions of the Wild Birds Directive, Member States' general ability to derogate is intended to provide some balance to the directive's

---

[75] By virtue of Article 11 Member States must "undertake surveillance" on the conservation status of habitats and species (particularly priority species and habitats). Pursuant to such surveillance and where they deem it necessary, Member States can take measures to make sure that the taking and exploitation of those Annex V species of wild fauna and flora is "compatible with their being maintained at a favourable conservation status"; Article 14.

[76] See Scott, *EC Environmental Law* (1998), p.11.

[77] Article 16(1).

[78] Article 16.

environmental objectives by allowing other interests to be taken into account but in carefully defined circumstances. It is however worthy of note that reasons for derogations under the Wild Birds Directive do not expressly include those of an economic or social nature. In specifically noting that reasons "of overriding public interest" can include reasons of a social or economic nature, the Habitats Directive certainly reflects the desire amongst Member States to be less restricted in the exercise of their discretion as to the appropriateness of derogations.

Habitat Protection

Each Member State must contribute to the Natura 2000 network "in proportion to the representation within its territory of the natural habitat types and the habitats of species"[79] noted in Annex I and II respectively. The network will enable certain sites to "be maintained, or where appropriate, restored at a favourable conservation status".[80] A process leading to the eventual establishment of "Special Areas of Conservation" (SACs) will contribute to this network. The Natura 2000 network is to comprise three types of site:

A. Sites Hosting Natural Habitat Types noted in Annex I

Over 150 habitat types noted in Annex I may either be in danger of disappearing, or have a small natural range due, for example, to regression. These habitats include cypress forests, salt meadows, reefs, estuaries, peat bogs and alpine rivers. The network will also comprise outstanding representative examples of the Community's following biogeographical areas – Alpine, Atlantic, Boreal, Continental, Macaronesian, and Mediterranean.[81] The conservation status of such a habitat type will be regarded as "favourable" when

- *its natural range and area it covers within that range are stable or increasing, and*

- *the specific structure and functions which are necessary for its long-term maintenance exist and are likely to continue to exist for the foreseeable future, and*

- *the conservation status of its typical species is favourable.*[82]

The assistance of the European Environment Agency in helping to determine whether a particular conservation status is "favourable" will no doubt be of importance in the future.

---

[79] Article 3(2).

[80] Article 3(1).

[81] Article 1(c)iii.

[82] Article 1(e). See *infra* n.83 and accompanying text as to when the conservation status of typical species is to be considered favourable.

B. Sites Hosting the Habitats of Rare, Vulnerable or Endangered Species noted in Annex II

Over 700 animal and plant species are listed in Annex II as being in need of protection either because they are endangered, vulnerable or rare. These species include the harbour porpoise, certain bats and dragonflies, as well as the lynx. Their conservation status will be regarded as "favourable" when

- *population dynamics data on the species concerned indicate that it is maintaining itself on a long-term basis as a viable component of its natural habitats, and*

- *the natural range of the species is neither being reduced nor is likely to be reduced for the foreseeable future, and*

- *there is, and will probably continue to be, a sufficiently large habitat to maintain its populations on a long-term basis.*[83]

As with "favourable" conservation status of habitats, actually defining the conservation status of species may prove controversial and the role of environmental data supplied by the European Environment Agency can add clarity to any future disagreement between Community institutions and Member States.

C. Special Protection Areas Classified under the Wild Birds Directive

Each area designated as a SPA under the Wild Birds Directive will also form part of the NATURA 2000 network. A total area greater than the size of the Benelux countries has already been designated as SPAs.[84]

The interlinking Natura 2000 network is to be established in three stages:

Member States Draw up National Lists of Suitable Sites

Member States are obliged under Article 4(1) to draw up national lists indicating those sites within national territory in which Annex I habitats are located, and those which host Annex II species. These lists are to be passed to the Commission with relevant site information. In drawing up these national lists, Member States are obliged to carry out a scientific assessment identifying suitable habitats within their territory. The Court of Justice has ruled that, although Member States have a margin of discretion in proposing sites, they "must do so in compliance with the criteria laid down by the directive",[85] and has summarised the criteria noted in Annex III (Stage 1) in the following terms:

---

[83] Article 1(I)

[84] European Commission, *supra* n.1, p.7.

[85] Case C-71/99 *Commission* v *Germany* [2001] ECR I-5811.

The relevant criteria are the degree of representativity of the natural habitat type on the site, the area of the site covered by the natural habitat type and its degree of conservation, the size and density of the population of the species present on the site, their degree of isolation, the degree of conservation of their habitats and, finally, the comparative value of the sites.[86]

Certain "priority natural habitats", like alluvial forests, dry heaths, bog woodland areas and lagoons, and "priority species," such as wolverines, and certain seals and ferns, are marked by asterisks in both Annexes I and II. The directive regards the Community as having a particular duty towards these priority habitats and species not only because they are in danger of disappearing or becoming extinct, but also due to the fact that the Community bears a special responsibility for their protection bearing in mind the proportion of their natural range which falls within Member States' territory. In their national lists Member States must specifically highlight these priority natural habitats and species.

Can economic, social or cultural issues be taken into account by Member States in drawing up their lists? Bearing in mind the *Lappel Bank* ruling in which the ECJ stipulated that a Member State is not authorised to take into account economic requirements when designating a SPA under the Wild Birds Directive, there is a degree of strength in the argument that the designation process for the two other types of site which will comprise the Natura 2000 network (areas hosting natural habitat types in Annex I and habitats of the species listed in Annex II) should similarly not involve the consideration of economic interests, particularly bearing in mind that the assessment criteria in Annex III does not expressly indicate that economic considerations can be taken into account in this process.[87] Definitive light has now been shed on this particular issue by the ECJ in *R v Secretary of State for the Environment, Transport and the Regions ex p. First Corporate Shipping Ltd.*[88] The case concerned the proposed inclusion of the Severn Estuary by the British Government in its national list. Seeking judicial review of this decision, First Corporate Shipping Ltd, the statutory authority for the Port of Bristol and a substantial employer and owner of land in the area, argued that when deciding which sites to propose to the Commission under Article 4(1) and the boundaries of such sites, account must be taken of economic, social and cultural requirements by virtue of Article 2(3). It will be recalled that the latter notes

measures taken pursuant to this Directive shall take account of economic, social and cultural requirements and regional and local characteristics.

---

[86] *Ibid*, para.25.
[87] See Harte, *supra* n.49, p.175.
[88] C-371/98 [2000] ECR I-9235.

This argument was contested by not only the Commission, but also the British Government and the WWF, all of whom relied on the *Lappel Bank* case.[89] Whilst of the opinion that the *Lappel Bank* is inapplicable to an issue relating to the Habitats Directive, Advocate General Léger concluded in his opinion that at this initial stage "the discretion of the Member States as to the choice of sites to propose to the Commission is very limited",[90] and precludes a Member State taking into account economic, social and cultural requirements or regional and local characteristics in drawing up national lists and defining site boundaries. This proved to be a convincing argument, the ECJ concluding that to allow otherwise would mean that "the Commission could not be sure of having available an exhaustive list of sites eligible as SACs, with the risk that the objective of bringing them together into a coherent European ecological network might not be achieved".[91] In effect, the ruling accepted that this stage in the establishment of Natura 2000 is akin to a fact-finding operation in which Member States shall, by means of their national lists, inform subsequent deliberations.

All Member States have proposed some sites as part of their national lists. The United Kingdom has for instance included in their list the sea cliffs around Tintagel, Marsland and the Clovelly coast as they are representative of "vegetated sea cliffs of the Atlantic and Baltic coasts" noted in Annex I as being a type of natural habitat whose conservation requires designation, and which are additionally habitats for a variety of rare plants noted in Annex II. Other habitats nominated within the UK include Ben Nevis, an example of alpine limestone natural grassland noted in Annex I and the habitat of rare mossy saxifrage, and the New Forest which is host to a range of endangered habitats, including bog woodland areas, as well as being known as an important habitat of the stag beetle. Additionally both the Wash, covering more than 100,000 hectares on the English east coast and noted for its mudflats and saltmarsh areas, and Lundy Island, just 3500 hectares in area but particularly important as its underwater reefs support rare coral, form part of the UK's list of habitats nominated.[92]

National lists should have been adopted by Member States and passed to the Commission by 11 June 1995. It is therefore disappointing to note that, as at April 2002, none of the Member States had submitted a completely coherent national list.[93] The Commission is becoming increasingly concerned that various Member States have provided inadequate contributions to the Natura 2000 network and/or insufficiently transposed the directive into national law.[94] Indeed, in late 2001 the

---

[89] Opinion of the Advocate General Léger [2000] ECR I-9235.

[90] *Ibid*, para.40.

[91] Para.24 of the judgment.

[92] See *The Independent*, 21 June 1999, p.8.

[93] See European Commission's "Barometer" *supra* n.58.

[94] See, for example, European Commission press releases "Habitats Directive: Commission takes further steps against several Member States", 11/1/2000, and "Habitats Directive: Commission moves against the Netherlands, Portugal, Italy, UK, Germany and Sweden", 6/8/2001.

ECJ delivered judgments against France,[95] Ireland[96] and Germany[97] respectively deeming that they had failed to fulfil their obligations under Article 4(1) by not transmitting the full list of sites and relevant information on such sites to the Commission. However, it would be wrong to conclude that progress is not being made; clearly Member States have failed to deliver adequate lists on time but in 1998 and 1999 "steady progress [continued] to be made in improving the overall level of Member State contributions",[98] and over 14,900 proposed sites covering close to more than 430,000 square kilometres had been submitted by April 2002.[99]

Commission Establishes a List of Sites of "Community Importance"

The second stage in establishing the network involves the Commission evaluating the significance of each of the sites on the national lists. By virtue of Article 4(2) the Commission is obliged to draw up a draft list of "sites of Community importance" from the sites proposed by the Member States. A site of Community importance refers to an area which contributes significantly

> *to the maintenance or restoration at a favourable conservation status of a natural habitat in Annex I or of a species in Annex II and may also contribute significantly to the coherence of Natura 2000 ... and/or contribute significantly to the maintenance of biological diversity within the biogeographic region or regions concerned.*

> *For animal species ranging over wide areas, sites of Community importance shall correspond to the places within the natural range of such species which present the physical or biological factors essential to their life and reproduction.*[100]

The relative importance of sites noted in national lists must therefore be assessed by the Commission assisted by the European Environment Agency's Topic Centre on Nature. All those sites identified by Member States as areas host to priority habitats and/or species are automatically to be regarded as of Community importance.[101] The lack of discretion in this respect takes into account the particular sensitivity of such areas and species. It is important therefore to stress that sites hosting priority habitats and species will automatically become areas of Community importance regardless of the impact such classification will have on social, economic and cultural factors. However a Member State whose sites hosting priority habitats or species cover more

---

[95] Case C-220/99 *Commission* v *France* [2001] ECR I-5831.

[96] Case C-67/99 *Commission* v *Ireland* [2001] ECR I-5757.

[97] Case C-71/99 *Commission* v *Germany* [2001] ECR I-5811.

[98] European Commission press release "Habitats Directive: Commission takes further steps against several Member States", 11/1/2000.

[99] See European Commission's "Barometer", *supra* n.58.

[100] Article 1(k).

[101] Annex III, Stage 2(1).

than five per cent of their territory can ask the Commission to apply the relevant criteria flexibly.[102]

For other habitats and species noted in Annexes I and II but not regarded as falling within the definition accorded priority status, the Commission, in agreement with each Member State, will determine a draft list of sites of Community importance taking into account criteria noted in Annex III (Stage 2). The criteria include the relative value of the site at national level, the geographical situation of the area in relation to migration routes of those species in Annex II and whether it belongs to a continuous ecosystem situated on both sides of one or more internal Community frontiers, the total area of the site, the number of Annex I habitats and Annex II species on the site in question, and the area's global ecological value.[103] Clearly not all sites hosting non-priority habitats and species and nominated by Member States will be chosen as of Community importance,[104] and it is certainly arguable that in the compiling of the draft list non-environmental factors of a social, economic or cultural nature could be taken into account as far as the non-priority sites are concerned.[105]

The draft list of sites of Community importance must then be formally adopted; the process is not a simple one. A committee consisting of expert representatives from the Member States, and chaired by the Commission in a non-voting capacity,[106] must give an opinion on the draft. If the committee gives approval by a qualified majority vote, the Commission can then move to adopt the list. If the list does not gain the approval of the committee, the matter moves to the Council which has power to act by qualified majority.[107]

The list of sites of Community importance was to have been established by the middle of June 1998 but this proved impossible due to insufficiencies in national lists submitted to the Commission. The delay on the part of Member States can partly be put down to national inefficiencies, but also underlines a realisation that eventual designation as a SAC would impose numerous legal restrictions on activities within such protected areas which, judging by the approach in cases brought before it relating to the Wild Birds Directive, the ECJ will seek to uphold when the need arises. Only the list of sites of Community importance for the Macaronesian biogeographical region had been adopted by the end of 2001.[108] The Macaronesian biogeographical region constitutes the archipelagos of the Azores, Madeira and the Canary Islands situated in the Atlantic Ocean.

---

[102] Article 4(2).

[103] Annex III, Stage 2(2)

[104] Ball, "Has the UK Government Implemented the Habitats Directive properly?" in Holder (ed.), *The Impact of EC Environmental Law in the United Kingdom* (1997), p.219.

[105] Advocate General Léger's opinion in *R* v *Secretary of State for the Environment, Transport and the Regions ex p. First Corporate Shipping Ltd* supports the notion that such non-environmental factors can be taken into account in this instance; *supra* n.89.

[106] Article 20.

[107] Article 21.

[108] Commission Decision of 28 December 2001 Adopting the List of Sites of Community Importance for the Macaronesian Biogeographical Region, OJ 2002 L5/16.

It is of interest to note that where a site does not appear on a national list but is one hosting a "priority" species or a "priority" habitat, the Commission, on the basis of reliable scientific information, will initiate a consultation procedure with the relevant Member State if it is of the opinion that the protection of the site concerned is crucial to the maintenance of the priority habitat type, or to the protection of the priority species concerned.[109] In this context the information supplied to the Commission by the European Environment Agency, and in particular its Topic Centre on Nature, will again no doubt prove to be of vital importance. The stated purpose of this bilateral exercise is to compare the scientific data used by both the Commission and the Member State.[110] No reference is made to the need to discuss non-scientific data such as that relating to economic or social issues.

The establishment of this consultation procedure under the Habitats Directive between the Member State concerned and the Commission as to areas and species with priority status is possibly to be preferred to the cumbersome initiation of infringement procedures.[111] If however the bilateral consultation process fails to facilitate an agreement within a six-month period, the Commission is obliged to forward a proposal on selection of the site to the Council who will make the decision as to whether it should become part of Natura 2000. The directive notes that the Council will act unanimously in making this decision, but surely it will be difficult to obtain such a level of consensus? The Member State which does not wish to see part of its territory within the network will vote against inclusion and, in such circumstances, unanimity can only be obtained if all other Member States disagree with the Commission and actually vote to exclude the site. In effect, the Member State which does not wish to see a site in its territory designated with priority status would seem able to block its inclusion.[112] Much therefore depends on the outcome of the consultation process between the Commission and the State concerned, but problems are envisaged where, despite persuasive scientific evidence, a Member State opposes selection of the site for reasons that may in fact be of an economic or social nature.

Member States must Designate Sites as "Special Areas of Conservation"

When an area has been designated as a site of Community importance, the relevant Member State must designate the site as a "Special Area of Conservation" (SAC) as soon as possible and certainly within six years, priority in this designation process being given to sites of particular importance for the maintenance or restoration of an

---

109 Article 5(1).
110 *Ibid.*
111 We have noted that under the Wild Birds Directive Member States have been slow on occasions to designate SPAs despite the fact that sites have clearly satisfied ecological criteria.
112 See Ball, *supra* n.104, p.219.

Annex I habitat type or Annex II species, and to the overall coherence of the Natura 2000 network.[113] The six-year phase-in period is designed to allow Member States to introduce appropriate protection measures over time, and therefore to spread both the administrative and financial burden that these measures will necessitate. Once designated by the Member State in question as an SAC, "necessary conservation measures" must apply to the site,[114] although the precise detail of such measures is a matter for the State concerned.

Any conservation measures must however "correspond to the ecological requirements of the natural habitat types in Annex I and the species in Annex II present on the sites".[115] Particular attention must therefore be paid by Member States to the fact that the action it takes must be appropriate to the needs of the individual habitat or species on site. These ecological requirements will clearly vary according to the species or habitat in question,[116] and the Commission has indeed noted that the needs of a species may in fact differ according to the time of year:

> *... for the bats included in Annex II ... the ecological requirements differ between the period of hibernation (when they rest in underground environments, in hollow shafts or in dwellings) and the active period, from spring onwards (during which time they leave their winter quarters and resume their activities of insect hunting).[117]*

Although the directive gives Member States up to six years in which to designate an area as an SAC and therefore to have introduced detailed conservation measures relating to the site, it is important to stress that as soon as a site has been placed on the list of sites of Community importance (possibly as long as six years before designation as a SAC), the area is subject to specific obligations, namely the provisions of Articles 6(2), (3) and (4) of the directive.[118] These provisions of the Habitats Directive also apply to sites after they have been designated as SACs, and, by virtue of the amendment to the original Article 4(4) of the Wild Birds Directive

---

[113] Article 4(4).

[114] Article 6(1). In accordance with Article 2(2) they must be "designed to maintain or restore, at a favourable conservation status, natural habitats and species of wild fauna and flora of Community interest". According to Article 6(1), the necessary conservation measures can either be adopted as "statutory, administrative or contractual measures" or "if need be, appropriate management plans".

[115] Article 6(1).

[116] *European Commission, Managing NATURA 2000 Sites: the Provisions of Article 6 of the Habitats Directive* (2000), p.18. This document is available on the Internet at http://europa.eu.int/comm/environment/nature/art6_en.pdf.

[117] *Ibid.*

[118] See Scott, *supra* n.76, p.115; obligations therefore flow from the time a site is included on the Community list in contrast to the Wild Birds Directive where obligations arise where a site has not been designated as a SPA but should have been (see *Santona Marshes* case). In this way, the Habitats Directive increases the influence of Member States as to the sites which must be afforded protection as, although the Commission draws up the draft, the list of sites of Community importance requires the endorsement of either the committee of experts established by Article 20 or the Council, both of which comprise representatives of the Member States themselves; *ibid.*

adopted following the *Leybucht Dykes* case,[119] to SPAs designated under the Wild Birds Directive.[120] It should be noted that Article 7 of the Habitats Directive amends the first sentence of Article 4(4) of the Wild Birds Directive,[121] replacing it with 6(2), (3) and (4) of the Habitats Directive.

Article 6(2):

Member States shall take appropriate steps to avoid, in the special areas of conservation, the deterioration of natural habitats and the habitats of species as well as disturbance of the species for which the areas have been designated, in so far as such disturbance could be significant in relation to the objectives of the directive.

Although the specific nature of the envisaged measures to be adopted is a matter for the discretion of individual Member States, they are legally obliged to introduce conservation measures to prevent deterioration of habitats. In addition, measures must avoid disturbance but only where this "could be significant in relation to the objectives of this directive". There is no definition of "significant" in the directive but Member States must bear in mind that the aim of the measure is to "contribute towards ensuring biodiversity through the conservation of natural habitats and of wild fauna and flora",[122] and that a significant disturbance would certainly take place if such disturbance adversely impacts upon the favourable conservation status of a species.[123] It is also worth reiterating that there is no need to prove conclusively the disturbance to be "significant" but merely to show that it "could be significant" in the sense that it has the potential to be so.[124]

With specific regard to the Wild Birds Directive, it is worthy of note that both the original version of Article 4(4) of this measure and its amended version therefore require Member States to take steps to avoid deterioration of habitats classified as SPAs. Indeed, the Court of Justice has held France to be in breach of its obligations in this respect by allowing those areas of the Poitevin Marsh designated as SPAs to deteriorate to the extent that the numbers of wintering ducks in the Baie de l'Aiguillon and Pointe d'Arcay areas of the Marsh had fallen from over 67,000 in the period 1977-86 to just 16,551 for the period 1987-96.[125]

---

[119] See *supra* text accompanying nn. 66-69.

[120] Interestingly the ECJ has ruled that Articles 6(2), (3) and (4) do not however apply to those ornithologically important sites which have not as yet been classified as SPAs under the Wild Birds Directive but which ought to have been so designated – in such instances, these areas still fall under the stricter regime set up by the first sentence of Article 4(4) of the Wild Birds Directive; Case C-374/98 *Commission v France supra* n.41, para.47.

[121] Originally the first sentence of Article 4(4) Wild Birds Directive noted that "*Member States shall take appropriate steps to avoid pollution or deterioration of habitats or any disturbances affecting the birds, in so far as these would be significant having regard to the objectives of this Article*".

[122] Article 2(1).

[123] European Commission, *supra* n.116, pp.28-29. For definition of "favourable conservation status", see *supra* n.83 and accompanying text.

[124] European Commission, *supra* n.116, p.27.

[125] Case C-96/98 *Commission v France supra* n.41, para.39.

Article 6(3):

Any plan or project not directly connected with or necessary to the management of the site but likely to have a significant effect thereon, either individually or in combination with other plans or projects, shall be subject to appropriate assessment of its implications for the site in view of the site's conservation objectives. In the light of the conclusions of the assessment of the implications for the site and subject to the provisions of [Article 6(4)], the competent national authorities shall agree to the plan or project only after having ascertained that it will not adversely affect the integrity of the site and, if appropriate, after having obtained the opinion of the general public.[126]

This provision too suffers from a lack of clarity. What plans or projects fall within the remit of this article's obligations? It is likely that the provision affects plans or projects which are not related to the conservation management of the site,[127] and would for instance include transport schemes, general development plans, and plans relating to the management of waste.[128] When is such a project or plan to be deemed "likely to have a significant impact" on the site? This would seem to be a matter for Member State discretion, although the exercise of such discretion must clearly bear in mind the specific conservation objectives for the site concerned, and, it is submitted, be based purely on ecological factors. The ruling in *Commission* v *France*[129] lends a degree of support to this submission, the ECJ rejecting the French Government's argument that the level of discretion given to Member States allowed it to waive the need for impact assessment because of the low cost of a project or the particular nature of the work planned. This ruling must surely be correct, but has served to highlight the willingness of a Member State to exploit any ambiguity in the text of the directive in an attempt to justify its own national implementation of the directive's provisions.

In the process of determining whether the plan or project proceeds, the national authorities need only consult the general public "if appropriate". It is unfortunate that clearer guidance is not forthcoming from the measure as to when the public can participate. It is however submitted that, if the *project* in question falls within the application of the 1985 Directive on the Assessment of the Effects of Certain Public and Private Projects on the Environment,[130] the public must be consulted in the

---

[126] In a press release issued on 6 January 2000 the Commission indicated that it had sent a reasoned opinion to Portugal for its failure to respect habitat safeguards concerning the Abrilongo dam and irrigation project which impacts on the Campo Maior SPA, an area which plays host to a variety of endangered birds such as the little bustard, black-bellied sandgrouse and lesser kestrel. One such habitat safeguard included the need to carry out an assessment of projects likely to have significant effects; Commission press release IP/00/4, 6/1/00. See also the decision to send Sweden a reasoned opinion in late 1999 on the basis that its national legislation failed to require an assessment where a project is likely to have significant effects on a SPA; Commission press release IP/99/789, 25/10/99.

[127] European Commission, *supra* n.116, pp.31-32.

[128] *Ibid*, p.31.

[129] Case C-256/98 [2000] ECR I-2487, at *para*.39.

[130] Directive 85/337 OJ 1985 L175/40 as amended by Directive 97/11 OJ 1997 L72/5.

assessment process in accordance with the terms of that directive. Nevertheless, not all works that might be carried out in a protected area will fall within Annex I or II of the 1985 EIA Directive,[131] in which case it will be a matter for the competent authorities at national level to determine whether members of the public need to be given a chance to voice their views. Alternatively, if a *plan* or *programme* is deemed likely to have a significant effect on a site, an environmental assessment must be carried out in accordance with Directive 2001/42 on the Assessment of the Effects of Certain Plans and Programmes on the Environment (SEA directive),[132] and the public must be consulted in accordance with the provisions of such measures.

Article 6(4) (first paragraph):

If, in spite of a negative assessment of the implications for the site and in the absence of any alternatives, a plan or project must nevertheless be carried out for imperative reasons of overriding public interest, including those of a social or economic interest, the Member State shall take all necessary compensatory measures to ensure that the overall coherence of Natura 2000 is protected. It shall inform the Commission of the compensatory measures adopted.

This exemption provision applies when the assessment of the implications for the site is negative. It has been specifically included in the Habitats Directive by Member States in the aftermath of the *Leybucht Dykes* case, and is intended to negate the judgment's impact. It will be recalled that the *Leybucht Dykes* judgment held that a reduction in the size of a SPA could not be justified on economic or recreational grounds, and that only in very limited circumstances related to public health or safety could such a reduction be contemplated. This exemption clause seeks to strike a balance between conservation interests and other important public interests while taking into account the measure's overall objectives.

Following an assessment of the proposed activity in question, if it is found that a site will be adversely affected, the plan or project can nevertheless proceed but only if three conditions are met: first, the Member State in question must be satisfied there are no alternative solutions; secondly, the Member State concerned must introduce compensatory measures to ensure the continued coherence of Natura 2000; and thirdly, the activity is deemed necessary for "imperative reasons of overriding public interest". Although the provision expressly stipulates that social or economic interests can amount to "imperative reasons of overriding public interest", it is clear that other interests can potentially also be so regarded.

---

[131] Kramer, *Focus on European Environmental Law* (1997), p.249. See further n. 17 and accompanying text of the chapter on Environmental Impact Assessment (chapter 5).

[132] See Article 3(2)b of Directive 2001/42 on the Assessment of the Effects of Certain Plans and Programmes on the Environment OJ 2001 L197/30. This SEA Directive is considered in greater depth in the chapter on Environmental Impact Assessment (chapter 5).

A higher degree of protection is in theory afforded however in the second paragraph of Article 6(4) to sites which are host to "priority" habitat types and/or species. It will be recalled that these particular types of habitats and species are those which are not only in danger of disappearing or endangered, but are also given priority status due to the Community's special responsibility to protect them bearing in mind the proportion of their natural range which falls within the territory of the Community's Member States. If a site includes either priority habitat or priority species, the second paragraph of Article 6(4) notes that

> *the only considerations which may be raised are those relating to human health or public safety, to beneficial consequences of primary importance for the environment or, further to an opinion from the Commission, to other imperative reasons of overriding public interest.*

The level of protection therefore afforded to priority habitats or species seems in principle more akin to the protection given to SPAs in the *Leybucht Dykes* judgment.[133] However, special note should be made that the reasons of overriding public interest expressly mentioned in the second paragraph are not exclusive. Indeed, following the first three opinions given by the Commission under the procedure in this second paragraph, it is now quite clear that in the Commission's view social or economic interests can in fact amount to reasons of overriding public interest even though the issue relates to the protection of a priority habitat or species.[134] The two Commission opinions given in 1995 concerned two sections of the proposed A20 motorway designed to create a link post-reunification between the former and "new" German Lander with a view to encouraging economic development in Mecklenburg-Western Pomerania where unemployment in early 1995 was almost twice as much as the average in the "old" Lander. The motorway also forms part of the trans-European road network[135] which is intended to link isolated regions of the Community to central regions in order to underpin the economic and social cohesion of the Community.

The proposed route of the A20 crossed two areas of particular environmental importance; both the Trebel and Recknitz Valley, and the River Peene Valley are SPAs under the Wild Birds Directive and, as such, now form part of Natura 2000 under the provisions of the Habitats Directive. They are additionally host to a variety of priority natural habitats including bog woodland, fens and residual alluvial forests. It was clear from the environmental impact assessment carried out by the German Government that the route of the motorway could potentially have an adverse impact on these habitats.

---

133 Ball, *supra* n.104, p.220. There are no birds noted under the Habitats Directive as "priority species". Nevertheless if a SPA hosts a priority natural habitat site, that area will fall within those sites to which the Habitats Directive gives greater protection under Article 6(4).

134 Commission opinions of this nature are non-binding. If a future opinion decides against a Member State's proposals, the national authorities in question can decide nonetheless to proceed with the project.

135 See Council Decision 93/629/EEC OJ 1993 L305/11.

Both areas being SPAs, it seems very unlikely that the A20 project would have been allowed to proceed under the terms of the original Article 4(4) of the Wild Birds Directive read in the light of the *Leybucht Dykes* judgment.[136] Even under the provisions of Article 6(2) of the Habitats Directive, Germany would *prima facie* have been in breach of their obligation to prevent deterioration of protected areas.[137] However, inserted at the insistence of Member States following the *Leybucht Dykes* case, the exemption clause in Article 6(4) proved the project's "saving grace". Germany was of the view that the project was justified on economic and social grounds. As the areas concerned were host to priority natural habitat sites and those imperative reasons of overriding public interest expressly noted in the second paragraph of the exemption clause were of no direct relevance, the only manner in which Germany could proceed with the project was by complying with the conditions of Article 6(4) as they relate to alternative means and compensatory measures, and by additionally obtaining an opinion from the Commission as to the project's compatibility with the overall purpose of the Habitats Directive.

Taking into account not only that the Mecklenburg-Western Pomerania area had "Objective 1" status as far as EC Structural Funds support was concerned, but also the very high unemployment rates in the area and the part to be played by the A20 in the trans-European road network, the Commission concluded that the two sections of motorway were justified. In effect, the route of the A20 was acceptable for social and economic reasons which on the specific facts amounted to imperative reasons of overriding public interest. It is uncertain to what extent the Commission itself looked into the issue as to whether the construction of the A20 would bring about the desired economic and social benefits.[138] Certainly the balance of evidence supports the notion that the road had the potential to bring improvements in this regard, although in general when giving Article 6(2) opinions the Commission must be careful not to be seen to allow any interest automatically to be regarded as an imperative reason of public interest which overrides environmental considerations.[139] Nollkaemper has indeed advocated a balancing of interests approach in which "a project that is of great economic public interest but involves only minor adverse effects to the protected area in question should be treated differently than a project with marginal economic public interests but important detrimental effects on ecological values".[140]

Certainly the Commission did look closely at the issue of "alternative means" – it agreed with the German Government that there were no alternatives to the route that crossed the Trebel and Recknitz Valley, but carefully scrutinised the four alternatives

---

[136] Nollkaemper, *supra* n.65, at p.277.
[137] *Ibid.*
[138] *Ibid.*, at p.280.
[139] *Ibid.*
[140] *Ibid.*

in the River Peene valley. As a result the least damaging alternative route with no impact on priority habitats was chosen instead of the original path of the A20 which would have "directly affected bog woodland over a stretch of approximately 150 metres".[141] No priority habitat sites were in fact affected by the chosen crossing of the Peene east of Jarmen.

As for compensatory measures, it is apparent from the wording of Article 6(4) that measures must be taken to ensure the overall coherence of Natura 2000. As far as the route crossing the Trebel and Recknitz Valley was concerned, the Commission was satisfied that the German Government was in principle willing to make suitable compensatory measures to ensure the overall coherence of Natura 2000.[142] As to the Peene crossing, it was apparent that several species of Community interest would be affected, including the otter, beaver, kingfisher and large copper butterfly, but the Commission was satisfied that Germany intended to carry out compensatory measures including the restoration or creation of a variety of habitat types in an alternative site in the Peene valley. The Commission stressed that the creation or restoration of these habitat areas had to be undertaken at the same time as the A20 construction works to ensure compensatory measures were introduced at the earliest opportunity. In addition, noise barriers were to be erected along the route of the motorway with the intention of limiting disturbance to nocturnal animals, and reducing light attraction from headlights.[143]

Another Commission opinion, issued in April 2000, was again made at the request of Germany and concerned the proposed extension of the Daimler Chrysler Aerospace Airbus GmbH (DASA) plant in Hamburg-Finkenwerder.[144] The project was supported by the German Government and involved the building of an extension to the existing DASA construction sites to allow the assembly of part of the so-called "Super Jumbo", the Airbus A3XX passenger aircraft which, once built, will be the largest passenger plane in the world. The project would impact on 170 hectares of a 750 hectare SPA known as the Muhlenberger Loch, a recognised wetland of international importance for ten migratory birds and six Annex I species under the Wild Birds Directive. Additionally the site formed part of Germany's national list of sites under the Habitats Directive playing host to a priority habitat, two other Annex I habitats, one priority plant species and five Annex II fish species. The estimated loss of approximately 20 per cent of this wetland area would no doubt impact not only on the movement and feeding of various wild birds, but also its rare priority marshland habitat and priority plant species (*Oenanthe conioides*) endemic to the upper Elbe estuary.

---

141 Para.3.1 of the River Peene opinion. See also Nollkaemper, *supra* n.65, at p.281.
142 Commission opinion 95/C 178/03, OJ 1995 C178/3.
143 Commission opinion 96/15/EC, OJ 1996 L 6/14.
144 Commission opinion K(2000) 1079, 19 April 2000 (as yet unpublished in the Official Journal).

The German Government indicated that in its view the project was justified by compelling reasons of overriding public interest. First, the project would create jobs in the Hamburg area mitigating previous job losses in the aircraft assembly industry, and would additionally have a positive economic and social impact in neighbouring areas, particularly Schleswig-Holstein and Lower Saxony. Germany also highlighted the beneficial impact of the project on the wider European aircraft industry in the sense that it would promote cooperation within the industry and foster technical progress. Airbus Industrie, the company launching the A3XX project, is made up of four European partners [BAe Systems (UK), Matra Aerospatiale (France), DASA (Germany) and CASA (Spain)], and has estimated that the project will generate 60,000 jobs in Europe.[145] The Commission opinion notes that the German Government had balanced the detrimental impact of the project on the wetland area against its positive social and economic effects and, having taken into account the fact that the project affected just a part of the Muhlenberger Loch, had concluded that the positive aspects of the project outweighed the negative impact.

It is difficult to say however whether the Commission simply accepted the German Government's approach in concluding that the project was indeed justified for overriding reasons of public importance, although there is perhaps little doubt that the proposed project itself will have considerable beneficial social and economic effects over a number of years.[146] However the extent to which the Commission carried out its own evaluation of alternative sites is unclear. The opinion simply notes DASA's and the German Government's conclusion that no alternative sites were suitable; three other sites in the Hamburg area were considered but the German authorities viewed these alternatives as inappropriate bearing in mind the technical demands of the project. It was claimed that only if the project proceeded in an area next to the existing DASA works could optimal use be made of the existing skilled workforce and premises; in essence the project would otherwise have proved to be an inefficient use of resources, and have jeopardised the projects's viability by reducing the estimated productivity gains.

Perhaps the most worrying aspect of the opinion is that the Commission would seem to have judged the project to be justified without being totally satisfied that compensatory measures proposed by Germany were sufficient. The German authorities planned to re-establish or create wetland areas on three alternatives sites in the area. However, the Commission was unable comprehensively to judge whether such actions and their timing were enough to ensure the coherence of the Natura 2000 network as Germany had not completed their national list of sites in accordance with the provisions of Article 4(1) of the Habitats Directive, and, more

---

[145] See *The Independent* (UK), 24 June 2000, p.4.

[146] There is some debate however as to whether the A3XX will attract enough buyers, one newspaper report noting that "critics say airports will not be able to cope with the A3XX, residents will not put up with its noise and passengers will not warm to the experience of flying with so many people"; *The Independent* (UK), 24 June 2000, p.4.

particularly, had not given sufficient information on alternative sites for the priority plant species (*Oenanthe conioides*) affected by the DASA works extension into Muhlenberger Loch. This being the case, it is submitted that it would have been tactically appropriate for the Commission to have declined to offer their opinion until Germany had provided it with sufficient information to evaluate thoroughly the suitability of planned compensatory measures. No doubt the Commission could bring infringement proceedings in the future against Germany if left unsatisfied as to the sufficiency of such compensatory measures, but by that time it will be too late to save the wetland area in question at Muhlenberger Loch.[147] Clearly the desire not to be seen to be placing any kind of obstacle in the way of a high profile project – which will, in theory, promote a type of "European champion" capable of competing against the Boeing Corporation in global markets – proved to be of paramount importance.

Only three opinions have to date been given by the Commission but some conclusions can nevertheless be drawn. It was to have been hoped that the second paragraph of Article 6(4) of the Habitats Directive would in practice have provided a level of protection to those European areas most in need of protection similar to that afforded in the *Leybucht Dykes* case to SPAs. However, to date the need for a Commission opinion which impacts on such priority areas and species has proved more akin to a procedural formality than an effective deterrent to those who wish to promote development in, or create other disturbance to, such areas.[148] Indeed, commenting on the Commission's first two opinions, Winter has noted that the Commission "yielded to stark pressure from German developmental interests".[149] Some sympathy must however be offered to the Commission in the sense that had it adopted a harder line at this time towards the protection of sites forming part of Natura 2000, Member States would have been even less inclined to supply comprehensive national lists of sites as required by Article 4(1) of the Habitats Directive, being fearful of the restrictions placed on the exercise of their discretion as to future development in such areas.[150] It remains to be seen whether a stronger stance will be adopted by the Commission once a comprehensive list of sites of Community importance has finally been adopted.

Some Concluding Remarks

The Sixth Environmental Action Programme highlights the protection of nature and biodiversity as one of four priority areas recognising the "responsibility to preserve

---

[147] See also Nollkaemper, *supra* n.65, at p.282-3.
[148] *Ibid.*, p.280.
[149] Winter footnote to Harte, *supra* n.49, p.180.
[150] See Nollkaemper, *supra* n.65, at p.280.

the intrinsic value of nature both for ourselves and for future generations".[151] The eventual establishment of a coherent interlinking Natura 2000 network will be of paramount importance to the protection of Europe's diminishing biodiversity,[152] and it has been estimated that it will eventually cover more than 12 per cent of territory in the Community.[153] Important headway has been made to date supported by assistance from the LIFE Nature fund which provided ECU 350 million to approximately 500 projects between 1992-1999.[154] However, it is a sobering thought to note that biodiversity continues to decline at an alarming rate, the Commission noting for example that approximately 25 per cent of wild bird species have "undergone a substantial decline in numbers over the last 20 years".[155] In the coming years, the accession of countries in Central and Eastern Europe will undoubtedly present further challenges bearing in mind that candidate countries "possess vast areas of untouched nature which contribute considerably to biological diversity in the whole of Europe".[156]

Member States' reluctance to endorse fully the objectives of the Wild Birds and Habitats Directives has clearly hindered the pace of progress.[157] Both the ECJ and the Commission have generally played their part in endeavouring to uphold the aims of both measures. Other actors in the regulatory chain, especially national courts, must also play their role. In this context, it is worth noting that certain provisions of the two measures may well have direct effect; for example, in relation to the Wild Birds Directive it is certainly arguable that Article 5 (containing certain prohibitions to protect birds), Article 6 (prohibition on sale), Article 7 (prohibition on hunting) and Article 8 (prohibition as to means of hunting) enjoy direct effect.[158]

In the English case of *R* v *Secretary of State for Trade and Industry ex parte Greenpeace Ltd*,[159] the High Court noted that the Habitats Directive was capable of being directly effective but was not more specific in this regard. This judgment has

---

151 Sixth Environmental Action Programme, "Environment 2010: Our Future, Our Choice" COM (2001) 31, p.30.

152 The Sixth Environmental Action Programme refers to the setting up of Natura 2000 as "the lynchpin of European policy to protect biodiversity and the ecosystems which support it"; *ibid*, p.33.

153 European Commission, *supra* n.4, p.7.

154 *Ibid*, p.8. See Regulation 1655/2000 concerning the Financial Instrument for the Environment (LIFE), OJ 2000 L192/1. For further information on the LIFE financial instrument see http://europa.eu.int/comm/life/nature.history.htm.

155 European Commission, "Report on the Application of Directive 79/409/EC on the Conservation of Wild Birds; update for 1996-98" COM 2002 146, para.2(3).

156 COM (98) 294, p.1.

157 One in three complaints to the Commission concerned nature conservation in the year 2000; European Commission, "Eighteenth Annual Report on Monitoring the Application of Community Law" COM 2001 309.

158 Wils, *supra* n.46, p.239. Also Kramer, *Focus on European Environmental Law* (1992), p.164. Note however that the ECJ seems to have inferred that Article 9 of the Wild Birds Directive concerning the power to derogate also has direct effect; Case C-118/94 *Associazione Italiana per il WWF* v *Regione Veneto supra* n.33, para.19. In relation to Article 4(1) Wild Birds Directive, see *supra* n.47.

159 [2000] Env LR 221. On this case see the analysis by Jans (2000) 12(3) JEL 385-390.

however proved to be more important in relation to questions as to the geographical application of the measure and, as such, has provided a timely reminder of the important influence national courts can bring to bear on national implementation. In relation to the geographical application of the Habitats Directive, Article 2(1) notes that

[t]he aim of this Directive shall be to contribute towards ensuring biodiversity through the conservation of natural habitats and of wild fauna and flora in the European territory of the Member States to which the Treaty applies.

The UK Government argued that it could legally carry out its licensing functions for oil exploration without reference to the Habitats Directive as this measure was only applicable within its sovereign territory (which included its 12-mile territorial sea). Greenpeace however disagreed and sought judicial review of the Secretary of State's decision that licences would be granted to oil companies to search and bore for oil in the North East Atlantic, specifically in an area which forms part of the UK's Continental Shelf and its declared Economic Fishing Zone.

By virtue of Article 77(1) of the Law of the Sea Convention,

[t]he coastal state exercises over the continental shelf sovereign rights for the purpose of exploring it and exploiting its natural resources.

The area therefore is not regarded as within the confines of the UK's sovereign territory but is a locality beyond territorial seas within which the UK exclusively exercises specific sovereign rights. Concerned at the potential impact of the oil companies' activities on cetaceans and coral forming reefs, Greenpeace claimed that the UK Government would act illegally if it failed to consider the provisions of the Habitats Directive in the licensing process.

Adopting a purposive approach to the issue of geographical scope, Mr Justice Kay agreed with Greenpeace in deciding that the Directive did apply to the UK's Continental Shelf and to the superjacent waters up to a 200-mile limit from the baseline from which the territorial sea is measured. In coming to this conclusion, the High Court in particular took into account Greenpeace's argument that the aims of the directive were "more likely to be achieved if the geographical scope extends to the continental shelf and its superjacent waters": cetaceans are listed in Annex IVa and are known to spend much of their time not in territorial seas but in waters beyond such confines; and the coral forming reef *lophelia pertusa* (not specifically noted in the Directive although "reefs" are mentioned in Annex I) is also more likely to be found outside the 12-mile territorial sea limits. The national court therefore concluded that

a directive which includes in its aims the protection of ... lophelia pertusa and cetaceans will only achieve those aims, on a purposive construction, if it extends beyond territorial waters.

As such, the UK Government could not legally exercise its offshore licensing function without taking into account and applying the provisions of the Habitats

Directive. In the perceived absence of sufficient political will among Member States to ensure the overall coherence of Natura 2000, the High Court's enlightened approach in this case is to be applauded as an indication that national courts may be prepared to play their part in ensuring that the Community's environmental objectives are eventually realised in this area.

This chapter has particularly highlighted that the Wild Birds Directive and the Habitats Directive clearly impact on the exercise of national discretion with regard to planning and development processes within Member States. In the next chapter we turn our attention to the Community's measures relating to impact assessment which also have a significant bearing on issues relating to the use of land at the national, regional and local levels.

Select Bibliography

Baldock, "The Status of SPAs for the Protection of Wild Birds" (1992) 4(1) JEL 139.

Ball, "Has the UK Government Implemented the Habitats Directive Properly?" in Holder (ed.), *The Impact of EC Environmental Law in the United Kingdom* (1997), pp. 215-227.

Birnie, "The European Community and Preservation of Biological Diversity" in Bowman and Redgwell (eds.), *International Law and the Conservation of Biological Diversity* (1996), pp.211-234.

European Commission, *Managing NATURA 2000 Sites: the Provisions of Article 6 of the Habitats Directive* (2000).

European Commission, *Natura 2000* (European Commission DG Environment's Nature Newsletter).

Freestone, "The Enforcement of the Wild Birds Directive: a Case Study" in Somsen (ed.) *Protecting the European Environment: Enforcing EC Environmental Law* (1996), pp. 229-250.

Haigh, *Manual of Environmental Policy* (looseleaf), chapter 9.2

Harte, "Nature Conservation: The Rule of Law in European Community Environmental Protection" (1997) 9(1) JEL 139.

Nollkaemper, "Habitat Protection in European Community Law: Evolving Conceptions of a Balance of Interests" (1997) 9(2) JEL 271.

Owen, "The Application of the Wild Birds Directive beyond the Territorial Sea of European Community Member States" (2001) 13(1) JEL 39.

Reid, "Nature Conservation Law" in Holder (ed.) *The Impact of EC Environmental Law in the United Kingdom* (1997), pp.199-214.

Scott, *EC Environmental Law* (1998), chapter 6.

Wils, "The Birds Directive 15 Years Later: a Survey of the Case Law and a Comparison with the Habitats Directive" (1994) 6(2) JEL 218.

Chapter 5

Environmental Impact Assessment

Environmental impact assessment (EIA) refers to a process which seeks to provide the relevant decision-making authority with the requisite information on a specific project proposal enabling its likely environmental impact to be assessed before a decision is made as to its future operation. In this process the developer collects and makes available information relating to the environmental impact of a proposed project. This information, together with comments gathered in a subsequent consultation process with relevant competent authorities and the general public, is considered and taken into account by the decision-maker in deliberations as to the viability of the development. The process therefore allows a proposal's environmental impact to be assessed in advance of the decision as to its future operation, for possible alternatives to the proposed project to be scrutinised, and for impact on the environment to be mitigated or eliminated in the event of the project being allowed to proceed. EIA is therefore anticipatory in nature seeking to minimise environmental harm and in this sense endorses the preventive principle. It is also seen as a vitally important tool to promote sustainable development by facilitating the integration of environmental protection requirements into the land-use/planning process. Where there is likely to be significant environmental impact, decisions should be made with full knowledge of relevant environmental considerations.

However, it is important to stress, although EIA is intended to highlight the negative effect of proposed projects on the environment, it should not be seen as a process which prohibits certain types of development which potentially have significant deleterious environmental impact. The process must be seen as operating in a political context in which other factors of an economic, social or political nature may well outweigh those of an environmental nature.[1] Sheate notes that EIA "is not and should not be the sole determinant of the decision to be made, but the decision should be one which is made more transparent by the EIA process".[2] Decision-making should be improved by taking into account the environmental impact of projects, and the worst fears of the general public can be reduced by both making available accurate information on a project's environmental consequences and taking into account justifiable public concern.

---

[1]   Wood, *Environmental Impact Assessment: a Comparative Review* (1995), pp.2-3.

[2]   Sheate, *Environmental Impact Assessment: Law and Policy - Making an Impact II* (1996), p.26.

The concept of environmental impact assessment was first endorsed in the United States following the adoption of the 1969 National Environmental Policy Act (NEPA) which required all major federal actions significantly affecting the quality of the environment to be subject to an assessment as to their environmental impact. In effect, proposals for legislation and other activities by federal agencies with a significant environmental impact had to be made subject to an assessment, and agencies were obliged to produce a document to be made available for public review noting the results of the analysis. The concept of impact assessment has now been widely endorsed internationally.[3] In a Community context, the seeds of action can be traced back to the first EC Action Programme on the Environment which affirmed the need to take into account effects on the environment at the earliest possible stage in the planning and decision-making process.[4]

The EC and Impact Assessment

Council Directive on the Assessment of the Effects of Certain Public and Private Projects on the Environment ("the directive")[5] was adopted in 1985, and came into effect on 3 July 1988. The Commission was obliged to report on the measure's application and effectiveness in July 1990,[6] but this review was in fact delayed until April 1993 due to the lack of information sent by Member States as to their experiences in implementation.[7] The 1993 report assessed progress under the directive in the period July 1985 – July 1991, and its findings were taken into account in the drafting of an amending proposal.[8] Council Directive 97/11/EC ("amending directive") was subsequently adopted in early 1997.[9]

Article 2(1) of the directive as amended obliges Member States to implement national measures

to ensure that before consent is given, projects likely to have significant effects on the environment by virtue, inter alia, of their nature, size or location are made

---

[3] Gilpin in his work published in 1995 noted that 31 countries had introduced assessment requirements and a further seven had legislation pending, *Environmental Impact Assessment: Cutting Edge for the Twenty-First Century* (1995), p.3.

[4] OJ 1973 C112/1.

[5] Council Directive 85/337/EEC OJ 1985 L 175/40. The measure was formally notified on 3 July 1985.

[6] Article 11(3).

[7] Report from the Commission on the Implementation of Directive 85/337/EEC on the Assessment of the Effects of Certain Public and Private Projects on the Environment, COM(93)28 final.

[8] COM(93)575.

[9] Council Directive 97/11/EC, OJ 1997 L73/5. Member States were obliged to transpose this measure by 14 March 1999.

subject to a requirement for development consent and an assessment with regard to their effects.[10]

Both public and private projects likely to have significant environmental impact fall within the embrace of the directive. However, the measure does not cover projects relating to national defence,[11] nor does it apply to projects adopted by a specific act of national legislation.[12] Moreover, "in exceptional circumstances" a Member State may exempt a particular project from the provisions of the directive.[13] In such a situation the Member State concerned must consider whether another form of assessment is appropriate and whether information collected in such an assessment should be made available to the public. Both the public and the Commission must be informed and told of the reasons for the exemption, and the Commission is obliged to inform the other Member States of the exemption.

The environmental impact assessment process introduced by the directive can be integrated into existing planning consent procedures or other procedures to be established as the respective Member States see fit.[14] Essential elements in the EIA process are:-

• a determination by the competent authority as to whether the project is likely to have significant effects on the environment ("*screening*");

• provision of information by the developer on the project which is deemed likely to have significant environmental effects including the project's potential impact on the environment;

• a subsequent process of consultation with the general public, and agencies with environmental responsibilities (and neighbouring Member States if the project has a transboundary impact);

• having identified and assessed the effect of the project on the environment, a final decision on the future of the project is to be taken by the relevant competent authority.

---

10   Article 2(1).
11   Article 1(4).
12   Article 1(5) which further notes that in the case of such projects "the objectives of [the] directive, including that of supplying information, are achieved through the legislative process". This exemption was inserted at the insistence of the Danish government which was concerned that the requirements of the directive would otherwise encroach unnecessarily upon Denmark's sovereignty; see Haigh, *Manual of Environmental Policy*, 11.2-6. In Case C-435/97 *WWF* v *Autonome Provinz Bozen* [1999] ECR I-5613 the Court of Justice stipulated that Article 1(5) exempts projects from the requirements of the directive subject to two conditions: "[t]he first requires the details of the project to be adopted by a specific legislative act; under the second, *the objectives of the directive*, including that of supplying information, *must* be achieved through the legislative process" (para. 57)[emphasis added]; see also Case C-287/98 *State of the Grand Duchy of Luxembourg* v *Linster et al.* [2000] ECR I-6917, paras.49-59.
13   Article 2(3). See Case C-392/96 *Commission* v *Ireland* [1999] ECR I-5901 on Ireland's infringement of the obligation to implement correctly Article 2(3) in national legislation (paras.84-87).
14   Article 2(2) as amended. In addition, under Article 2(2)a (inserted by the amending directive), Member States may introduce a single procedure to fulfil the requirements of the EIA directive and the Directive on Integrated Pollution Prevention and Control [OJ 1996 L257/26].

"Screening"; Deciding which Projects Require Assessment

Only projects likely to have significant effects on the environment are subject to EIA; a project which has an effect but not a *significant* effect would not need to be assessed within the EIA process. It is therefore of great importance to clarify what projects would be regarded as giving rise to likely significant environmental effect. The text of the directive is in fact vague as to what amounts to "significant" and merely refers to significance being assessed with regard to the "nature, size or location"[15] of the project. However some assistance in this respect is given in that a list of projects set out in Annex I are deemed to be "significant" in their impact.[16] These projects must therefore be subject to mandatory impact assessment and *inter alia* include crude oil refineries, nuclear power stations, installations for the reprocessing of irradiated fuel, installations for extracting asbestos, chemical installations, motorways, thermal power stations, waste incinerators, landfill sites for hazardous waste, and iron and steel smelting works. The amending directive has extended the number of projects falling within Annex I, adding the following: waste disposal installations for the incineration or chemical treatment of non-hazardous waste with a capacity exceeding 100 tonnes per day; groundwater abstraction schemes where the annual volume of water abstracted is equivalent to or exceeds 10 million cubic metres; certain works for the transfer of water resources and for the treatment of waste water; gas extraction projects; large dams; gas, oil and chemicals pipelines of more than 40km in length; large scale intensive pig and poultry rearing projects; pulp and paper plants; quarries and open-cast mining where the surface of the site exceeds 25 hectares; overhead electric power lines of more than 15km in length; and installations for storing petrol and chemical products with a capacity of 200,000 tonnes or more.

But what of proposals for projects not noted in Annex I? A large number of projects which may have a significant impact on the environment are noted in Annex II. These would only be made subject to an assessment following a determination by the Member State in question that they would be likely to have significant environmental effects. Member States, or more specifically the "competent authorities" allocated responsibility by the Member States, are therefore given a wide discretion as to whether Annex II projects are subject to the requirements of the directive. The determination will be made on a case-by-case basis allowing for the appraisal of individual projects against certain guidelines, or through the application of thresholds or criteria set and applied by the Member State.[17]

---

15   Article 2(1).
16   Article 4(1).
17   Article 4(2) as amended. Member States may decide to apply a combination of these procedures for projects listed in Annex II. However where Member States set thresholds or criteria, the preamble to the amending directive makes clear that "Member States should not be required to examine projects below those thresholds or outside those criteria on a case-by-case basis".

Annex II projects are grouped under the following headings:

• agriculture, silviculture and aquaculture

• extractive industry

• energy industry

• production and processing of metals

• mineral industry

• chemical industry not included in Annex I

• food industry

• textile, leather, wood and paper industry

• rubber industry

• infrastructure projects

• other projects

• tourism and leisure

• modifications to Annex I and II projects likely to have a significant adverse environmental impact.[18]

Annex II projects *inter alia* include intensive fish farms, underground mining operations, hydroelectric projects, shipyards, pesticide production plants, slaughter houses, tanneries and holiday villages. The amending directive added the following: wind farms, manufacture of ceramic products such as roof tiles and bricks by the process of burning, coastal works to combat erosion and maritime work capable of altering the coastline, installations for the recovery or destruction of explosives, ski-runs, permanent campsites and theme parks.

In carrying out a case-by-case assessment of a specific project, or in determining criteria or thresholds, the selection criteria added by the amending directive and specified in Annex III must be taken into account by the Member State concerned. Annex III criteria fall under three headings:

---

[18]   A modification to an Annex I project may therefore be regarded as an Annex II project. However see also Case C-431/92 *Commission v Germany* [1995] ECR I-2189 which concerned the building of a new block to the existing Grosskrotzenburg thermal power station. The new block would have had a heat output of 500 megawatts. Annex I includes thermal power stations with a heat output of 300 megawatts. The German Government argued that the new block, despite having a capacity in its own right of considerably more than 300 megawatts, was not an Annex I project as it was simply a modification to an existing Annex I project. This argument was rejected by the ECJ noting that all power stations with a heat output of 300 megawatts or more must undergo EIA as an Annex I project regardless of whether they are separate constructions or linked in some way to existing constructions (see paras.34-36 of the judgment). Where therefore a project can be identified in its own right as an Annex I project, it will be treated as such despite being a modification to an existing Annex I project.

• *characteristics* of the project (ie. size, production of waste, risk of accidents and pollution);

• *location* (environmental sensitivity of geographical areas likely to be affected by the project); and

• *potential impact* having regard to the project's magnitude, the probability of impact, its transfrontier impact, complexity, duration and reversibility.

The addition of the criteria in Annex III by the amending directive is a positive step towards establishing a formal screening process. Under *location* criteria, for example, Annex III expressly notes that a relevant selection criteria is whether a project impacts on national nature reserves, or protected areas under the Wild Birds and Habitats directives.[19] It is to be hoped that the application of Annex III criteria will lead to a greater degree of consistency in the exercise by relevant competent authorities of their discretion as to the need for EIA for Annex II projects. In this respect, the Commission's 1993 report on implementation of the directive had interestingly highlighted the wide diversity of thresholds at that time: in France approximately 5500 assessments were carried out each year in the late 1980s due to the fact that France had established low thresholds; in the UK around 200 assessments were made each year in the same period due to the higher thresholds introduced.[20] In the Netherlands the average dropped to approximately 65 assessments per year, while in Portugal this figure was just 12 each year.[21]

The determination as to whether an Annex II project requires an assessment and the reasoning behind it must be made available to the public.[22] This is to be welcomed as it will improve the chances of seeking judicial review of the competent authority's decision before national courts.[23]

---

19   Nevertheless if a proposed project were seemingly to be located in a position which would impact on a protected area under the Wild Birds or Habitats Directives, whereas the competent authority must take into account this fact, the preamble to the amending directive makes clear that this "does not imply necessarily that projects in those areas are to be automatically subject to an assessment". In effect therefore the screening criteria must be taken into account but a decision can then be made that EIA would nonetheless be inappropriate as the project fails to have a likely significant impact, the Member States "in accordance with the subsidiarity principle" being in "the best position to apply [Annex III] criteria in specific instances" (preamble to the amending directive).

20   European Commission, *supra* n.8, p.38.

21   *Ibid.* Too often it would seem that individuals with little experience have been allowed to make decisions as to the need for assessment. See for instance research by Wood and Jones in relation to the practice of twelve local planning authorities in the UK which had not determined that an EIA was appropriate at all from July 1988 to December 1989. It revealed that thirty cases not considered as being appropriate for EIA perhaps should have been as other local planning authorities applied the assessment procedures in similar cases. In the great majority of these cases, the research concludes that relatively junior planning officers, largely ignorant of the directive and national implementing measures, made the final decision; Wood and Jones, *Monitoring Environmental Assessment and Planning* (1991), pp.19-21.

22   Article 4(4) as amended.

23   On whether the competent authority under the terms of the original directive was obliged to give reasons for not requiring environmental assessment in relation to a specific project see *R v Secretary of State for the Environment, Transport and the Regions, and Parcelforce ex p. Anthony Marson* [1999] 1 CMLR 268 in which the UK's Court of Appeal held that the decision by the Secretary of State that the building of a mail sorting project by Parcelforce near Coventry airport "would not be likely to have significant effect on the environment" could not be quashed for lack of further reasoning.

Information to be Submitted by a Developer

All Annex I projects and those in Annex II which are deemed by the national competent authority to fall within the remit of the directive are to be assessed in the light of their direct and indirect effect on the environment, and more specifically on the following:

• human beings, fauna and flora;

• soil, water, air, climate and the landscape;

• material assets and the cultural heritage; and

• the interaction between these factors.[24]

Developers *may* request the advice of the competent national authority on the nature or scope of the information to be provided before submitting an application.[25] If a developer makes such a request, amendments to the directive now oblige the competent authority to consult other relevant authorities with environmental responsibilities before giving its opinion.[26] The process under the directive as amended does however fall short of the formal obligatory "scoping" procedure utilised in the United States of America in which the public and interested bodies come to an agreement at an early stage prior to the formal assessment as to the issues deemed to have significant relevance to the environment and which therefore require detailed investigation in the assessment.[27] This formal procedure allows the "scope" of the EIA process to be defined in advance of the submission of any statement or report on the project, and helps to ensure that the range of environmental impacts covered in the process is comprehensive.

It is of interest to note however that the amending directive provides that Member States *may* require their respective national competent authorities to give an opinion on the nature or scope of the information to be provided by the developer, even if such an opinion is not requested by the developer.[28] This again falls short of an obligation to introduce a formal mandatory scoping procedure, but allows a Member State to establish such a procedure should it wish to do so. National legislation in the Netherlands for instance requires scoping to take place with project-specific guidelines being formulated for each assessment. These guidelines include the types of environmental effect which should be covered in the assessment, the planning policies applicable, the alternatives to the proposed project, and the local conditions which must be described in the assessment.[29]

---

24   Article 3 as amended.
25   Article 5(2) as amended.
26   *Ibid.*
27   See Wood, *supra* n.1, pp.22-23, and on scoping generally pp.130-142.
28   Article 5(2) as amended.
29   Wood, *supra* n.1, pp.136-137.

The scoping process in respect of a waste incineration plant jointly proposed by the regional government of Twente and the Overijssel regional electricity company provides a useful example of the Dutch approach. Following the publication of an outline of the proposed project in April 1993, the Dutch EIA Commission provided the competent decision-making authority with draft scoping guidelines which were also made public. In principle such draft guidelines need not be adopted by the competent authority which makes the final decision on the project, but in practice often are. Guidelines of this sort are widely acknowledged to cover all relevant environmental effects, a reflection of the high esteem in which the experienced Dutch EIA Commission is held.[30] The EIA Commission's advice noted the need to consider a number of alternatives for the design of the project, and also highlighted atmospheric pollution as the most significant potential environmental threat, particularly the issue as to how the plant was to comply with carbon dioxide emission standards. The plant's perceived impact on soil and water, noise pollution, and safety issues were also issues upon which the EIA Commission felt the assessment should focus. Information subsequently supplied by the joint developers in an environmental impact statement covered all aspects of the scoping guidelines, and the final decision was taken by the competent authority in March 1994 to grant the plant the relevant licenses. Advice given on scoping ensured that the relevant environmental issues raised by the developers' proposal were addressed and alternatives identified. As such, the scoping procedure provided a valuable focus for the assessment process.[31]

Professionals and researchers have recommended the adoption of a Community-wide scoping requirement similar to the Dutch model which would establish a checklist of matters that need to be covered in specific assessments.[32] Time and expense would also be saved as matters deemed not to be relevant to a particular project's impact can be excluded at an early stage. An early draft of the amending directive put forward by the Commission included a duty on competent authorities to define the scope of information to be provided in consultation with other relevant authorities and developers. It is to be regretted that this formal duty on the part of the competent authorities was put to one side in the final version of the amending directive.[33]

At the Member State's discretion, to be exercised in the light of the nature of the particular project, the environmental features likely to be affected by it, and also the reasonableness of requiring information in the light of current knowledge and

---

[30] See Wood, "EIA in the Netherlands: a Comparative Assessment" in Commission for Environmental Impact Assessment (the Netherlands), *Environmental Impact Assessment in the Netherlands: Experiences and Views by and to the Commission for EIA* (1996), p.7.

[31] See Commission for Environmental Impact Assessment (the Netherlands), *EIA-Methodology: Scoping of Alternatives - a Study Based on Ten Representative Cases* (1994), pp.27-28.

[32] European Commission, *supra* n.8, p.22.

[33] See ENDS Report January 1996, p.40.

methods of assessment, the developer is obliged to supply the information noted in Annex IV.[34] The latter *inter alia* includes an outline of the main alternatives taken into account by the developer and the reasons for his/her choice, a description of the main production processes, an estimate of the type and quantity of pollution resulting from the proposed project once operational, detail of those aspects of the environment likely to be significantly affected, and of measures envisaged to prevent or reduce adverse environmental effects. Member States therefore exercise a level of discretion in determining the amount of information required of the developer, but, as a basic minimum, developers are obliged to supply:[35]

• a description of the project comprising information on the size, design and site;

• a description of the measures envisaged to avoid, reduce and, if possible, remedy significant adverse effects;

• the data required to identify and assess the main effects which the project is likely to have on the environment;

• an outline of the main alternatives studied by the developer and reasons for his/her choice; and

• a non-technical summary of this information.

The requirement that developers must provide an outline of the main alternatives studied was added by the amending directive. Prior to this change, Member States exercised discretion as to whether or not the developer should identify alternatives in this way. This particular amendment must be seen as a significant improvement in the EIA procedure particularly when one bears in mind that EIA reports often insufficiently covered alternatives.[36] The 1993 Commission report on implementation noted that Denmark, Germany, Greece and the Netherlands obliged developers to provide some information on alternatives, but other Member States either made provision of this information optional or made no reference at all to the issue.[37]

---

[34]   Article 5(1) as amended.

[35]   Article 5(3) as amended.

[36]   The research carried out by Wood and Jones of the EIA Centre, University of Manchester, was completed before the amending directive was adopted and concluded that "the lack of coverage of alternatives was reported in a number of Member States and this was explained by the fact that this is not required by legislation. Where alternatives were covered, this mainly related to site selection. Mitigation measures were not always covered in the reports and, where they were, details provided about their implementation and effectiveness were often limited", *supra* n.21, p.9.

[37]   European Commission, *supra* n.8, p.22.

Consultation with the General Public, and Agencies with Environmental Responsibilities

While the developer is compiling the required information, Member States are obliged where necessary to ensure relevant information held by any authority is made available to the developer.[38] The developer is therefore encouraged to utilise a wide range of sources when compiling relevant information. Once the developer has compiled and submitted the required information relating to the impact of the proposed project, the information must be made available in a consultation process. This consultation process is an essential component of the EIA process as it provides an opportunity for the public to contribute to the decision-making process by expressing their concern or approval. Members of the public and those authorities likely to be concerned by the project due to their environmental responsibilities must be given an opportunity to scrutinise, review and comment on information supplied by the developer before development consent is granted.[39] Consultation of this nature identifies the concerns of the public and agencies, and provides an invaluable source of relevant information. Member States are however obliged to respect national practices and provisions relating to industrial and commercial secrecy in the consultation process.[40]

Involvement of the local community affected by the proposed project is seen as particularly valuable. The Sixth Environmental Action Programme talks in terms of "empowering citizens" in the decision-making process by involving local people in that process, and Sheate has noted that locals

> *will be the people who know their own local environment and will be able to identify key areas of concern. Those concerns and fears may, in some cases, prove to be ill-founded, but if they are not identified at the earliest opportunity, they may arise at a much later stage when they are more likely to lead to conflict. By involving the public as early as possible issues may be identified which 'experts' might not have considered important.*[41]

The original text of the directive had noted in Article 6(2) that the public had to be "given the opportunity to express an opinion before the project is initiated". In certain cases (i.e. in Greece and sometimes in France) this had been interpreted as allowing the public to comment *after* consent had already been given – in effect at the appeal stage.[42] It is to be welcomed therefore that the directive as amended now

---

[38] Article 5(4) as amended.
[39] Article 6(1) & (2) as amended. Member States are obliged to designate those authorities to be consulted for these purposes either in general terms or on a case-by-case basis (Article 6(1)).
[40] Article 10.
[41] Sheate, *supra* n.2, p.83.
[42] European Commission, *supra* n.8, p.27.

clearly stipulates that the public must be given opportunity to comment "before the development consent is granted".[43] Further developments to improve public participation are expected. With a view to implementing the second pillar of the 1998 Aarhus Convention on Access to Information, Public Participation in Decision-making and Access to Justice in Environmental Matters,[44] the Commission has put forward a proposal which seeks to ensure public intervention at an early stage in the decision-making process.[45]

Projects with a Transboundary Impact

In accordance with the terms of the Convention on Environmental Impact Assessment in a Transboundary Context,[46] if a Member State is aware that a project is likely to have significant transboundary environmental effects in another Member State, the Member State in whose territory the project is to be carried out should notify the affected neighbouring country of the project, and provide information on its potential transboundary impact.[47] Information on the nature of the decision which may be taken is also to be provided.[48] Any Member State affected in this way must then be given a reasonable period of time to assess whether it wishes to be involved in the particular EIA process.[49]

---

[43] Article 6(2) as amended.
[44] 38 ILM 517 (1999)
[45] COM (2000) 839. A Common Position was adopted by the Council on 25 April 2002 (OJ 2002 C170/22). Under the terms of the Common Position, the public shall be informed early in the decision-making process of the following: the request for development consent; the fact that the project is subject to the EIA procedure; details of the competent authorities responsible for taking the decision, those from which information can be obtained, those to which comments can be submitted, and time frames for giving comments; the nature of the possible decision; an indication as to availability of information gathered under Article 5; times and places where information will be made available; and details of arrangements made for public participation. Additionally, the public affected or likely to be affected or having an interest in the decision (the "public concerned" which includes environmental NGOs) must be given the information gathered under Article 5, the main reports and advice issued to the competent authority, and information relevant other than that already supplied to the public. The public concerned must be given "early and effective opportunities to participate in the environmental decision-making procedures" and in particular "be entitled to express comments and opinions when all options are open to the competent authority ... before the decision on the request for development consent is given". The Common Position also seeks to ensure that the public concerned has access to "fair, equitable, timely and not prohibitively expensive" legal procedures allowing challenges to be made to the legality of acts which are subject to the public participation procedures of the directive. This access to review procedure will therefore place an obligation on Member States to provide access to justice in this respect not only for individuals affected by the decision, but also for environmental NGOs. On the implications of the Aarhus Convention on EC law, see Davies, "Public Participation, the Aarhus Convention, and the European Community" in Zillman, Lucas and Pring (eds.), Human Rights in Natural Resource Development: Public Participation in the Sustainable Development of Mining and Energy Resources (2002), pp.155-185.
[46] The Community signed the Espoo Convention on Environmental Impact Assessment in a Transboundary Context (OJ 1992 C104) on 25 February 1991. The treaty is reproduced in 30 ILM 800 (1991).
[47] Article 7 as amended.
[48] *Ibid.*
[49] *Ibid.*

In the event that a neighbouring Member State wishes to become involved in the process, it must be sent the information compiled by the developer.[50] This information must then be made available to the general public and relevant agencies in the country likely to be affected in a transboundary context, and an opportunity given to forward their opinions before development consent is granted.[51] In addition, consultations on a governmental level must take place between the Member States concerned as to the potential transboundary impact of the project and the measures to be taken to reduce such impact.[52]

Deciding Whether to Give Approval to a Project

The directive is firm in the obligation it lays down that all information gathered from the developer, and in the consultation process with the general public, relevant authorities and other Member States, must be taken into account in the development consent procedure.[53] However, a Member State is not legally obliged to refuse consent for a proposed project which potentially has a severely damaging impact on the environment. Having made a decision, the relevant competent authority is however obliged to inform the public of the content of that decision. If approval is given, any conditions to which it is made subject must also be made public.[54] In addition, the competent authorities must also make available a description of the main measures to mitigate adverse environmental effects.[55]

The Interpretation of the Directive's Requirements by the Court of Justice

Either in cases brought before it by the Commission in infringement proceedings against Member States, or referred to it by national courts seeking preliminary rulings, the ECJ has been given opportunities to deliberate on the requirements of the directive. In doing so it has been prepared to adopt a purposive approach to interpretation as in *Aannemersberdrijf PK Kraaijeveld BV et al v Gedeputeerde Staten van Zuid-Holland*[56] where the Netherlands State Council requested a preliminary ruling on certain issues which had been raised in a national action

---

[50] Article 7(2) as amended. The Common Position noted *supra* at n.45 provides that the "public concerned" in the territory of the affected Member State should be given the opportunity to "participate effectively" in decision-making concerning the project. It also specifies the information which must be provided to the neighbouring state (this is largely in line with the information outlined *supra* n.45 to be given to the public and public concerned in the country in which the project might be put into operation).

[51] Article 7(3)a and 7(3)b as amended.

[52] Article 7(4) as amended.

[53] Article 8 as amended.

[54] Article 9 as amended.

[55] Article 9(1) as amended.

[56] Case 72/95 [1996] ECR I-5403.

brought before it by Aannemersberdrijf PK Kraaijeveld BV ("Kraaijeveld"). The latter was seeking annulment of a decision by the South Holland Provincial Executive which had given approval to a local zoning plan relevant to the reinforcement of dykes. Under the plan the waterway to which Kraaijeveld importantly had access would cease to be linked to navigable waterways. Without this access, the future of Kraaijeveld's business would have been put in jeopardy. The national case had raised the issue of whether the proposed works on the Merwede dyke should have been subject to an environmental assessment under the terms of the directive; no assessment had been carried out as the size of the works fell below the minimum thresholds established in Dutch legislation.

A specific question upon which the national court sought a ruling was whether the expression "canalisation and flood-relief works" in Annex II of the directive should be interpreted as including work on a dyke. The Dutch Government argued that there was a distinction to be drawn between on the one hand "canalisation and flood-relief works" which would regulate water flow or were intended to benefit river navigation, and on the other hand dyke reinforcement works which merely involved increasing the height of embankments with sand or clay; the former were Annex II projects, the latter were not. As such, according to the Dutch Government's argument, the works in issue were not Annex II projects and simply fell outside the requirements of the directive. The ECJ looked first to a comparison of the various language versions of the directive and found divergence in meaning. In the absence of a uniform interpretation, the ECJ looked to the purpose and general scheme of the directive. Adopting this purposive approach the ECJ underlined the importance of the directive in concluding that the measure was broad in scope and purpose and, as such, applied to all works for retaining water including reinforcement works on dykes which ran alongside waterways.

The nature of this interpretation has importance beyond the case in hand as it is likely to be indicative of the ECJ's approach to the interpretation of Annex II projects in general.[57] Indeed, the ECJ proceeded in the same case to adopt a purposive approach once again noting the directive's "very broad scope" in determining that modifications to existing Annex II projects must also be regarded as Annex II works in their own right, despite no express mention of the need to subject such projects to the requirements of the original directive.[58] To decide otherwise, according to the ECJ, would have undermined the measure's purpose by allowing modification works to evade the need for assessment even though they

---

[57] See "The Penelope Project" comment on the case at http://www-penelope.et.ic.ac.uk/penelope/library/Libs/EURO/dyke/dyke_s.htm.

[58] Although the original directive noted that modifications to Annex I projects must be treated as Annex II projects, the legislation was silent as to modifications to existing Annex II projects.

were likely to have a significant impact on the environment. The ECJ's conclusions in this respect are significant bearing in mind that the Commission's 1993 report on implementation of the directive had indicated that there was divergence in Member States' practice, some interpreting Annex II to include modifications to existing Annex II projects, while others treated such modifications as falling outside the requirements of the directive.[59] The drafting of the original text of the directive can be criticised for failing to address the issue of modifications to Annex II works, but the purposive approach again adopted by the ECJ underlines its determination to interpret the measure's requirements broadly. The vagueness of the original directive has in fact now been clarified by the amending directive which includes in Annex II not only modifications or extensions to Annex I works which may have significant adverse environmental effects, but also Annex II projects of a similar nature.

National Discretion in Establishing Criteria/Thresholds

It will be recalled that Member States are offered discretion to establish criteria or thresholds necessary to determine which projects are to be subject to assessment. The ECJ has been instrumental in establishing the limits of this discretion. The Commission had held the view that the existence of national criteria/thresholds does not exempt Member States from undertaking an actual examination of projects to ascertain whether they are likely to have significant effects on the environment. However this view was rejected in the *Kraaijeveld* case, the ECJ noting that "a Member State would have no interest in fixing specifications, thresholds and criteria if, in any case, every project had to undergo an individual examination". This is now underlined in the directive as amended, the preamble to the amending directive noting that Member States "should not be required to examine projects below those thresholds or outside those criteria on a case-by-case basis".

However, while the ECJ has acknowledged that Member States have a measure of discretion in establishing criteria/thresholds,

> *the limits to that discretion are to be found in the obligation set out in Article 2(1) that projects likely ... to have significant effects on the environment are to be subject to an impact assessment.*[60]

Clearly national thresholds/criteria may not in principle exempt whole classes of Annex II projects in advance.[61] Only where entire classes of Annex II projects could be regarded on the basis of a comprehensive assessment to be not likely to have significant effects on the environment can an entire class of project be exempted in

---

59   European Commission, *supra* n.8, p.18.
60   Case 72/95 *supra* n.56, para.50.
61   Case C-133/94 *Commission* v *Belgium* [1996] ECR I-2323, paras.42-43.

advance.[62]

What if a Member State has not gone as far as to exempt an entire class of project falling within Annex II, but instead established criteria/thresholds at such a level that in practice an entire class is exempted in advance from the requirements of the directive? In *Commission v Ireland*[63] the ECJ made it clear that a Member State exceeds the limits of its discretion in so doing unless all the projects so excluded could, when viewed as a whole, be regarded as not being likely to have significant environmental effects. This is particularly relevant where Member States establish a criterion of project size and do not take into account the cumulative impact of a number of individual projects. For example, Ireland had established a threshold of 70 hectares for initial afforestation projects; an assessment would only have to be carried out if the area involved, either itself or when taken with any adjacent area planted by the applicant within the previous three years, amounted to an area more than 70 hectares. The ECJ held that such a threshold exceeded the limits of Ireland's discretion as such projects

> *encouraged by the grant of aid, may be implemented in proximity to one another without any impact assessment at all being carried out, if they are conducted by different developers who all keep within the threshold of 70 hectares over three years.*[64]

It is equally clear from this case that where a Member State sets thresholds which only take into account the *size* of the projects without also taking into account their *nature* and *location*, as required by Article 2(1) of the directive, the Member State exceeds the limits of its discretion.[65] Even a small scale project can have a significant impact on the environment if located in an area particularly sensitive to change. Again the ECJ used afforestation as an example:

> *[W]hen carried out in areas of active blanket bog, it entails, by its nature and location the destruction of the bog ecosystem and the irreversible loss of biotypes that are original, rare and of great scientific interest.*[66]

Following this ruling Member States may set a number of thresholds according to

---

62   See Case C-435/97 *WWF et al* v *Autonome Provinz Bozen et al*, *supra* n.12, para. 49. Additionally, where a Member State exempts a specific project from the directive's requirements, an onus is placed on the national courts to review whether, on the basis of the individual examination carried out by the national authorities which resulted in the project's exclusion from the requirements of the directive, the relevant national authorities had correctly assessed the significance of the environmental effects of the project.

63   Case C-392/96 *supra* n.13.

64   Para. 79 of the judgment.

65   Para. 65 of the judgment.

66   Para. 69 of the judgment.

size of projects but these should also be applicable by reference to nature and location.

Issues Relating to the Date of Entry into Force of the Directive

In *Bund Naturschutz in Bayern E.V and Richard Stahnsdorf et al v Freistaat Bayern, Stadt Vilsbiburg and Landkreis Landshut* the Court of Justice was requested by the Bavarian Higher Regional Administrative Court to give a preliminary ruling.[67] The dispute before the Bavarian court related to the construction of two sections of the B15 federal highway jointly accounting for ten kilometres of its length. The Bavarian Highways Department as developer of the Annex I road project had lodged applications for the plans for the two sections on 7 September 1988 and 9 November 1989 respectively. National legislation implementing the directive had been enacted but came into force on 1 August 1990, long after the 3 July 1988 deadline by which time the directive should have been transposed. The plans had therefore been submitted before national legislation came into force, but after the time for national implementation of the terms of the directive.

German implementing law laid down rules under which pending consent procedures were exempt from the directive's requirements if the project in question had already been notified to the general public before 1 August 1990. The ECJ was asked to rule as to whether the directive allowed a Member State to waive its requirements in this way for projects for which the consent procedure had been initiated after 3 July 1988, but before entry into force of national implementing measures. The ECJ held that a Member State was not entitled to, as to rule otherwise "would result in an extension of the deadline of 3 July 1988 and would be contrary to the obligations under the directive".[68] The judgment itself is unsurprising and is noteworthy more for what the ECJ failed to address – the issue of "pipeline" cases.[69] The German court *inter alia* asked whether the directive should be interpreted as meaning that

> *Member States were under an obligation to take by 3 July 1988 the measures necessary to ensure that all public projects which fell within the ambit of the directive and for which development consent was granted for the first time after that date were in accordance with the requirements of the directive.*

The issue submitted by the national court could therefore be interpreted as asking

---

[67] Case C-396/92 [1994] ECR I-3717.

[68] Para. 19 of the judgment. See also Case C-150/97 *Commission v Portugal* [1999] ECR I-259, and Case C-81/96 *Burgemeester en wethouders van Haarlem merliede en Spaarnwoude et al v Gedeputeerde Staten van Noord-Holland* [1998] ECR I-3923.

[69] See "The Penelope Project" comment on the case at:
http://www-penelope.et.ic.ac.uk/penelope/library/Libs/EURO/bund/bund_s.htm.

whether Member States were obliged to regard as falling within the remit of the directive not only projects which were initiated after 3 July 1988, but also those projects for which plans had been submitted or formal discussions begun before the 3 July 1988 deadline, but for which final consent had not been granted before this deadline. The latter type of project has become known as "pipeline" projects in the sense that they were under consideration – or in the pipeline – before the directive's deadline date, but the final decision had not been made by 3 July 1988. The Court of Justice simply sidestepped the issue of projects for which consent procedures were already under way by 3 July 1988, preferring to give no indication as to whether the directive applied to pipeline projects on the basis that the issue before the German court did not fall within this type of project. The plans for the two motorway projects had after all been submitted in September 1988 and November 1989 respectively and the consent procedure commenced after the directive's deadline for implementation.

But what if those plans had been submitted in March 1988 and the final consent given after the 3 July 1988 deadline for implementation? The Commission held the view that, in the absence of any specific transitional provision in the directive itself, no final consent could be legally given after 3 July 1988 to any project likely to have significant environmental effects without satisfying the requirements of the directive.[70] The original directive was deficient in not addressing the issue and this led to confusion which could have been avoided if greater attention had been paid in the drafting of the measure.[71] It was left to the Court of Justice in *Commission* v *Germany*[72] to indicate that

> *the date when the application for consent was formally lodged ... constitutes the sole criterion which may be used. Such a criterion accords with the principle of legal certainty and is designed to safeguard the effectiveness of the directive.*[73]

In effect, the ECJ decided that the consent procedure begins when an application for consent is formally lodged. The directive will not apply where an application for consent has been formally lodged before 3 July 1988.

---

[70]   See generally on pipeline related issues, Kunzlik, "Environmental Impact Assessment: the British Cases" (1995) 4(12) EELR pp.336-344 which analyses the Commission's initial concern over various UK projects, including the Twyford Down M3 motorway extension and the M11 link road. See also "Brussels Ups the Stakes on Environmental Assessment" ENDS Report 201 (October 1991) pp.14-17.

[71]   See Sheate, *supra* n.2, pp.181-131. See also the English case *Twyford Parish Council* v *Secretary of State for the Environment and the Secretary of State for Transport* [1993] Env. L.R. 37 in which McCullough J. held that "pipeline" projects were not required to be covered by the procedure established by the directive; "[h]ad it been intended that the directive was to cover pipeline cases one would have expected it to have said so and to have stated how the gathering and considerations of the information was to affect the stages that had already passed" (p.45 of the judgment). See also *Secretary of State for Transport* v *Haughian et al* [1997] Env LR 59.

[72]   Case C-431/92 [1995] ECR I-2189.

[73]   Para. 32 of the judgment.

However, consider the situation where consent for a project was obtained before 3 July 1988 but no progress was made on the project's construction. What if a fresh application for consent is then required under relevant national law due to the delay in initiating the project, this renewed application being made after 3 July 1988? Would the requirements of the directive apply to the fresh application? In the *Burgemeester* case[74] the ECJ addressed this issue. First, the ECJ reiterated that the directive does not apply where the application for consent for a project was formally lodged before 3 July 1988 noting that

> *the directive is primarily designed to cover large-scale projects which will most often require a long time to complete. It would not be appropriate for the relevant procedures, which are already complex at national level and which were formally initiated prior to the date of the expiry of the period for transposing the directive, to be made more cumbersome and time-consuming by the specific requirements imposed by the directive, and for situations already established to be affected by it.*[75]

However where a fresh application had been made after the directive became effective, the requirements of the directive had to be fulfilled otherwise the effectiveness of the measure would be compromised.

Importantly the drafters of the amending directive learnt from the difficulties that had arisen from the failure to address the issue in the original directive. Article 13(2) of the amending directive stipulates that if a request for development consent is submitted before 14 March 1999, the provisions of the original directive will continue to apply.

Implementation of Obligations Relating to Projects with a Transboundary Impact

As noted earlier, Article 7 as amended stipulates that if a Member State is aware that a project is likely to have significant transboundary environmental effects in another Member State, the Member State in whose territory the project is to be carried out should notify the affected neighbouring country of the project, and provide information on its potential transboundary impact as well as information on the nature of the decision which may be taken. In the event that a Member State does wish to become involved in the consent process, it must be sent the information compiled by the developer. In *Commission v Belgium*[76] the Commission brought infringement proceedings against Belgium claiming that the Flemish region and the

---

[74] Case C-81/96 *supra* n.68.

[75] Para. 24 of the judgment.

[76] Case 133/94 [1996] ECR I-2323. See also Case C-392/96 *Commission v Ireland, supra* n.13, paras.91-95, the ECJ finding against Ireland for failing to implement Article 7.

region of Brussels had failed to transpose obligations relating to works with transboundary impact. The ECJ found against Belgium, having little time for an argument put forward that the region of Brussels did not have to implement formally these obligations as Brussels' geographical location precluded the establishment of industrial installations capable of having a transboundary effect on neighbouring countries. The ruling in this respect is of course correct; there are few who now argue against the potential long-range environmental impact of local projects.

"Direct Effect" of the Directive's Provisions

In the *Kraaijeveld* case the national court which had submitted the preliminary reference asked for guidance from the Court of Justice as to whether the obligation placed on Member States by virtue of Article 2(1), to adopt measures to ensure that projects likely to have significant environmental effects are made subject to an impact assessment, was directly effective. Both the applicant and the Commission were of the opinion that Article 2(1) was capable of direct effect and therefore could be relied upon by individuals before national courts. Advocate General Elmer agreed, identifying the individual's right to express an opinion in the assessment process as a right to be upheld in the absence of correct national implementation. The obligation in Article 2(1) was "sufficiently precise" in the sense it unequivocally obliged Member States to make certain projects subject to assessment, and "unconditional" in the sense that the discretion afforded to Member States to designate a project as significant does not entitle a Member State to

> *implement the provision in such a way that the discretion is subject to the application of fixed rules which in general exclude the environmental impact assessment of certain projects. The Member States can certainly lay down criteria but cannot invalidate the obligation to exercise the prescribed discretion.*[77]

The Court of Justice did not expressly speak in terms of the direct effect of the directive but noted that in circumstances where an individual claims that a Member State has exceeded the discretion given to it under a directive as to form and method of implementation, national courts should examine the issue in the light of the Community measure and set aside national implementing provisions found by it to exceed the discretion afforded by the directive.[78] In circumstances where national law allowed courts to raise of their own motion pleas based on national law which have not been raised by the parties, national courts must examine whether national authorities had exceeded the limits of their discretion in setting thresholds/criteria

---

[77] Para. 73 of Advocate General Elmer's opinion.
[78] See also Case C-287/98 *State of the Grand Duchy of Luxembourg* v *Linster et al.*, *supra* n.12, paras.37-39.

even when the issue has not been brought up by the parties. If discretion has been exceeded and national laws set aside, the authorities of the Member State would be obliged to ensure that projects are examined to assess whether they are likely to have significant environmental effects, and, if so, to subject such projects to assessment in accordance with the terms of the directive.

More recently in answer to a question as to whether Article 4(2)[79] in conjunction with Article 2(1) was directly effective, the ECJ in *WWF* v *Autonome Provinz Bozen*[80] confirmed its *Kraaijeveld* ruling stating that

[w]here the discretion conferred by those provisions has been exceeded by the legislature or administrative authorities of a Member State, individuals may rely on those provisions before a court of that Member State against the national authorities and thus obtain from the latter the setting aside of the national rules or measures incompatible with those provisions.[81]

A strong argument can certainly be made that those provisions which place an obligation on Member States to carry out environmental assessment of Annex I projects in accordance with the directive's requirements are indeed directly effective; the provisions of the directive are clear and unconditional in this respect and the right of an individual, forming part of the "public concerned" (Article 6 [2]), to be given an opportunity to express an opinion in the process must be upheld before national courts.[82]

In relation to requirements of the directive concerning Annex II projects, it has been suggested that the ECJ's indication in *Kraaijeveld* and *WWF* v *Autonome Provinz Bozen* that national courts can set aside national legislation which exceeds the discretion afforded by the directive is arguably something other than an endorsement of the notion that Article 2(1) (read in conjunction with Article 4 [2]) is therefore directly effective. Judge Edward, one of the judges in the *Kraaijeveld* case has, in a personal capacity, noted since this ruling that the ECJ did not follow Advocate

---

[79] "Projects of the classes listed in Annex II shall be made subject to an assessment ... where Member States consider that their characteristics so require. To this end Member States may ... specify certain types of projects as being subject to an assessment or may establish the criteria and/or thresholds necessary to determine which of the projects of the classes listed in Annex II are to be subject to an assessment" (unamended Article 4 [2]). For comment on the amended Article 4(2) see n.17 and accompanying text.

[80] Case C-435/97 *supra* n.12.

[81] *Ibid.*, para.71.

[82] See also Kramer, *Focus on European Environmental Law* (1992), pp.166-167. In the English case of *Berkeley* v *Secretary of State for the Environment et al*, Lord Hoffmann noted that "[t]he directly enforceable right of the citizen which is accorded by the Directive is not merely a right to a fully informed decision on the substantive issue. It must have been adopted on an appropriate basis and that requires the inclusive and democratic procedure prescribed by the directive in which the public, however misguided or wrongheaded its views may be, is given an opportunity to express its opinion on the environmental issues"; [2000] 3 WLR 420, p.430.

General Elmer's approach in the case, and that the ability to set aside national law was "not direct effect in a traditional sense and it would perhaps be as well to find another formula in order to avoid confusion".[83] In the light of the *Kraaijeveld* judgment, Jans however talks in terms of a "review of lawfulnss as a form of direct effect".[84] What is quite clear is that where Member States have exceeded their discretion in relation to Annex II projects (by for instance exempting an entire class of Annex II project either expressly or in practice from the directive's requirements without determining whether the class of project has likely significant environmental effects), individuals can rely on the provisions of the directive before national courts to set aside conflicting national implementing measures. National courts are therefore placed under an obligation to take an active role in determining whether Member States have exceeded their discretion in setting thresholds. If it is found that the limits to Member State discretion have been exceeded, competent national authorities must take the measures necessary to determine whether the project or projects are likely to have a significant effect, and, if so, to carry out an assessment. However, if a Member State correctly exercises its discretion in establishing criteria or thresholds concerning Annex II projects, and applies such criteria/thresholds in practice, the exercise of national discretion in this way must be regarded as beyond reproach.

Research on the Impact of the EIA Process

An indication as to the practical impact of the directive can be gained from relevant research. The Commission's 1993 report on implementation which had looked at assessments up to July 1991 indicated that there were "a substantial number [of reports] in most Member States which are not of a satisfactory standard".[85] Common failings included failure to look at alternatives and to incorporate mitigating measures into project design at an early stage in the consent process, lack of experience of staff, and unsatisfactory scoping.[86]

---

83   Judge Edward, "Foreword" to Holder (ed.), *"The Impact of EC Environmental Law in the UK"* (1997), at *xiv*. See Scott, *EC Environmental Law* (1998), p.217.

84   Jans, *European Environmental Law* (2000), pp.178-179.

85   European Commission, *supra* n.8, p.42.

86   *Ibid.*, p.43. Research on reports submitted between 1988-1993 by the Institute of Terrestrial Ecology and Oxford Brookes University has also highlighted poor quality of reports; ENDS Reports 270 (July 1997), p.10.

Concerned at these findings, the Commission engaged the EIA Centre at the University of Manchester to carry out an evaluation of certain impacts of the EIA procedure. This report was published in late 1996 prior to the adoption of the amending directive.[87] In evaluating the quality of EIA reports, researchers looked at eight reports from each of the following Member States: Belgium, Denmark, Greece, Ireland and Portugal. In addition 24 reports from each of the following countries were analysed: Germany, Spain and the UK. Half of these EIA reports had been carried out in either 1990 or 1991. The remainder were completed in the period 1994-96. In this way the researchers were able to compare the quality of the reports over the two periods of time, and encouragingly concluded that the number of satisfactory reports improved from 50 per cent to just over 70 per cent.[88] However the majority of the satisfactory reports were only "just satisfactory" and clearly there remains room for continued improvement.[89] The improvement in the overall quality of reports was attributed to several factors,[90] which included:

• changes to national implementing legislation which had brought about improvements;

• use by developers of consultants experienced in the EIA process[91];

• more effective scoping.

The research also highlighted that there was clear evidence that the EIA process had brought about modifications to project proposals. A review of 18 projects from Germany, Spain and the UK concluded that on average just over two changes to projects in Spain and the UK, and over three modifications to German projects, were made as a result of impact assessment. In Germany and the UK, most of these modifications were made before the environmental statement was produced by the developer, although in Spain the majority of changes to project proposals came about at the decision-making stage.[92] Most changes in the German and Spanish projects reduced impact on fauna and flora, while in the UK modifications were mainly of a visual nature.[93] Suggestions made by the report to increase the adoption

---

[87] Wood, Barker, Jones and Hughes, *Evaluation of the Performance of the EIA Process* (1996) vol.1 (Main Report) and vol.2 (Member States Reports).

[88] *Ibid.*, p.5. The quality of EIA reports in six of the eight Member States improved over time; however in two countries (Belgium and Denmark) the quality of reports remained unchanged with only 25 per cent of Belgian reports and 50 per cent of Danish reports attaining the standard of overall satisfactory quality. Research carried out by the University of Manchester's EIA Centre and published in 1991 concluded that many environmental statements in the UK were inadequate. As part of the research 24 case studies were examined and it was found that nearly two thirds (15 of the 24) did not meet the requirements of UK implementing regulations and were held "not to be in broad compliance with the EC Directive"; see Wood and Jones, *supra* n.21, pp.31-35.

[89] Wood, Barker, Jones and Hughes, *supra* n.87, p.12.

[90] *Ibid.*, pp.18-20.

[91] The report calls for the accreditation of EIA consultants describing such a move as "especially relevant at a time of acute competition within the environmental consultancy field"; *ibid.*, p.22.

[92] *Ibid.*, pp.25-26.

[93] *Ibid.*, p.28.

of meaningful modifications included making sure scoping took place so that developers are made aware at an early stage that changes may be required, a greater discussion of alternatives in the EIA process, and improvement in public participation guaranteeing a more wide-ranging list of alternatives to the proposed project.[94]

The report acknowledged that the amending directive would assist in improving the effectiveness of the EIA process in the Community but, in addition, recommended *inter alia* the introduction of formal checks by Member States on the quality of EIA reports, and formal scoping requirements. In this context, it is of interest to note the launch of the International Commission for Impact Assessment (ICIA) in September 2002.[95] This independent international body will offer non-binding advice on the sufficiency of information provided in environmental impact assessments. In effect, the ICIA will give a second opinion on the quality of information but only where the government concerned has given its consent. The idea for such a body was first mooted in the Brundtland report in the context of providing much needed expertise to developing states,[96] but failed to win sufficient political support at that time. More recently the idea has attracted backing, the European Commission *inter alia* voicing its support for the proposed role of the ICIA. It is intended that the ICIA provides advisory assistance not only in relation to impact assessments in developing states, but also in respect of assessments in other countries including EC Member States.

The EIA Centre's 1996 report also highlighted the need for the monitoring of projects which have been approved to assess whether agreed modifications have indeed been implemented; the directive as amended makes no reference to the need to carry out post-project monitoring despite reference being made to it in an unpublished draft of the amending directive.[97] In recent years the adoption of a Community-wide obligation has been advocated which would establish an open review process enabling those involved in EIA to learn lessons from previous assessment processes.[98] Sheate has noted that

> *[o]nly by the knowledge, experience and understanding gathered as a result of post-project monitoring can the effectiveness of the earlier EIA processes, ie. identification and assessment of impacts, be seen. Predictions made in an environmental statement need to be tested against the reality once that project has been built. That information should then inform best practice, government*

---

94   *Ibid.*, p.34-37.
95   The ICIA is online at http://www.geocities.com/ICIAOS/ICIA.
96   World Commission on Environment and Development, *Our Common Future* (1987).
97   Sheate, *supra* n.2, p.112.
98   European Commission, "Evaluation of the Performance of the EIA Process" Final Report, vol.1 (1998), p.22.

guidance and local authority attitudes to future EIAs, including the scope of issues that should be addressed, alternatives, mitigation measures, monitoring requirements and the effectiveness of particular methodologies.[99]

Provision for post-project monitoring would seem to have been dropped from the text of the amending directive as a result of Member State unease that it lengthened the EIA process, and placed unreasonable burdens on competent authorities and developers.[100] Nevertheless conditions can of course be attached to a consent for a project and such a condition could include the need for compliance monitoring.[101] In Denmark monitoring after the giving of consent and construction of works is part of the ongoing approval process carried out by local authorities and has had a positive impact.[102] A formal report review process is also required in the Netherlands.

Strategic Environmental Assessment

At the 1992 Rio UN Conference on Environment and Development the Commission expressed the need to broaden the reach of EIA to the policy-making and planning stages.[103] Such a process has been termed "Strategic EIA" or "SEA", and is intended to ensure that strategic decisions are made having taken into account environmental considerations. There is merit in the notion that impact assessment is of limited use if it only applies to specific projects as many key issues will already have been determined at an earlier stage. Gilpin poignantly notes that

[m]atters difficult or impossible to settle at the project level relate to the cumulative effects of other projects within the same or related programmes; to transportation decisions governing the modal split between road and rail movement; to energy policies relating to power generation; to greenhouse strategies; and to natural resource conservation and management.[104]

The need to establish a system of SEA can be shown in the following example. Let us suppose that a Member State decides to embark on a programme of motorway building. Under the EIA project-based process each individual motorway project would be subject to an individual assessment. However, fully to appreciate the potential cumulative impact of the proposed roads would have required an SEA of the entire road-building programme. Implementation of SEA becomes in effect the first tier of assessment, and EIA the second.[105]

---

99   Sheate, *supra* n.2, p.111.
100 *Ibid.*
101 See European Commission, *supra* n.8, p.32.
102 *Ibid*, p.55.
103 See Gilpin, *supra* n.3, p.76.
104 *Ibid*, p.172. On the merits of strategic environmental assessment, see Sheate, *supra* n.2, chapter 11.
105 See Sheate, "From EIA to SEA: Sustainability and Decision-making" in Holder (ed.) *Impact of EC Environmental Law in the UK* (1997) pp.270-271.

In June 2001 agreement was finally reached on the content of the Strategic Environmental Assessment Directive (SEA Directive).[106] The directive is to be welcomed as it complements the project-specific EIA Directive by seeking to provide an environmental assessment framework in relation to certain plans and programmes likely to have significant environmental impact. As such, it endeavours to ensure that potential impact on the environment is taken into account at an earlier stage in the planning procedure than required under the EIA Directive. In this way, it seeks to further the process towards sustainable development, the measure's stated objective being to

> *provide for a high level of protection for the environment and to contribute to the integration of environmental considerations into the preparation and adoption of plans and programmes with a view to promoting sustainable development ... .*[107]

National implementation of the directive's provisions is required by 21 July 2004. The measure stipulates that an environmental assessment will be carried out during the preparation of a plan and programme which is likely to have significant environmental effects. Its requirements relate particularly to plans and programmes prepared for a closed list of sectors, namely agriculture, forestry, fisheries, energy, industry, transport, waste management, water management, telecommunications, tourism, town and country planning or land use and which establish the framework for the future development consent of Annex I and II projects as noted in the EIA Directive.[108] These plans or programmes are therefore deemed likely to have significant effects on the environment and would generally be subject to systematic environmental assessment. However, Article 3(3) notes that plans and programmes which fall within this closed list of sectors but which "determine the use of small areas at local level" will only require environmental assessment if a Member State determines that they are likely to have significant environmental effects.[109] No guidance is given as to what area could be regarded as "small" in nature and it is submitted that too much discretion has been given to Member States which may wish to exploit this loophole. Similarly, if a "minor" modification is made to plans within the closed list, Member States can determine whether the minor change in question is likely to have significant environmental effects.[110] But what actually amounts to a "minor" modification is a matter which the relevant national authority can determine.

---

[106] Directive 2001/42/EC on the Assessment of the Effects of Certain Plans and Programmes on the Environment OJ L197/30.

[107] Article 1.

[108] Article 3(2)a. Note also that plans and programmes which require assessment under Articles 6 and 7 of the Habitats Directive will require an environmental assessment in accordance with the provisions of the SEA Directive (Article 3(2)b).

[109] Article 3(3). Member States can either decide on a case-by-case basis or by identifying types of plans and programmes (or by combining these two approaches).

[110] *Ibid.* In this respect, Member States can either decide on a case-by-case basis or by identifying types of plans and programmes (or by combining these two approaches).

What of plans or programmes which set the framework for development consent of projects but which are not noted in the closed list? In relation to such other plans and programmes, Member States can assess whether they are likely to have significant environmental effects either on a case-by-case basis or by specifying types of plans or programmes, or by combining both of these approaches. Annex II sets out the criteria to be taken into account in determining whether such a plan is likely to have a significant effect. Annex II criteria include an assessment of the characteristics of the plan or programme, of the environmental effects and of the area likely to be affected. These criteria should also be taken into account when determining whether the types of plans referred to in Article 3(3) require assessment. Despite the guidance provided by Annex II, it must however be concluded that a high degree of discretion is given to Member States to determine whether such plans or programmes are likely to have significant environmental effects and therefore require assessment.[111] Nevertheless, where a Member State determines that a plan or programme should not be assessed, the reasons for this determination must be made available to the public.[112] This obligation to give reasons was inserted at the insistence of the European Parliament, the latter correctly taking the view that this would make the decision-making process more transparent. The need to give reasons will facilitate public scrutiny – and perhaps even judicial review – of screening determinations.

Let us assume that a plan or programme requires an assessment. This being the case, an "environmental report" needs to be drawn up identifying the significant environmental effects of implementing the plan or programme concerned, as well as the reasonable alternatives available.[113] Although Annex I refers to the type of information which should be included in the environmental report, the latter need only contain the

> *information which may reasonably be required taking into account current knowledge and methods of assessment, the contents and level of detail in the plan or programme, its stage in the decision-making process and the extent to which certain matters are more appropriately assessed at different levels in that process in order to avoid duplication of the assessment.*[114]

This provision therefore also affords a high degree of discretion to Member States. The latter are obliged to "ensure that environmental reports are of a sufficient quality to meet the requirements of [the SEA directive]",[115] but it is submitted that a Member State acting in bad faith may nevertheless allow assessment at the plan or programme level to be largely cursory in nature.

---

111 Article 3(4). Member States can in this regard either decide on a case-by-case basis or by identifying types of plans and programmes (or by combining these two approaches). They are nevertheless obliged to take into account the criteria noted in Annex II in their determination as to whether a plan or programme is likely to have significant effects.

112 Article 3(7).

113 Article 5(1).

114 Article 5(2).

115 Article 12(2).

What of the consultation process? Relevant authorities (designated by Member States due to their particular environmental responsibilities), as well as the public (including relevant NGOs in accordance with national legislation or practice) must be consulted. They are to be given an early and effective opportunity to comment on the draft plan or programme and the environmental report before a final decision is made.[116] In a situation in which a Member State considers that the implementation of a plan or programme is likely to have significant effects on the environment in another Member State, it must forward the draft proposal and the environment report to the Member State in question.[117] Similarly, where a Member State which is likely to be significantly affected asks to be involved in the consultation process, it should be consulted.

The report and results of consultations (including those consultations as to transboundary effects) must be taken into account by the relevant national authority during the preparation of the plan or programme and before its formal adoption.[118] Once a decision has been taken, Member States are obliged to ensure that the public and any Member State consulted in the process are informed of the content of the plan or programme adopted, as well as the manner in which environmental considerations have been integrated into the final decision. Also, the reasons why the plan or programme was favoured over and above reasonable alternatives should be given.[119] At the instigation of the European Parliament, Member States are also obliged to monitor the significant environmental effects of the implementation of plans and programmes so that unforeseen adverse effects can be identified and remedial action taken.[120]

In general terms, the SEA Directive could have gone further by obliging Member States to carry out environmental impact assessment on national, regional and local *policy decisions* thus covering the entirety of the planning process. This particular option however attracted criticism from some Member States including France, Germany and the UK who believe such a measure to be impractical despite the fact that, for instance, New Zealand[121] and Slovakia[122] have strived to endorse such a system with some success. In the legislative procedure prior to the adoption of the SEA Directive, the European Parliament had endeavoured to amend the proposal in such a way that it made specific reference to the fact that the Commission in its first report on the application and effectiveness of the directive would have been able to put forward proposals for future amendment which might have been linked to

---

[116] Articles 6(1) and 6(2).

[117] Article 7(1).

[118] Article 8.

[119] Article 9.

[120] Article 10.

[121] See generally Sheate, *supra* n.2, pp.159-168.

[122] Economic Commission for Europe's Committee on Environmental Policy, "Key Issues in the Implementation of Article 7 on Plans, Programmes, and Policies, and Article 8 on Regulations and Laws", doc.CEP/WG.5/2000/10 (2/5/2000), pp.5-6.

extending the SEA process to policies.[123] In the adopted measure the Commission must indeed issue a report on the application of the measure (before 21 July 2006), but no express mention has been made as to the possibility of the report including recommendations on extending SEA to policies.

Plans and programmes covered by the obligations in the SEA Directive include those subject to preparation and/or adoption by an authority at the national, regional or local level, or which are prepared by an authority for adoption through a legislative procedure by Parliament or government.[124] At the insistence of the European Parliament, such plans or programmes include those co-financed by the European Community. However, the SEA Directive includes a temporary derogation for plans and programmes co-financed under the Community's Structural Funds.[125] This was in part due to the fact that most of the decisions as to such funding in the current programming period of the Structural Funds (2000-2006) would have already been made by the time compliance with the SEA Directive is required. However the derogation is stated only to apply until the end of the current programming period. Moreover, the Commission is obliged to report on the relationship between the SEA Directive and the Structural Funds.[126] This report will be taken into account when the Commission drafts a new proposal for legislation concerning future financial support from the Structural Funds. It is to be hoped that plans and programmes in the next programming period are indeed made subject to the provisions of the SEA Directive thereby facilitating the further integration of environmental protection requirements into this important area of Community activity.[127]

Some Conclusions

Ambiguity in the terms of the EIA Directive has given rise to problems of

---

[123] See European Parliament Committee on the Environment, Public Health and Consumer Policy, session document A5-0196/2000 of 13 July 2000.

[124] Article 2(a) notes

"Plans and programmes" shall mean plans and programmes, including those co-financed by the European Community, as well as any modifications to them:

- which are subject to preparation and/or adoption by an authority at the national, regional or local level, or which are prepared by an authority for adoption through a legislative procedure by Parliament or Government, and

- which are required by legislative, regulatory or administrative provisions.

[125] Article 3(9).

[126] Article 12(4).

[127] The current programme provides for *ex-ante* environmental evaluation but falls some way short of a full strategic assessment; see Article 41(2)b of Council Regulation 1260/1999 laying down general provisions on the Structural Funds (OJ 1999 L161/1). Of Structural Fund programmes prior to the current programme, Scott noted that relevant legislation was "laconic as regards the place of environmental considerations in development planning"; *EC Environmental Law* (1998), p.143.

implementation in most Member States.[128] In particular, exercise of the wide discretion given to Member States in determining whether environmental assessment is required for Annex II projects has been far from uniform. However, the Court of Justice, in interpreting the terms of the directive, has endeavoured to ensure that the exercise of national discretion in this respect does not frustrate the aim of the directive;[129] if a project is likely to have significant effects on the environment, an impact assessment must be carried out before development consent is granted. The amending directive will improve assessment procedures by establishing a formal screening process with the addition of the criteria in Annex III, and in requiring developers to provide an outline of the main alternatives to the proposed project. It is also to be welcomed that the directive as amended now expressly stipulates that the public must be given an opportunity to comment on the proposed works before the development consent is granted. However some issues remain unresolved, including the lack of a formal scoping requirement to identify the types of environmental effect which should be covered in the assessment, as well as the specific local conditions which must be addressed in the process. The adoption of a formal post-project monitoring obligation under the EIA Directive would also improve the overall effectiveness of the assessment procedure.[130] In this respect, there may well be lessons which other Member States can learn from the review body established in the Netherlands, the Dutch EIA Commission. Comprising experts on activities subject to assessment, this independent authority guides the assessment process by playing a role in the scoping and reviewing of projects, and in generally maintaining the quality of the assessment process.[131]

---

[128] In 2000 one in every four complaints to the Commission concerned environmental impact assessment; European Commission, "Eighteenth Annual Report on Monitoring the Application of Community Law" COM 2001 309.

[129] See Macrory in ENDS Report 297 (October 1999), p.59.

[130] See Sheate, "The EIA Amendment Directive 97/11/EC - A Small Step Forward?" (1997) 6(8/9) EELR pp.235-243, at p.243.

[131] See Commission for Environmental Impact Assessment (the Netherlands), *Environmental Impact Assessment in the Netherlands: Experiences and Views by and to the Commission for EIA* (1996). For the Commission's website, see http://www.eia.nl.

Select Bibliography

Alder, "Environmental Impact Assessment - the Inadequacies of English Law"(1993) 5(2) JEL 203.

Cerny and Sheate, "Strategic Environmental Assessment: Amending the EA Directive"(1992) 22(3) Environmental Policy and Law, pp.154-159.

Colombo, Artola, Gervasi, Haq and Melaki, *An Analysis of Environmental Impact Studies of Installations for the Treatment and Disposal of Toxic and Dangerous Waste in the EU* (1996) [Joint Research Centre report].

Commission for Environmental Impact Assessment (the Netherlands), *Environmental Impact Assessment in the Netherlands: Experiences and Views by and to the Commission for EIA* (1996).

European Commission, *Report on the Implementation of Directive 85/337/EEC on the Assessment of the Effects of Certain Public and Private Projects on the Environment*, COM(93)28 final.

Gilpin, *Environmental Impact Assessment: Cutting Edge for the Twenty-First Century* (1995).

Glasson, Therivel and Chadwick, *Introduction to Environmental Impact Assessment*, 2nd ed. (1999).

Haigh, *Manual of EC Environmental Policy* (looseleaf), chapter 11.

Kunzlik, "Environmental Impact Assessment: the British Cases"(1995) 4(12) EELR pp.336-344.

Lambrechts, "Environmental Impact Assessment" in Winter (ed.) *European Environmental Law: a Comparative Perspective* (1996), chapter 5.

Lee (ed.) (1992) 7(3) Project Appraisal - Special Issue on Strategic Environmental Assessment.

Macrory, "Environmental Assessment and EC Law"(1992) 4(2) JEL pp.298-304.

Salter, European Environmental Law (looseleaf) vol.II, chapter 5.

Sheate, *Environmental Impact Assessment: Law and Policy - Making an Impact II* (1996).

Sheate, "The EIA Amendment Directive 97/11/EC - A Small Step Forward?"(1997) 6(8/9) EELR pp.235-243.

Ward, "The Right to Effective Remedy in EC Law and Environmental Protection: a Case Study of UK Judicial Decisions Concerning the Environmental Assessment Directive"(1993) 5(2) JEL pp.222-244.

Wood, *Environmental Impact Assessment: a Comparative Review* (1995).

Wood, Barker, Jones and Hughes, *Evaluation of the Performance of the EIA Process* (1996) vol. 1 (Main Report) and vol. 2 (Member States Reports).

Wood and Jones, *Monitoring Environmental Assessment and Planning* (1991).

Chapter 6

Environmental Protection and the Free Movement of Goods

Supporters of the principle of free trade and environmentalists are often perceived as pursuing different agendas and objectives. Free traders stress the clear economic benefits to be gained from increased competition in global markets,[1] while to environmentalists it is all too apparent that increased economic growth brought about by such liberalisation of trade can place severe pressures on the natural environment.[2] Polarisation of the debate is said to be exacerbated by a perceived clash of cultures between the two opposing camps, Jackson noting that environmentalists would wish to encourage the influence of non-governmental organisations and participation of the public in as open a policy-making process as is possible, whilst the free trade lobby "tend to operate more in secret or use non-public processes in the habit of traditional diplomacy and elites".[3] This clash of cultures has purportedly increased distrust and confusion between trade and environmental specialists.[4] However, to look at the relationship between trade and the environment solely as an antagonistic one beyond reconciliation would be misleading. The opening up of a market to an environmentally sensitive product previously unknown in that region may serve both to liberalise trade between nations and offer greater protection to the environment. Neither interest is compromised and trade and environment policies can be seen to be "mutually supportive", a vital element in the pursuit of sustainable development.[5]

More usually however a satisfactory balance needs to be struck between the promotion of unrestricted trade between States and the need to protect the environment. Let us imagine a State introduces a measure which bans the sale of a product in its territory unless the product can be recycled. This may well amount to a restriction of trade between it and a neighbouring State whose producers do not manufacture recyclable goods. The State introducing this trade related measure is likely to have done so in response to the perceived risks to the environment of

---

1   On the economic benefits of the common market and of the internal market see El-Agraa (ed.), *The European Union: History, Institutions, Economics and Policies* (1998) pp.14-15, and pp.158-162 respectively.

2   Trebilcock and Howse, *The Regulation of International Trade* (1999), p.395.

3   Jackson, "Greening the GATT: Trade Rules and Environmental Policy" in Cameron, Demaret and Geradin (eds.), *Trade and the Environment: The Search for Balance* (1994), Vol I, pp.39-40.

4   *Ibid*, p.40.

5   See Gothenburg European Council conclusions (15 and 16 June 2001), press release 200/01, p.5.

unrestricted trade in the market place. It has placed restrictions on trade between it and a trading partner for the good of the environment. The measure's impact may be beneficial environmentally by immediately affording greater protection to the domestic environment. In the longer term it may also encourage research and development into the use of environmentally friendly products by both domestic and foreign manufacturers. This would be of benefit not only to the domestic natural environment, but also to the state of the environment in other countries where such environmentally friendly products may be sold in the future. The measure would be justifiable in principle. On the other hand a trade related environmental measure may in fact be one principally designed to protect the domestic market from foreign competition; a "disguised restriction on trade" which purports to be environmental in nature but in fact is purely protectionist. If so, the measure is likely to be unjustifiable.

At the centre of the worldwide trading regime lies the multilateral 1994 Agreement Establishing the World Trade Organization (WTO Agreement)[6] which seeks to regulate the international movement of goods, persons, services and capital in such a way as to ensure the promotion of non-discriminatory trade practices and free competition. The WTO Agreement's preamble refers to the aim of "optimal use of the world's resources in accordance with the objective of sustainable development, seeking both to protect and preserve the environment and to enhance the means for doing so". Various panel decisions have attempted to strike a satisfactory balance between the principle of free trade and national measures seemingly introduced to afford environmental protection.[7]

At a regional level, the European Community has also addressed the issue. Securing the free movement of goods is an essential ingredient in the move to market integration. The free movement of goods is one of the EC Treaty's fundamental

---

[6]   WTO, *The Legal Texts: The Results of the Uruguay Round of Multilateral Trade Negotiations* (1999). The Final Act of the Uruguay Round *inter alia* includes the Agreement establishing the WTO [30 ILM 13 (1994)], the General Agreement on Trade and Tariffs 1994 [33 ILM 28 (1994)], and the Understanding on Rules and Procedures Governing the Settlement of Disputes [33 ILM 112 (1994)].

[7]   For example see WTO Panel Decision on US-Import Prohibition of Certain Shrimps and Shrimp Products 37 ILM (1998) 834 together with WTO Appellate Body Report on the same case 38 ILM (1999) 118, and the following General Agreement on Trade and Tariffs (GATT) Panel Decisions: US Restrictions on Import of Tuna ("Tuna-Dolphin I") 30 ILM (1991) 1594; US Restrictions on Imports of Tuna ("Tuna-Dolphin II") 33 ILM (1994) 839; and EC-Measures Affecting Asbestos and Asbestos-Containing Products WT/DS135/AB/R(2001). On the WTO and Community law see Scott, *EC Environmental Law* (1998), pp.93-105. See generally on the WTO/GATT regime, Petersmann (ed.), *International Trade Law and the GATT/WTO Dispute Settlement System* (1997), Kreuger (ed.), *The WTO as an International Organization* (1998), and Jackson, *The World Trading System* (1997). Also see the WTO website at http://www.wto.org.

principles.[8] This chapter will focus on the extent to which Member States retain competence to protect the environment where national environmental measures conflict with the free movement of goods. It will seek to introduce the reader to the case law and issues relating to non-fiscal measures which hinder market access, although it is accepted that the imposition of fiscal measures can also potentially restrict free movement.[9]

The Application of Articles 28-29 EC

In situations where the Community has not occupied the field, Member States are free to introduce their own national environmental legislation but only in so far as it is compatible with the relevant primary Community law including Articles 28-30 EC. Article 28 EC (ex Article 30 EC) seeks to eliminate physical and technical (i.e. non-fiscal) measures imposed by Member States which restrict the free movement of goods in the Community noting that

> *Quantitative restrictions on imports and all measures having equivalent effect shall be prohibited between Member States.*

Quantitative restrictions (QRs) have been defined by the ECJ as "measures which amount to a total or partial restraint of ... imports, exports or goods in transit".[10] Any measure which, for instance, imposes an absolute ban on the importation of a product, or a partial ban in the form of a limit on the volume or number of such

---

8   The issue as to what exactly constitutes "goods" was discussed in the *Walloon Waste* case (Case C-2/90 *Commission v Belgium* [1992] ECR I-4431). The Commission had brought an action against Belgium seeking a declaration that a decree passed by the Belgian region of Wallonia was incompatible with the schemes and principles established in existing EC legislation on the disposal of waste, and with primary Community law. However the Belgian Government contended that addressing the measure's compatibility with Article 28 EC as it related to non-hazardous non-recyclable waste was in fact inappropriate as waste which was neither recycled nor re-used had no intrinsic commercial value. Indeed, such waste only had a negative value in that the producer or importer would have to pay for its disposal. The Belgian Government argued that it could not therefore be regarded as a "good." In this regard, it relied on the judgment in *Commission v Italy* where the Court had indicated that within the meaning of goods "must be understood products which can be valued in money and which are capable, as such, of forming the subject of commercial transactions" (Case 7/68 [1968] ECR 423, at para.2). This Belgian contention was dismissed by both the Advocate General and the ECJ, the latter indicating that goods were "objects which are shipped across a frontier for the purposes of commercial transactions, whatever the nature of those transactions" (para.26 of the judgment). The ECJ therefore underlined that the term "goods" is to be broadly defined to include any object forming the subject of a commercial transaction whether or not it has a commercial value. For general comment on *Walloon Waste*, see Hancher and Sevenster (1993) 30 CMLRev 351, Von Wilmowsky (1993) 30 CMLRev 541, and Geradin (1993) 18 ELRev 144.

9   Article 25 EC prohibits the imposition of customs duties and charges having equivalent effect, whereas Article 90 EC prohibits discrimination in internal taxation against imported goods. For a discussion as to national fiscal measures and the free movement of goods see Ziegler, *Trade and Environmental Law in the European Community* (1996) pp.37-39 and pp.53-60, and Jans, *European Environmental Law* (2000) pp.224-232.

10   Case 2/73 *Geddo v Entenazionale Risi I* [1973] ECR 865 at para.7.

products, falls within the prohibition of Article 28 EC. Article 29 EC (ex Article 34) notes an identically worded provision relating to restrictions on exports thereby prohibiting national measures which discriminate against exports.[11]

Most of the ECJ's jurisprudence concerning Article 28 EC relates not so much to the imposition of QRs, but rather to the matter of "measures having equivalent effect to a quantitative restriction" (MEQRs). No definition of MEQRs is included in the Treaty, and it was left to the ECJ in *Procureur du Roi v Dassonville*[12] to define such measures as

> *[A]ll trading rules enacted by Member States which are capable of hindering, directly or indirectly, actually or potentially, intra-Community trade.*[13]

This "*Dassonville*" formula places emphasis not on the form or intent of the national measure in question, but on its effect. If the effect of a measure is to establish an obstacle to market access, it is *prima facie* prohibited under Article 28 EC. Importantly, it applies whether a measure discriminates between domestic and imported goods ("distinctly applicable"), or pertains to all products regardless of origin ("indistinctly applicable"). In *Rewe-Zentrale AG* v *Bundesmonopolverwaltung für Branntwein* (the "*Cassis*" case),[14] the ECJ underlined that the latter were also capable of falling within the Article 28 EC prohibition. German national law had stipulated that fruit liquers like "Cassis de Dijon" could not be marketed in Germany if they did not contain at least 25 per cent alcohol content. "Cassis de Dijon" was freely marketed in France, but only contained between 15-20 per cent of alcohol. A German court asked the ECJ whether the national rule was consistent with Article 28 EC (ex Article 30). The rule in question was indistinctly applicable in the sense it was an origin-neutral technical rule which applied to both imported and German goods. The *Cassis* judgment proceeded on the basis that, even in the absence of discrimination against imports, the German rule restricted access to the German market and was therefore incompatible with Article 28 EC (ex Article 30) unless it was necessary to protect a legitimate interest or "mandatory requirement".

The ECJ in *Cassis* provided an invaluable boost to the pursuit of market integration by adopting an approach which assumed equivalent basic health and safety standards throughout the Community in the absence of harmonisation. In effect, a Member State could not in principle deny market access to goods which were lawfully produced and marketed in another Member State on the grounds that the

---

[11] However, Article 29 EC has been interpreted differently by the ECJ in that non-discriminatory rules which apply equally to both exports and to goods intended for the domestic market do not fall within its prohibitory effect; see Case 15/79 *Groenveld BV v Produktschap voor Vee en Vlees* [1979] ECR 3409, para.7. See also *infra* n.88 and accompanying text.

[12] Case 8/74 [1974] ECR 837.

[13] Para.5 of the judgment.

[14] Case 120/78 [1979] ECR 649.

product failed to comply with its own national technical rules. However, it became apparent over time that the broad definition of MEQRs as outlined in *Dassonville* and *Cassis* had proved a catalyst for an over-abundance of national actions challenging a very wide range of national trade rules.[15] There was a clear need for guidance as to the precise scope of the prohibition on free movement of goods, and the opportunity to re-define and restrict the outer margins of the scope of Article 28 EC was taken by the ECJ in *Keck*. A French law prohibiting the resale of goods at a loss was judged to fall outside the scope of ex-Article 30 (Article 28 EC). The ECJ emphasised that

> *contrary to what has previously been decided, the application to products from other Member States of national provisions restricting or prohibiting certain selling arrangements is not such as to hinder directly or indirectly, actually or potentially, trade between Member States within the meaning of the Dassonville judgment, provided that those provisions apply to all affected traders operating within the national territory and provided that they affect in the same manner, in law and in fact, the marketing of domestic products and of those from other Member States.*[16]

The ECJ ruled that national marketing rules meeting these conditions did not prevent market access for imports, nor did they impede access more than they impeded access of domestic goods.[17] They therefore fell outside the scope of Article 28 EC.[18] All distinctly applicable measures continued to fall within the Article 28 EC prohibition. However, post-*Keck* in the absence of discrimination, national rules relating to *marketing circumstances* (such as Sunday trading rules and those regulating advertising) no longer fall within Article 28 EC as they apply an equal burden on all products which have already achieved market access. These measures only deny a trader an opportunity to sell a product,[19] and national authorities are

---

15   For an account as to the confusion caused by the question of whether Sunday-trading laws were compatible with ex-Article 30 EC (now Article 28), see Arnull, "What Shall We Do On Sunday?" (1991) 16 ELRev 112. See also Case 145/88 *Torfaen BC v B & Q* [1989] ECR 3851. It would seem that rules of this type now fall within the "selling arrangements" referred to in Keck.

16   Joined Cases C-267, C-268/91 *Keck* [1993] ECR I-6097, para.16.

17   *Ibid*, para 17.

18   On the potential implications of *Keck* in an environmental context, see Temmink, "From Danish Bottles to Danish Bees: The Dynamics of Free Movement of Goods and Environmental Protection - a Case Law Analysis" 1 *Yearbook of European Environmental Law* (2000), pp.73-77. On the general ramifications of Keck, see Chalmers, "Repackaging the Internal Market - the Ramifications of the *Keck* Judgment" (1994) 19 EL Rev 385, Reich, "The November Revolution of the European Court of Justice: *Keck, Meng and Audi* revisited" (1994) 31 CMLRev 459, Weatherill, "Some Thoughts on How to Clarify the Clarification" (1996) 33 CMLRev 885, and Barnard, "Fitting the Remaining Pieces into the Goods and Persons Jigsaw?" (2001) 26 ELRev 35.

19   See Arnull, Dashwood, Ross and Wyatt, *Wyatt and Dashwood's European Union Law* (2000) p.332.

exclusively competent to regulate such issues.[20] On the other hand, indistinctly applicable national rules establishing *product requirements* (such as regulations determining product form, size, content, presentation, packaging and labelling) do fall within Article 28 EC.[21]

Clearly any product standard introduced for environmental reasons still falls within the Article 28 EC prohibition, as does any ban on imports introduced for the same reasons.[22] In the *Danish Bees* case,[23] for example, the Danish Government had argued that national law prohibiting the keeping of certain bee species on the Danish island of Laesø had to be regarded as a selling arrangement within the meaning of the *Keck* judgment. This argument was refuted by the Court as the national law at issue concerned the "intrinsic characteristics of the bees"[24] and did not therefore amount to a selling arrangement. The national rules were characterised as pertaining to the product in question, and were not to be regarded as merely affecting marketing circumstances. However, post-*Keck* a national ban on the television advertising of a product which has a particularly detrimental environmental impact might not now fall within the Article 28 EC prohibition, but instead be regarded as a selling arrangement as long as it did not affect the marketing of imported goods differently from that of the equivalent domestic product.[25] An indistinctly applicable restriction on where certain environmentally hazardous goods may be sold, and by whom, is also likely to fall outside the scope of Article 28 EC.[26]

Although now limited to a certain extent by the ECJ in *Keck*, the "*Dassonville*" formula has ensured that the scope of the Article 28 EC prohibition is broad in nature. Consequently, a great number of national rules which restricted or potentially restricted market integration have been eliminated on the grounds that

---

[20] For example, see Case C-401 and C-402/92 *Tankstation 't Heukste vof and J.B.E Boermans* [1994] ECR I-2199 (in which Article 28 EC was judged not to apply to Dutch rules concerning the compulsory closing of shops), and Case C-412/93 *Leclerc-Siplec* v *TF1 Publicite SA and M6 Publicite SA* [1995] ECR I-179 (in which the ECJ concluded that Article 28 EC did not apply to French rules prohibiting the broadcasting of adverts concerning the distribution of fuel).

[21] See for instance, Case C-470/93 *Verein gegen Unwesen in Handel und Gewerbe Koln* v *Mars GmbH* [1995] ECR I-1923.

[22] See Jans, *supra* n.9, p.236.

[23] Case C-67/97 *Criminal Proceedings against Ditlev Bluhme* [1998] ECR I-8033. For comment see Denys (1999) 8 EELR 82.

[24] Para.21 of the judgment.

[25] Jans, *supra* n.9, p.236. "Selling arrangements" have certainly been held by the Court to include advertising restrictions; see, for example, Case C-292/92 *Hünermund* v *Landesapothekerkammer Baden-Württemberg* [1993] ECR I-6787. Note however that the rule in question might indeed relate to selling arrangements but still be within Article 28 EC if the measure has a greater impact on the marketing of products from other Member States than on national products; see Cases C-34-36/95 *Konsumentombudsmannen* v *De Agostini (Svenska) Forlag AB and TV-Shop i Sverige AB* [1997] ECR I-3843.

[26] See C-319/92 *Commission* v *Hellenic Republic* [1995] ECR I-1621 in which a non-discriminatory law regulating the outlets which may sell baby milk powder was held to fall outside Article 28 EC.

they constituted MEQRs.[27] Even where a case is confined on its specific facts to a single Member State and accordingly there appears to be no cross-border connection, the ruling in *Pistre* case has underlined that the prohibition in Article 28 EC is still applicable if the national measure in question is at least capable of being applied to imported products.[28] Moreover, even a restriction on a small percentage of imports into a Member State will fall within the prohibitory effect of Article 28 EC. For example, in *Danish Bees*[29] a national measure banning the keeping of bees only applied to an island covering just 0.3 per cent of Danish territory. Nonetheless, the measure fell within the prohibition in Article 28 EC.

In addition, a Member State fails to fulfil its obligations under Article 28 EC not only where it itself introduces national rules which impact on trade, but also where it fails to adopt proportionate and necessary measures to prevent private individuals from hindering and blocking the free movement of goods. In *Commission v France* (*"Spanish Strawberries"* case),[30] French farmers had systematically impeded the free movement of fruit and vegetables (such as Spanish strawberries and Belgian tomatoes) in protest against the importation of agricultural products originating in other Member States. A variety of violent acts committed in France, such as the interception and destruction of lorries carrying fruit and vegetable products, had created obstacles to intra-Community trade. Serious incidents had taken place over a ten-year period. On certain occasions the French police were conspicuous by their absence even though they had been warned of the likelihood of demonstrations. Some acts of vandalism had been filmed but only a very small number of perpetrators had been successfully identified and prosecuted.

Although France enjoyed a margin of discretion in determining the appropriateness of measures to eliminate such obstacles, the measures enacted by the French Government had been "manifestly inadequate" to secure free trade in agricultural products.[31] The ECJ held that Article 28 EC read in conjunction with Article 10 EC (which provides that Member States must take all appropriate measures to ensure fulfilment of Community law obligations) required that France take the necessary measures to ensure that the fundamental freedom of the free movement of goods was respected in its territory.[32] Denys correctly notes that the *Spanish Strawberries* case

---

[27] Measures which have been deemed by the ECJ to be MEQRs include rules introduced in Ireland which prohibited the import and sale of "Irish" souvenirs manufactured abroad unless such objects were marked with an indication that they were manufactured outside Ireland (Case 113/80 *Commission v Ireland* [1981] ECR 1625), the German restriction on the use of a particular product designation to domestic products despite the fact that such products were not unique and were capable of being produced outside Germany (Case 12/74 *Commission v Germany* [1975] ECR 181), and the "Buy Irish" campaign which appealed to nationalistic feelings in encouraging the purchase of domestic products rather than imported goods (Case 249/81 *Commission v Ireland* [1982] ECR 4005).

[28] Case C-321-324/94 *Criminal Proceedings against Jacques Pistre at al* [1997] ECR I-2343.

[29] Case C-67/97 *supra* n.23.

[30] Case C-265/95 [1997] ECR I-6959. See comment by Jarvis (1998) 35 CMLRev 1371, and by Denys (1998) 7(6) EELR 176.

[31] *Ibid*, para.52.

[32] *Ibid*, para.32.

is likely to have implications of an environmental nature. For example, bearing in mind that all types of waste are to be regarded as "goods",[33] the adequacy of a Member State's response to a blockade by private individuals which impedes the free movement of hazardous waste may well be subject to review.[34]

Residual Competence of Member States to Restrict the Free Movement of Goods

EC market integration allows producers to trade throughout the Community without the fear of access to a particular Member State's market being blocked by a national measure. However it is recognised that it remains appropriate for a Member State to erect barriers to trade and hence hinder the move to market integration when the effects of free trade impact on certain specific national interests. The restrictive effect on free trade of measures introduced by Member States to safeguard such national interests is deemed acceptable due to the particular importance of the interest requiring protection. These interests are found in Article 30 EC, and in the ECJ's application of the "rule of reason".

Article 30 EC

Article 30 EC (ex Article 36 EC) can be relied upon to justify restrictions on the free movement of goods on certain limited grounds constituting fundamental requirements recognised by EC Law:

> *The provisions of Article 28 and 29 shall not preclude prohibitions or restrictions on imports, exports or goods in transit justified on grounds of public morality, public policy or public security; the protection of health and life of humans, animals or plants; the protection of national treasures possessing artistic, historic or archaeological value; or the protection of industrial and commercial property. Such prohibitions or restrictions shall not, however, constitute a means of arbitrary discrimination or a disguised restriction on trade between Member States.*

The ECJ has traditionally interpreted the grounds of justification in Article 30 EC restrictively. The free movement of goods is a fundamental principle of the Community and, as such, justifications to measures that restrict free trade are limited to those grounds specifically mentioned in Article 30 EC. The ECJ has consistently refused to extend such heads of justification.[35]

---

[33] See discussion *supra* n.8.

[34] Denys, *supra* n.23, p.180.

[35] See Case 113/80 *supra* n.27 in which the Court of Justice refused to accept the Irish Government's argument that consumer protection should be regarded as a justification for discriminatory trade restrictions under Article 30 EC.

Environmental protection is certainly not a ground for justification under Article 30 EC. However, it may be possible to justify a national measure which seeks directly to protect "*health and life of humans, animals or plants*" and which may therefore have a positive impact on the environment. In *Nijman*, for instance, a Dutch ban on a certain type of pesticide was held by the ECJ to be justified under Article 30 EC as the pesticide in question had a particularly harmful effect on humans and animals.[36] In the *Toolex*[37] case a Swedish ban on the use of trichloroethylene for industrial purposes was deemed justified on grounds of the protection of health of humans.[38] Additionally, in the *Danish Bees* case a Danish measure prohibiting the introduction and keeping of bees other than native brown bees on the Danish island of Laesø was justified as it aimed to protect the health and life of indigenous brown bees by ensuring that the native population would not gradually disappear through interbreeding.[39]

The Member State seeking to justify a measure which constitutes an obstacle to market access bears the burden of proving that the interest referred to in Article 30 EC actually is under threat from the importation of goods from another Member State. The Community's environmental policy has however endorsed the precautionary principle and there is a compelling argument that the adoption of a precautionary approach would allow a Member State to satisfy this burden of proof by showing that the interest requiring protection was highly likely to be threatened in this way; conclusive scientific proof would not be required.[40] Indeed such an approach could be said to be broadly in line with the manner in which the ECJ has approached issues where there is a degree of scientific uncertainty. For example, in *Officier van Justitie* v *Koninklijke Kassfabriek Eyssen BV*[41] a cheese producer questioned the legitimacy of a Dutch ban on the use of nisin as a preservative in processed cheese intended for the domestic market. Nisin is an antibiotic which acts to preserve cheese by slowing down the process of deterioration. The Dutch prohibition was clearly a MEQR but could it be justified to protect the health of humans? In other Member States the addition of the preservative in cheese was either unregulated or authorised without restriction subject to maximum concentration levels. Respected research had been carried out by bodies such as the Food and Agriculture Organization as to the potential harm caused by the antibiotic,

---

[36] Case 125/88 *Criminal Proceedings against Nijman* [1989] ECR 3533. See also Case C-400/96 *Criminal Proceedings against Jean Harpegnies* [1998] ECR I-5121 in which a Belgian ban on a biocidal product being placed on the market was held to be capable of justification to protect human health and life.

[37] Case C-473/98 *Kemikalieinspektionen* v *Toolex Alpha AB* [2000] ECR I-5681. See comment by Heyvaert (2001) 13(3) JEL 392.

[38] The Court in *Toolex* makes reference to the fact that "the health and life of humans rank foremost among the property or interests protected by [ex] Article 36"; para.38 of the judgment.

[39] Case C-67/97 *supra* n.23.

[40] See Jans, *supra* n.9, p.242. Article 174(2) notes Community policy on the environment shall *inter alia* "be based on the precautionary principle".

[41] Case 53/80 [1981] ECR 409.

but no absolute conclusions had been drawn. There was clearly legitimate doubt on the issue and no unanimous scientific consensus. In view of the uncertainty as to whether nisin was harmful, the Court concluded that a Member State should be allowed to protect the health of its public by prohibiting the substance even though other countries were not concerned about the health risks involved.

A measure is only capable of justification where it directly affects or immediately threatens the health or life of humans, animals or plants. However, the ECJ generously applied these grounds in the *Danish Bees* case. The introduction of non-native bees would not necessarily have endangered the life of any of the existing native bees, but would have led to the native strain's gradual disappearance over a longer period of time. The national measures in question were nonetheless justifiable in the ECJ's opinion as

> *measures to preserve an indigenous animal population with distinct characteristics contribute to the maintenance of biodiversity by ensuring the survival of the population concerned. By doing so, they are aiming at protecting the life of those animals and are capable of being justified under [Article 30] of the Treaty.*[42]

This judgment adopted a surprisingly broad definition to the protection of "*health and life of humans, animals or plants*" by allowing a national measure intended to protect a distinct strain of animal to be justified if faced with a threat of extinction which is "more or less imminent, or *even in the absence of such risk, on account of a scientific or other interest in preserving the pure population at the location concerned*".[43] After *Danish Bees* it might be argued that a national protection measure which simply intends to conserve biodiversity may be justified under Community law even though it seeks to offer protection where there is not necessarily an immediate direct danger to the health and life of animals.[44] However, even bearing in mind this generous application of Article 30 EC, it is very important to stress that action to protect the health and life of humans, animals or plants is certainly not as broad a justification for national action as the need to protect the environment. It is difficult to imagine that the introduction of many national measures of an environmental nature, such as an eco-labelling strategy or a requirement that goods should meet certain recycling criteria, are capable of justification under Article 30 EC as they would not be regarded as necessary to

---

[42] Case C-67/97 *supra* n.23.

[43] *Ibid*, para.34 (emphasis added).

[44] Denys, *supra* n.23, p.88. It is of interest to note that the fact that the Danish measure prohibited the keeping and importation of bees into only a part of its territory did not prevent the rule being regarded as a measure having equivalent effect requiring justification; non-native bees were excluded from the Danish island of Laesø whether they came from abroad or from other parts of Denmark. A measure can still be regarded as a measure of equivalent effect even where it negatively impacts upon certain domestic products as well as imported goods (see para.20 of the judgment and Joined Cases C-1/90 and C-176/90 *Aragonesa de Publicidad v Departamento de Sanidad* [1991] ECR I-4151, para.24).

protect health and life of humans, animals or plants from a genuine or legitimate threat.[45]

Mandatory Requirements and the "Rule of Reason"

The effect of the ECJ's traditionally strict interpretation of the exhaustive justifications in Article 30 EC has been limited by the judgment in *Cassis*. Under the *Cassis de Dijon* formula, restrictions on the importation of goods for failure to comply with national technical rules will be deemed necessary and appropriate in exceptional circumstances where there is no other way of protecting a "mandatory requirement" recognised by the ECJ:

> *Obstacles to movement within the Community resulting from disparities between the national laws relating to the marketing of the products in question must be accepted in so far as those provisions may be recognized as being necessary in order to satisfy mandatory requirements relating in particular to the effectiveness of fiscal supervision, the protection of public health, the fairness of commercial transactions and the defence of the consumer.[46]*

The adoption of the *Cassis de Dijon* formula or "rule of reason" by the Court of Justice should be seen as an acknowledgement that the restrictive impact of Article 28 EC on Member States' domestic competence had been very considerable indeed. The scope of Article 28 EC required softening to a certain degree. If necessary to satisfy a mandatory requirement, a national measure which restricts free trade would now fall outside the scope of Article 28 EC.

However, according to the traditional approach of the ECJ, the rule of reason developed in *Cassis* only applies in circumstances where the measure in question is indistinctly applicable, in that no distinction is made in the measure's application between imported and domestic goods.[47] Where free trade has been restricted, only in the absence of discrimination could certain justifications not mentioned in Article 30 EC be entertained. Distinctly applicable measures are regarded as measures which are far more likely to be part of a protectionist national agenda and are therefore not justifiable under the rule of reason. If a measure is "distinctly applicable" in the sense that it only applies to imports, the ECJ's traditional approach has been that the rule of reason will not apply and the exhaustive heads of justification in Article 30 EC remain the only manner in which the national measure can be justified. We will return to this issue in later discussion, but suffice to say at

---

45   Kramer, *Focus on European Environmental Law* (1997) pp.184-185.
46   Case 120/78 *supra* n.14, para.8 of the judgment.
47   See Weatherill and Beaumont, *EU Law* (1999), p.576, and pp.578-580 for more general discussion.

this stage that the ECJ has in recent years shown signs that it is perhaps moving away from its traditional approach towards an acceptance that distinctly applicable measures can indeed be justified under one of the mandatory requirements.

In the *Cassis* judgment the ECJ had indicated that the mandatory requirements mentioned were by no means exhaustive although it remained unclear at this stage whether the need to protect the environment would be acknowledged at a later date as an addition to the list. In the case of *Procureur de la République* v *Association de Défence des Brûleurs de l'Huile Usagées* (*"Waste Oils"* case)[48] a request for a preliminary ruling was made by a French Court on the interpretation and validity of Directive 75/439 on the disposal of waste oils.[49] The judgment amounted to an acknowledgement that the need to protect the environment can potentially limit the impact of Article 28 EC.[50] The French national court asked for a preliminary ruling as to whether the directive was in conformity with the principles of freedom of trade, free movement of goods and freedom of competition. The directive imposed an obligation on Member States to ensure the safe collection and disposal of waste oils, preferably by recycling. To this end, the measure provided that, in circumstances where the directive's aims could not otherwise be achieved, a Member State could establish zones within its territory within which one or more undertakings would carry out the collection and/or disposal of waste oils. The directive therefore clearly placed limits on free trade, particularly bearing in mind that any such undertaking would have required a permit to be granted to it prior to disposing of waste oil.

The request for a preliminary ruling was an issue addressing the compatibility of an existing piece of harmonising Community legislation with the general principle of free trade, rather than the applicability of Article 28 EC to a unilateral national measure introduced in the absence of such legislation. Nevertheless the case is of general importance as the judgment stated that

the principle of freedom of trade is not to be viewed in absolute terms but is subject to certain limits justified by the objectives of general interest pursued by the Community provided that the rights in question are not substantively impaired.[51]

Importantly the ECJ further indicated that

[t]here is no reason to conclude that the directive has exceeded those limits. The directive must be seen in the perspective of environmental protection, which is one of the Community's essential objectives. It is evident ... that any legislation dealing with the disposal of waste oils must be designed to protect the

---

[48] Case 240/83 [1985] ECR 531.

[49] Council Directive 75/439/EEC on the Disposal of Waste Oils, OJ 1975 L 194/23.

[50] See Opinion of Advocate General Sir Gordon Slynn in Case 302/86 *Commission* v *Denmark* ("Danish Bottles") [1988] ECR 4607, at 4622.

[51] Para.12 of the judgment.

environment from harmful effects caused by the discharge, deposit or treatment of such products.[52]

The measures were deemed acceptable as they were not discriminatory, nor disproportionate in the sense that they did not go "beyond the inevitable restrictions which are justified by the pursuit of the objective of environmental protection, which is in the general interest".[53] The judgment underlined the ECJ's previous jurisprudence that even a fundamental Community right, such as freedom of trade, could be limited by Community legislation, but only if measures prescribed by such legislation were justified by the objectives of general interest pursued by the Community. It is of great significance to note that the judgment in this case acknowledged that environmental protection is one of those "essential objectives" of the Community (even though at the time of the judgment the Treaty made no specific reference to the need for environmental protection).[54]

The landmark case of *Commission* v *Denmark* (*"Danish Bottles"*)[55] provided the ECJ with an opportunity to deliberate on a national environmental measure seemingly in conflict with the provisions of Article 28 EC. The ECJ's ruling in *Danish Bottles* expressly confirmed for the first time that the mandatory requirements referred to in the *Cassis de Dijon* case did include matters relating to environmental protection. The ECJ's judgment took into account its ruling in the *Waste Oils* case which had noted that environmental protection was one of the Community's essential objectives. The ECJ was also influenced by the Single European Act which had established an "Environmental Title" and underlined the need to preserve, protect and improve the quality of the environment. Bearing in mind the *Waste Oils* case and the impact of the Single European Act, the ECJ came to the conclusion that environmental protection must be regarded as a "mandatory requirement" within the *Cassis de Dijon* formula.[56] In effect, a national measure introduced to enhance environmental protection was capable of legitimately restricting the free movement of goods in the absence of common Community rules. This acknowledgment crucially ensures the possibility of justifying more wide-ranging protection for the environment under the *Cassis* formula than under Article

---

[52] Para.13 of the judgment.

[53] Para.15 of the judgment.

[54] See also Kramer, *European Environmental Law Casebook* (1993), pp.13-15.

[55] Case 302/86 *supra* n.50.

[56] Para.9 of the judgment. Several years prior to this judgment the Commission had recognised that environmental protection was a mandatory requirement; see "Communication from the Commission concerning the judgment given by the Court of Justice on 20 February 1979 in Case 120/78 ('Cassis de Dijon')" OJ 1980 C256/2. Advocate General Sir Gordon Slynn in his opinion delivered on 24 May 1988 also expressed the view that "national measures taken for the protection of the environment are capable of constituting 'mandatory requirements' recognised by the judgment in 'Cassis de Dijon' as limiting the application of [ex] Article 28 of the Treaty in the absence of Community rules", [1988] ECR at p.4622. For a more recent recognition that restrictions on the free movement of goods can be justified by the need to protect the environment, see Case C-314/98 *Snellers Auto's BV* v *Algemeen Directeur van de Dienst Wegverkeer* [2000] I-8633 at para.55 (on the legitimacy of Dutch rules defining criteria for the determination of the date on which a vehicle was first authorised for use on the public highway).

30 EC. However, as previously mentioned, traditionally the national measure would have to apply to domestic and imported products alike (be indistinctly applicable).

The Striking of a Balance: the Application of the "Proportionality" Principle

Even if the ECJ is satisfied that a national measure which restricts trade does so in order to protect the health or life of humans, animals, or plants, or to protect a mandatory requirement, that measure must also satisfy the "proportionality" principle. The national measure in question may only impose a restriction on imports which is suitable for the attainment of the desired objective, proportionate to the risk posed, and the least restrictive of trade necessary to attain the legitimate aim. In *Commission* v *Germany*,[57] for instance, the ECJ concluded that a national measure introduced to protect the life of native crayfish was capable of falling within the justification offered by Article 30 EC. But the precise nature of the measure, a total ban on the import of live crayfish, went beyond that which was necessary to fulfil the objective of the measure. The German Government had argued that the import prohibition was required to protect native crayfish from disease, but the Court took the view that other measures could also have afforded protection in a manner less restrictive on free trade (such as the submitting of imported crayfish consignments to health checks). On the other hand, in *Danish Bees* the setting up of a protection area within which the keeping of bees other than Laesø brown bees was banned did satisfy the proportionality test. The conservation of biodiversity through special protection areas had been endorsed under both international and Community law and, bearing in mind that the disappearance of the native Laesø brown bee was a real possibility without effective action, the Danish action was deemed to be "an appropriate measure in relation to the aim pursued".[58]

It can certainly be argued that, in applying the proportionality principle, the Court is placed in a position in which it determines the legitimate level of environmental protection to be afforded.[59] The *Danish Bottles* case provides a good example. National rules applicable to the marketing of beer and soft drinks placed an obligation on manufacturers and importers to set up a deposit-and-return scheme for empty containers. In this way bottles could be refilled and used again. In assessing whether these rules were "necessary" to achieve their environmental objectives, the ECJ concluded that the establishing of the deposit-and-return scheme for empty containers was

---

[57] Case C-131/93 [1994] ECR I-3303.

[58] Case C-67/97 *supra* n.23, para.37.

[59] Maduro has underlined the responsibility placed on the Court in determining whether a measure is proportionate in the following terms: *"To have the Court balance the costs and benefits of a certain provision under a test of proportionality means, to a great extent, making it responsible for defining the appropriate regulatory policy"*; "Reforming the Market or the State? Article 30 and the European Constitution: Economic Freedom and Political Rights" (1997) 3 ELJ 55, at p.60.

an indispensable element of a system intended to ensure the re-use of containers and therefore appears necessary to achieve the aims pursued by the contested rules. That being so, the restrictions which it imposes on the free movement of goods cannot be regarded as disproportionate.[60]

The ECJ had sympathised with the Danish Government's efforts to protect the environment. The deposit-and-return scheme was necessary to satisfy the mandatory requirement of environmental protection and was deemed to be acceptable.

However, the Danish rules also required that the vast majority of producers and importers had to use containers approved by the Danish Government. There were good environmental reasons for this. Under the approved containers scheme, a bottle could be returned to any retailer of beverages rather than just to the retailer who sold the drink. The Court acknowledged that it therefore ensured a maximum rate of re-use and "a very considerable degree of protection to the environment".[61] The marketing of beer and soft drinks in containers which had not received approval was very limited as a volume restriction on the marketing of such containers by a producer in any given year had been imposed. Under the non-approved container scheme, a deposit-and-return scheme still applied but bottles could only be returned to the retailer who sold the drink. The scheme was therefore capable of affording environmental protection albeit to a lesser degree.

Approval of more than approximately thirty types of container under the approved containers scheme was not envisaged "since the retailers taking part in the system would not be prepared to accept too many types of bottles owing to the higher handling costs and the need for more storage space".[62] It was therefore possible that a container could be denied approval even though it was capable of being re-used. If approval was not forthcoming, a foreign producer would have had to either make or buy containers of a variety that had been approved. In this respect, the Court took the view that the Danish Government had introduced an unjustifiable restriction on the free movement of goods by restricting the volume of a product which could be marketed each year in non-approved containers. This aspect of the national measure was disproportionate as the objective of affording protection to the environment could have been achieved in a manner less restrictive to the free movement of goods. The system for approved containers clearly offered a higher degree of protection to the environment than the non-approved scheme. However, the non-approved containers system did involve a "deposit-and-return" and was therefore also capable

---

[60]   Case 302/86 *supra* n.50, para.13.
[61]   Para.20 of the judgment.
[62]   Para.15 of the judgment.

of protecting the environment to a certain extent. Although the ECJ did not specifically refer to Advocate General Slynn's view that the degree of protection afforded to the environment "must be at a reasonable level",[63] it is hard to disagree with the argument that the Court endorsed such an approach.[64] Such a "reasonable" level of protection certainly did not equate to the highest level of protection possible.

It is certainly difficult to second-guess the Court's deliberations as to proportionality with accuracy. For example, in *Commission v Germany*[65] the ban on the import of live crayfish failed the proportionality test even though it was subject to certain discretionary derogations. This prompted one commentator to note correctly that

> *[i]t seems fair to say that a presumption exists against the proportionality of total bans. Rather than making importation impossible subject to discretionary derogations, it seems that where a Member State proceeds on the basis of freedom of importation subject to derogations, it has better chances of passing the obstacle of Articles [28-30].*[66]

However, clearly a total ban can be a proportionate response in certain circumstances as in *Danish Bees*, and the *Safety Hi-Tech* case[67] in which a Community prohibition on the use and marketing of HCFCs was deemed to be an appropriate response. In addition, the Swedish ban on the use of trichloroethylene for industrial purposes in the *Toolex* case[68] was deemed justified on grounds of the protection of health of humans. The Court evidently exercises a considerable degree of discretion in the application of the proportionality test, Heyvaert commenting that "it remains exceedingly difficult to pin down, let alone predict, what exactly makes national interventions necessary and proportional".[69] Indeed, the ECJ in the *Walloon Waste* case avoided the issue of proportionality in its ruling completely.

The Mandatory Requirements and Distinctly Applicable Measures

The ECJ has traditionally been at pains to underline that distinctly applicable measures cannot be justified under the *Cassis* rule of reason.[70] A distinctly applicable measure can only be justified under one of the grounds in Article 30 EC.

---

63   *Supra* n.50, at p.4626.

64   Geradin, "Balancing Free Trade and Environmental Protection - the Interplay Between the European Court of Justice and the Community Legislator" in Cameron, Demaret and Geradin, *supra* n.3, p.210.

65   Case C-131/93 *supra* n.57.

66   Somsen's case-note comment in (1995) 4(7) EELR 214 at p.217.

67   Case C-284/95 *Safety Hi-Tech Srl v S. & T. Srl* [1998] ECR I-4301. The ban was introduced to protect the ozone layer under Regulation 3093/94 (OJ 1994 L333/1).

68   Case C-473/98 *supra* n.37.

69   See Heyvaert's comment on the *Toolex* case; 13(3) JEL (2001) 392 at p.402.

70   Oliver has however argued that "it would be both simpler and more logical to treat the mandatory requirements as additions to the heads of justification in Article 30"; "Some Further Reflections on the Scope of Articles 28-30 EC" (1999) 36 CMLRev 783, pp.799-804., p.804.

Environmental protection cannot therefore be taken into account when assessing the legality of a distinctly applicable national measure. However, the *Walloon Waste* case might be regarded as an exception to this approach. The national decree in question effectively banned the import of waste into the Walloon region from the Member States and other regions of Belgium.[71] In this context it is important to appreciate that the Belgian measure was a genuinely environmental one adopted to prevent the importation into Wallonia of waste from areas which had more stringent regulatory controls than Wallonia. The ECJ accepted the Belgian Government's argument that the measure was undoubtedly necessary to protect the environment noting that

> *in view of the abnormal large-scale inflow of waste from other regions for tipping in Wallonia, there was a real danger to the environment, having regard to the limited capacity of that region.*[72]

The ECJ concluded that the Walloon policy of dealing only with its own waste was deemed necessary "by imperative requirements of environmental protection".[73] In essence, by treating the Walloon decree as an indistinctly applicable measure capable of justification under the rule of reason, the restriction on inter-state trade was deemed necessary to satisfy the mandatory requirement of the protection of the environment. However, this decision is a surprising and controversial one. Both the Commission and the Advocate General had argued that the decree was a distinctly applicable measure as it was origin-specific. This must be correct. Quite simply, the measure did not apply to both domestic and imported waste products in a like manner. As such, the decree could surely only be justified by reference to one of the headings in Article 30 EC? The ECJ took a different view, declaring that the measure was indistinctly applicable and therefore necessary to satisfy a mandatory requirement under the rule of reason.[74] The judgment notes that

> *Imperative requirements can indeed be taken into account only in the case of measures which apply without distinction to both domestic and imported products. However, in assessing whether or not the barrier in question is*

---

[71]   There were a limited number of exceptions. Article 1 of the decree, for example, banned the "storage, tipping or dumping of foreign waste" from outside of Wallonia "except in depots annexed to an installation for the destruction, neutralisation and disposal of toxic waste". Article 2 provided that the Walloon Regional Executive was empowered to grant derogations from the provisions of Article 1 for a limited time period and only when justified "by reference to serious and exceptional circumstances". Article 3 banned storage, tipping or dumping of waste from Belgium's other regions, Flanders and Brussels, unless an agreement had otherwise been made with such regions.

[72]   Para.31 of the judgment.

[73]   Para.32 of the judgment.

[74]   This was despite ruling in a previous case that the restrictive effect of a measure which favoured goods from a particular region of a Member State rendered the measure distinctly applicable and incapable of such justification; Case C-21/88 *Du Pont de Nemours Italiana SpA v Unita sanitaria locale No. 2 di Carrara* [1990] ECR I 889 (paras. 11-14 of the judgment); see Hancher and Sevenster, "Case Note on Case C-2/90 *Commission v Belgium*" (1993) 30 CMLRev 351.

discriminatory, account must be taken of the particular nature of waste. The principle that environmental damage should as a matter of priority be remedied at source ... entails that it is for each region, municipality or other local authority to take appropriate steps to ensure that its own waste is collected, treated and disposed of; it must accordingly be disposed of as close as possible to the place where it is produced, in order to limit as far as possible the transport of waste".[75]

The "rectification at source" principle therefore discouraged the transport of waste. Authorities had the responsibility to dispose of waste locally. Taking this into account as well as the differences in nature of waste produced in different areas, the ECJ concluded that the Belgian decree could not be termed as discriminatory.[76] The measure was therefore necessary to satisfy a mandatory requirement under the rule of reason established in *Cassis de Dijon*.

It is important to note that the ECJ was at pains to stress that there was still a distinction to be made between distinctly applicable measures which can only be justified under the narrowly interpreted provisions of Article 30 EC, and indistinctly applicable measures to which the rule of reason could be applied. However, by controversially classifying the measure as indistinctly applicable, the ECJ was able to apply the rule of reason. The Court's reasoning is not very convincing. It failed, for example, to elaborate on the nature of the differences in waste produced in different areas, and why those differences should impact on the issue as to whether the measure was or was not discriminatory.[77] In addition, it is doubtful if the national measure was compatible with the proportionality principle. The decree had introduced a ban on imports of waste into Wallonia. Surely there was an "alternative means" to such a blanket ban which would also have afforded protection to the environment but which would have been less restrictive on trade?[78] The judgment avoided all discussion as to proportionality.

The ECJ in *Walloon Waste* had no wish to strike down the Wallonian decree, particularly bearing in mind the growing political importance and influence of the Community's environmental policy. The ECJ had therefore engaged in a process which can be criticised because of its unconvincing nature, but which was calculated

---

[75] Para.34 of the judgment.

[76] Para.36 of the judgment.

[77] The ECJ had also noted that the principle of rectification at source "is consistent with the principle of *self-sufficiency* and *proximity*" set out in the Basel Convention on the control of Transboundary Movements of Hazardous Wastes and their Disposal (see paragraph 36 of the judgment). But Hancher and Sevenster question the relevance of the Basel Convention to the issue bearing in mind that that treaty applies only to the regulation of hazardous waste; *supra* n.74, at p.363. Usher also questions its applicability in a matter which concerns trade between Member States rather than trade between the Community and non-EC countries; Usher "Trade-Related Environmental Measures in the External Relations of the EC", in Cameron, Demaret and Geradin, *supra* n.3, pp.274-275. The EC became a party to the Basel Convention on 8 May 1994 following deposit of ratification.

[78] See Geradin, *supra* n.3, p.213.

to produce the desired result.[79] The ECJ held that the measure as it related to non-hazardous materials was justifiable for environmental reasons and simply avoided the need to expand the application of the rule of reason to distinctly applicable measures by declaring the Walloon decree to be non-discriminatory. To have expanded the applicability of the rule of reason to distinctly applicable measures would have greatly encouraged efforts in the future to justify national measures adopted not so much to satisfy mandatory requirements, but rather for protectionist reasons. In simply sidestepping the matter by declaring the measure to be an indistinctly applicable one, the national measure remained in place and the ECJ underlined its strict application of the rule of reason to non-discriminatory measures only. The ECJ's decision was a practical one. For policy reasons a national measure introduced for admirable environmental reasons was deemed to be justified.[80] However, the ECJ had undermined the coherence of its approach in this area. The Walloon decree was clearly discriminatory despite the ECJ's efforts to convince otherwise.

More recently, rulings such as *De Agostini*[81] and *Decker*[82] have fuelled speculation that the ECJ might be prepared to justify a distinctly applicable measure under the rule of reason without the need for the type of convoluted argument evidenced in *Walloon Waste* in relation to the nature of a national measure's application. In a purely environmental context, certain cases might also be interpreted as indicating that the Court is less concerned to determine issues in strict accordance with established *Cassis* jurisprudence, that the need for environmental protection should only be taken into account in the case of indistinctly applicable measures under the rule of reason. For instance, the German legislation in question in *Aher-Waggon* required that aircraft previously registered in another Member State had to comply with stricter national noise regulations than those imposed by relevant Community legislation.[83] By contrast, those aircraft registered in Germany prior to the implementation of Community law retained their German registration even though they did not now meet the requirements of German law. The surprising aspect of the judgment is that the ECJ showed no inclination in its ruling to classify the national measure in question as either distinctly or indistinctly applicable before recognising that it "may be justified by considerations of public health *and environmental*

---

[79]   Weatherill and Beaumont, *supra* n.47, p.591 where this process is described as "reasoning in reverse".

[80]   See generally Gormley, "Free Movement of Goods and the Environment" in Holder (ed.), *The Impact of EC Environmental Law in the UK* (1997) at pp.299-301, and Weatherill, *Law and Integration in the European Union* (1995), pp.243-245.

[81]   Case C-34-36/95 *supra* n.25.

[82]   Case C-120/95 *Decker* v *Caisse de Meladie des Employés Privés* [1998] ECR I-1831.

[83]   Case C-389/96 *Aher-Waggon GmbH* v *Germany* [1998] ECR I-4473.

protection".[84] Whilst "public health" is of course to be regarded as an Article 30 justification and a mandatory requirement, the need to protect the environment is traditionally only relevant to indistinctly applicable measures under the *Cassis* formula. If however it is accepted that the measures at issue were distinctly applicable, why did the ECJ intimate that it might be justified not only for reasons relating to public health, but also relating to environmental protection? The national law clearly restricted trade within the Community,[85] and looked discriminatory in nature favouring domestic aircraft over imported aircraft. The Court was not however drawn on this point. Without the benefit of the ECJ's opinion as to whether the German measures were distinctly or indistinctly applicable, it is impossible to draw hard and fast conclusions as to the Court's future willingness to apply the rule of reason's mandatory requirements to a distinctly applicable measure.[86]

In June 1998, a matter of days before the *Aher-Waggon* ruling, the ECJ in *Chemische Afvalstoffen Dusseldorp BV et al* v *Minister van Volkshuisvesting, Ruimtelijke Ordening en Milieubeheer* was given the opportunity to deliberate as to the legitimacy of a measure which placed restrictions on exports contrary to Article 29 EC.[87] As noted earlier, Article 29 EC prohibits national measures which discriminate against exports. However, the jurisprudence of the ECJ has underlined that non-discriminatory rules applying equally to both exports and to goods intended for the domestic market do not, it appears, fall within its prohibitory effect.[88] In effect therefore the *Cassis de Dijon* rule of reason is incapable of being applied to export restrictions that conflict with Article 29 EC as any measure which contravenes this Treaty provision must be distinctly applicable. This of course means that an export restriction can be justified for reasons relating to the protection of *"health and life of humans, animals or plants"* or other grounds noted in Article 30 EC, but never for an environmental reason which falls outside this Article 30 exception. This distinction has been criticised for being "formalistic" in nature,[89] and for this reason the ruling in *Dusseldorp* is of much interest.

The Dutch measure in question restricted the export of waste for recovery to those exports which would be subject to a superior processing operation abroad, or to situations where there was insufficient capacity for processing waste in the Netherlands. Dusseldorp had unsuccessfully applied to the Dutch Ministry of the Environment for an authorisation to export oil filters and related waste to Germany

---

84 Para.19 of the judgment. See in particular Temmink, *supra* n.18, pp.91-92.

85 Para.18 of the judgment.

86 See Scott, "Trade and Environment in the EU and WTO" in Weiler (ed.), *The EU, the WTO and the NAFTA* (2000) at p.130.

87 Case C-203/96 [1998] ECR I-4075. See generally comment by Notaro (1999) 36 CMLRev 1309.

88 See Case 15/79 *Groenveld BV* v *Produktschap voor Vee en Vlees, supra* n.11, para.7. See also Case 237/82 *Jongeneel Kaas* v *The State (The Netherlands) and Stichting Centraal organ Zuivelcontrole* [1984] ECR 483. This approach has been criticised; see generally Oliver, *supra* n.70.

89 Temmink, *supra* n.18, p.92.

for processing by Factron. Its application had been rejected on the basis that processing by Factron was not of a superior quality to that performed by AVR Chemie, the solely authorised operator dealing in the management of such waste in the Netherlands. Dusseldorp challenged the validity of the export restriction claiming that it was incompatible with Article 29 EC (ex Article 34). Clearly the ECJ formed the opinion that this was a measure which fell within the prohibition of ex-Article 34 (Article 29 EC) noting that

> *[Ex] Article 34 prohibits quantitative restrictions on exports, as well as all measures having an equivalent effect. According to the settled case-law of the Court, it concerns national measures which have as their specific object or effect the restriction of patterns of exports and thereby the establishment of a difference in treatment between the domestic trade of a Member State and its export trade, in such a way as to provide a particular advantage for national production or for the domestic market of the State in question ... [I]t is plain that the object and effect of ... [the national] provision is to restrict exports and to provide a particular advantage for national production.*[90]

The national measure therefore was evidently distinctly applicable and yet it is arguable that the ECJ raises the possibility of justifying such a measure on the basis of the need to protect the environment. Intriguingly and controversially, the ECJ noted that "[e]ven if the national measure in question could be justified by reasons relating to the protection of the environment",[91] before going on to reject the national measure's legality due to its purely economic nature. The ECJ therefore ruled that, in accordance with its established case law, the national action was in fact incompatible with Community law as the Dutch Government's justification for the measure was purely of an economic nature and therefore incapable of justifying a barrier to free movement of goods. However, the ruling left open the issue as to whether the measure could have been justified by reason of the need to protect the environment had the Dutch Government's action been motivated by non-economic objectives. To have determined in this way would of course have served to undermine the basis of its jurisprudence since *Cassis de Dijon* that only *indistinctly applicable* national laws are capable of being deemed to be acceptable in so far as their provisions are necessary to satisfy mandatory requirements. Surely such a measure could never be justified by environmental protection requirements, but only

---

90   Case C-203/96 *supra* n.87, paras.40 and 42 of the judgment.
91   Para.44 of the judgment.

by justifications as noted in Article 30 EC? In the *Walloon Waste* case, the decree in question was clearly discriminatory but the ECJ went to great length to assert otherwise and apply the rule of reason. In *Dusseldorp*, no such pretence was made to conceal the discriminatory nature of the national measure and yet the ECJ did not dismiss the possibility of justification on environmental protection grounds in accordance with its existing jurisprudence.[92] On the one hand, the ECJ certainly did not definitively assert that the rule of reason could be applied. Equally it did not dismiss its applicability, prompting Notaro correctly to note that

> *it can be maintained that the original distinction between discriminatory and non-discriminatory measures is nowadays blurred, especially when it has to be applied to environmental measures. The ECJ seems conscious that the derogation granted by Article 30 EC for the protection of health and life of humans, animals and plants, is too narrow to grant adequate environmental protection.*[93]

After *Dusseldorp* we were accordingly left in some doubt as to the possible relevance of the rule of reason to discriminatory national measures introduced to protect the environment. In the subsequent *Kobenhavns Kommune* judgment, the ECJ would have seemed to clarify the matter by initially indicating that "protection of the environment cannot serve to justify any restrictions on exports."[94] However, the ruling went on to confuse the issue. In specifically ruling as to whether national restrictions on the export of building waste could be justified by the need to protect the environment, the ECJ noted the non-hazardous nature of the waste in question and the fact that no argument had been put forward that it was harmful to the environment. The judgment then proceeds to stipulate that

> *[i]n those circumstances, restrictions on exports contrary to [ex] Article 34 of the Treaty, such as those alleged in the main proceedings, cannot be justified by the need to protect the environment...*[95]

But what if the waste in question had posed a threat to the environment? The ruling could be read as implying that an export restriction might be justified for purely environmental reasons if the restriction sought to prevent the export of waste that posed an environmental threat. In its concluding remarks as to whether the export restriction was justified, the ECJ noted that it could not be justified

---

92   See Notaro, "The New Generation Case Law on Trade and the Environment" (2000) 25 ELRev 467, at 479.
93   *Ibid.* See also on this issue, French, "The Changing Nature of 'Environmental Protection': Recent Developments Regarding Trade and the Environment in the European Union and the World Trade Organization" (2000) vol. XLVII Netherlands International Law Review 1, at pp.22-25, and Van Calster, "Export Restrictions - a Watershed for Article 30" (2000) 25 ELRev 335, at 350.
94   Case C-209/98 *Entreprenoerforeningens Affalds/ Miljoesektion (FFAD) v Kobenhaven Kommune* [2000] ECR I-3743, para.48.
95   Para.50.

on the basis of [ex] Article 36 of the Treaty or in the interests of environmental
protection ... in the absence of any indication of danger to the health or life of
humans, animals or plants or danger to the environment.[96]

Surely this therefore leaves open the possibility that a restriction on exports might
be justifiable for environmental reasons if the waste was of such a nature that it
would cause environmental damage?[97]

The case of *PreussenElektra*[98] is also of considerable interest, lending weight to the
argument that the ECJ is indeed now prepared to justify certain distinctly applicable
measures in the interests of environmental protection. German law had been
introduced to promote the use of electricity from renewable sources. More
specifically, an obligation had been placed on regional electricity distribution
undertakings to buy electricity from renewable energy sources in their area of supply
at fixed minimum prices. In effect, distribution undertakings had to purchase
electricity produced from renewable sources in Germany – the purchase obligation
in question did not extend to electricity produced from renewable energy sources
outside Germany. The measure was potentially capable of hindering intra-
Community trade by reducing demand for electricity produced in other Member
States. Although therefore it was a MEQR on imports contrary to the Article 28 EC
prohibition, could it be justified under Community law? There were evidently sound
environmental reasons for the domestic measure, but the rule appeared to be
distinctly applicable as it treated electricity generated in Germany differently from
imported electricity. If the Court's traditional approach was to be applied,
presumably the mandatory requirements could not be invoked to justify the
measure? Advocate General Jacobs in *PreussenElektra* however argued for a more
flexible approach with regard to the imperative requirement of environmental
protection – just because a measure was discriminatory should not rule out the
possibility of justification for environmental reasons. Furthermore, citing the
Court's rulings in *Dusseldorp* and *Aher-Waggon*, the Advocate General stipulated
that "there are indications that the Court is reconsidering its earlier case-law".[99] For
reasons of legal certainty, he called on the Court to clarify whether directly
discriminatory measures could be justified by mandatory requirements.[100]

The *PreussenElektra* judgment spelt out in some detail that the measure promoting
the use of electricity from renewable sources was indeed appropriate for sound

---

[96]   Para.51.

[97]   Notaro, "European Community Waste Movements: the Copenhagen Waste Case" (2000) 9(11)
EELR 304 at p.311.

[98]   Case C-379/98 *PreussenElektra AG* v *Schhleswag AG* [2001] ECR I-2099.

[99]   Para.227 of Advocate General Jacobs' opinion.

[100]   *Ibid*, para.229. He regarded the reasoning in the *Walloon Waste* case as flawed since no regard should
have been given to whether a measure was appropriate in assessing whether it was discriminatory;
para.225.

environmental reasons,[101] before adding that the German approach was also designed to protect the health and life of humans, animals or plants. However, it is noticeable that the ECJ did not follow its classic case law approach of determining whether or not the measure was distinctly or indistinctly applicable before considering possible justifications. Although the Court had certainly justified a measure which appeared discriminatory on environmental grounds, the judgment gave no clear guidance as to whether the measure in question was distinctly or indistinctly applicable. Accordingly, we still await the clarification which AG Jacobs had called for. While the Court remains reluctant formally to provide this clarity, it fascinatingly supported its assertion that the German measure was justified by making reference to the fact that Article 6 EC placed an obligation to integrate environmental protection requirements into the definition and implementation of all Community policies.[102] It would appear that the Court had therefore used the integration principle to interpret the Community's primary law on free movement of goods in such a way that an environmental justification could be applied to a measure which seemed to be distinctly applicable.

French aptly raised the question whether the judgments in *Aher-Waggon* and *Dusseldorp* amounted to "an initial step in recognising the artificiality of the division between Article 30 EC exemptions and the need to protect the environment?"[103] *Kobenhavns Kommune* and *PreussenElektra* can only be regarded as rulings that seemingly provide further evidence that the Court is prepared to look sympathetically on national measures introduced for sound environmental reasons despite their distinctly applicable nature.[104]

Member States' Regulatory Competence After the Adoption of Harmonising Legislation

Where a matter is regulated in a harmonised manner at Community level, action by Member States must be assessed in the light of that measure.[105] The content and nature of the harmonising measure determines the extent to which Member States

---

101 The Court noted that promotion of renewable energy may assist in the reduction of greenhouse gas emissions "which are amongst the main causes of climate change which the European Community and its Member States have pledged to combat"; para.73 of the judgment.

102 Para.76 of the judgment.

103 French, *supra* n.93, p.24.

104 Mortelmans, "Towards Convergence in the Application of the Rules on Free Movement and on Competition" (2001) 38 CMLRev 613, at p.636.

105 For example, see Case C-324/99 *DaimlerChrysler AG* v *Land Baden-Wurttemberg* [2001] ECR I-9897, at paras.42 and 43. The harmonisation process encourages market integration by removing national measures which impose legal trade barriers. The latter are replaced by a harmonised legal regime which abolishes market distortions and affords a minimum level of protection applicable in all Member States. Unilateral action by a Member State can prove to be the catalyst for a harmonisation measure; see Kramer in relation to such national measures including the German eco-label scheme *supra* n.45, pp.54-56.

can take action at the national level, if at all. In other words, relevant Community secondary legislation determines the boundary between national and Community competence. In the *Walloon Waste* case, for example, the Commission brought an action against Belgium seeking a declaration that a decree passed by the Belgian region of Wallonia was incompatible with the schemes and principles established in existing EC legislation on the disposal of waste, and with primary Community law.[106] We have already noted that, in so far as certain types of waste were not covered by the provisions of existing Community legislation (*non-hazardous* waste was not comprehensively covered by Community legislation at that time), Member States were free to introduce their own national environmental rules as long as they were compatible with ex-Articles 30-36 (now Articles 28-30 EC). In effect, where the Community had yet to enter the field, national action had to be assessed in the light of primary Community law. However, the Community had indeed entered the field in relation to the shipment of *hazardous* waste by adopting Directive 84/631 which made provisions for the establishing of a supervision system for the transfrontier shipment of certain types of hazardous waste.[107]

In so far as the Belgian measure affected hazardous waste, its legitimacy had to be evaluated in the light of Directive 84/631 which had introduced a detailed harmonised system for the storage, treatment or tipping of toxic and dangerous waste.[108] The Walloon decree in question amounted to an outright ban on all shipments of hazardous waste into the Walloon region from other regions of Belgium and from Member States. Its legitimacy had to be assessed in the light of the aforementioned directive. The complete system of regulation established by the directive detailed the particular manner in which Member States could interrupt the trade in hazardous waste. The Court held that the Walloon decree was incompatible with this system as it had adopted a blanket prohibition on waste transfer, rather than the approach endorsed under the directive which only provided for prohibitions of particular movements in certain circumstances. A general prohibition was out of line with the scope of the comprehensive system established by the harmonising directive.

Importantly, justification under Article 30 EC or the "rule of reason" is no longer possible where Community legislation makes provision for the necessary measures to protect those fundamental requirements recognised by Community law in Article

---

[106] Case C-2/90 *supra* n.8.

[107] Council Directive 84/631/EEC on the Supervision and Control within the European Community of the Transfrontier Shipment of Hazardous Waste OJ 1984 L326/31 as amended. Now repealed by Council Regulation 259/93 on the Supervision and Control of Shipments of Waste within, into and out of the European Community OJ 1993 L30/1.

[108] Advocate General Jacobs noted in the *Walloon Waste* case that "Directive 84/631 establishes a detailed, uniform system for the supervision and control of the transfrontier shipment of dangerous waste. As the Court has indicated, where in application of [ex]Article 100 of the Treaty, Community directives and the appropriate checks must be carried out and the measures of protection adopted within the framework outlined by the harmonizing directive"; para.19 of Advocate General's opinion.

30 EC or acknowledged as a mandatory requirement under the "rule of reason". The *Hedley Lomas*[109] case provides an example of this long-established principle. UK authorities had refused to grant a licence for the export of a quantity of live animals to Spain. This refusal was based on the belief that some slaughterhouses in Spain were failing to comply with the provisions of Directive 74/577 on the Stunning of Animals before Slaughter.[110] The refusal to issue an export licence was a quantitative restriction on exports contrary to ex-Article 34 (Article 29 EC). Furthermore, it could not be justified on the grounds of the protection of health and life of animals, as recourse to [ex] Article 36

> *was no longer possible where Community directives provide for harmonisation of the measures necessary to achieve the specific objective which would be furthered by reliance upon this provision.*[111]

The nature of the Community harmonising measure was "exhaustive" in the sense that applicable Community secondary legislation had secured the framework for the appropriate protection of the interest in question, and Member States were precluded from taking action in the area capable of justification under Article 30 EC.[112] To put it another way, the relevant Community legislation formed the framework within which national legislation had to be assessed as to its compatibility with Community law.[113]

In assessing whether or to what extent Member States can derogate from the directive, it must be determined which harmonisation method or technique has been adopted in the harmonising measure. Certain measures introduce a system of "total harmonisation" by fixing common uniform standards, whilst others apply the "minimum harmonisation" technique. If the Community measure is an example of total harmonisation, the power of Member States to introduce a separate national system of regulation by way of derogation is abolished apart from in those defined situations allowed by the harmonising measure. In *Walloon Waste*, for example, Directive 84/631 had established a comprehensive system of regulation with regard to the shipment of hazardous waste. Member States had lost the ability to regulate other than in the manner established by the Community's comprehensive system of regulation. The technique of total harmonisation produces the least obstacles to the functioning of the market by establishing identical rules applicable throughout the

---

[109] See Case C-5/94 *R v MAFF ex parte Hedley Lomas* [1996] ECR I-2553, para.18. See comment by Oliver (1997) 34 CMLRev 666.

[110] OJ 1974 L316/10.

[111] Para.18 of the judgment.

[112] On the other hand, the ECJ in *Toolex* (Case C-473/98 *supra* n.37) found that a Swedish prohibition against the use of trichloroethylene was capable of justification under Article 30. The scope of Community rules had not prevented the Member States from regulating the use of trichloroethylene. For example, although Directive 76/769 imposed restrictions on the marketing and use of certain dangerous substances and preparations listed in the Annex to that measure, trichloroethylene did not appear in that list. The scope of the measure therefore provided no hindrance to the regulation of that substance by Member States.

[113] Slot, "Harmonisation" (1996) ELRev 378, at p.388.

Community. It has been particularly used as a harmonising technique in legislation determining product standards.

Rather than adopting the total harmonisation approach, environmental directives commonly allow for differentiated integration by adopting "minimum harmonisation" in which measures seek to establish minimum standards only.[114] The Community has indeed entered the field but harmonisation is to be regarded as a minimum allowing Member States to impose more stringent national requirements. In effect, stricter national rules are not pre-empted and uniformity of standards is not necessarily envisaged even after harmonisation. The judgment in *Hans Honig* v *Stadt Stockach* provides an example of a judgment relating to a measure utilising the minimum harmonisation technique.[115] Directive 88/166 established standards for the protection of laying hens kept in battery cages. A German farmer took the view that German law requiring that cages larger than those required under the directive was incompatible with the harmonising measure. The ECJ disagreed ruling that the letter and purpose of the directive allowed Member States to establish stricter national rules relating to the cage area for laying hens than the standards in the harmonising measure. The directive was to be interpreted as only establishing minimum standards. Stricter national rules were not pre-empted; they were permitted even though it would allow inequalities in competition to continue. The Community and the Member States both enjoyed competence in this area.

The Community can certainly adopt the technique of total harmonisation for secondary legislation adopted under Article 95 EC.[116] However, numerous directives adopted under Articles 95 EC have expressly indicated that Member States can adopt more stringent standards as the measure has only established minimum standards. Such express provision in an environmental directive would not however be required if the legal base for the measure is Article 175 EC. Article 176 EC notes that

> *[t]he protective measures adopted pursuant to Article 175 shall not prevent any Member State from maintaining or introducing more stringent protective standards. Such measures must be compatible with this Treaty. They shall be notified to the Commission.*

This is a specific acknowledgement that measures adopted under the Environment Title set minimum standards only. Member States are free to adopt or maintain more stringent protective measures even if the relevant Community measure fails specifically to indicate that they may do so.

---

[114] See Article 7(2) of Directive 76/160/ EEC on the Quality of Bathing Water (OJ 1976 L31/1) and also Article 9 of Directive 79/923/EEC on the Quality of Shellfish Waters (OJ 1979 L281/47).

[115] Case C-128/94 [1995] ECR I-3389.

[116] The reader should however be reminded that, if a measure is adopted under Article 95 EC, Member States do enjoy a right to maintain, or introduce national provisions in defined circumstances for certain reasons which include those relating to the protection of the environment (Articles 95(4) and (5)EC). See further chapter 2.

Where the minimum harmonisation technique has been adopted, it is important to stress that any national measures imposing more stringent standards must be compatible with primary Community law. National measures setting such higher standards must therefore be assessed as to their compatibility with Articles 28-30 EC. The *Aher-Waggon*[117] case provides an example of the ability of Member States to legislate in the event of minimum harmonisation. National legislation in Germany required that aircraft previously registered in another Member State could not be registered in Germany unless they complied with stricter national noise emission regulations than those imposed by relevant Community legislation.[118] By contrast, those aircraft registered in Germany prior to the implementation of such Community law were exempt from these standards. The ECJ noted that Directive 80/51 as amended clearly established minimum standards only "as is shown by the words 'in accordance with requirements which are at least equal to the applicable standards' which appear in Article 3(1)".[119] As such, the relevant Community rules allowed Member States to set their own stricter noise limits as long as they were compatible with primary Community law, particularly Articles 28-30 EC. The German rules amounted to a barrier to trade within the Article 28 EC prohibition but were in principle capable of justification. In this sense, it could be said that Community secondary legislation had set the "floor" for national action below which Member States could not sink, whilst Community primary law established the "ceiling" in the sense that more stringent national measures had to comply with the rules relating to Article 28 EC.[120]

---

117 Case C-389/96 *supra* n.83.

118 Directive 80/51 (OJ 1980 L18/26) as amended by Council Directive 83/206 (OJ 1983 L117/15).

119 Para.15 of the judgment.

120 See Weatherill, *supra* n.80, p.153, and Scott, *supra* n.86, p.129. However, the approach in *Aher-Waggon* (in which more stringent standards were acceptable as long as they were compatible with primary Community law) is hard to reconcile with the judgment in *Compassion in World Farming* (Case C-1/96 [1998] ECR I-1251). In accordance with Article 11(2) of Directive 91/629, the UK had applied within its territory stricter provisions than laid down in the said Community measure. Advocating a ban on the export of live calves from the UK, Compassion in World Farming (CIWF) argued that such a quantitative restriction on exports could be justified under Article 30 EC in order to protect the health of those calves which would otherwise have been exported to other Member States with less stringent welfare standards than the UK. The ECJ ruled to the contrary. Directive 91/629 had made provision for the necessary measures to achieve the specific interest (protection of the health of animals) which would have been furthered by reliance on Article 30 EC. The ECJ therefore regarded the standards set in the directive as exhaustive in nature (para.56). Hence, recourse to Article 30 EC was precluded despite the fact that it was acknowledged that the directive only established common minimum standards for the protection of calves. Comparing the different approaches to more stringent national measures in *Aher-Waggon* and in *Compassion*, it has been suggested that the ECJ is inclined to deem a directive setting only minimum standards to be "exhaustive" in nature (thereby precluding recourse to Article 30) where more stringent national measures are designed to have extra-territorial application (as in *Compassion in World Farming*); see Scott, *supra* n.86 at p.131, and discussion in Dougan, "Minimum Harmonisation and the Internal Market" (2000) 37 CMLRev 853, at p.874. For further comment on the *Compassion* case, see Van Calster (2000) 25 ELRev 335.

Some Concluding Remarks

In situations where national environmental measures are upheld by the ECJ, they are deemed appropriate in the circumstances pending potential replacement by Community harmonising legislation. It must be appreciated however that harmonisation of all aspects relating to the environment is not expected, the Commission noting with regard to Community law in general that

> *experience has shown that ... relying on a strategy based totally on harmonisation would be over-regulatory, would take a long time to implement, would be inflexible and could stifle innovation.*[121]

Cases will therefore continue to come before the ECJ in which the latter must deliberate as to a Member State's competence to regulate its own environment both in the absence of harmonisation and once the Community has entered the field.

Whether or not a national measure which aims to protect environmental interests in another Member State (extra-territorial application) is capable of justification has been an issue of some debate. In *Gourmetterie Van den Burg*,[122] *Hedley Lomas*[123] and *Compassion in World Farming*[124] the ECJ avoided the need to rule on the extra-territorial applicability of Article 30 EC by stipulating that a Member State cannot rely on Article 30 EC justifications where existing Community legislation harmonises measures necessary to achieve the specific objective which would be furthered by reliance on that Treaty provision.[125] However, in the *Kobenhaven Kommune* case,[126] the ruling appears to back the argument that a national measure which aims to protect environmental interests in another Member State may be justified under Article 30 EC.[127] The case raised questions as to the legality of Danish municipal measures which, contrary to Article 29 EC, effectively prohibited producers of non-hazardous building waste from exporting it. In ruling as to whether an Article 30 EC derogation could justify the measures, the ECJ noted that such a justification

> *would be relevant if the fact that building waste was shipped over a greater distance, as a consequence of being exported, and processed in a Member State other than that in which it is produced represented a danger to the health and life of humans, animals or plants. In the present case however the waste in question is non-hazardous waste and nothing has been put forward to show there is a danger to the health and life of humans, animals or plants.*[128]

---

[121] European Commission, *Completing the Internal Market COM* (85) 310, para.64.

[122] Case C-169/89 [1990] ECR I-2143, paras. 8-9.

[123] Case C-5/94 *supra* n.109, paras. 18-19.

[124] Case C-1/96 *supra* n.120.

[125] For comment see Jans, *supra* n.9, pp.265-267, and Notaro, *supra* n.92, pp.487-489. See also Scott, *supra* n.7, pp.79-85, and in Weiler (ed.), *supra* n.86, pp.131-133.

[126] Case C-209/98 *supra* n.94.

[127] See Notaro, supra n.97 at p.310.

[128] Paras. 45-46 of the judgment.

Without explicitly indicating that a measure introduced to protect the environment of another Member State could be justified under Article 30 EC, it might be argued that by making reference to distance to be travelled, partly in another country, the ECJ remains open to the possibility of extra-territorial application allowing a measure to be justified which bans the export of hazardous waste with a view to reducing potential risk to the environment outside the exporting state.[129]

This chapter has served to introduce the reader to the manner in which the ECJ has struck a balance between the need for environmental protection and free trade. In the next chapter, attention will focus on the EC's waste management strategy in which a variety of measures have been adopted at the Community level which seek also to strike that balance between ensuring the effective functioning of the internal market on the one hand, and providing adequate protection for the environment on the other.[130]

[129] Notaro, supra n.97 at p.311.
[130] 'See' as noted Laurence, *Waste Regulation Law* (1999), p.5.

Select Bibliography

Coleman, "Environmental Barriers to Trade and EC Law" (1993) 2(11) EELR 295.

Demiray, "The Movement of Goods in a Green Market" (1994) LIEI 73.

French, "The Changing Nature of 'Environmental Protection': Recent Developments Regarding Trade and the Environment in the European Union and the World Trade Organization" (2000) XLVII Netherlands International Law Review 1.

Geradin, "Trade and Environmental Protection: Community Harmonization and National Environmental Standards" 13 *Yearbook of European Law* (1993) 151.

Gormley, "Free Movement of Goods and the Environment" in Holder (ed.) *The Impact of EC Environmental Law in the UK* (1997) 289.

Hancher and Sevenster, "Case C-2/90 *Commission* v *Belgium*" (1993) 30 CMLRev 351.

Jans, *European Environmental Law* (2000), pp.101-121 and chapter 6.

Kramer, "Environmental Protection and Article 30 EEC Treaty" (1993) 30 CMLRev 111.

Kramer, "Environmental Protection and Trade: the Contribution of the European Union", *Focus on European Environmental Law* (1997), pp.44-77.

Kromarek, "Environmental Protection and the Free Movement of Goods: The Danish Bottles Case" (1990) 2(1) JEL 89.

Notaro, "The New Generation Case Law on Trade and the Environment" (2000) 25 ELRev 467.

Oliver, *Free Movement of Goods in the European Community* (1996).

Oliver, "Some Further Reflections on the Scope of Articles 28-30 EC" (1999) 36 CMLRev 783, pp.799-804.

Scott, *EC Environmental Law* (1998) pp.64-85.

Sexton, "Enacting National Environmental Laws More Stringent Than Other States' Laws in the European Community" (1991) 24 Cornell International Law Journal 563.

Temmink, "From Danish Bottles to Danish Bees: The Dynamics of Free Movement of Goods and Environmental Protection - a Case Law Analysis" 1 *Yearbook of European Environmental Law* (2000) 61.

Van Calster, "Export Restrictions - a Watershed for Article 30" (2000) 25 ELRev 335.

Von Wilmowsky, "Waste Disposal in the Internal Market: the State of Play after the ECJ's Ruling on the Walloon Import Ban" (1993) 30 CMLRev 541.

Weatherill, *Law and Integration in the European Union* (1995), pp.239-245.

Chapter 7

Waste Management in the Community

The Community's waste management strategy seeks to strike a balance between two important interests. Bearing in mind that the ECJ has determined that wastes must be regarded as "goods",[1] and that a significant amount of cross-border waste movement takes place each year, efforts must be made to ensure that the functioning of the internal market is not distorted.[2] Equally however, there is an obvious need to attain a high level of environmental protection by discouraging the relentless generation of waste. The amount of waste generated within the Community continues to increase, the European Environment Agency indicating that

> *[r]eported total waste generation in OECD Europe increased by nearly 10% between 1990 and 1995. Approximately 2000 million tonnes of municipal waste was generated in 1995, equivalent to 420 kg/person/year.*[3]

The Community's approach to waste management is founded on the fact that a balance must therefore be struck between the need to ensure the functioning of the internal market on the one hand, and to attain a high level of environmental protection on the other. If a successful balance is reached, the Community's waste management strategy can contribute significantly to the pursuit of sustainable development, the Commission noting that "waste production is one of the best indicators of our progress" towards this long-term goal.[4]

---

[1] Case C-2/90 *Commission* v *Belgium* (*Walloon Waste* case) [1992] ECR I-4431 discussed at length in chapter 6. It will be recalled that the Court of Justice held that waste – whether recyclable or not – is a "good", the free movement of which must not in principle be impeded within the Community. However, the ECJ went on to indicate that free movement of waste can be limited bearing in mind that the principle that environmental damage should as a priority be rectified at source implies waste should "be disposed of as close as possible to the place where it is produced, in order to limit as far as possible the transport of waste" (para.34), and that this principle "is consistent with the principles of self-sufficiency and proximity set out in the Basel Convention on the control of transborder movements of hazardous waste and their disposal, to which the Community is a party" (para.35). See later discussion in this chapter on the principles of self-sufficiency and proximity and on the Basel Convention.

[2] See Laurence who notes that "the total amount of cross-border waste movements of hazardous wastes (not all wastes) has been estimated as being about 100,000 annually, or approximately one movement every five minutes"; Laurence, *Waste Regulation Law* (1999), p.5.

[3] European Environment Agency, *Europe's Environment - the Second Assessment* (1998), p.130. Interestingly, "Germany and France were the largest contributors to the approximately 42 million tonnes per year of hazardous waste reported ... for the period around 1994"; *ibid.*

[4] European Commission, *EU Focus on Waste Management* (1999).

This chapter will first seek to highlight the main objectives of the Community's waste management strategy drawn up by the Commission in 1989 and subsequently reviewed in 1996.[5] The basic obligations imposed on Member States by the "Framework Directive" on waste will then be outlined. The difficulties experienced in defining what exactly constitutes "waste" will subsequently be addressed, before attention turns to the hazardous waste regime and the regulation of waste shipments. Next, discussion moves on to assess the legal requirements surrounding waste management processes. Landfill and incineration are two of the main forms of waste disposal and the regimes governing these processes will therefore be highlighted. Lastly, we shall analyse those measures adopted at the Community level in relation to a number of particular waste streams.

Waste Management Objectives

The Community's waste management policy is underpinned by three key objectives: prevention, recovery and safe disposal of waste. The Commission talks in terms of a hierarchy of aims with prevention being the priority, followed by recovery and then lastly safe disposal.[6] The choice is not however to be determined exclusively on environmental grounds – whilst the best environmental solution should be considered, account should also be taken of economic and social costs.[7]

The most effective manner in which to eradicate or reduce the impact of waste on both the environment and human health is to prevent waste being generated in the first place. This can be achieved by *inter alia* using clean technologies, prohibiting or limiting dangerous substances (such as heavy metals) in products, improving consumer information and providing education. Waste prevention is the central objective of the Community's waste policy, and clearly underlines the need to integrate environmental concerns into the production process.[8] In this context, the 1996 review of the Community's 1989 strategy underlined that in certain scenarios the concept of "producer responsibility" will be of future importance. Producers will need to take responsibility for the environmental impact of their products, thereby encouraging them to bear in mind the need to prevent waste at the design stage. We will note later that producer responsibility has been endorsed in the sphere of end-of-life vehicles and will no doubt play an important part in the future management of other waste streams.

---

5   European Commission, "A Community Strategy for Waste Management" SEC (89) 934 final. See also the 1996 review; European Commission, "Communication from the Commission on the Review of the Community Strategy for Waste Management COM (96) 399" (subsequently adopted in a 1997 Council resolution, OJ 1997 C 76/1). The strategy does not cover radioactive waste; see however COM (94) 66 on radioactive waste management strategy.

6   See COM (96) 399.

7   *Ibid.*

8   The introduction of the eco-labelling system is designed to complement this approach by highlighting to the consumer those products of an environmentally friendly nature; Regulation 1980/2000 on a Revised Community Eco-label Award Scheme OJ 2000 L 237/1.

In the event that waste is unavoidably generated, it should be recovered. In this way materials can be re-used, or alternatively, waste can either be recycled (material recovery) or utilised as a source of energy (energy recovery).[9] As a result, the generation of waste will be kept to a minimum. If waste can neither be prevented nor recovered, it should be disposed of safely, generally by means of incineration or landfill. We shall note that these means of waste disposal produce their own environmental problems which must be minimised by effective regulation.

The Framework Directive on Waste Management

The legal structure for waste management throughout the Member States is established in Directive 75/442 on Waste as amended which takes as a base a high level of environmental protection.[10] The original directive was adopted in 1975 but was amended in 1991 to take account of experience gained by the Member States in the intervening period. The "Framework Directive" on waste is referred to as such as it establishes basic obligations that underpin waste management in the Community, but also envisages the introduction of more specific rules on the management of particular types of waste by means of other directives (so called "daughter" directives).[11] Unless specific legislation states to the contrary, the provisions of the Framework Directive have relevance to all classes of waste.

Prevention, Recovery and Disposal

Article 3 of the Framework Directive places a duty on Member States which, together with the obligations in Article 4, can be seen to be reflective of the Community's general philosophy on waste management policy. Firstly, Article 3 places an obligation on Member States to introduce national measures to encourage the prevention or reduction of waste production and its harmful nature.[12] For example, the introduction of clean technology is encouraged which makes less use of scarce resources, as is the development of products which make no contribution or the smallest possible contribution to the generation of harmful waste. Secondly, measures are to be adopted by Member States to encourage the recovery of waste by either recycling, re-use, reclamation or other processes to extract secondary raw

---

[9] The 1996 review of the community's strategy stipulated that the recovery of materials should take precedence over energy generation.

[10] Directive 75/442 OJ 1975 L194/39 amended by Directive 91/156 OJ 1991 L78/32 and Decision 96/350 OJ 1996 L135/32.

[11] Article 2(2) notes that "specific rules for particular instances or supplementing those of this directive on the management of particular categories of waste may be laid down by means of individual directives"; Article 2(2).

[12] Article 3(1)a.

materials, or the use of waste as a source of energy.[13] Additionally, Article 4 of the measure imposes a legal obligation on all Member States to take the necessary domestic measures to ensure that waste is either recovered or disposed of without endangering human health and without using processes which might harm the environment. More particularly, recovery or disposal of waste should not cause a risk to the environmental media or fauna and flora. Neither should it cause a nuisance through noise or odours, or adversely affect the countryside. The dumping, abandonment or uncontrolled disposal of waste must be prohibited.

A system of management must therefore be introduced by Member States for waste recovery and disposal, but it will be recalled from earlier discussion in chapter 3 on the doctrine of "direct effect" that the ECJ has ruled that Article 4 merely "indicates a programme to be followed and sets out the objectives which the Member States must observe".[14] It therefore defines a framework for action to be taken by Member States,[15] but cannot confer rights on individuals to be upheld before national courts as the provision is not sufficiently unconditional nor sufficiently precise in nature to be directly effective.

Self-sufficiency and Proximity in Relation to Waste Disposal

An integrated network for the disposal of waste must be established at the Community level and, if possible, at the national level. The setting up of this network undoubtedly reduces the need for the transportation of waste for disposal over long distances. Article 5 endorses the principle of "self-sufficiency" in obliging Member States to establish an integrated network of disposal installations taking account of the best technology not involving excessive costs.[16] The network must enable the Community as a whole to be "self-sufficient" in the disposal of that waste generated inside the EC, and for Member States to progress in such a way that they each individually move towards self-sufficiency as far as the disposal of waste is concerned. However, account will be taken of geographical considerations, and also of the fact that certain types of waste require disposal at specialist sites which may not be established in each and every Member State. Member States may cooperate with other Member States in the establishing of this network where necessary or advisable.

---

[13]   Article 3(1)b. Article 3(2) notes that Member States are obliged to inform the Commission of any measures which they propose to take to meet the aims established by Article 3(1)a and 3(1)b. However the ECJ has confirmed that failure to so notify will not give "individuals any right which they may enforce before national courts in order to obtain the annulment or suspension of national rules falling within the scope of that provision"; Case C-159/00 *Sapod Audic* v *Eco-Emballages SA* [2002] ECR I-5031 at para.62.

[14]   Case C-236/92 *Comitato di Coordinamento per la Difesa della cava et al.* v *Regione Lombardia et al.* [1994] ECR I-483. The ECJ has subsequently concluded however that certain obligations are imposed on Member States under Article 4 even though Article 4 is not directly effective; see Case C-365/97 *Commission* v *Italy* [1999] ECR I-7773, paras. 65-67.

[15]   Ibid, para.14.

[16]   Article 5(1).

In addition, the "proximity" principle is endorsed in that the waste management network established must enable waste to be disposed of locally in one of the nearest appropriate disposal sites using the most appropriate methods and technologies to ensure a high level of protection for the environment and for public health.[17] The proximity principle seeks to ensure that waste is locally and efficiently disposed of rather than sent to another region or country where it could be dealt with more cheaply, but in a less environmentally sensitive manner. The application of the self-sufficiency and proximity principles are aims to be achieved in relation to waste disposal only.[18] Their inapplicability to waste destined for recovery can be explained by the desire not to limit cross-border opportunities to recover waste.

Waste Management Plans

In order to achieve the objectives established in Articles 3, 4 and 5, relevant national competent authorities are obliged to draw up national waste management plans.[19] As a minimum, these plans must identify the type, quantity and origin of waste to be recovered or disposed of, general technical requirements, special arrangements for particular wastes, and suitable disposal sites or installations. Member States can take measures to prevent waste movements which are inconsistent with these national plans.[20]

Permit System

Having established broad objectives and obligations in relation to the management of waste, the Framework Directive additionally places an obligation on Member States to ensure that, for the main part,[21] any "holder"[22] of waste has it handled by a private or public waste collector or by an undertaking carrying out disposal or recovery operations noted in Annex IIA or B.[23] In typical "command and control" fashion, the disposal or recovery of waste is prohibited unless the undertaking involved in such an operation is duly licensed under a licensing system. This licensing system must be put in place by the Member States. "Disposal operations" noted in Annex IIA, such as landfill sites or incineration plants, can therefore only legally operate having obtained a permit from the relevant national competent

---

17 Article 5(2).
18 See Case C-203/96 *Chemische Afvalstoffen Dusseldorp BV* v *Minister van Volkhuisvesting, Ruimtelijke Ordening en Milieubeheer* [1998] ECR I-4075, para.34. See also the case report by Jans (1999) 11(1) JEL 121.
19 Article 7(1).
20 Article 7(3).
21 Alternatively, the holder of waste should recover or dispose of the waste concerned "in accordance with the provisions of this Directive"; Article 8.
22 Defined as "the producers of waste or the natural or legal person in possession of it"; Article 1(c).
23 Article 8.

body.[24] Conditions imposed in these permits shall relate to the types and quantity of waste to be disposed of, the technical requirements of the operation, and the security precautions that need to be imposed.[25] Authorisations will also regulate the type of treatment method to be pursued, and the disposal site itself.[26] Permits should therefore impose conditions of operation and any application for a permit can be refused, particularly if the method of disposal is environmentally unacceptable.[27] Those undertakings carrying out any of the "recovery operations" noted in Annex IIB, such as recycling, re-using oil and the use of waste to generate energy, must also obtain a permit, although the directive provides no indication of what exactly such an authorisation should cover.[28]

By virtue of Article 11, an establishment which disposes of their own waste at the place of production and undertakings which carry out their own recovery operations may be exempted from the need to obtain a permit. However, such an exemption can only be granted if competent authorities have general rules in place governing such types and quantities of waste, as well as the conditions under which any exemption may apply. Any exempted undertaking must be registered with the national competent authority,[29] and, in addition, the types or quantities of waste and the methods of disposal or recovery must be such that the conditions of Article 4 are met (i.e. waste is recovered or disposed of without endangering human health and in a manner which could not cause environmental harm).

As for professional waste collectors, transporters, dealers or brokers, Article 12 stipulates that they must be registered with the relevant national competent authority. Disposal and recovery operations must keep records of waste processed by them,[30] and, together with all exempted undertakings, waste collectors, transporters, dealers and brokers, must be made subject to "appropriate" periodic inspections.[31]

---

24   Article 9.
25   Some waste management operations – including hazardous waste facilities with more than 10 tonnes capacity per day, and municipal waste incinerators with a capacity of more than 3 tonnes per hour – fall within the remit of Council Directive 96/61 concerning Integrated Pollution Prevention and Control (OJ 1996 L257/26) [IPPC Directive]. Under the provisions of the IPPC Directive, existing operations of this type which undergo "substantial change" and any new facilities require a permit before operating. A permit would *inter alia* take account of the impact of the facility on all three environmental media. Existing operations which do not undergo substantial changes must comply with the terms of the IPPC Directive by 30 October 2007.
26   Article 9(1).
27   Article 9(2).
28   Article 10.
29   Article 11(2).
30   Article 14.
31   Article 13.

Polluter Pays

The Framework Directive endorses the polluter pays principle. The cost of waste disposal must be borne by the holder who has waste handled by a waste collector or an authorised disposal operator, and/or by the previous holder or producer of the product from which waste is produced.[32] However, it is much to be regretted that the measure gives no guidance whatsoever as to the manner in which the principle should be implemented in this context.[33] This is another example of vagueness in a Community measure which makes effective implementation difficult.

Progress on Implementation

Some insight into the general implementation of the Framework Directive can be gained from the Commission's report on implementation covering the period 1995-97.[34] Under the provisions of the Framework Directive as amended, Member States are obliged to report on implementation to the Commission every three years to enable the Commission to draw up a consolidated report.[35] It is therefore unfortunate that four Member States, Greece, Italy, Spain and Portugal, did not see fit to submit their individual reports at the appropriate time, and the Commission's consolidated report is therefore incomplete. The findings of the report in part make disappointing reading as the quality of the national waste management plans would seem to be unsatisfactory;[36] neither Greece nor Luxembourg had notified the Commission of any national plan, whilst plans in almost all other States (the exception being Austria) were not comprehensive in the sense that they covered only a proportion of the territory concerned or did not encompass all the necessary types of wastes.[37] More encouragingly Member States indicated that they were largely self-sufficient in the disposal of waste,[38] but, on a less positive note, there is clearly a concern that the definition of waste had only been properly transposed in a minority of Member States.[39] This particular finding is indicative of perhaps the most apparent failing in the Community's waste management strategy – the lack of a comprehensive definition of "waste".

---

[32] Article 15.

[33] Chalmers poignantly notes that this general provision "illustrates all the weaknesses of the 'polluter pays principle' as a mechanism for ascribing responsibility. Joint responsibility is established for the costs of disposal, yet no mechanism is provided for the apportionment of those costs. There will frequently be persons who are simply unidentifiable. For such persons the incentives simply do not exist to modify their behaviour"; "Community Policy on Waste Management - Managing Environmental Decline Gently" 14 *YEL* 257 (1995), at p.271.

[34] COM (1999) 752.

[35] Article 16.

[36] COM (1999) 752, p.12.

[37] In this respect, it is to be welcomed that the European Environment Agency's Topic Centre on Waste is involved in the drafting of a guideline for waste management plans which Member States will be invited to follow; *ibid.*

[38] *Ibid*, p.15.

[39] *Ibid*, p.9.

What is "Waste"?

Whilst clearly the Framework Directive envisages the establishment of a tightly regulated waste industry, waste management has in part been undermined by the absence of a conclusive definition as to what actually constitutes "waste" for the purposes of the Framework Directive. It is impossible to point to an intrinsic quality common to all forms of waste, and a substance viewed as waste by some may be regarded as a valuable raw material by another.[40] The original definition of waste in the directive noted that "waste means any substance or object which the holder disposes of or is required to dispose of pursuant to the provisions of national law in force".[41] "Disposal" was defined broadly as including not only "the collection, sorting, transport and treatment of waste as well as its storage and tipping above or under ground", but also "the transformation operations necessary for its re-use, recovery or recycling".[42] This definition of waste lacked precision and led to differing interpretations at national level as to those substances to be covered by the system of control introduced by the Framework Directive.[43] Though clearly the system of control to be established was intended to be wide in scope,[44] the original directive failed to provide for a common terminology for waste.

An amendment to the directive proved necessary to address this definitional issue, the preamble of Directive 91/156 which amended the original Framework Directive noting that "common terminology and a definition of waste are needed in order to improve the efficiency of waste management in the Community". Furthermore, it contained an acknowledgement that any lack of consistency in national laws on waste disposal and recovery can affect not only the quality of the environment, but also interfere with the functioning of the internal market. Directive 91/156 redefined "waste" in the following terms:

> *[A]ny substance or object in the categories set out in Annex I which the holder discards or intends or is required to discard.*[45]

---

40   See Bell and McGillivray, *Environmental Law* (2000), pp.486-487.

41   Article 1(a).

42   Article 1(b).

43   See Laurence, *supra* n.2, p.46.

44   See Joined Cases 372/85 to 374/85 *Ministere Public* v *Oscar Traen and others* ECR [1987] 2141 at para.7.

45   Article 1(a) as amended. Certain substances and objects are expressly excluded from the definition of waste under the Framework Directive, Article 2(1) as amended noting the following exclusions:-

    (a) gaseous effluents emitted into the atmosphere;

    (b) where there are already covered by other legislation:

        (i) radioactive waste;

        (ii) waste resulting from prospecting, extraction, treatment and storage of mineral resources and the working of quarries;

        (iii) animal carcases and the following agricultural waste: faecal waste and other natural, non-dangerous substances used in farming;

        (iv) waste waters, with the exception of waste in liquid form;

        (v) decommissioned explosives.

The first condition therefore is that the substance must fit within one of the Annex I categories which include:

- production or consumption residues not otherwise specified below *(Q1)*

- off-specification products *(Q2)*

- products whose dates for appropriate use has expired *(Q3)*

- materials spilled, lost or having undergone other mishap, including any materials, equipment, etc contaminated as a result of the mishap *(Q4)*

- materials contaminated or soiled as a result of planned actions (e.g. residues from cleaning operations, packing materials, containers, etc) *(Q5)*

- unusable parts (e.g. reject batteries, exhausted catalysts, etc) *(Q6)*

- substances which no longer perform satisfactorily (e.g. contaminated acids, contaminated solvents, exhausted tempering salts, etc) *(Q7)*

- residues of industrial processes (e.g. slags, still bottoms, etc) *(Q8)*

- residues from pollution abatement processes (e.g. scrubber sludges, baghouse dusts, spent filters, etc) *(Q9)*

- machining/finishing residues (e.g. lathe turnings, mill scales, etc) *(Q10)*

- residues from raw materials extraction and processing (e.g. mining residues, oil field slops, etc) *(Q11)*

- adulterated materials (e.g. oil contaminated with PCBs, etc) *(Q12)*

- any materials, substances or products whose use has been banned by law *(Q13)*

- products for which the holder has no further use (e.g. agricultural, household, office, commercial and shop discards) *(Q14)*

- contaminated materials, substances or products resulting from remedial action with respect to land *(Q15)*

- any materials, substances or products which are not contained in the above categories *(Q16)*

The list is informative but only to a certain degree; the final category *(Q16)*, for example, lacks all drafting precision.[46]

The Framework Directive as amended placed an obligation on the Commission to "draw up ... a list of wastes belonging to the categories listed in Annex I. This list will be periodically reviewed and, if necessary, revised".[47] This list, known as the

---

[46] Kramer is of the view that this Q16 category "includes literally any substance or object"; see *European Environmental Law Casebook* (1993) p.275.

[47] Article 1(a).

"European Waste Catalogue", was originally adopted by the Commission in December 1993,[48] but was replaced in May 2000 by a revised list with effect from January 2002.[49] Both the original 1993 list and its revised form are wide-ranging, but neither list is exhaustive as they can be reviewed and revised if necessary. Furthermore, even if substances fall within the categories in Annex I or appear in the revised European Waste Catalogue, this is not to be regarded as conclusive that they represent "waste" in all circumstances. Materials are considered to be waste only where the definition of waste in Article 1(a) of Directive 75/442 is met. Tyres, sawdust, bricks and photographic fixer solutions are, for example, noted in the original European Waste Catalogue and in its revised form, but are not to be regarded as waste unless the second condition in Article 1(a) is met, namely that the holder must either *discard* them, intend to do so, or be required to do so.[50] Whether or not an object should be classified as waste should therefore be deduced from the holder's actions – if he is to "discard" the object, it is to be categorised as "waste" under the Framework Directive.[51] No definition is however given in the Framework Directive of the term "discard".

Whilst it is evident that a broad definition of "waste" is envisaged, a lack of clarity as to its precise meaning continues to provide difficulties in national implementation of the directive and its subsequent daughter directives. This ambiguity is another good example of vagueness in environmental measures which has served to hamper effective implementation.[52] Defining the term "discard" has proven particularly difficult. A particular issue arises in the scenario where an industrial process produces a by-product which can be recovered or reused. Should the recovery or reuse of the by-product be regarded as an operation relating to "waste", and therefore falling within the strict system of regulation established under Community Law? We will note that this is an issue which has been raised before the ECJ on several occasions. In its jurisprudence, the Court has undoubtedly experienced difficulties in seeking to uphold the environmental objectives of the Framework Directive, while at the same time endeavouring to ensure that industry is not over-regulated.[53]

---

[48] Commission Decision 94/3 Establishing a List of Wastes Pursuant to Article 1(a) of Council Directive 75/442 on Waste, OJ 1994 L5/15.

[49] Commission Decision 2000/532 replacing Decision 94/3 Establishing a List of Wastes Pursuant to Article 1(a) of Council Directive 75/442 on Waste and Council Decision 94/904 Establishing a List of Hazardous Waste Pursuant to Article 1(4) of Council Directive 91/689 on Hazardous Waste, OJ 2000 L226/3. This decision has been amended by Commission Decisions 2001/118 (OJ 2001 L47/1) and 2001/119 (OJ 2001 L47/32), and by Commission Decision 2001/573 (OJ 2001 L203/18).

[50] See Framework Directive, Article 1(a). This is acknowledged in Decision 94/3, and also in Decision 2000/532 which replaced Decision 94/3. For example, the Annex to Decision 2000/532 notes that "the inclusion of a material in the list does not mean that the material is a waste in all circumstances. Materials are considered to be a waste only where the definition of waste in Article 1(a) of Directive 75/442 is met".

[51] See, for example, Case C-9/00 *Palin Granit Oy* [2002] ECR I-3533, para.22.

[52] Tromans, "EC Waste Law - A Complete Mess?" [2001] 13(2) JEL 133, at p.141 at n.34. See also general discussion on quality of directives in chapter 3.

[53] Cheyne, "The Definition of Waste in EC Law" (2002) 12(1) JEL 61, at p.65.

To what extent has the ECJ seen fit to define the term "discard"? Certainly in its case law the ECJ has indicated that the original definition of waste includes substances which the holder disposes of even where these substances are capable of economic reutilisation.[54] In addition, the ECJ has also confirmed this to be the case in relation to the current definition of waste.[55] An object is therefore not only waste if it is "thrown away" being of no economic value - it can still fall within the system of control and supervision established by the Framework Directive if discarded by an owner for value to a commercial recovery operation. Even waste that has an economic value must be regulated to ensure the Framework Directive's objective of ensuring a "high level of protection and effective control"[56] is achieved. Nevertheless, this determination hardly amounts to a comprehensive definition of the concept of "waste" or the term "discard".

In the absence of a comprehensive definition of the term "discard", the opinion of Advocate General Jacobs in *Criminal Proceedings against Euro Tombesi et al* provided a focus of much debate.[57] In his view, the definition of waste was "imprecise and open-ended" and some practical rules were required if operators in the waste industry were to be given the legal certainty they required.[58] In this respect, AG Jacobs put forward the view that there was in fact "little to be gained by considering the normal meaning of the term 'discard'" as the word under the directive had acquired a "special meaning":[59]

> *It is clear from the provisions of the Directive ... that the term 'waste' and the regulatory system of the Directive extend both to substances or objects which are disposed of and to those which are recovered. Thus the term 'discard' employed in the definition of waste in Article 1(a) has a special meaning encompassing both the disposal of waste and its consignment to a recovery operation. The scope of the term "waste" therefore depends on what is meant by 'disposal operation' and 'recovery operation'*[60] [emphasis added].

---

[54] See joined Cases C-206/88 and C-207/88 *Criminal Proceedings against Vessoso and Zanetti* [1990] ECR I-1461 at para.8. See also Case C-359/88 *Criminal Proceedings against Zanetti et al* [1990] ECR 1509 in which the ECJ noted that "national legislation which defines waste as excluding substances and objects which are capable of economic reutilization is not compatible" with the Framework Directive (para.13).

[55] See for instance Case C-422/92 *Commission v Germany* [1995] ECR I-1097, paras.22-23.

[56] Preamble to Directive 91/156 amending the Framework Directive.

[57] Joined Cases C-304/94, C-330/94, C-342/94 and C-224/95 [1997] ECR I-3561.

[58] Advocate General Jacobs' opinion in *Criminal Proceedings against Euro Tombesi et al* [1997] ECR I-3561, para.56.

[59] Advocate General Jacobs' opinion, para.50.

[60] *Ibid.*

This approach to providing a definition of "waste" became known as the "*Euro Tombesi* bypass",[61] and sidestepped the importance of the ambiguous word "discard" which had proved hard to define.[62] Instead, it preferred to place emphasis on the disposal operations noted in Annex IIA and the recovery operations noted in Annex IIB. According to the Advocate General, "[t]he sole question is whether the substance at issue is subject to a disposal or recovery operation within the meaning of Annex IIA or IIB".[63] In effect, if the substance is subject to such an operation or an analogous operation, it is "waste" and falls within the scope of the supervision regime established by the directive. In this context Advocate General Jacobs argued that if a substance is transferred to another person and in its existing form is subject to continued used by the latter – as when a second-hand car is sold to a new owner – it is not "recovered".[64] In essence, it is not "waste" as it is not made subject to a processing operation making it suitable for continued use. Laurence rightly points out that such an approach "would ensure that many substances which are used directly in industrial processes do not fall within the definition of waste" and would therefore not be subject to the directive's regulatory regime.[65] For instance, scrap metal which is placed directly into a smelting furnace in an operation producing iron and steel would not constitute "waste" as it had not been made subject to an Annex IIB recovery operation before being re-used.[66] It would be regarded simply as a raw material rather than as waste as it is to be re-used in its existing form without processing.[67] On the other hand, scrap metal which is crushed by a scrap metal collector for future use in an industrial process is "waste" as, prior to being re-used, it was made subject to a recovery operation.[68]

The "*Euro Tombesi* bypass" was designed to provide national courts, national regulators and industry with some much needed guidance to distinguish "waste" from a non-waste product. The approach is not however totally flawless as the Advocate General himself acknowledged.[69] In particular, whilst it certainly deflects attention from the significance of the ambiguous word "discard", it places emphasis on "disposal and recovery operations" which are not comprehensively defined in the

---

[61] Van Calster, "The EC Definition of Waste: *Euro Tombesi* Bypass and Basel Relief Routes", European Business Law Review May/June 1997, p.137.

[62] See Cheyne and Purdue, "Fitting Definition to Purpose: the Search for a Satisfactory Definition of Waste" [1995] 7(2) JEL 149.

[63] Advocate General Jacobs' opinion, para.57. See also on this point Laurence, *supra* n.2, p.83

[64] Advocate General Jacobs' opinion, para.52.

[65] Laurence, *supra* n.2, p.83

[66] *Ibid.*

[67] This was a view held by the UK Government in the Tombesi case; see Advocate General's opinion, para 48. On the issue of substances which are "raw materials" rather than "waste", see Veldkamp "Community Waste Policy and the Internal Market: Conflicting Interests?" in Faure, Vervaele and Weale, *Environmental Standards in the European Union in an Interdisciplinary Framework* (1994), at p.223.

[68] See Laurence, *supra* n.2, pp.83-84.

[69] See Advocate General's opinion, paras.53-55.

directive. Advocate General Jacobs indeed noted that the wording of both Annex IIA and B "suggests these lists are merely illustrative and based on existing experience" in that Annex IIA refers *inter alia* to disposal operations "such as they occur in practice", and Annex IIB is intended to include recovery operations "as they are carried out in practice".[70] Additionally, some recovery operations noted in Annex IIB did not fit easily into a restricted definition of recovery endorsed in the "bypass" which excludes products passed to another person and put to continued use in their existing form.[71] Category R8 for example referred to the re-use of oil,[72] and R9 to "use principally as a fuel",[73] both being operations which do not necessarily involve treatment or processing of a substance prior to use in another industrial process.

The ECJ in *Euro Tombesi* certainly did not expressly endorse the Advocate General's opinion in its judgment, merely seeing fit to reconfirm for the purposes of the issue at hand that the directive as amended established a waste management system which covered *"all objects and substances discarded by their owners, even if they have a commercial value and are collected on a commercial basis for recycling, reclamation or re-use"*.[74] Some however have taken the view that the *Euro Tombesi* judgment implicitly adopted the bypass,[75] and certainly there would seem to be a general endorsement of the AG Jacobs' approach in that the ECJ preferred to concentrate on addressing the concepts of disposal and recovery, rather than the concept of "discard". Indeed, in the subsequent case of *Inter-Environnement Wallonie ASBL v Region Wallonne*[76] the ECJ expressly linked the term "discard" to the concepts of disposal and recovery in the following terms:

> *[I]t follows from the wording of Article 1(a) of Directive 75/442, as amended, that the scope of the term "waste" turns on the meaning of the term "discard". It is also clear from the provisions of Directive 75/442, as amended, ... that the term "discard" covers both disposal and recovery of a substance or object.*[77]

However, the rulings in *Euro Tombesi* and *Inter-Environnement Wallonnie* certainly did not advocate that a substance is waste *only* if it undergoes either an Annex IIA disposal or IIB recovery operation.[78]

---

[70] *Ibid*, para.51.

[71] See Advocate General's opinion, para.53.

[72] See Purdue, "The Distinction between Using Secondary Raw Materials and the Recovery of Waste: the Definition of Waste" (1998) 10(1) JEL 116, at p.139. Note that Commission Decision 96/350 replaced the original Annexes IIA and IIB (OJ 1996 L135/32) – as a consequence "oil refining and other reuses of oils" now constitutes category R9.

[73] See comment by van Rossem (1998) 10(1) JEL at p.142. "Use principally a fuel or other means to generate energy" now constitutes category R1 (see Commission Decision 96/350 *supra* n.72).

[74] Para.52 of the judgment.

[75] Van Calster, "The Legal Framework for the Regulation of Waste in the EC" 1 *Yearbook of European Environmental Law* (2000) 161, at p. 166.

[76] Case C-129/96 [1997] ECR I-7411.

[77] Paras.26 and 27 of the judgment.

[78] See Laurence, *supra* n.2, p.86.

The ECJ was provided with another opportunity to clarify the definition of waste in *ARCO Chemie Nederland/ Epon*.[79] The Dutch national court raised certain questions relating to whether use of "LUWA-bottoms" and wood chips as fuel amounted to the discarding of these objects. LUWA-bottoms are by-products of ARCO's manufacturing process to be used primarily as a fuel in the cement industry, whilst the wood chips were to be transformed into wood powder and used by Epon as a fuel to generate electricity. Clearly the LUWA-bottoms and wood chips were to undergo a recovery operation noted in Annex IIB ("use principally as a fuel or other means to generate energy"), but did this mean that the objects were "waste"?

The judgment first underlined that the term "waste" turned on the meaning of "discard",[80] and that the latter particularly includes the disposal and recovery of an object.[81] However this certainly did not amount to an approval of the "bypass" approach as there was no endorsement of the notion that a substance is waste only if it is made subject to a disposal or recovery operation noted in Annex IIA and B. Indeed the ECJ specifically went on to undermine the "bypass" approach of AG Jacobs by stipulating that it cannot be conclusively determined that a substance has been "discarded" just because it undergoes an Annex IIA or B operation.[82] In this respect, the judgment noted that certain methods noted in Annex IIB categories could apply to the use of raw materials rather than waste substances.[83] Annex IIB for example referred to "use principally as a fuel or other means to generate energy" which could apply to the burning of fuel oil, gas or kerosene, and also to "spreading on land resulting in benefit to agriculture or ecological improvement" which might apply to use of fertilisers.[84] In effect, whether or not a substance has been discarded (and is therefore "waste") cannot be conclusively determined simply by reference to whether it undergoes an Annex II process.

What light, if any, did the ECJ shed on the meaning of the term "discard"? Bearing in mind the Framework Directive's objective to ensure the protection of human health and the environment, as well as the Community's environmental policy objective to aim at a high level of protection based on the precautionary principle and that preventive action should be taken,[85] the ECJ indicated that the concept of waste "cannot be interpreted restrictively".[86] Having said that, clearly Member States are free to determine presumptions with regard to issues defined in

79   Cases C-418/97 and C-419/97 *ARCO Chemie Nederland Ltd* v *Minister van Volkshuisvesting, Ruimtelijke Ordening en Milieubeheer and Vereniging Dorpsbelang Hees, Stichting Werkgroep Weurt and Vereniging Stedelijk Leefmilieu Nijmegen* v *Directeur van de dienst Milieu en Water van de provincie Gelderland* [2000] ECR I-4475.
80   Para.46 of the judgment.
81   Para.47 of the judgment.
82   Para.49 of the judgment.
83   Para.50 of the judgment.
84   *Ibid.*
85   Para.39 of the judgment.
86   Para.84 of the judgment.

Community directives. However, any such presumption would not be allowed to restrict the scope of the Framework Directive inappropriately. The ECJ went on to determine that it would be inappropriate, for example, to conclude that use of a substance (such as LUWA-bottoms) did not constitute "discarding" merely because it could be recovered in an environmentally responsible manner for use as a fuel without substantial treatment.[87] Additionally, while acknowledging that evidence in determining whether a substance has been discarded may be provided by the fact that use as a fuel is a common method of recovering waste and that a particular substance is commonly thought of as waste, the final determination as to whether the substance is indeed waste must be made in the light of all circumstances "regard being had to the aim of the directive and the need to ensure that its effectiveness is not undermined".[88]

The request for a preliminary reference in *ARCO Chemie Nederland/Epon* had also asked the ECJ to deliberate as to whether the substance being a main product or simply a residue is of relevance in determining if it has been discarded. Importantly, the Court indicated that certain circumstances might be evidence that something has been discarded particularly where the substance is a production residue.[89] For example, that no use for that residue substance other than disposal can be envisaged,[90] or the fact that special environmental precautions have to be taken when the residue substance is used may be seen as evidence of discarding.[91] However, the final determination had to be made bearing in mind all the circumstances and the aim of the directive.

The *ARCO Chemie Nederland/Epon* judgment and the ECJ's earlier jurisprudence have underlined that the concept of waste is to be interpreted broadly in the light of the Framework Directive's objective of ensuring a high level of environmental protection. Instead of establishing an exhaustive definition, the ECJ has placed the onus on national courts to determine on a case-by-case basis whether or not a substance should be regarded as waste, and accordingly made subject to relevant regulatory standards. In this sense, the ECJ has favoured the need for environmental protection at the risk of distorting the functioning of the internal market.[92] The more recent ruling in *Palin Granit Oy*[93] provides some evidence to support this notion. Leftover stone from granite quarrying activities was to be stored for an indefinite period of time awaiting possible use (for example, in the building of breakwaters or harbours). The ECJ recalled that its judgment in *ARCO Chemie Nederland/Epon* had

---

[87] Para.65 of the judgment.
[88] Para.73 of the judgment.
[89] Para.84 of the judgment.
[90] Para.86 of the judgment.
[91] Para.87 of the judgment.
[92] See Tromans, *supra* n.52, p.145.
[93] Case C-9/00 *supra* n.51.

noted the importance of determining whether the matter in issue was a production residue. If it is a residue rather than the operator's primary objective in the production process, it may provide evidence that the subject-matter is waste. The leftover stone was indeed a secondary product, not being the primary end-product of Palin Granit's operations. The Court therefore acknowledged strength in the argument put forward by the Commission that the leftover stone was waste being "residues from raw materials extraction and processing" (Q11 of Annex I to the Framework Directive). On the other hand, the Court noted that, even where a substance at issue is not the primary aim of the operation, a counter-argument could validly be made that such goods or raw materials resulting from the extraction process could be regarded not as a residue, but rather as a by-product which is not intended to be discarded, and which the holder intends to market or exploit on favourable terms in another process without further processing before re-use.

Which of these perfectly plausible arguments was to prevail? The Court recalled that the concept of waste was to be interpreted widely to minimise environmental harm. As a consequence, the ECJ noted that

> *the reasoning applicable to by-products should be confined to situations in which the reuse of the goods, materials or raw materials is not a mere possibility but a certainty, without any further processing prior to reuse and as an integral part of the production process.*[94]

On the facts, the re-use of the leftover stone was far from certain. If it was to be re-used, such re-use was only foreseeable in the long term. The stone was therefore likely to be stored long-term placing a burden on the holder, and was potentially a cause of environmental pollution.[95] As such, the Court concluded that leftover stone which was to be stored for an indefinite length of time awaiting only possible re-use amounted to "waste" under the Framework Directive as the holder discarded or intended to discard such stone. In applying the notion that the likelihood of re-use without further processing was a criterion to be taken into consideration, the Court concluded that the leftover stone was waste. As such, it had chosen the line of argument which provided the least possibility of causing environmental harm.

---

[94] Para.36. The Court additionally stated that, if a substance will possibly be re-used without further processing, and there is also a financial advantage to be gained by the holder for so re-using, the chances are high that the substance will be re-used in this way. In these circumstances, the substance would not be regarded as one that the holder would "discard" but rather as a "genuine product"; para 37.

[95] Para.38. Advocate General Jacobs had agreed with the Finnish government's argument that the stockpiling of stones for an indefinite period of time could lead to noise and dust pollution, and would constitute an eyesore on the countryside. The Court clearly had sympathy with this viewpoint in concluding that, even if the stone of itself did not pose a risk to human health or the environment, the stockpiling of such stone was a source of environmental harm and pollution in circumstances where the re-use of the stone was "neither immediate nor even always foreseeable"; para.49.

A comprehensive definition of "waste" still remains elusive with the inevitable result that certain disparities between Member States' laws on waste recovery and disposal will continue to arise. Cases will no doubt continue to come before national courts attempting to determine the borderline between waste and non-waste products. These must be determined on a case-by-case basis. There is equally little doubt that requests for preliminary rulings of the ECJ will continue to be made on this issue. Indeed, a request for such a ruling in the English case of *Mayer Parry Recycling Ltd* is pending at the time of writing.[96]

Hazardous Waste

Bearing in mind the inherent nature of hazardous waste, the Community has seen fit to adopt specific legislation relating to its management. Council Directive 91/689 on hazardous waste ("Hazardous Waste Directive") replaced the 1978 Directive on toxic and dangerous waste,[97] and imposes a stricter degree of supervision on the disposal and recovery of hazardous waste than afforded to waste under the general terms of the Framework Directive. Whilst the general rules of the Framework Directive remain applicable to hazardous waste, its application is subject to the terms of the Hazardous Waste Directive.

Mixing of Waste

Member States must ensure that undertakings which dispose of, recover, collect or transport hazardous waste do not mix different types of hazardous waste, nor mix any hazardous waste with non-hazardous waste.[98] If waste is already mixed, it should be separated where economically and technically possible.[99] In addition, Member States must ensure that, wherever hazardous waste is tipped, the waste is recorded and identified.[100] These requirements clearly have been introduced for safety reasons.

---

[96] Case C-444/00. The issue to be determined by the ECJ concerns whether scrap metal, used potentially as a feedstock in steel mills, should be regarded as "waste" under the Framework Directive.

[97] Directive 91/689/EEC (OJ 1991 L377/20) which replaced Directive 78/319/EEC (OJ 1978 L84/43).

[98] Article 2(2). These requirements are subject to a derogation that mixing can take place but only if waste is recovered or collected in accordance with Article 4 of the Framework Directive in that such an operation must not endanger human health or harm the environment. Such an operation would need to satisfy the relevant permit requirements in the Framework Directive.

[99] Article 2(4).

[100] Article 2(1).

Permit Requirements

Any undertaking which carries out their own waste *disposal* operations at the place of production must obtain a permit before doing so.[101] Contrary to Article 11 of the Framework Directive, no derogations are allowed. On the other hand, any undertaking which *recovers* hazardous waste, while normally required to obtain a permit, need not do so as long as the undertaking is registered with the national competent authority,[102] and operates without endangering human health or in a way which could cause environmental harm. However, this derogation is only applicable where a Member State has adopted general rules listing the type and quantity of waste and establishing specific conditions for recovery operations.[103] The adoption of such rules has not proved to be an option which Member States have widely endorsed.[104]

Other Obligations

Not only must undertakings which are involved in a hazardous waste disposal or recovery operation be subject to periodic inspections in accordance with Article 13 of the Framework Directive, but producers of hazardous waste must also be regularly inspected.[105] This is intended to ensure effective regulation at the beginning of the life cycle. Additionally, not only must those involved in hazardous waste disposal or recovery keep full records on hazardous waste handled by them, but also producers and transporters of hazardous waste are so obliged.[106]

Member States have the responsibility to ensure that hazardous waste is properly packaged and labelled when collected, transported or temporarily stored.[107] Also, Member States must adopt hazardous waste management plans either within the general waste management plans which must be adopted under the terms of the Framework Directive, or as separate plans.[108] In addition, in times of emergency or grave danger Member States must ensure that hazardous waste is dealt with without causing a threat to the public or the environment. In such instances, temporary derogations from the terms of the hazardous waste directive would be allowed as long as the Commission is informed.[109]

---

[101] Article 3(1).

[102] Article 3(3).

[103] Article 3(2). On a Member State's failure to comply with this requirement, see Case C-65/00 *Commission* v *Italy* [2002] ECR I-1795.

[104] In its report on implementation of the directive covering the period 1995-97, the Commission noted that none of the Member States who supplied information on implementation had established general rules to facilitate the making of such exemptions; COM (99) 752.

[105] Article 4(1).

[106] Article 4(2).

[107] Article 5(1).

[108] Article 6(1). On failure to comply with this obligation, see Case C-292/99 *Commission* v *France* [2002] ECR I-4097.

[109] Article 7(1).

What Exactly is "Hazardous Waste"?

Clearly therefore a more stringent regime exists for the control and supervision of hazardous waste, but what types of waste qualify as hazardous? The Hazardous Waste Directive makes reference to a list to be drawn up at a later date of those substances which possess one or more of the properties mentioned in Annex III of the directive.[110] The Annex III properties which render a substance "hazardous" *inter alia* include being carcinogenic, highly inflammable, explosive, of an oxidising nature, corrosive, infectious or harmful. The "Hazardous Waste list" was eventually adopted in 1994,[111] and included substances such as sulphuric acid and ammonia from inorganic chemical processes, CFCs from coolants, and insulation materials containing asbestos. In all, over two hundred types of waste were included on the list.

However, the list was certainly not to be regarded as fully comprehensive bearing in mind that Article 1(4) of the Hazardous Waste Directive notes that when a Member State considers that any other waste displays Annex III properties, such substances should also be regarded as hazardous.[112] The measure therefore expressly allows Member States to introduce more stringent measures. In such circumstances, the Member States concerned must notify the Commission which must then examine as to whether the list should be reviewed to include the substance. In effect, a substance is "hazardous" not only if noted on the Hazardous Waste list, but also – within the specific Member State concerned – if a Member State considers it to display any of the Annex III properties.[113] This is an added complication which potentially has internal market implications particularly bearing in mind that, by the beginning of 1999, the Commission had received 471 notifications from Member States in this way.[114] If, after being notified of a Member State's view that certain waste displays a property listed in Annex III, the Commission takes the view that the hazardous waste list should be amended to take account of the notification, the waste in question is consequently to be treated as hazardous in nature throughout the Community as a whole.[115]

---

[110] Article 1(4).

[111] Council Decision 94/904 OJ 1994 L356/14.

[112] Article 1(4).

[113] Case C-318/98 *Re Criminal proceedings against Fornasar, Strizzolo, Toso, Mucchino, Peressutti and Chiarcosso* [2000] ECR I-4785, paras.45 and 48.

[114] COM (1999) 752, p. 35.

[115] Case C-318/98 *Re Criminal proceedings against Fornasar, Strizzolo, Toso, Mucchino, Peressutti and Chiarcosso, supra* n. 113, para.49.

The Hazardous Waste list is repealed with effect from January 2002 by a new list which takes account of previous notifications by Member States on hazardous waste, and also establishes a single Community list of wastes incorporating the European Waste Catalogue.[116] Wastes considered as hazardous display one or more of the Annex III properties and are marked by an asterisk on the revised list.[117] But this new list is also far from comprehensive in nature as Article 1(4) of the Hazardous Waste Directive still applies.[118] Furthermore, the new list notes that Member States are allowed "in exceptional cases" to treat an otherwise non-hazardous waste as displaying an Annex III characteristic and, as such, as being hazardous in nature.[119] Conversely, a Member State, in exceptional circumstances and on the basis of documentary evidence supplied by the holder of waste, can decide that a waste does not display an Annex III property. In these circumstances, it can treat that waste substance as not being hazardous in nature even though the revised list states otherwise. All such decisions by Member States must be notified on a yearly basis to the Commission, the latter being under an obligation to examine whether the list of wastes and hazardous wastes should be revised in the light of such national determinations.[120] Overall, the present rules do not therefore promote uniformity and consistency in defining hazardous waste. This inevitably has internal market implications presenting real practical problems for those handling and dealing in waste throughout the Member States.

Regulating the Shipment of Waste

If insufficiently regulated, market forces may facilitate the movement of waste from those countries demanding high environmental standards where treating waste is expensive, to those states with lower standards where costs are minimised. Council Regulation 259/93 establishes a system of supervision for the shipment of waste within, into and out of the Community ("Shipment of Waste Regulation").[121] It seeks to implement the Community's international obligations in this field, namely the

---

[116] Commission Decision 2000/532 *supra* n. 49.

[117] Unless it is domestic waste. Under Article 1(5) of the Hazardous Waste Directive, domestic waste is exempt from its provisions. In an exchange of emails with the author in late 2001, the Information Centre in DG Environment noted that "the Commission does not consider it a priority to amend the hazardous waste directive to include hazardous waste into its scope or to establish specific rules for this type of waste".

[118] For an example of an amendment to the revised list of waste introduced in the light of notifications by Member States pursuant to Article 1(4) of Council Directive 91/689 on Hazardous Waste, see Commission Decision 2001/118 amending Decision 2000/532 as regards the list of wastes (OJ 2001 L47/1).

[119] Commission Decision 2000/532 *supra* n.49, Article 3.

[120] *Ibid.* An added complication is that the inclusion of any material on the original hazardous waste list or on the revised list does not mean it is always to be regarded as "waste" – it must additionally meet the definition of waste in Article 1(a) of the Framework Directive.

[121] OJ 1993 L30/1. Annex II, III and IV have most recently been amended by Commission Decision 1999/816/EC, OJ 1999 L316/45. Annex V has most recently been amended by Commission Regulation 2557/2001, OJ 2001 L349/1. The Shipment of Waste regulation replaced the poorly implemented Council Directive 84/631 on the Supervision and Control within the EEC of the Transfrontier Shipment of Hazardous Waste as amended (OJ 1984 L326/31).

Basel Convention on the control of hazardous wastes and their disposal (Basel Convention),[122] the Lomé IV Convention,[123] as well as action in this sphere by industrialised countries within the Organisation of Economic Cooperation and Development (OECD). Of particular relevance in the OECD context is the 1992 OECD Council Decision on the transfrontier movement of waste destined for recovery operations (1992 OECD Decision)[124] which has provided a framework for the control of such waste movements.

The Shipment of Waste Regulation defines waste by reference to the definition provided in the Framework Directive on waste.[125] Therefore not only hazardous waste but also all other waste falls within its remit.[126] The Regulation is a highly intricate piece of legislation which makes important distinctions between waste shipped for disposal and that destined for recovery.[127] In principle, the regulation endorses the notion that the transfrontier shipment of waste for disposal should be very limited indeed, whilst the shipment of waste for recovery purposes should be effectively controlled but more widely accepted within the industrialised world.[128]

---

[122] 28 ILM 649 (1989); OJ 1993 L39/3. The Community and all Member States have ratified the Basel Convention. See generally Kummer, "The Basel Convention: Ten Years On" (1998) 7(3) RECIEL 227. For the treaty regime's website, see http://www.basel.int/.

[123] OJ 1991 L229/3. Article 39 of this treaty introduces a ban on the export of hazardous and radioactive waste from the EC to 70 African, Caribbean and Pacific (ACP) countries; see Laurence, *supra* n.2, p.222. In the context of this Convention, see the resolution on hazardous waste adopted by the Lomé IV treaty's Joint Assembly between African, Caribbean and Pacific States and the EU in relation to the ban on the export of hazardous waste from OECD to non-OECD states introduced under the Basel Convention with effect from January 1998, OJ 1997 C308/61.

[124] OECD C(92)39 [as now amended by Decision C(2001) 107]. This decision constitutes a multilateral agreement under Article II of the Basel Convention; see Kummer, *International Management of Hazardous Waste* (1995) pp.159-163. For the OECD's website, see http://www.oecd.org.

[125] Article 2(a).

[126] The Regulation does however specifically exclude from its remit certain shipments including shipments of radioactive waste (regulated by Directive 92/3/Euratom OJ 1992 L35/24), waste generated by ships and offshore platforms provided "such waste is the subject of a specific binding international instrument", civil aviation waste, waste shipped to the EC in accordance with the 1991 Madrid Protocol on Environmental Protection to the Antarctic Treaty, and other wastes referred to in Article 2(1)b of the Framework Directive "where they are already covered by relevant legislation" (such as wastes from quarries, animal carcasses and decommissioned explosives).

[127] All permitted shipments under the Shipment of Waste Regulation must however be accompanied by a financial guarantee or equivalent insurance covering costs of shipment, disposal or recovery in situations where, for some reason, the notifier is unable to bear such costs; Article 27(1).The guarantee will come to an end as soon as a relevant certificate has been signed and sent confirming that the shipment has been disposed of or recovered "in an environmentally sound manner" or that, in the case of transit through the EC, the waste has left the Community; Article 27(2).

[128] This being the case, the judgment in Case C-6/00 *Abfall Service AG (ASA)* v *Bundesminister fur Umwelt, Jugend and Familie* [2002] ECR I-1961 is of considerable interest. The ECJ determined that the deposit of waste in a disused mine did not necessarily amount to an act of "disposal" for the purposes of the Framework Directive. The shipment of filling waste could therefore be construed as waste destined for recovery and as falling within the more relaxed shipment system. The ruling stipulated that "[t]he deposit must be assessed on a case-by-case basis to determine whether the operation is a disposal or a recovery operation within the meaning of [the Framework Directive]. Such a deposit constitutes a recovery if its principal purpose is that the waste serve a useful purpose in replacing other materials which would have had to be used for that purpose".

In defining "disposal" and "recovery", the definitions in the Framework Directive apply.[129] The detailed requirements of the Regulation do not apply to shipments of waste *within* a Member State. However, Member States must introduce "an appropriate system for the supervision and control of shipments of waste within their jurisdiction ... [which] should take account of the need for coherence with the Community system established by this Regulation".[130]

The system established by the Shipment of Waste regulation in relation to waste for disposal will first be addressed.

Waste for Disposal

Shipments of waste between Member States   Member States can importantly introduce national measures in compliance with the principles of non-discrimination and proportionality to "prohibit generally or partially or to object systematically to shipments of waste".[131] These measures must be notified to the Commission which will in turn inform the other Member States. In effect, national measures can be introduced to enable Member States to be self-sufficient in relation to the disposal of waste – any such measure must be adopted "to implement the principles of proximity, priority for recovery and self-sufficiency at Community and national levels"[132] in accordance with the Framework Directive.[133] This ability to prohibit certain waste shipments underlines the importance placed on the proximity and self-sufficiency principles in the Community's waste management strategy.

Those shipments which are permitted are made subject to a system of supervision based on prior notification.[134] The "notifier" (entity shipping the waste) must notify the relevant competent authority for the area in which the shipment will be received ("competent authority of destination"). The notifier must also send a copy of the notification to the relevant competent authorities of dispatch and of transit, as well as to the undertaking to which the waste will be shipped ("consignee"). The

---

[129] It will be recalled that the Framework Directive notes that "disposal" includes the operations in Annex IIA, and "recovery" as covering operations in Annex IIB. If the competent body of dispatch disagrees with the exporter of certain waste as to its classification as either waste for recovery or for disposal, the former should oppose the shipment by making an objection to the misclassification; Case C-6/00 *Abfall Service AG (ASA)* v *Bundesminister fur Umwelt, Jugend and Familie, supra* n.128.

[130] Article 13(2).

[131] Article 4(3)(a)I.

[132] *Ibid.* In circumstances where a national measure restricts exports in this way, the measure need not also be subject to a further and separate review of its compatibility with Articles 29 and 30 EC; *DaimlerChrysler AG* v *Land Baden-Wurtemberg* [2001] ECR I-9897.

[133] This would not however be applicable in circumstances where such small quantities of hazardous waste are produced in a Member State of dispatch that it would render the establishing of a specialist disposal operation in that country uneconomic; Article 4(3)(a)ii. The Member State of destination must liaise with the Member State of dispatch in such circumstances to resolve the issue. If no solution is found, the matter can be referred to the European Commission which will decide the matter.

[134] See generally Article 3.

notification must be in the form of a standard consignment note issued by the competent authority of dispatch, and is intended to make relevant competent authorities aware of shipments and their final destination.[135] In this way, the competent authorities can take the appropriate measures to protect human health and the environment.

The consignment note is to be completed by the notifier and includes details as to the source, composition and quantity of the waste being shipped. Information must also be given as to the route of the shipment and arrangements for insurance cover against damage to third parties. In addition, the notifier must give information as to the measures which will be taken to ensure safe transport, as well as full details of the disposal centre which will accept the waste for disposal (location, type and duration of authorisation). The relevant disposal centre must have the technical capacity to deal with the waste in question in such a way that the disposal operation presents no danger to human health or the environment. In addition, the notifier and the consignee must enter into a contract in which the former undertakes to take the waste back if the shipment has not been carried out as planned or has been made contrary to the Shipment of Waste Regulation. The contract must include an obligation on the part of the consignee to send a certificate to the notifier that the waste has been disposed of in an environmentally sound way no later than 180 days from receipt of the waste.[136]

On receipt of the notification, the competent authority of destination must send an acknowledgement to the notifier, and copies to the consignee and other relevant competent authorities. It then has 30 days in which to make a decision as to whether the shipment will be formally allowed (with or without conditions) or refused.[137] A decision authorising the shipment can only be made in the absence of any objections it may have or which are aired by other competent authorities. Any conditions must be entered into the consignment note, and must not discriminate in that they must not be more stringent than those laid down in respect of similar shipments occurring wholly within their jurisdiction.

Competent authorities of dispatch and destination may raise reasoned objections to shipments if intended shipments fail to comply with the terms of the Framework Directive. These objections must be made in order to implement the principle of self-sufficiency in waste disposal at Community and national levels, to ensure that

---

[135] Commission Decision 94/774 Concerning the Standard Consignment Note referred to in Council Regulation 259/93 on the Supervision and Control of Shipments of Waste within, into and out of the European Community OJ 1994 L310/70.

[136] Shipment of Waste Regulation, Article 3(6).

[137] See generally Article 4.

shipments are in accordance with waste management plans adopted pursuant to the Framework Directive, and in situations where the installation has to dispose of waste from a nearer source and the competent authority has given priority to this waste.[138] In addition, competent authorities of dispatch, destination and transit can raise reasoned objections to a shipment where the notifier or consignee has previously been found guilty of illegal trafficking, or where the shipment fails to comply with national laws relating to environmental protection, public order, public safety or health protection, or with relevant international legal obligations of the Member State concerned.[139] The competent authorities of dispatch and transit have 20 days in which to raise objections or establish conditions concerning the transport of waste in its jurisdiction.

Any shipment of waste for disposal can only be made once the notifier has received the relevant express authorisation from the competent authority of destination.[140] If authorisation is forthcoming, the notifier must insert the date of the shipment in the consignment note, and send copies to all relevant competent authorities three working days before the shipment commences its journey. Within three working days of receiving the shipment, the consignee must inform the notifier and competent authorities, and must subsequently send a certificate of disposal to these parties no later than 180 days after receipt of the waste.[141] The certificate of disposal must confirm that the shipment has been disposed of in an environmentally sound manner.[142]

Exports of waste from Member States to non-EC countries The general rule is that the shipment for disposal of any type of waste – hazardous or non-hazardous – is prohibited.[143] The rationale for this ban is provided by the need to protect the environment of non-EC countries from unscrupulous undertakings which may otherwise have been tempted to send waste out of the Community to avoid the high cost of disposing of waste inside the EC. In effect, implementation of the principle of self-sufficiency prevents wastes being exported out of the Community to non-EC countries.

An exception to the general rule applies to shipments to those European Free Trade Agreement (EFTA) countries that have ratified the Basel Convention.[144] Even then,

---

[138] Article 4(3)(b).

[139] Article 4(3)(c).

[140] Article 5(1).

[141] See Articles 5(5) and 5(6).

[142] Article 27(2)

[143] Article 14(1)

[144] Article 14(1).

if either the EFTA state concerned itself bans imports of such wastes or has not given its written consent to the specific import of waste, or if the competent national authority of dispatch believes the consignment will not be managed in an environmentally sound manner, the exports of waste are also to be prohibited.[145] If waste is indeed sent to an EFTA country for disposal, the competent authority of dispatch is obliged to require that the waste must be "managed in an environmentally sound manner throughout the period of shipment and in the state of destination".[146] A system of supervision is established based on prior notification and is generally akin to the system noted above relating to shipments of waste between Member States. For instance, competent authorities of dispatch and transit in the Community may raise objections based on Article 4(3).[147] One of the notable differences is that the competent authority of dispatch has a period of 70 days following dispatch of the acknowledgement to make its decision.[148]

Import of waste into Member States from non-EC countries The general rule is that the Community prohibits the import of waste for disposal. However, if the exporting state is an EFTA country party to the Basel Convention, or a country either party to the Basel Convention or which has concluded an agreement with the Community and/or Member States guaranteeing that disposal will take place in an authorised centre which complies with environmentally sound management standards, the ban on import of waste does not apply.[149] A system of prior authorisation is applicable; any shipment must be authorised by the competent authority of destination which, together with the competent authority of transit, can raise objections based on Article 4(3) or lay down conditions.[150] The competent authority of destination must place a ban on the importation of any waste into its jurisdiction if it is of the view that the waste in question will not be managed in an environmentally sound manner once within its jurisdiction.[151]

---

[145] Article 14(2).

[146] Article 14(3).

[147] Article 15(3).

[148] Article 15(2).

[149] Article 19(1)b. Alternatively, the third indent of Article 19(1)b notes that imports can be admitted into a particular Member State from other countries which have concluded bilateral agreements with the specific Member State in question prior to the application of the Shipment of Waste Regulation. Any such agreement would have to be compatible with Community legislation and guarantee that the disposal of the waste in question is carried out in an authorised centre and complies with requirements for sound environmental management.

More controversially, the fourth indent of Article 19(1)b indicates that imports can be admitted from countries with which individual Member States have signed agreements after the date of application of the Shipment of Waste Regulation. Article 19(2) notes that any such agreement is only legitimate in "exceptional cases for the disposal of specific waste where such waste will not be managed in an environmentally sound manner in the country of dispatch".

[150] Article 20(3).

[151] Article 19(4).

Next our discussion will focus on the regime established in relation to the shipment of waste for recovery.

Waste for Recovery

Concerning proposed shipments of waste intended for recovery operations, the Regulation does not distinguish between non-hazardous and hazardous waste by reference to the European Waste Catalogue. Instead the Regulation has served to complicate the issue by adopting the three-tier system utilised in the 1992 OECD Decision in that the applicable approach depends on whether the waste is categorised as being in the "Green" list (noted in Annex II of the Regulation), "Amber" list (Annex III) or "Red" list (Annex IV). The shipment of those wastes noted on the Green list (such as scrap paper or metal, and silk and cotton textile waste) are subject to the least control as they are regarded as causing least harm to human health and the environment. Such a shipment is in large part excluded from the provisions of the Shipment of Waste Regulation,[152] and shipment management is minimal.

Those on the Amber list (such as waste oils, brake fluids, sewage sludge and pig manure) and Red list (such as asbestos dusts, PCBs, peroxides other than hydrogen peroxide, and waste consisting of or contaminated with PCBs) are regarded as hazardous and are therefore subject to stricter supervision, the Red list substances being subject to the strictest control due to their particularly harmful properties. In general terms, proposed shipments of Amber and Red list waste must be notified in advance by sending a consignment note to the relevant competent authorities in the country of destination allowing the latter to make a considered decision as to whether the shipment should proceed.[153]

Shipments of waste between Member States[154]   In relation to shipment of waste on the Green list, the competent national authority of destination's prior consent to such a shipment is not required although each shipment must be accompanied by information on the shipment such as the type and quantity of waste being transported and its point of destination.[155] Such waste would not in theory present a

---

[152] Article 1(3)a.

[153] But how should "mixed" waste be classified? In Case C-192/96 *Beside BV and I.M. Besselsen* v *Minister van Volkshuisvesting, Ruimtelijke Ordening en Milieubeheer* [1998] ECR I-4029 the ECJ ruled that Green list waste mixed with a "small quantity of materials not referred to on that list" constituted "municipal/household waste" under the Amber list (para.34). But what exactly would constitute a "small quantity"? The ruling is unclear and affords national courts a large degree of discretion; see Van Calster, *supra* n.75, p.195.

[154] The detailed requirements of the Regulation do not apply to shipments of waste within a Member State. However, Article 13(2) notes that Member States must introduce "an appropriate system for the supervision and control of shipments of waste within their jurisdiction ... [which] should take account of the need for coherence with the Community system established by this Regulation".

[155] Article 11.

risk to the environment as long as it is recovered appropriately in accordance with the provisions of the Framework Directive.[156]

If a waste on the Amber or Red list is to be transported for recovery in another Member State, a system of notification applies similar to the notification procedure in relation to the shipments of waste for disposal. A contract for example must be concluded between the notifier and the consignee for the recovery of waste providing *inter alia* that the former must take back any waste if the shipment has not been completed, and in which the consignee assumes the obligation to send a certificate to the notifier that the waste has been recovered in an environmentally sound way no later than 180 days from receipt of the waste.[157] Notification must be made by means of a consignment note informing the competent national authority of destination of relevant information such as the quantity of the substance involved, those measures to be taken to ensure safe transport, the planned method of recovery and the recovery operation's location.[158] Financial guarantees are needed,[159] and the competent national authority of dispatch and destination can object to the shipment by giving reasoned objections within 30 days following the giving of an acknowledgement to the notifier of receipt of the notification. An objection may indicate, for instance, that the shipment appears not to comply with the terms of the Framework Directive, or does not satisfy national rules as to environmental protection or public safety.[160] Transfrontier shipment of waste on the Red list must always receive written prior consent of the competent national authority of destination.[161] The movement of Amber list waste for recovery requires prior consent but is simplified in that such approval can be tacit,[162] Laurence correctly

---

[156] Recovery operations must therefore comply with the permit requirement introduced by Article 10 of the Framework Directive.

[157] Article 6(6).

[158] Article 6(5).

[159] Article 27(1).

[160] Article 7(4)a:

The competent national authority of destination and dispatch may raise reasoned objections to the planned shipment:

- in accordance with Directive 75/442/EEC, in particular Article 7 thereof, or

- if it is not in accordance with national laws and regulations relating to environmental protection, public order, public safety or health protection, or

- if the notifier or the consignee has previously been guilty of illegal trafficking. In this case, the competent authority of dispatch may refuse all shipments involving the person in question in accordance with national legislation, or

- if the shipment conflicts with obligations resulting from international conventions concluded by the Member State or Member States concerned, or

- if the ratio of the recoverable and non-recoverable waste, the estimated value of the materials to be finally recovered or the cost of the recovery and the cost of the disposal of the non-recoverable fraction do not justify the recovery under economic and environmental considerations.

Article 7(4)b notes that competent authorities of transit may raise reasoned objections based on the second, third and fourth indents of Article 7(4)a.

[161] Article 10.

[162] Article 8(1).

noting that "this is in obvious contrast to international shipments for disposal, where the onus is upon the notifier to receive the competent authority's formal approval prior to the shipment".[163] Tacit consent expires after one year.

Interestingly, there is no provision equivalent to that concerning waste for disposal which would specifically allow a Member State to ban or limit transfrontier movement of waste for recovery in order to implement the principles of proximity or self-sufficiency. In line with the provisions of the Framework Directive, these principles apply only to disposal of waste. The ECJ explained this distinction in its judgment in *Chemische Afvalstoffen Dusseldorp BV* v *Minister van Volkhuisvesting, Ruimtelijke Ordening en Milieubeheer*:

> *Only waste for recovery can contribute towards implementation of the principle of priority for recovery ... It was in order to encourage such recovery in the Community as a whole, in particular by eliciting the best technologies, that the Community legislature stipulated that waste of that type should be able to move freely between Member States for processing, provided that transport poses no threat to the environment. It therefore introduced for intra-Community shipment of that waste a more flexible procedure, which does not reflect the principles of self-sufficiency and proximity.*[164]

The *Dusseldorp* case also underlined that, although the Regulation was adopted under the Environmental Title and consequently Member States could in principle introduce more stringent rules, ex Article 130t EC did not permit a Member State to extend the application of the proximity or self-sufficiency principles to waste for recovery when such national rules created a barrier to exports incompatible with the EC Treaty.[165]

Exports of waste from Member States to non-EC countries As to the export of Green list waste, the Commission was obliged by the Regulation to inform non-OECD countries as to the content of the list, and to request confirmation from these countries that such waste was not controlled in those countries.[166] As previously noted, the export of Green list waste between Member States is generally excluded from the obligations as to supervision under the Regulation due to the minimal environmental risk involved. Clearly however certain non-EC countries may take a different view or prefer simply not to become a destination point for EC waste, and the Regulation had to take this into account. Certain non-EC states indicated that they would not under any circumstances accept Green list waste for recovery, and, as a result, the export of such waste is prohibited.[167] Other states did not respond to

---

[163] See Laurence, *supra* n.2, p.262.

[164] Case C-203/96 *supra* n.18, para.33.

[165] For further discussion of this case, see chapter 6.

[166] Article 17(1).

[167] Council Regulation 1420/1999, Article 1 and Annex A, OJ 1999 L166/6. At the request of the country of destination the control procedures can be amended.

the Commission's queries – export to such countries is not prohibited but is nevertheless subject to a system of control in which the written consent of the country of destination must be forthcoming in the case of each planned shipment.[168] Some states indicated that they would accept Green list waste but only subject to specific export arrangements.[169]

Concerning the export of hazardous waste for recovery, the Community was the chief instigator of Decision III/1 of the Conference of the Parties of the Basel Convention. This 1995 decision promoted a ban on hazardous waste exports from OECD to non-OECD countries with effect from 1 January 1998. The Community has implemented the ban on such exports.[170] Any waste which falls within Annex V of the Shipment of Waste Regulation falls within this export ban.[171] But what of shipments to countries to which the OECD Decision applies? The export of Amber and Red list waste from the Community to recovery operations in such OECD states is still allowed.[172] Only where any such state has banned the import of all such wastes or not given its consent to a specific import, or where the competent authority of dispatch believes the waste will not be managed in accordance with environmentally sound methods, will the shipment be prevented.[173] In respect of the export of Amber list waste to countries to which the 1992 OECD Decision applies, the procedure is the same as is applicable to the shipment of waste between Member States for recovery.[174] The notifier must therefore complete a consignment note and send this to the relevant competent authority in the OECD state in question as well as copies to the competent authority of dispatch (and transit if applicable). If no objection is lodged within the 30-day period, the shipment may proceed. For Red list waste, formal written permission is needed.[175]

---

[168] *Ibid*, Article 2 and Annex B.

[169] As noted in Commission Regulation 1547/1999, OJ 1999 L185/1. This measure has been amended on occasion at the request of the country of destination, most recently by Commission Regulation 2243/2001 in relation to Cameroon, Paraguay and Singapore (OJ 2001 L303/11).

[170] As implemented by Council Regulation 120/97, OJ 1997 L22/15. See also Wirth, "Trade Implications of the Basel Convention Amendment Banning North-South Trade in Hazardous Wastes" (1998) 7(3) RECIEL 237.

[171] Annex V to the Shipment of Waste Regulation (as most recently defined by Commission Regulation 2557/2001 OJ 2001 L349/1) identifies the "hazardous waste" which falls within the prohibition.

[172] Shipment of Waste Regulation, Article 16(1)a as amended by Article 1 of Regulation 120/97 *supra* n.170.

[173] Shipment of Waste Regulation, Article 16(3)a and b.

[174] Shipment of Waste Regulation, Article 17(4). Where such waste is exported to countries to which the 1992 OECD Decision does not apply, the provisions of Article 17(8) are applicable. These are analogous in large part to the provisions of Article 15 on the export of waste for disposal to non-EC countries. All exports of waste to African, Caribbean and Pacific (ACP) countries is prohibited unless it has initially been sent to the EC for processing and is being sent back to the ACP state of origin (Article 18).

[175] Shipment of Waste Regulation, Article 17(6).

Import of waste into Member States from non-EC countries   The general rule is that the Community prohibits the import of waste for recovery. However, in similar fashion to the exemption applicable to the ban on the import of waste for disposal discussed above, if the exporting state is an OECD state to which the 1992 OECD Decision applies, or a country either party to the Basel Convention or which has concluded an agreement with the Community and/or Member States guaranteeing that recovery will take place in an authorised centre which complies with environmentally sound management standards, the ban on import of waste does not apply.[176] Where Red and Amber list waste is imported into Member States from OECD states party to the 1992 Decision, control measures apply as are applicable to the shipment of waste for recovery between Member States.[177] Where waste is imported into Member States from states to which the 1992 OECD Decision does not apply, a system of prior authorisation is applicable; any shipment must be authorised by the competent authority of destination which, together with the competent authority of transit, can raise relevant objections.[178]

Having addressed the highly complex system regulating the shipment of waste, discussion now turns to the regulation of waste treatment processes.

Waste Treatment Processes

The two most commonly utilised methods of processing waste are landfill and incineration. It is precisely because both of these processes bring about negative environmental consequences that the Community's waste management strategy places a priority on the need to prevent waste generation and also on waste recovery operations. However, if waste has to be disposed of by landfill and incineration,[179] it must be disposed of in such a manner which minimises harmful effects on the environment.

---

[176] Article 21(1). Alternatively, the second indent of Article 21(1)b notes that imports can be admitted into a particular Member State from other countries which have concluded bilateral agreements with the specific Member State in question prior to the application of the Shipment of Waste Regulation. Any such agreement would have to be compatible with Community legislation and guarantee that the disposal of the waste in question is carried out in an authorised centre and complies with requirements for sound environmental management.

The third indent of Article 21(1)b indicates that imports can be admitted from countries with which individual Member States have signed agreements after the date of application of the Shipment of Waste Regulation. Article 21(2) notes that any such agreement is only legitimate "where a Member State deems such agreements or arrangements necessary to avoid any interruption of waste treatment" prior to the Community entering into an agreement with the non-EC country in question.

[177] Shipment of Waste Regulation, Article 22(1).

[178] Shipment of Waste Regulation, Article 22(2). Relevant objections are noted in Article 7(4) discussed above.

[179] The process of incineration can also be regarded as a recovery process – whilst some plants are built principally to burn/destroy waste, others are designed to carry out the twin purpose of burning waste and recovering energy; see Laurence, *supra* n.2, p.234.

Landfill

Notwithstanding the Community's stated aim to encourage either the prevention of waste or its recycling/reuse before considering the need to turn to the option of safe disposal, the majority of municipal and hazardous waste in the Member States is presently disposed of in landfills.[180] Landfill can be environmentally harmful in a number of ways. The accumulation of methane gas generated from decomposing biodegradable waste is a hazard, and its subsequent migration is a contributing cause to the greenhouse effect. Decomposing landfill waste is said to be responsible for 32 per cent of the overall methane release in the Community.[181] In addition, liquid which percolates through the site ("leachate") can interact with the landfilled waste and pollute surrounding soil, groundwater and surface water. Council Directive 99/31 on the Landfill of Waste ("Landfill Directive")[182] aims as far as possible to prevent or reduce risks to public health and harmful environmental effects caused by landfill disposal, and is one of the most significant waste management directives passed to date. The Landfill Directive was adopted in April 1999 and the deadline for transposition was mid-July 2001.

Authorisation Each landfill site must be in receipt of a formal authorisation prior to operating. This operating permit can only be issued by the competent national authority if the project satisfies the general requirements of the directive which include stringent technical requirements designed to ensure that the site is suitably located and managed to minimise environmental harm.[183] In addition, the directive requires that appropriate measures be taken to prevent accidents once the site is operational.[184]

Life-cycle management Efforts have also been made to ensure that measures are in place which relate to the entire life-cycle of landfill sites. The applicant for a permit must have a financial security in place prior to the commencement of disposal operations to ensure that the directive's provisions are respected in full.[185] Notably this security must cover not only obligations relating to operational practice, but also after-care provisions – once a site has been closed, the operator of the site remains responsible for monitoring landfill gas accumulation and analysing groundwater around the site for as long as the national competent authority feels the site is likely to cause an environmental hazard.[186] The measure also seeks to ensure that Member States carry out effective sampling, monitoring and measuring of operations at

---

180 European Commission, *supra* n.4.
181 Haigh, *Manual of Environmental Policy* (looseleaf), 5.11-6.
182 OJ 1999 L182/1.
183 See Annex I.
184 Article 8(a)iii.
185 Article 8(a)iv.
186 Article 13(d).

landfill sites, and that sites are located in suitable places with natural geological barriers to prevent the spreading of pollution to soil and water.

Classification of sites   Landfills must additionally be classified as sites either for hazardous, non-hazardous or inert waste thereby reducing potentially harmful effects of waste mixing.[187] Certain waste, such as inflammable, explosive, liquid and infectious clinical waste, cannot be landfilled. In addition, waste to be placed in landfill sites must be pre-treated to reduce its size, or to make it easier to handle.[188] The risk of leaching of hazardous substances from the landfill to the surrounding environment can in this way be reduced.

Reducing reliance on landfill as a method of disposal   It will be recalled that the waste management strategy stipulates that disposal of waste is a last resort. In line with this policy, the directive very importantly obliges Member States to reduce the amount of biodegradable municipal waste disposed of by landfill,[189] and instead to ensure that this type of waste is recycled, reused or recovered. It is this aspect of the directive which is guaranteed to bring about the most impact on the Member States' waste management strategies. By July 2006, biodegradable municipal waste being sent to landfill must be reduced to 75 per cent of the total amount by weight of such waste produced in 1995.[190] By July 2009, such waste must be reduced to 50 per cent of the amount produced in 1995.[191] By July 2016, biodegradable municipal waste being sent to landfill must be reduced to 35 per cent of the 1995 amount.[192] If a Member State in 1995 landfilled more than 80 per cent of its municipal waste, they may postpone these targets for a period of not more than four years.

Apart from endeavouring to reduce the environmental impact of disposal by landfill, the other aim of the directive is therefore to discourage landfill disposal as a method of dealing with waste. Member States are obliged to ensure that the cost of establishing and operating a landfill site, as well as the expense involved in its eventual closure and after-care for a period of at least 30 years, is covered by charges made by operators of sites. These charges will be met by those who choose to dispose of waste on the sites in question. In this way, the directive aims to place a financial disincentive in the path of the latter, and it is hoped that generators of waste will seek alternatives to disposal such as re-use or recycling.[193]

---

[187] Article 6.

[188] Article 6(a). Inert waste however may not need treatment if "not technically feasible". Other waste may not require treating if such treatment would not result in a reduction in its size or its potential risk to humans and the environment.

[189] "Municipal waste" is defined as "waste from households, as well as other waste which, because of its nature or composition, is similar to waste from households"; Article 2.

[190] Article 5(2)a.

[191] Article 5(2)b.

[192] Article 5(2)c.

[193] See Forster, "The Landfill Directive: How Will the UK Meet the Challenge?" (2000) 9(1) EELR 16, at p.18.

Incineration

The other main means of processing waste is by incineration. This involves the passing of waste through a process of intense thermal treatment to reduce the amount of waste. The residue from the process can either be recycled or more safely disposed of. Incineration is not however without its harmful effects – particular concern has been raised in recent years as to the high level of dioxins and furans, as well as atmospheric emissions of heavy metals, sulphur dioxide, nitrogen oxide and carbon monoxide produced in incineration operations.[194] The Community has therefore seen fit to establish regulatory rules in this area. In June 1989 two directives were adopted to reduce and control atmospheric emissions of pollutants from existing and new municipal waste incineration plants.[195] Both measures established emission limit values for certain pollutants, requirements for the design and operation of incineration plants, and the obligation to monitor the concentration levels of combustion gases. In December 1994 a further directive was adopted to reduce harmful effects on the environment and human health of hazardous waste incineration.[196]

Over time it became clear that more stringent controls were required particularly as the Landfill Directive is increasing the cost of processing waste by landfilling, thereby potentially placing greater emphasis on the use of incineration as a means of waste disposal.[197] In particular, the emission limit values pertaining to the incineration of non-hazardous waste required tightening. Directive 2000/76 on the incineration of waste is a single text which will repeal the 1989 directives and the 1994 Directive on Hazardous Waste Incineration as of the end of 2005.[198] Whether the waste being incinerated is hazardous or not, common limit values for emissions to the atmosphere are established. In addition, the directive sets common emission limit values for discharges to the aquatic environment caused by the cleaning of exhaust gases. There are however different obligations as to the monitoring of waste on reception at the incineration plant. Whilst a general obligation is placed on the operator of the plant to prevent or limit negative environmental effects and direct risks to public health, in the case of hazardous waste additional obligations include

---

[194] For example, emissions from incineration are believed to be responsible for 36 tonnes of mercury per year and 16 tonnes per year of cadmium throughout the EC; Umweltbundesamt, *European Atmospheric Emission Inventory of Heavy Metals and Persistent Organic Pollutants for 1990* (1997) cited in COM (2000) 347 at p.7.

[195] Council Directive 89/429/EEC on the Reduction of Pollution from Existing Municipal Waste Incineration Plants OJ 1989 L203/50, and Council Directive 89/369 on the Prevention of Air Pollution from New Municipal Waste Incineration Plants OJ 1989 L163/32.

[196] Council Directive 94/67/EC on the Incineration of Hazardous Waste OJ 1994 L365/34.

[197] Glinski and Rott, "Waste Incineration - Legal Protection in European Environmental Law" (2000) 12(2) JEL 129, at 129-130. The UK Government issued its draft waste strategy in June 2000 and placed emphasis on the need to build new incinerators instead of landfill as a method of disposal; see ENDS Report 296, September 1999, p.18-19.

[198] OJ 2000 L332/91.

the need to assess the suitability of the waste for incineration at the specific plant in question, and to observe the necessary precautions that need to be taken when handling such waste.

The 1989 directives apply to incineration facilities, but not to co-incineration plants (plants which primarily produce energy and which use waste as a fuel). By contrast, the 2000 directive covers both incineration and co-incineration plants. The latter applies to all new plants from the end of 2002, and all existing plants must comply with the directive by the end of 2005. Detailed operating conditions are designed to ensure that all plants are built and operate in a manner which prevents atmospheric emissions causing significant ground-level air pollution (suitable stacks are to be built), and which ensures that heat generated from the incineration process is recovered as far as possible. No plant will operate without a permit, and no permit will be provided unless the facility's proposed measurement techniques for emissions to water and the atmosphere comply with certain requirements. If a permit is granted, it will specifically note the categories and quantity of waste which may be treated by the plant, and the applicable sampling and measuring procedures to follow. In addition, the directive places an obligation on Member States to ensure that incineration residues are minimised and, where appropriate, recycled.

Waste Streams

We noted earlier in the chapter the importance of the Hazardous Waste Directive. A variety of other specific rules have been adopted on the management of particular types of waste thereby supplementing the framework established by the Framework Directive. We will note that these measures seek to increase the amount of waste which is recovered, and often to eliminate or reduce the amount of hazardous materials used in the manufacture of products.

Packaging and Packaging Waste

Much packaging is discarded as soon as goods have been purchased and becomes packaging waste. Packaging waste often contains non-biodegradable substances rendering it unsuitable for landfill, and can produce emissions of a harmful nature when incinerated. The directive on packaging and packaging waste (Packaging Waste Directive)[199] therefore introduces measures which are designed to prevent or

---

[199] Council Directive 94/62 on Packaging and Packaging Waste OJ 1994 L365/10. See generally Reid, "The Packaging and Packaging Waste Directive" 4(8) EELR 239, and Long, "The Single Market and the Environment: the European Union's Dilemma - the Example of the Packaging Directive" 6(7) EELR 214.

reduce the impact of "packaging"[200] or "packaging waste"[201] on the environment of Member States and also of third countries.

Preventing the production of packaging waste, encouraging the re-use of packaging, and the recycling or other recovery of packaging waste are important environmental objectives of this measure. However it must also be appreciated that the regulation of the management of packaging or packaging waste will undoubtedly have a significant impact on the functioning of the internal market. That the Packaging Waste Directive was adopted under the internal market provision of ex Article 100a EC is reflective of this fact, and also of the measure's non-environmental objective to harmonise national measures with a view to avoiding obstacles to trade within the internal market.[202] If packaging complies with the provisions of the directive, access to the market should not be impeded by any Member State.[203]

The application of the measure is broad in nature in that it applies to all packaging placed on the market in the EC, and all packaging waste whether used or released at industrial, commercial, office, shop, service, household or any other level regardless of the material used.[204] Crucially, Member States are obliged to ensure that collection/return systems are set up for used packaging, as well as re-use or recovery (including recycling) operations.[205] In this way, where packaging cannot be prevented, it should be re-used, recycled or recovered, so reducing the total amount of packaging waste that must be disposed of by landfill or incineration. It should however be noted that the directive broadly reflects the approach endorsed more generally in the Community's waste management strategy; Article 1(2) stipulates that the directive

> *lays down measures aimed, as a first priority, at preventing the production of packaging waste and, as additional fundamental principles, at reusing packaging, at recycling and other forms of recovering packaging waste and hence, at reducing the final disposal of such waste.*

Preventive action is therefore a priority. Member States are placed under a general obligation noted in Article 4(1) to implement preventive measures in addition to those more specific measures it must take in relation to packaging waste under Article 9 discussed below. The nature of the measures required to prevent packaging under Article 4(1) is left very much to the discretion of the Member State concerned

---

200 "Packaging" is defined in Article 3 of the Packaging Waste Directive as "all products made of any materials of any nature to be used for the containment, protection, handling, delivery and presentation of goods, from raw materials to processed goods, from the producer to the user or the consumer. 'Non-returnable' items used for the same purposes shall also be considered to constitute packaging".

201 "Packaging waste" is defined in Article 3 of the Packaging Waste Directive as "any packaging or packaging material covered by the definition of waste in Directive 75/442/EEC excluding production residues".

202 Reid, *supra* n.199, p.240.

203 Article 18.

204 Article 2(1).

205 Article 7(1) a and b.

although measures must be in line with the directive's environmental and internal market objectives.[206] The aforementioned Article 9 is more precise in placing the burden on Member States to ensure that by the end of 1997 packaging can only be put on the market if it complies with the "essential requirements" of the directive including those noted in Annex II. The Annex II requirements *inter alia* include reference to the fact that packaging should be manufactured only if its weight and volume are "limited to the minimum adequate amount to maintain the necessary level of safety, hygiene and acceptance for the packed product and for the consumer".

Re-use, recycling and other forms of recovery are regarded as "additional fundamental principles".[207] Article 5 notes that Member States can encourage re-use systems for packaging.[208] In addition, Member States are obliged to ensure that packaging meets certain requirements as to composition and suitability for recovery, re-use and recycling. Obligations include the need to ensure that packaging is designed to allow it to be re-used or recovered, and the obligation to minimise the environmental impact of packaging when it is disposed of.[209]

A recovery target of between 50 per cent as a minimum and 65 per cent as a maximum by weight of packaging waste is also established which had to be met by 30 June 2001 by all Member States apart from Greece, Ireland and Portugal.[210] Recovery can take various forms including material recycling, incineration with energy recovery, and composting. In an interim report published in 1999,[211] the Commission encouragingly noted that the "minimum target of 50 per cent has already been achieved by most of the Member States which were to comply with this target by June 2001".[212] Austria, Belgium, Denmark and the Netherlands had in fact

---

[206] Article 4(2) notes that the Commission will assist in promoting prevention by encouraging the setting of suitable European standards in accordance with Article 10. Article 10 notes that these standards will relate to the essential requirements in Annex II. Five standards were approved by the European Committee for Standardisation (CEN) in 2000 as harmonised standards. When packaging has been produced in accordance with a harmonised standard, references for which have been published in the Official Journal, the packaging in question is presumed to be in compliance with Annex II essential requirements. Objections were however raised by Belgium and Denmark that certain of the standards did not meet some of the essential requirements. The Commission gave due consideration to the objections and noted that in its view three of the standards indeed did not meet the essential requirements. As a consequence, they were not published in the Official Journal. The two other standards were published; see Commission Decision 2001/524 OJ 2001 L190/21. One of these two published standards was deemed to meet Annex II requirements in full, the other in part only. CEN has been urged to improve the standards which did not meet the essential requirements.

[207] Article 1(2).

[208] For discussion on the introduction of mandatory re-use quotas, see Reid, *supra* n.199, pp.218-219.

[209] Article 9 and Annex II.

[210] Article 6(a). These three countries must meet the target by 31 December 2005 at the latest.

[211] COM (1999) 596.

[212] *Ibid*, p.20.

exceeded the 65 per cent maximum recovery target and Germany and Sweden had reached the 65 per cent limit.[213] Not so encouragingly, both Italy (35 per cent) and the UK (34 per cent) fell well below the minimum recovery target rate.[214]

Within the 50 to 65 per cent target, the directive additionally sets a specific material recycling target of 25 to 45 per cent by weight of the totality of packaging materials in packaging waste with a minimum of 15 per cent by weight of each packaging material. This target also had to be met by most Member States by the end of June 2001 (although Greece, Ireland and Portugal needed only to reach the target by the end of 2005 bearing in mind *inter alia* their relatively low level of packaging consumption).[215] In its 1999 report the Commission noted that the minimum target of 25 per cent by June 2001 had in fact already been reached by those Member States which were bound by it,[216] and the maximum target has been reached by Austria, Belgium, Germany, the Netherlands and Sweden. Italy (32 per cent), Luxembourg (33 per cent) and the UK (30 per cent) had recycling rates only just above the minimum target rate.

On the re-use of packaging, the directive did not establish firm targets but the Commission's report concludes that approximately a third of soft drinks, mineral water and wine packaging is re-used in the Community taken as a whole.[217] Re-use is far more commonplace however in northern rather than southern Member States. In Denmark for instance re-use rates of over 90 per cent for mineral water packaging, over 80 per cent for soft drinks packaging and almost 100 per cent for beer containers has been reached.[218]

If a Member State establishes a national programme going beyond the targets set in the directive, they must follow a procedure which seeks to ensure any such national measure is being followed in the interest of a high level of environmental protection, avoids distortion of the internal market and does not hinder compliance by other Member States with the directive. The latter criterion seeks to ensure that a given Member State's capacity to recycle or recover is not hindered by an influx of packaging waste from another Member State. Any such national programme must also not constitute an arbitrary means of discrimination or a disguised restriction on trade. By virtue of Article 6(6) the Commission must be informed of any such

---

[213] Under Article 6(6) Member States can establish their own specific targets to ensure a high level of environmental protection as long as the measures avoid distortions of the internal market; see *infra* text accompanying nn.219-220.

[214] *Supra* n.211, p.20.

[215] Additionally a minimum recycling rate of 15 per cent by weight for each packaging material must be reached. The Commission's report notes that the "only material for which the recycling rate is still, in several countries, below the rate set ... is plastic"; *ibid*, p. 20.

[216] The recycling target rate does not apply to Ireland, Portugal or Greece. Greece had in fact already achieved the minimum target while Portugal had only a three per cent recycling rate.

[217] *Supra* n.211, p.19.

[218] *Ibid*.

programme and, after verification of the measures in cooperation with Member States, to confirm that the measures comply with the said requirements. To date, the Commission, having consulted with the Member States, has seen fit to confirm Austrian and Dutch measures exceeding the maximum target for recycling,[219] as well as Belgian measures exceeding both recovery and recycling maximum target rates.[220]

It is evident that the Packaging Waste Directive has proved successful in establishing far greater recovery and recycling. The measure amounted to a compromise between those Member States in which collection facilities and recycling/recovery targets had already been established, and those States where this was not the case. Part of this compromise was to set the targets noted above, but to appreciate that these were initial targets only; a second set of targets had to be agreed upon covering a second five-year period to 2006.[221] With this in mind, the Commission's 2001 proposal to amend the directive seeks *inter alia* to establish a set of objectives to be met by 2006 including an overall recovery target of between 60 per cent and 75 per cent (as opposed to the 2001 target of 50 to 65 per cent), and an overall recycling target of between 55 per cent and 70 per cent (as opposed to the 2001 target of 25 to 45 per cent).[222]

Batteries and Accumulators

Like the Packaging Waste Directive, the Directive on Batteries and Accumulators Containing Dangerous Substances seeks to strike a balance between the need to protect the environment and ensure the functioning of the internal market.[223] This particular daughter directive to the Framework Directive prohibits the sale from the beginning of 2000 of batteries and accumulators containing specific levels of mercury.[224] Moreover, batteries and accumulators which are not capable of being re-used must be collected separately to facilitate recovery or disposal.[225] In addition, a marking scheme must be set up drawing attention to the need for such separate collection.[226] On the other hand and in order to prevent market distortions, Member States are not allowed to ban or restrict the marketing of batteries and accumulators which comply with the directive's provisions.[227]

---

[219] See Commission Decision 1999/42 OJ 1999 L14/24 (Austria) and Commission Decision 1999/823 OJ 1999 L321/19 (Netherlands).

[220] Commission Decision 1999/652 OJ 1999 L257/20 (Belgium).

[221] Article 6(3)b.

[222] COM (2001) 729.

[223] Directive 91/157 (OJ 1991 L78/38) as amended by Directive 93/86 (OJ 1993 L264/51) and Directive 98/101 (OJ 1999 L1/1).

[224] Batteries containing more than 0.0005% of mercury by weight (apart from button cells and batteries composed of button cells with a mercury content of no more than 2% by weight); Article 3(1) as amended by Directive 98/101.

[225] Article 4(1).

[226] Article 4(2). See amending Directive 93/86 which established the details of this marking system.

[227] Article 9.

Member States are additionally obliged to make sure that an efficient and separate collection scheme is established for batteries and accumulators,[228] and to draw up certain programmes which are to be reviewed and updated at least every four years taking into account technical progress, and economic and environmental considerations. These programmes must achieve stated objectives: to reduce the heavy metal content of batteries (mercury, cadmium and lead); to promote marketing of batteries containing smaller volumes of dangerous substances; and gradually to reduce spent batteries in household waste which contain certain levels of heavy metal content.[229] The programmes should also promote research into the reduction of heavy metals in batteries, and achieve the objective of separate collection.

On the whole, implementation of the directive has been disappointing. A number of enforcement actions have been successfully brought by the Commission against Member States for non-transposition of the directive,[230] and for failure to introduce the required comprehensive national programmes.[231]

End-of-Life Vehicles

Each year in the UK alone 1.8 million end-of-life vehicles (ELVs) are discarded either at the end of their natural life (approximately 12-13 years) or having been damaged in accidents.[232] On a Community-wide basis, ELVs generate between 8 and 9 million tonnes of waste annually.[233] The End-of-Life Vehicles Directive[234] attempts to minimise the environmental impact of ELVs by endorsing the notion of "producer responsibility" in the sense that producers are obliged to take responsibility for their product once it has been discarded as waste by the consumer.

---

[228] Article 7.

[229] Article 6. The types of batteries which must be gradually reduced are noted in Annex I (as amended by Directive 98/101).

[230] See Case C-303/95 *Commission* v *Italy* [1996] ECR I-3859, Case C-236/96 *Commission* v *Germany* [1997] ECR I-6397, and Joined Cases C-282/96 and 283/96 *Commission* v *France* [1997] ECR I-2929.

[231] See Case C-347/97 *Commission* v *Belgium* [1999] ECR I-309, Case C-298/97 *Commission* v *Spain* [1998] ECR I-3301, Case C-215/98 *Commission* v *Hellenic Republic* [1999] ECR I-4913, and Case C-178/98 *Commission* v *France* [1999] ECR I-4853.

[232] House of Commons Select Committee on Trade and Industry, Report on End-of-Life Vehicles Directive (HC 299), para.9 [report published on 6 December 2001]. Between 200,000 and 300,000 of these vehicles reach end-of-life as a result of damage in accidents; *ibid*.

[233] See preamble to the End-of-Life Vehicles directive, para.1.

[234] Directive 2000/53/EC on End-of-Life Vehicles, OJ 2000 L269/34 (as amended by Commission Decision 2002/525 amending Annex II of Commission Decision 2000/53 [OJ 2002 L170/81]. A "vehicle" is defined as any vehicle designated as category M1 or N1 as defined in Annex IIA of Directive 70/156/EEC on the approximation of laws relating to the type-approval of motor vehicles and their trailers (OJ 1970 L42/1) as amended, and three-wheeled motor vehicles as defined by Directive 92/61/EEC (OJ 1992 L225/72) but not including three-wheeled tricycles. Three-wheeled vehicles are in fact given an exemption from many of the measure's provisions; see Article 3(5). Manufacturers producing less than 500 vehicles each year are also exempt from certain provisions; see Article 3(3). An "end-of-life vehicle" is a vehicle which is waste in accordance with Article 1(a) of the Waste Framework Directive.

In this way, producers are given an incentive to prevent waste at source, to promote greater recycling of their product, and to integrate environmental considerations into the design stage to a larger extent than has been the case in the past.[235]

Adopted in September 2000, the measure endorses the prevention of waste generation "as a first priority", and, additionally, to encourage the re-use, recyclability and other forms of recoverability of ELVs and their components.[236] Vintage cars kept in "a proper and environmentally sound manner, either ready for use or stripped into parts" do not fall within the scope of the measure.[237]

Preventing waste generation With a view to preventing waste generation, Member States are obliged to "encourage":

- vehicle manufacturers, as well as material and equipment manufacturers, to limit the use of hazardous materials and to reduce such use as far as possible.[238] In this way there will be less need to dispose of hazardous waste and the re-use and recovery of vehicles will be facilitated;

- the design and production of new vehicles which facilitate the dismantling, re-use and recovery (particularly recycling) of ELVs;[239]

- greater use of recycled materials in the manufacture of vehicles (thus stimulating a market for such materials).[240]

Member States must also ensure that vehicle materials and components which are marketed after 1 July 2003 do not contain certain dangerous heavy metals: cadmium, lead, mercury or hexavalent chromium.[241]

Role of economic operators In addition to seeking the avoidance or prevention of waste, the directive also endeavours to ensure that all "economic operators" active in the life-cycle of vehicles improve their environmental performance.[242] "Economic operators" are defined as "producers, distributors, collectors, motor vehicle insurance companies, dismantlers, shredders, recoverers, recyclers and other treatment operators of end-of-life vehicles, including their components and

---

[235] The directive additionally seeks to ensure that distortions of competition are avoided and the functioning of the internal market is safeguarded.

[236] Article 1.

[237] Preamble, para.10. A "vintage" car refers to "historic vehicles or vehicles of value to collectors or intended for museums"; *ibid*.

[238] Article 4(1)a.

[239] Article 4(1)b.

[240] Article 4(1)c.

[241] Article 4(2)a. The use of these heavy metals may however be unavoidable. If so, they can be utilised in the limited circumstances noted in Annex II (for example, lead solder in electronic circuit-boards is presently allowed). The Commission is to keep the application of Annex II under review taking account of technical and scientific progress (see Article 4(2)); see the amending Decision 2002/525 in this respect (OJ 2002 L170/81).

[242] Article 1.

materials".[243] They must establish systems for the collection of ELVs, and, as far as is technically possible, for the waste used parts removed when passenger cars are repaired.[244] A particular onus is placed on those economic operations which are directly involved in the treatment of ELVs. Some small dismantling facilities will undoubtedly find it very difficult to comply with the minimum technical requirements established for treatment and storage sites.[245]

Any facility wishing to treat ELVs must be duly authorised in accordance with the Waste Framework Directive,[246] and satisfy the following minimum obligations:

- Vehicles must be stripped in such a manner as to reduce adverse environmental impact before further treatment.[247]

- Stripping and storage operations must be carried out so that vehicle parts can, where appropriate, be re-used and recovered.[248]

- Hazardous materials must be removed so as to ensure that they do not contaminate other waste from ELVs which is subsequently shredded. In this way, hazardous materials will not find their way to incineration plants or landfill operations.[249]

In addition, the removal of batteries, fuel, oils, antifreeze and air-conditioning fluids, as well as the neutralising of air-bags (so-called "depollution") of ELVs must be carried out "as soon as possible".[250] This obligation is an innovative one as far as practice in certain Member States is concerned; for instance, prior to the adoption of the directive, most ELVs in the UK were not subject to any form of depollution before being shredded or otherwise processed.[251]

Recovery, re-use and recycling Member States must also take measures to encourage the re-use of component parts, recovery of those which cannot be used, and a preference to recycling when environmentally viable.[252] In this regard, vehicle

---

243 Article 2(10).

244 Article 5(1).

245 These technical requirements are noted in Annex I. Sites for treatment must, for example, have impermeable surfaces for appropriate areas to minimise the impact of spillage, as well as appropriate storage facilities for tyres, dismantled spare parts, batteries, and vehicle fluids.

246 Article 6(2).

247 Article 6(3)a.

248 Article 6(3)c.

249 Article 6(3)b.

250 Article 6(3).

251 House of Commons Select Committee on Trade and Industry, *supra* n.232, para.21.

252 Article 7(1) notes that Member States are obliged to adopt "measures to encourage the re-use of components which are suitable for re-use, the recovery of components which cannot be re-used and the giving of preference to recycling when environmentally viable ... " "Recovery" means any operation provided for in Annex IIB of the Framework Waste Directive; Article 2(8). "Recycling" is defined as "the reprocessing in a production process of the waste materials for the original purpose or for other purposes but excluding energy recovery"; Article 2(7).

manufacturers must ensure that their products are designed in an appropriate manner to achieve quantified targets for re-use, recycling and recovery. Approximately 75 per cent of the metal content of ELVs are currently recycled. By 2006, re-use and recovery must be increased to 85 per cent by average weight per vehicle and year, and must rise by 2015 to 95 per cent. In relation to re-use and recycling, the target to be met by 2006 is 80 per cent by average weight per vehicle and year rising to 85 per cent by 2015.[253] Targets of a less rigorous nature can be set in relation to vehicles manufactured before 1980.[254] The meeting of these targets should be facilitated by the fact that Member States must ensure that vehicle manufacturers use material coding standards to aid the identification of components and materials suitable for re-use and recovery in the dismantling process.[255]

Collection and treatment Member States must additionally ensure the provision of "adequate" collection facilities to avoid the environmentally unsound discarding of ELVs. Also, economic operators must establish the systems for collection of such vehicles.[256] All ELVs must be transferred to duly authorised treatment facilities,[257] and Member States are also obliged to establish a system under which a "certificate of destruction" is issued to the owner of the ELV on the transfer of vehicles to duly authorised treatment facilities.[258] Only once such a certificate has been issued can the ELV be deregistered. While authorised treatment facilities will be able to issue the "certificate of destruction", Member States may also permit vehicle manufacturers, dealers and collectors to issue these certificates on behalf of the undertaking providing treatment facilities, but only where it is guaranteed that the ELV is transferred to an authorised treatment facility.[259]

Financial costs Who will pay for the take-back of ELVs? It is clear that the last owner of the vehicle will not be responsible.[260] Regardless of the fact that the ELV may indeed have no market value, any car placed on the market before July 2002 must be capable of being delivered to an authorised treatment facility free of charge from January 2007.[261] The last owner of a vehicle placed on the market after 1 July 2002 must be in a position also to so deliver the car as from 1 July 2002.[262] A

---

[253] See Articles 7(2)a and b.

[254] In relation to the targets set for 2006, Member States can establish lower percentage figures for cars made before 1980. However, these rates must not be lower than 75 per cent for re-use and recovery, and not lower than 70 per cent for re-use and recycling. The Commission must be informed and reasons given.

[255] Article 8(1).

[256] Article 5(1).

[257] Article 5(2).

[258] Minimum requirements for these certificates have been established; see Commission Decision 2002/151/EC (OJ 2002 L50/94).

[259] Article 5(3).

[260] Article 5(4).

[261] Article 12(2) and 5(4). Member States can determine that delivery of ELVs is not fully free of charge if the vehicle in question "does not contain the essential components of a vehicle, in particular the engine and the coachwork, or contains waste which has been added to the end-of-life vehicle"; Article 5(4).

[262] *Ibid.*

Member State may even bring these dates forward if it so wishes.[263] To have made the last owner financially responsible would have severely undermined the directive's environmental objectives and encouraged even greater numbers of abandoned cars. Rather than the financial burden falling on the owner of the ELV, the directive stipulates that vehicle manufacturers or importers must "meet all, or a significant part of, the costs of implementation of this measure" in line with the idea that producers should take greater responsibility for their product even at the end of its life-cycle.[264] A degree of discretion is therefore given to Member States in determining who shall pay, but the directive ensures at least an element of producer responsibility in that vehicle manufacturers must contribute significantly. Clearly any costs imposed on vehicle manufacturers will be passed on to original purchasers of cars; the vehicle manufacturer MG Rover has estimated that its car prices would need to rise by as much as £500 if it was to assume total responsibility for the cost of processing ELVs.[265] The directive is therefore a good example of an innovative market-based approach to regulation in which waste costs are internalised. The concept of "producer responsibility" can in this context be said to be linked to the principle of "polluter pays".

Consumer information Clearly the directive intends to influence the design and method of production of vehicles to allow greater recycling and re-use. Furthermore, it intends to bring a discernible influence on consumer behaviour and attitudes. Prospective buyers of vehicles must be given certain information by manufacturers to enable them to make an informed choice. Information to be provided relates to the design of vehicles and their components with regard to future recovery and recyclability, the environmentally sound treatment of ELVs, and the development of ways to re-use, recycle or recover ELVs and component parts. Consumers must also be given information on progress made to reduce waste for disposal and to increase recovery and recycling rates.[266]

Electrical and Electronic Waste

Mindful of the fact that six million tonnes of waste electrical and electronic equipment (WEEE) was generated in 1998 and that by 2012 the volume of such waste is likely to have doubled,[267] the Commission proposed a directive relating to

---

[263] Article 12(3).

[264] Article 5(4).

[265] House of Commons Select Committee on Trade and Industry, *supra* n.232, para.32.

[266] Article 9(2).

[267] COM (2000) 347. This document also proposes a directive to substitute the use of certain hazardous substances (particularly heavy metals such as lead, mercury, cadmium and chromium) in electrical and electronic equipment from January 2008; a Common Position was adopted in this respect in December 2001, and a directive adopted in January 2003 (OJ 2003 L37/19).

electrical and electronic waste in 2000.[268] The proposal aimed to encourage the re-use or recycling of equipment rather than its disposal in landfill or by incineration. In this sense it therefore complements the Community's waste management strategy and measures on landfill and incineration discussed earlier.

As well as having clear environmental aims, the proposal also aimed to facilitate the functioning of the internal market. Austria, Belgium, Denmark, Italy, the Netherlands and Sweden have all introduced national legislation in this area and, unless a harmonised structure is introduced, divergent national approaches could encourage the transboundary movement of electrical and electronic equipment to those Member States which have less costly management systems.[269]

The Directive on Waste Electrical and Electronic Waste was adopted in January 2003.[270] In particular, as with the waste management of ELVs, the principle of producer responsibility is endorsed in that designers and producers of electrical and electronic equipment are encouraged to facilitate repair, re-use, disassembly and recycling of their products.[271] More particularly, consumers are encouraged to return electrical and electronic equipment (such as household appliances, computers, radios and video games) for recovery. To facilitate this process, distributers must offer to take back old equipment from private households without charge when the consumer buys new equipment of a similar type to replace it. Separate collection facilities must also be established where final holders and distributers can return private household waste and other waste equipment free of charge. For equipment other than private household waste, Member States are obliged to ensure producers provide for its collection.

Bearing in mind that a significant amount of the heavy metals content of municipal waste is attributable to their use in batteries, the obligation placed on Member States to establish a collection system for electronic and electrical waste is designed to complement the Batteries Directive.[272] We have noted that the latter obliges Member States to develop programmes with a view to reducing the heavy metal content (such as cadmium, lead, mercury) of batteries, and as part of these programmes to provide for the separate collection of spent batteries and accumulators for recovery or controlled disposal. However the Commission has noted that "as up to 90 per cent of consumer batteries are integrated in electrical and electronic equipment without being removed by the consumer prior to disposal of the equipment",[273] the separate collection of WEEE is essential to minimise the environmental impact of heavy metals from batteries.

---

268   *Ibid*, at p.4.

269   *Ibid*, at p.5.

270   OJ 2003 L37/24.

271   For example, the directive sets specific targets for rate of recovery; Article 7.

272   *Supra* n.267, at p.21.

273   *Ibid*.

Producers will assume physical responsibility in that they are obliged to set up systems for the effective treatment of waste. The treatment process must as a minimum include the removal of certain components or substances (such as CFCs, batteries, PCBs and toner cartridges). WEEE should also be recovered, priority being given to re-use of whole appliances.

Importantly, producers from 13 August 2005 must also assume financial responsibility by paying for collection from collection facilities, as well as the treatment, recovery and disposal of WEEE. In this way producers must largely accept financial responsibility for the products they manufacture, and as a result should be encouraged to adapt product designs to ensure that waste management costs are kept to a minimum.[274] Whilst producers will clearly seek to increase prices to accommodate their extra financial burden, independent consultants have estimated that prices would only be expected to rise between one and three per cent.[275] Such a rise is likely to have a minimal impact on sales particularly as research has shown that the demand for certain electrical equipment such as fridges, washing machines and televisions is inelastic.[276]

Sewage Sludge Used in Agriculture

Sewage sludge is an important fertiliser due to its richness in both phosphorous and nitrogen. The use of sludge in agriculture should be regarded as a type of recycling which reduces the need to dispose of sludge by means of landfill or incineration. It is anticipated that its use as a fertiliser will become even more attractive in future years due to the impact of the Landfill Directive which will make disposal of sewage sludge by landfill more expensive.[277] The increased use of sewage sludge in agriculture would be in line with the Community's waste management hierarchy of aims – given that sewage sludge cannot be totally prevented, it should be recovered or re-used rather than disposed of.

Although sewage sludge can undoubtedly improve the quality of agricultural soil, it contains heavy metals harmful to soil, vegetation, animals and man. These harmful metals include cadmium, copper, nickel, lead, zinc, mercury and chromium. Whilst the spreading of sludge on soil offers a more favourable environmental option than landfill or incineration, its use in agriculture must therefore be carefully controlled. Heavy metals can be toxic to plants and animals, and the Sewage Sludge Directive therefore establishes mandatory limit values for these elements in soil.[278] Sludge

---

[274] *Ibid*, p.6.

[275] *Ibid*, p.35.

[276] *Ibid*.

[277] European Environment Agency, "Sewage Sludge - a Future Waste Problem?" (Indicator Fact Sheet Signals 2001 – chapter on waste).

[278] Council Directive 86/278 on the Protection of the Environment, and in Particular of the Soil, when Sewage Sludge is Used in Agriculture, OJ 1986 L181/6.

cannot be used where the concentration of heavy metals in soil exceeds these limits. In addition, Member States are placed under an obligation to treat sludge from sewage plants treating domestic or urban waste waters before spreading on agricultural soil. This is to ensure that health hazards are significantly reduced.

In its report covering the period 1995-97, the Commission noted that there were no outstanding problems with regard to the implementation of this directive,[279] although it had earlier seen fit to bring a successful action against Belgium for non-implementation.[280] Encouragingly, the Commission has indicated that the directive "has been quite successful in preventing crop contamination by pathogens because of the use of sludge on agricultural soils".[281] The Sixth Environmental Action Programme has underlined the need for a revised directive. Such a measure will no doubt seek to establish stricter limits for heavy metals in sewage sludge.

Ship-generated Waste

The directive relating to ship-generated waste and cargo residues was adopted in late 2000 to improve port reception facilities for this type of waste, and therefore to reduce the amount of waste being discharged into the sea by ships using ports in the Community.[282] The measure applies to the vast majority of ships although naval vessels are not covered. However, even naval vessels must deliver their waste in a manner consistent with the directive as far as it is "reasonable and practicable".[283] It makes no difference in the application of the directive if a ship flies the flag of a non-EC country – in the interest of preventing marine pollution, any such vessel is still bound by the measure.

All EC ports must provide adequate reception facilities to cater for the needs of the type of ships normally using the port without causing undue delay to those vessels.[284] All waste from vessels that use a Community port must be delivered to the relevant reception facility (unless the ship has adequate storage facilities to enable it to proceed to its port of delivery and off-load waste there).[285] Ships must give advance notice to the port authorities of intention to use the port facilities and of the quantity of waste in question.

---

[279] COM (99) 752.
[280] Case C-260/93 *Commission* v *Belgium* [1994] ECR I-1611.
[281] COM (99) 752.
[282] Directive 2000/59/EC OJ 2000 L332/81.
[283] Article 3.
[284] Article 4(1).
[285] Article 7(2).

The measure importantly endorses the "polluter pays" principle in that the cost of port reception facilities for ship-generated waste shall be met by the collection of fees from ships.[286] Whilst Member States have a level of discretion in establishing the exact nature of the fee system, all ships must contribute "significantly" to the cost of treating or disposing of waste regardless of whether they actually use the port reception facilities. In this way, masters of ships will be encouraged to use the facilities rather than dump waste illegally at sea. In essence, if they have to pay for the operation of the facilities, then why not make use of those facilities rather than discharge waste at sea? The cost of operating the facility could be met by the payment of harbour dues payable by all vessels using the port. The actual amount of the harbour due could reflect the size of the vessel.[287] To ensure effectiveness, Member States are obliged to carry out targeted inspections and to operate a penalty system for non-compliance.

PCBs/PCTs

Since the 1930s these manufactured chemicals were used as lubricants for electrical equipment or to make coolants. By the mid-1980s wide-scale commercial production had ceased due to public health concerns. Consumed by insect larvae and fish, PCBs can enter the food chain and are believed to impair immunity and capacity to reproduce. Exposure to high levels of PCBs may increase risk of certain cancers. Although production is largely a thing of the past, these chemicals do not break down easily and great care must be taken to avoid spillage from electrical equipment still in use which contain PCBs. In addition, an effective waste management system must be established when electrical equipment (such as transformers, switchwear and capacitators) are decommissioned. The 1996 Directive on the Disposal of PCBs/PCTs places Member States under an obligation to ensure that equipment containing PCBs is decontaminated or disposed of as soon as possible.[288] All undertakings dealing in decontamination and disposal must be properly licensed in accordance with the provisions of the Framework Waste Directive.

More specifically, the measure requires that any equipment containing more than 5 litres of PCBs must be properly labelled,[289] and decontaminated and/or disposed of by 2010.[290] In addition, inventories of such equipment had to be compiled, and summaries made available to the Commission by 16 September 1999 together with copies of national plans for the decontamination and/or disposal of inventoried equipment.[291] This compiling of inventories was required to facilitate assessment as

---

[286] Article 8.
[287] Article 8(2)a.
[288] Council Directive 96/59 OJ 1996 L243/31.
[289] Article 4(5).
[290] Article 3.
[291] Articles 4 and 11.

to whether the provision of disposal facilities was adequate. All Member States were also obliged to provide the Commission with an outline for the collection and subsequent disposal of equipment containing PCBs not subject to inventory (such equipment would only be slightly contaminated and of low risk). As with many of the EC's waste management measures, implementation has been poor. It is disappointing to note that the ECJ ruled against a number of Member States in 2002 for their failure to supply inventories and plans to the Commission.[292]

Waste Oils

Prior to the adoption of this directive in 1975, research had indicated that between 20 and 60 per cent of waste oils were being disposed of in an uncontrolled manner in some Member States.[293] The discharge, deposit or treatment of waste oils can cause significant environmental difficulties. The Waste Oils Directive as amended[294] defines "waste oils" as

> *any mineral-based lubrication or industrial oils which have become unfit for the use for which they were originally intended, and in particular used combustion engine oils and gearbox oils, and also mineral lubricating oils, oils for turbines and hydraulic oils* (Article 1).

With a view to preventing unnecessary damage, the measure obliges Member States to take the necessary measures to ensure such oils are collected and disposed of without causing harm to man or the environment.[295] The collection of waste oils is vital to the operation of the directive – if such oils are not collected, they will find their way to landfill sites or in some other way be dumped, placing strains on the environment.[296] In 1999 the Commission noted that 71 per cent of waste oils were collected, leaving 29 per cent illegally handled.[297]

With regard to waste oils management after collection, priority should be given to regeneration in which contaminants can be removed from waste oils to produce base oils.[298] This refining of waste oils is to be preferred to their combustion (in which waste oils are used as a fuel). In situations where oils are neither regenerated nor burned, they must be safely destroyed or either stored or tipped in a controlled manner.[299] A hierarchy is therefore created in which the first priority is regeneration,

---

[292] See Case C-46/01 *Commission* v *Italy* [2002] ECR I-2093 and Case C-177/01 *Commission* v *France* [2002] ECR I-5137.

[293] Haigh, *supra* n.181, 5.7-1.

[294] Directive 75/439 on the Disposal of Waste Oils (OJ 1975 L194/23) as amended by Directive 87/101 (OJ 1987 L42/43).

[295] Article 2.

[296] See COM (1999) 752.

[297] *Ibid.*

[298] Article 3(1).

[299] Article 3(2).

then combustion, and lastly safe treatment and disposal. There is however evidence that the hierarchy is not being respected, with only a minority of Member States claiming to regenerate a sizeable proportion of waste oils.[300] The burning of waste oils seems to be the preferred option due to its particular economic viability.[301]

In addition, Member States must prevent the following (Article 4):

- discharge into inland surface water, ground water, territorial sea and drainage system;

- deposit and/or discharge harmful to soil and any uncontrolled discharge of residues resulting from the processing of waste oils;

- any processing causing air pollution over and above that prescribed by existing provisions.

Any undertaking which disposes of oils must obtain a permit before doing so to ensure that these prohibitions are followed in disposal operations.[302] Additionally, where the directive's objectives already noted cannot be otherwise achieved, Member States can establish zones within which one or more undertakings will be obliged to carry out collection and/or disposal operations.[303] In this sense, Member States can grant to a given undertaking the exclusive right to collect and/or dispose of waste oils in a given area of its territory. However, the ECJ has ruled that this should not be interpreted in such a way that a Member State is free to establish barriers to the export of waste seeing as

the environment is protected just as effectively when the oils are sold to an authorized disposal or regenerating undertaking of another Member State as when they are disposed of in the Member State of origin.[304]

Those undertakings required to collect and/or dispose of waste oils in a given zone can be compensated for the services they render by means of indemnities. These indemnities can be financed by a charge on products which after use become waste oils, or on waste oils themselves in accordance with the "polluter pays" principle.[305] Any holder of waste oils must pass them to a duly authorised undertaking if he is unable to comply with the prohibitions in Article 4.[306] In addition, Member States

---

[300] See COM (1999) 752. See Case C-102/97 *Commission* v *Germany* [1999] ECR I-5051 in which the ECJ declared that Germany had failed to take measures to give priority to processing by regeneration.
[301] *Ibid.*
[302] Article 6(1).
[303] Article 5(2). This provision and the requirement that disposal undertakings obtain a permit (Article 6[1]) were deemed by the ECJ to be compatible with the principles of free trade, free movement of goods and of competition in the *ADBHU* case; Case 240/83 [1985] ECR 531.
[304] Case 172/82 *Inter-Huiles* [1983] ECR 555, para.14.
[305] Articles 14 and 15.
[306] Article 9.

must take measures to ensure that any regeneration operations do not cause avoidable damage to the environment.[307]

Some Concluding Remarks

Reflecting on the approach to waste management to date, the Sixth Environmental Action Programme positively notes that it has been "successful in improving the standards of waste management".[308] However, legislation has "so far failed to reduce the rising tide of waste volumes".[309] Waste prevention, both in terms of volume and its hazardous nature, therefore remains very much a priority. Implementation of waste management legislation has often been disappointing,[310] the current Environmental Action Programme making reference to the fact that "special attention will be given to significantly improving the implementation of existing measures by Member States".[311] Although some guidance has been provided by the ECJ, imprecise drafting of the definition of "waste" in the Framework Directive has undoubtedly led to difficulties in transposition, and continues to present practical difficulties for industry and waste management regulators. In this respect, efforts must be renewed within the Commission to cast light on the distinction between waste and non-waste substances.

With a view to gradually reducing the consumption of natural resources and assisting in the prevention of waste generation, the Commission launched its Green Paper on Integrated Product Policy (IPP) in early 2001. The latter was published intending to stimulate public debate on the adoption of an integrated approach to improve the environmental performance of products and to promote a wider market for "green" products.[312] It is likely that the coordinated use of a mix of instruments will be encouraged on a product-by-product basis seeking to target those stages of a product's life cycle which have a profound bearing on its environmental impact (such as the design, manufacturing, marketing stages).[313] Possible measures are numerous and range from legislation to the introduction of voluntary agreements.[314]

---

307 Article 7.

308 COM (2001) 32, p.54.

309 *Ibid.*

310 See European Parliament Resolution concerning COM (97) 23 (OJ 1998 C313/99). Underlining the poor implementation of waste legislation, the Commission on 23 July 2002 announced its decision to pursue infringement proceedings against ten Member States concerning their lack of implementation of waste laws; see Commission press release IP/02/1119.

311 *Supra* n.308.

312 COM (2001) 68.

313 Charter, Young, Collects-Young and Beltane, "Integrated Product Policy and Eco-Product Development" (discussion paper for the "Towards Sustainable Product Design Conference" [23-24 October 2000]).

314 *Ibid.*

The choice of instrument to be adopted under the IPP approach would depend on the state of the market in relation to a given product, but clearly the strategy would *inter alia* seek to modify pricing systems by internalising environmental costs in accordance with the "polluter pays" principle.[315]

The development of the Community's IPP policy initiative is at an early stage, but it would appear to seek to provide a more coordinated approach to the prevention of waste generation by allowing choices to be made between a mix of instruments on a case-by-case basis. It is intended that stakeholders involved in a particular stage of a product's life-cycle will take greater responsibility for their actions where decisions they make have a detrimental environmental impact at some other stage in the life-cycle. Although in theory a possibility, not all products would be targeted. Instead, action is likely to focus on specific products chosen for their particular environmental impact.[316]

The IPP approach seeks both to change the market behaviour of businesses and consumers. On the demand side, for example, increased consumer demand for green products could be encouraged by ensuring the provision of accurate and understandable information as to the environmental performance of products. The Commission would additionally hope to create markets for "green" products by encouraging the greening of public procurement activities. In relation to the supply side, economic incentives for businesses to produce environmentally friendly products are anticipated. Additional use of economic instruments is a possibility for instance (such as the introduction of a differentiated tax mechanism which might, for example, reduce VAT payable on eco-labelled produts). The Commission had hoped to publish a White Paper in late 2001on IPP but this is not now expected until some time in 2003.

Whilst the issue of waste management has been highlighted by the Sixth Environmental Action programme as a key area for attention over the coming years, the final chapter of this book will seek to introduce the reader to another area of fundamental importance: the issue of global warming.

---

[315] *Ibid.*

[316] The Green Paper notes that attention may also fall on the provision of certain services although the policy is largely product-related.

Select Bibliography

Chalmers, "Community Policy on Waste Management - Managing Environmental Decline Gently"14 YEL (1995) 257.

Cheyne, "The Definition of Waste in EC Law"(2002) 12(1) JEL 61.

Cheyne and Purdue, "Fitting Definition to Purpose: the Search for a Satisfactory Definition of Waste"(1995) 7(2) JEL 149.

Ermacoma, "Community Legislation and Jurisprudence in the Area of Waste Management: Recent Developments"(1998) 7(3) RECIEL 274.

Fluck, "The Term Waste in EU Law"(1994) 3 EELR 79.

Gallego, "Waste Legislation in the EU"(2001) 10 EELR 342.

Glinski and Rott, "Waste Incineration - Legal Protection in European Environmental Law"(2000) 12(2) JEL 129.

Haigh, *Manual of Environmental Policy* (looseleaf) chapter 5.

Kramer, *EC Environmental Law* (2000), chapter 9.

Kroepelien, "Extended Producer Responsibility - New Legal Structures for Improved Ecological Self Organisation in Europe"(2000) 9(2) RECIEL 165.

Kummer, *International Management of Hazardous Wastes* (1995).

Laurence, *Waste Regulation Law* (1999).

Lee, "New Generation Regulation? The Case of End-of-Life Vehicles"(2002) 11 EELR 114.

O'Keefe, "Transfrontier Shipments of Waste: a Bureaucrat's Dream"(2000) 9 EELR 10.

Onida, "Challenges and Opportunities in EC Waste Management: Perspectives on the Problem of End-of-Life Vehicles" 1 *Yearbook of European Environmental Law* (2000) 253.

Purdue, "The Distinction between Using Secondary Raw Materials and the Recovery of Waste: the Directive Definition of Waste"(1998) 10(1) JEL 116.

Tieman, "The Broad Concept of Waste and the Case of ARCO-Chemie and Hees-EPON"(2000) 9 EELR 327.

Tromans, "EC Waste Law - A Complete Mess?"(2001) 13(2) JEL 133.

Tufet-Opi, "Life after End-of-Life: The Replacement of End-of-Life Product Legislation by an European Integrated Product Policy in the EC" (2002) 12(1) JEL 33.

Van Calster, "The EC Definition of Waste: *Euro Tombesi* Bypass and Basel Relief Routes"(1997) (May/June) European Business Law Review 137.

Van Calster, "The Legal Framework for the Regulation of Waste in the EC" 1 *Yearbook of European Environmental Law* (2000) 161.

Chapter 8

The Legal Response to Global Warming

The "Greenhouse Effect"

The Intergovernmental Panel on Climate Change (IPCC) was established in 1988 by the World Meteorological Organization and the United Nations Environment Programme (UNEP) to assess the scientific basis and impact of climate change. In its Second Assessment Report published in 1996 the IPCC noted that "the balance of evidence suggests that there is a discernible human influence on global climate".[1] An increase in global surface temperature of between 1 and 3.5 degrees Celsius by 2100 was predicted when compared to 1990 temperatures, a "rate of warming [which] would probably be greater than any seen in the last 10,000 years".[2] The work of the IPCC is ongoing and its Third Assessment Report published in 2001 projected even larger temperature increases in the same period of between 1.4 and 5.6 degrees Celsius.[3]

The potential impact of climate change is wide-ranging. Average sea levels for example are expected to rise affecting island and low-lying countries globally,[4] the European Commission indicating that in Europe projected sea level rises

> would affect large stretches of the Netherlands, certain marshlands in England, the length of the German North Sea coast, coastal areas on the Black Sea, around the Po flood plain in Italy and the tidal flats (the Wadden Sea) on the west coast of Jutland in Denmark.[5]

An increase in the number of violent storms and floods are also projected, and it is estimated that between 50 and 90 per cent of glaciers in Europe will have disappeared by the end of the 21st century.[6] Moreover, the warmer climate is

---

[1] Doc FCCC/CP/1996/5/Add.1, p.8.

[2] *Ibid*, p.9. Whilst scientists disagree on the precise extent of the global temperature rise, most do agree that a rise must be expected.

[3] IPCC, *Climate Change 2001: the Scientific Basis* (2001), chapter 9.

[4] See generally Freestone, "International Law and Sea Level Rise", in Churchill and Freestone (eds.), *International Law and Global Climate Change* (1991), pp.109-126.

[5] European Commission, "Newsletter from Ritt Bjerregaard, the EU's Commissioner for the Environment", November 1997, p.1.

[6] European Commission, "Third Communication from the EC Under the UN Framework Convention on Climate Change", p.142 [SEC (2001) 2053 (20/12/2001) available on http://unfccc.int/resource/docs/natc/European Commission.

expected to lead to the deterioration of soil quality and greater flood risk throughout Europe, and "climate zones (and thus ecosystems and agricultural zones) could shift towards the poles by 150 - 550 km in the mid-latitude regions".[7] Such a shift would have a negative impact on numerous ecosystems and the conservation status of particular species.[8]

The so-called "greenhouse effect" is in part a quite natural phenomenon. Radiation emanating from the Sun reaches the Earth's atmosphere and, with the exception of certain harmful ultra-violet radiation filtered out in the stratospheric ozone layer, eventually reaches the surface of the Earth. Some of this energy is reflected back from the Earth's surface to the Earth's atmosphere where it is trapped by so-called "greenhouse gases" and brings about a warming effect. Since the Industrial Revolution this perfectly natural process has been intensified by certain human activities: atmospheric concentration of the main greenhouse gas, carbon dioxide, has for example increased by more than 30 per cent since 1750 largely as a result of the burning of fossil fuels and forest clearance;[9] methane and nitrous oxide concentrations have also increased considerably in the same period;[10] and, in addition, the use of hydro fluorocarbons, per fluorocarbons and sulphur hexafluride, whilst thought not to be contributing to a large extent to the global warming effect at present, are likely to have such an impact in the future if emissions continue to increase.[11]

The IPCC's first scientific assessment report was published in 1990 and served to underline the need for a global agreement to combat global warming.[12] Clearly the problem is transboundary in nature and necessitates an international effort and agreement to reduce its impact. Equally, however, effective regional and domestic policies must be devised to implement any international response. This chapter will first address the international legal treaty regime established to reduce greenhouse gas emissions, and to which the EC is an important and influential party. As such it will provide an insight into the Community as an actor on the international stage,[13] and present an essential overview of the regime within which the Community must take action to reduce greenhouse gases. Attention will then focus on key elements in

---

7   "Press Backgrounder" issued by Secretariat to the Climate Change Convention, 20 November 1997, p.1.

8   *Ibid.* On the impact of global warming on wildlife, see Bowman, "Global Warming and the International Legal Protection of Wildlife", in Churchill and Freestone (eds.), *supra* n.4, pp.127-146.

9   IPCC, *supra* n.3, chapter 1.

10   *Ibid.* Methane is released from the burning of fossil fuels and from the gastric processes of ruminants. It is also produced as a consequence of change in land-use to, for instance, rice production. Nitrous oxide concentrations have been increased in the main as a result of greater use of agricultural fertilisers.

11   UN Doc FCCC/CP/1996/Add. 1, p.7. Hydro fluorocarbons are frequently used as refrigerants, and coolants in air conditioning systems. Per fluorocarbons are used primarily in aluminium smelters, and sulphur hexafluride as an insulating medium in electric circuit breakers.

12   IPCC, *Climate Change: The IPCC Scientific Assessment* (1990). See also "IPCC First Assessment Report: Overview" (1991) 3(1) International Environmental Affairs, pp.64-84.

13   See further chapter 2 on EC as an international environmental actor.

the Community's internal strategy to implement the legally binding international obligations assumed by the EC under the international regime. It will be noted that action to date in the EC falls a long way short of that which is required, and necessitates a response which integrates environmental concerns into other policy spheres, especially the energy, transport, agriculture and industry sectors.

National Perspectives on Tackling Climate Change

Whilst a few states have in the past seen no reason to reduce emissions even if the IPCC's findings had been accurate,[14] most countries now accept the Panel's general conclusions and favour the adoption of a precautionary approach.[15] Much of the political debate on abatement measures is however polarised. As far as the developing world is concerned, certain low-lying developing states risk losing part of their territory as sea-levels rise. These states have formed the Alliance of Small Island States (AOSIS) which has called for wide-ranging cuts in emissions. By contrast, the economies of the Organisation of Petroleum Exporting Countries (OPEC) are heavily dependent on the continuing export of oil and natural gas, and therefore have a vested interest in limiting cuts in the global consumption of fossil fuels. Other developing countries, particularly the least developed countries, are also vulnerable from the effects of climate change particularly bearing in mind the high financial and social costs of adapting to the impact of global warming. They advocate that any internationally agreed measures should not hamper their continued economic development, and place responsibility on the developed world for the dramatic increase in emissions over the last century.

There are clearly also divisions within the developed world. For instance, the United States of America has traditionally feared the potentially enormous economic and social impact of a domestic strategy to reduce its dependency on cheap fossil fuels. It has also shown reluctance to embrace any internationally agreed programme which places it at a competitive disadvantage when compared to its economic competitors in the developing world. The USA has always been of the view that any concerted international programme to reduce emissions must not only place the onus on the developed world, but also impose timetabled emission reductions on the richer developing states, like India and China. The USA has received some support

---

[14] See Oberthur, "The Second Conference of the Parties" (1996) 26 (5) Environmental Policy and Law, pp. 146-147. Whilst there remains some doubt as to the precise extent of the effect of global warming on the planet, the Climate Change Convention notes that "Parties should take precautionary measures to anticipate, prevent or minimize the causes of climate change and mitigate its adverse effects"; Article 3(3).
[15] Oberthur, *ibid*, p.147. For a more detailed account of the growing international consensus on the impact of global warming since the 1960s, see Bodansky "The United Nations Framework Convention on Climate Change: A Commentary" (1993) 18 Yale Journal of International Law, pp.458-471.

from other developed countries including Japan, Canada, Australia and New Zealand in this respect. The EC and its Member States, on the other hand, have actively pursued a strategy which accepts that the developed world has contributed most to the problem of climate change and, as such, should take the lead in accepting legally binding emission reduction obligations. In this way, and by implementing policies which ensure compliance with reduction responsibilities, an example will have been set by the developed world to be followed hopefully at a later date by developing states when their economic and social circumstances allow. The Community's Member States have adopted common climate change negotiating stances in conjunction with the European Commission, and have been perceived as being a powerful counterbalance to the influence of the USA in talks throughout the 1990s.

United Nations Framework Convention on Climate Change

In December 1990 the United Nations General Assembly established the Intergovernmental Negotiating Committee (INC) with a view to drafting a framework treaty for signature in June 1992 at the United Nations Conference on Environment and Development (UNCED) in Rio.[16] The INC met five times between February 1991 and May 1992 and, after much hard bargaining,[17] the United Nations Framework Convention on Climate Change (Climate Change Convention) was adopted on May 9th 1992 and opened for signature in June 1992.[18] The treaty entered into force on 21 March 1994.[19] Over ten years after the adoption of the Climate Change Convention, there are more than 180 States Parties to the treaty.

The Community and all its Member States are legally bound as ratifying parties.[20] Becoming a party to binding international agreements in this way raises the profile of the EC as an international actor, and provides the EC's Member States with a powerful and influential collective voice within international legal regimes. By virtue of Article 174(4) of the EC Treaty, the Community possesses the ability to cooperate with third countries in the area of the environment although the Community's competence is not exclusive.[21] In a Community law context, the

---

16   United Nations General Assembly Resolution 45/212 of 21 December 1990.

17   See Bodansky, *supra* n.15, pp.474-491.

18   (1992) ILM 849. On the negotiations and text of the Climate Change Convention, see Bodansky, *supra* n.15, pp.451-558. See also Barrett, "The Negotiation and Drafting of the Climate Change Convention" in Churchill and Freestone (eds.), *supra* n.4, pp.183-200.

19   Entry into force took place ninety days after the fiftieth instrument of ratification as specified in Article 23 of the Climate Change Convention.

20   The EC signed the treaty on 13 June 1992 and ratified on 21 December 1993.

21   Exclusive Community competence excludes national competence; Member States are prevented from taking action in the area concerned. Exclusive competence is enjoyed by the EC in the areas of the common commercial policy, the common customs tariff and fisheries.

Climate Change Convention is therefore an example of a "mixed agreement" which covers subject matter in which the Community is competent, but also includes issues concerning which the Member States themselves retain competence. Negotiation, conclusion and implementation of the treaty therefore require joint action by both the Community and the Member States. In effect, competence is shared and no attempt was made in the Community's instrument of approval to the treaty to draw a line between the Community's competence and individual Member States' competence:

> *The European Economic Community and its Member States declare that the commitment to limit anthropogenic emissions set out in Article 4(2) of the Convention will be fulfilled in the Community as a whole through action by the Community and its Member States, within the respective competence of each.*[22]

In the text of the treaty the Community had long favoured the introduction of timetabled emission reductions which would bind industrialised countries. Although receiving support from *inter alia* the AOSIS coalition, it became clear that it was politically unrealistic to include such substantive obligations in the face of opposition from the United States and OPEC countries which felt that any introduction of specific emission reductions would be premature, and particularly harmful to their continued economic growth. Bearing in mind the importance of establishing an international regime which included as many countries as possible, particularly the world's largest emitter of carbon dioxide, the United States of America,[23] the treaty did not establish timetabled emission reduction targets. Instead an "ultimate objective" to stabilise emissions at a level which would no longer interfere in a harmful way with the global environment was agreed.

Though not satisfied with this weak commitment to stabilise, the EC and other like-minded states hoped that, when political will allowed, a timetable of specific emission reductions could be agreed upon at some time in the future by the adoption of a protocol to the treaty.[24] Such an approach has been adopted successfully within international legal regimes established to combat transboundary air pollution[25] and to reduce ozone-depleting substances[26] without alienating those states which contribute most to these problems. The Climate Change Convention therefore is "framework" in nature in the sense that it establishes an administrative structure, as well as a legal regime within which information is exchanged, obligations are placed on states to devise and implement policies and programmes, and regular meetings of the parties held in the form of "Conferences of the Parties" (COPs). It is in the

---

[22] Council Decision 94/69/EC OJ 1994 L33/11.

[23] USA is responsible for approximately 23 per cent of global emissions. By contrast Japan is responsible for approximately five per cent, Germany for almost four per cent and the UK for around three per cent.

[24] Article 17 of the treaty notes that the Conference of the Parties "may, at any ordinary session, adopt protocols to the convention". The Conference of the Parties meets on an annual basis (Article 7(4)).

[25] Convention on Long-Range Transboundary Air Pollution (1979) 18 ILM 1442 (LRTAP).

[26] Vienna Convention for the Protection of the Ozone Layer (1987) 26 ILM 1529 (Ozone Convention); Montreal Protocol on Substances that Deplete the Ozone Layer (1987) 26 ILM 1550.

periods leading up to and at the Conferences of the Parties during which negotiations can take place between states with a view to adopting protocols establishing timetabled reductions in greenhouse gases.

The treaty establishes general obligations that bind all parties, and other obligations that only apply to developed countries and the Community. All parties to the treaty are *inter alia* legally obliged to prepare national inventories of emissions of greenhouse gases,[27] to implement national programmes to reduce global warming,[28] to cooperate in preparing for adaption to the impacts of climate change,[29] and to promote scientific research.[30] Annex I Parties are additionally subject to more onerous obligations bearing in mind that the

> *largest share of historical and current global emissions of greenhouse gases has originated in developed countries, that per capita emissions in developing countries are still relatively low and that the share of global emissions originating in developing countries will grow to meet their social and development needs.*[31]

Annex I comprises the vast majority of the industrialised world and includes all EC Member States and the Community itself. Articles 4(2)a and 4(2)b of the Climate Change Convention oblige Annex I States to adopt national policies which

> *will demonstrate that developed countries are taking the lead in modifying longer-term trends in anthropogenic emissions consistent with the objective of the convention,*[32]

and to provide detailed reports on such policies

> *with the aim of returning individually or jointly to their 1990 levels ... carbon dioxide and other greenhouse gases not controlled by the Montreal Protocol.*[33]

These obligations are vague in nature and Sands has aptly commented that "[t]his is clearly something other than a provision requiring a mandatory return to a specified

---

27 Article 4(1)a of the Climate Change Convention.
28 Article 4(1)b of the Climate Change Convention.
29 Article 4(1)e of the Climate Change Convention.
30 Article 4(1)g of the Climate Change Convention.
31 Preamble, Climate Change Convention.
32 Article 4(2)a of the Climate Change Convention.
33 Article 4(2)b of the Climate Change Convention.
    The Montreal Protocol on Substances that Deplete the Ozone Layer (*supra* n.26) controls certain gases such as chlorofluorocarbons (CFCs) which have ozone depleting characteristics. The latter part of this chapter concentrates only on the efforts made by the Community to reduce those gases regulated by the Kyoto Protocol. The reader should note however that success in reducing ozone layer depleting substances (such as CFCs) will assist in reducing the global warming effect as they too are greenhouse gases. On the Community's legislation to reduce substances that deplete the ozone layer, see Haigh, *Manual of Environmental Policy: the EC and Britain* (looseleaf) at 6.12. See also Regulation 2037/2000 on substances that deplete the ozone layer, OJ 2000 L244/1.

earlier level by a specified date".[34] The Community's own unilateral political commitment in 1992 was stronger, pledging to stabilise carbon dioxide emissions by the year 2000 at 1990 levels.[35]

The text of the Climate Change Convention also places certain developed states under a responsibility to finance the "agreed full incremental costs" of transferring environmentally sound technology to developing states,[36] and of providing financial resources to enable developing states to fulfil their reporting requirements.[37] These financial responsibilities apply to the Community and those states in Annex II (Annex I Parties apart from the Central and Eastern European countries), and are designed to facilitate the fulfilling of general obligations under the treaty by developing nations. The financial commitment by Annex II States should be seen as an essential part of a package deal in which developing states agree to be bound by certain obligations in return for financial assistance to allay the cost of implementing their responsibilities.

As for further and future activities, the treaty underlined that action would need to take into account certain principles.[38] These importantly included States Parties' "common but differentiated responsibilities";[39] whilst all parties share certain common responsibilities in the context of global warming, the treaty stressed the particular onus placed on the developed countries in Annex I to be seen to be taking the lead to combat emissions.

International Developments Since the Adoption of the Climate Change Convention

The text of the Climate Change Convention provided for a review of the adequacy of both Articles 4(2)a and 4(2)b at the First Conference of the Parties. The inclusion of this review clause has played a catalytic role in the eventual adoption of the Kyoto Protocol. The INC reconvened after UNCED as part of the review, and met six times before the First Conference of the Parties was held in Berlin from 28 March to 7

---

[34] Sands, *Principles of International Environmental Law* (1995), p.277.

[35] In its instrument of approval the EC noted that "the Community and its Member States reaffirm the objectives set out in the [EC] Council conclusions of 29 October 1990, and in particular the objective of stabilization of CO_2 emissions by 2000 at 1990 level in the Community as a whole"; see Council Decision 94/69/EC OJ 1994 L33/11.

[36] Articles 4(3) and 4(5) of the Climate Change Convention. "Incremental costs" refer to the finance needed to bring about additional decreases in greenhouse gas emissions over and above those reductions from the operation of a project on a business-as-usual context.

[37] Article 4(3) of the Climate Change Convention.

[38] Article 3 of the Climate Change Convention.

[39] "The Parties should protect the climate system for the benefit of present and future generations of human kind, on the basis of equity and *in accordance with their common but differentiated responsibilities and respective capacities. Accordingly, the developed country parties should take the lead in combatting climate change and the adverse effects thereof*" (Article 3(1); emphasis added).

April 1995.[40] At the INC's meeting in February 1995 it became clear that AOSIS and most developed countries were of the opinion that the obligations assumed by industrialised countries were inadequate to fulfil the objective of the treaty. However there was opposition from the Russian Federation and OPEC countries to the adoption of a protocol detailing more rigorous commitments.[41] It was also apparent that a split had arisen amongst developed states between those that accepted any new commitments should bind only developed countries, and those states, including Australia, Canada, Japan, New Zealand and USA, which also wished to see the wealthier developing countries adopt new commitments. The adoption of any such commitments by non-Annex I States was strongly opposed by developing countries who were given support in their approach by the Community.[42]

The lack of consensus within the INC underlined that the adoption of a protocol at Berlin was not feasible. However, after much debate and argument, the Conference of the Parties did adopt the so-called "Berlin Mandate" in which it was acknowledged that the provisions of Articles 4(2) and 4(2)b were inadequate.[43] State Parties therefore agreed

> *to begin a process to enable [the taking of] appropriate action for the period beyond 2000, including the strengthening of the commitments of the Parties included in Annex I to the Convention (Annex I Parties) in Article 4, paragraph 2(a) and 2(b), through the adoption of a protocol or another legal instrument.*

Whereas the Berlin Mandate acknowledged that "the global nature of climate change calls for the widest possible cooperation by all countries and their participation in an effective and appropriate international response",[44] it also noted that the process would "not introduce any new commitments for Parties not included in Annex I".[45] The process was to begin without delay and be conducted as a matter of urgency.[46] The Ad hoc Group on the Berlin Mandate (AGBM) was established to conduct the process with a view to reporting to the 1996 Second Conference of the Parties on progress made,[47] and to conclude its work in 1997. In adopting the Berlin Mandate the international community had acknowledged the urgent need for the

---

[40]   On the Berlin Conference see Oberthur and Ott, "The First Conference of the Parties" (1995) 25 Environmental Policy and Law, pp.144-156, and Morgan, 6 *Yearbook of International Environmental Law* (1995), pp.225-230.

[41]   Oberthur and Ott, *supra* n. 40, p.145

[42]   *Ibid*, p.145.

[43]   Decision 1/CP.1 (UN Doc FCCC/CP/1995/7/Add.1).

[44]   *Ibid*, paragraph 1(e).

[45]   *Ibid*, paragraph 2(b).

[46]   *Ibid*, paragraph 6.

[47]   The Second Conference of the Parties was held in Geneva from 8 to 19 July 1996. A draft protocol had not been drawn up at this stage, and debate underlined the lack of consensus on the approach to be taken in any such protocol. In particular USA argued that new commitments by developing countries were required which the Group of 77 representing developing states strongly opposed. There was also no agreement on whether a timetable for emissions reductions should be adopted under the process or whether an overall objective was all that was required. See generally Oberthur, *supra* n.14, pp.197-198.

developed world particularly to make progress on adopting further commitments to address the climate change issue. This in itself must be regarded as a success for the Community and its allies in the developing world who had placed considerable political pressure on the USA to compromise.

Kyoto Protocol

The Third Conference of the Parties (COP3) to the Climate Change Convention was held from 1-11 December 1997 at Kyoto, Japan. Here the States Parties to the Convention adopted the Kyoto Protocol under which Annex I Parties agreed to reduce their collective emissions of six greenhouse gases by at least five per cent by 2008-2012 when compared to their 1990 emission levels.[48] Individual emission reduction commitments for Annex I Parties are detailed in Annex B of the Protocol.[49] Each of the Annex I Parties must make "demonstrable progress" in reaching those individual commitments by 2005.[50] At the time of writing, the Protocol is not as yet in force although it is anticipated that it will do so during the course of 2003.[51]

Much of the detail as to the practical arrangements for implementation of the Protocol (particularly in relation to its so-called "flexible mechanisms" and the compliance procedure) still had to be determined after Kyoto. Progress was made in this respect at COP6 where political agreement was reached on a range of issues in the "Bonn Agreements". That political consensus did not however include the USA, the Bush administration having declared in March 2001 that the Protocol was "fatally flawed" and its intention to withdraw from the process. The US government's decision to disengage has been put down to the fact that developing countries did not make specific emission reduction commitments under the Protocol. The Bush administration felt that this would place the US economy at a commercial disadvantage bearing in mind that, if the USA was to ratify Kyoto, it

---

[48] The six greenhouse gases are carbon dioxide, methane, nitrous oxide, hydro fluorocarbons, per fluorocarbons and sulphur hexafluoride.

[49] The commitment period stretches over a five-year period and is intended to provide greater flexibility for States Parties than a single target year. Countries in Annex I "undergoing the process of transition to a market economy" (Central and Eastern European States) may use a base year other than 1990 if already agreed by the Conference of Parties to the Climate Change Convention, or subsequently agreed by the Conference of the Parties to the Protocol. In 1996 the Conference to the Parties agreed that, for instance, Romania may use 1989 and Poland 1988 as their respective base years (UN Doc FCCC/CP/1996/L.13). Such flexibility is envisioned under Article 4(6) of the Climate Change Convention bearing in mind particular economic and social difficulties experienced in these countries. The Protocol specifically allows for a certain degree of further flexibility to such states in the implementation of their commitments (Article 3(6)).

[50] Article 3(2) of the Protocol.

[51] No single state can block the entry into force of the Protocol which will take place 90 days after "not less than 55 Parties to the [Climate Change] Convention, incorporating Parties included in Annex 1 which accounted in total for at least 55% of the total carbon dioxide emissions for 1990 of the Parties included in Annex I" have ratified (Article 24 of the Protocol). By 28 January 2003, the Protocol had received 104 ratifications or accessions from states accounting for 43.9 per cent of such total carbon emissions.

would need to ensure compliance with the emission reduction timetable to which the Clinton administration had agreed in the 1997 negotiations at Kyoto. Reference to the approach of the USA in subsequent discussion reflects the US government's approach prior to its withdrawal from the Kyoto Protocol process. Since March 2001 the USA has been a silent observer only in negotiations.

The withdrawal of the USA from the process was a major blow to the regime agreed upon at Kyoto, but convinced the EC and other states left inside the process that agreement as to the detail of the Protocol had to be reached soon if the process was to survive. In November 2001 at COP7 in Marrakesh the States Parties built on the "Bonn Agreements" in finalising an extensive set of decisions known as the "Marrakesh Accords" which can be regarded as a rulebook for the operation of the Protocol's legal regime.

Emission Reductions and the "EC Bubble"

Under the Kyoto Protocol, individual states' commitments to reductions are differentiated with a view to meeting the five per cent overall target. The EC's collective commitment to an eight per cent reduction is equal to the largest under the Protocol. The Clinton administration signed up to a seven per cent target, and Japan agreed to a six per cent reduction. The adoption of an emission reduction timetable prompted distinguished commentators to note that

> *the numerical targets – and in particular those of the US, the [Community] and Japan – represent the main achievement of the [Community] at Kyoto. It is probably fair to say that without the [Community's] insistence on high numbers, the targets ... would have been much lower.*[52]

Prior to Kyoto, the Community had indicated in March 1997 that its negotiating stance would be to advocate a 15 per cent reduction in three gases (carbon dioxide, nitrous oxide and methane) by 2010,[53] whilst the position of the USA by contrast was merely to stabilise.[54]

---

[52] Oberthur and Ott, *The Kyoto Protocol: International Climate Policy for the 21st Century* (1999), p.137. New Zealand, the Russian Federation and Ukraine will stabilise emissions at 1990 levels, whilst some states negotiated an actual increase in emissions. For instance, Australia may increase emissions by eight per cent and Norway by one per cent. Each of the industrialised countries targets are noted in Annex B to the Protocol.

The EC signed the Kyoto Protocol on 24 April 1998. In 1997 the Community was responsible for 16 per cent of the world's energy related carbon dioxide emissions at which time its population represented just six per cent of global population; see European Commission, "The Energy Dimension of Climate Change" COM (97) 196, at p.3.

[53] European Commission, "Climate Change - the EU Approach to Kyoto" COM (97) 481.

[54] Oberthur and Ott, *supra* n.52, p.118. The actual commitment to reduce emissions in six gases under the Kyoto Protocol is in fact equivalent to approximately a 13 per cent reduction if based on just the three gases referred to in the Community's negotiating position; European Commission press release IP/97/1106, 11/12/97.

Importantly, under the terms of the Kyoto Protocol industrialised countries may agree to take joint action to fulfil their emission reductions targets. If, for instance, two such parties, State A and State B, decide to act jointly, and have notified the Secretariat to that effect, they will be deemed to have fulfilled their emission reduction obligations if State A's and States B's joint emissions do not exceed the level of emissions assigned to both states under the Protocol.[55] Any agreement between the two countries must indicate the emission level attributed to each state concerned.[56] These provisions are of particular relevance to the EC and its Member States, and have been referred to as the "EC Bubble". The EC has indicated that its Member States will take advantage of this ability to burden-share which provides flexibility in implementation by allowing the wealthier Member States to accept much of the burden of reaching the overall EC target. Certain other Member States may even increase their emissions. The "burden-share" agreement will remain in force for the first commitment period (2008-2012), and if the EC fails to reduce greenhouse gases by eight per cent by 2008-2012, any Member State which fails to meet its allocated target under the "bubble" agreement and also the EC itself will be held legally responsible for such failure.[57]

In June 1998 the Council reached agreement on the manner in which the burden would be shared among the Member States, and these targets are noted in the Community's formally binding ratification decision of 2002:[58]

Belgium	-7.5%	Luxembourg	-28%
Denmark	-21%	Netherlands	-6%
Germany	-21%	Austria	-13%
Greece	+25%	Portugal	+27%
Spain	+15%	Finland	0%
France	0%	Sweden	+4%
Ireland	+13%	UK	-12.5%
Italy	-6.5%		

The Community's ability to utilise the "bubble" has attracted criticism from some non-EC developed countries as it undoubtedly provides a greater degree of flexibility in reaching emission targets; an EC Member State may fail to meet its own target under the burden-share agreement but, as long as the EC's overall target of eight per cent is reached, it will not be held to account internationally. In effect

---

[55] Article 4(1) and (2) of the Protocol.

[56] Article 4(1) of the Protocol. If State A and State B failed to meet their joint target level of emissions, each state would be legally responsible for its own emission levels as established in the joint agreement (Article 4(5)).

[57] Article 4(6) of the Protocol.

[58] OJ 2002 L130/1. See also Bulletin EU 6-1998, 1.3.141.

the individual Member State's own failure will have been compensated for by another Member State reducing its own emissions by a higher amount than envisaged under the burden-share agreement. On the other hand however, the use of the "bubble" establishes a considerable burden for a number of the most industrialised Member States of the Community in that they take on under the burden-share a level of emissions reduction which far exceeds the level applicable to their major non-EC competitors such as Japan. In this way the latter can in fact gain a competitive advantage over the wealthier EC Member States.[59]

Implementation of Policies and Measures by Industrialised Countries

In achieving the greenhouse gas emissions reductions specified in the Protocol, Annex I Parties, including the EC and its Member States, are legally obliged under Article 2(1)a of the Protocol to "implement and/or further elaborate policies and measures in accordance with its national circumstances" such as energy efficiency programmes, measures to protect carbon sinks and reservoirs, promoting sustainable agriculture, the promotion of renewable energy, removing subsidies for environmentally damaging activities, encouraging reforms to promote emission reductions, reducing greenhouse gas emissions in the transport sector, and controlling methane emissions through recovery and use in waste management. In so doing Annex I Parties will cooperate with each other to enhance the overall effectiveness of such policies,[60] and take into account the effect of such policies and measures on other states, especially those particularly vulnerable from the effects of global warming (such as AOSIS and OPEC countries).[61] By contrast to the rather general commitments contained in the Climate Change Convention relating to policies,[62] it is noticeable that the Protocol underlines the need for specific policies including reference to energy efficiency programmes. Such a proposal was rejected by OPEC countries in negotiations leading to the adoption of the Climate Change Treaty.[63] Reference to specific rather than general policies in the Protocol had been supported by the EC in particular.

---

[59] Ott, "Outline of EU Climate Policy in the FCCC - Explaining the EU-bubble", a presentation to the Symposium on "Climate Change and the Future of Mankind", 13/14 September 1997, Tokyo.

[60] *Ibid*, Article 2(1)b of the Protocol.

[61] *Ibid*, Article 2(3) of the Protocol. By virtue of the Marrakesh Accords, funding can be made available in developing countries from the Special Climate Change Fund (SCCF) and the Adaptation Fund (AF) to implement activities such as those relating to adaptation to climate change, supporting capacity building for preventive measures and strengthening national centres for rapid response to extreme weather conditions. Funding can also be obtained from the GEF (on the GEF see *infra* n.72) for implementation of adaptation activities in the developing world. The SCCF and AF are new and additional sources of funding to that provided by the GEF. The SCCF will finance a wide range of activities in addition to adaptation activities that are complementary to those funded by the GEF. The AF will finance adaptation projects in developing countries and will be financed from a share of proceeds on Clean Development Mechanisms (CDM) projects (on the CDM see *infra* nn. 79-84 and accompanying text). The Least Developed Countries Fund is also established under the Marrakesh Accords to support work programmes in least developed nations.

[62] See Articles 4(1) and (2)a of the Climate Change Convention.

[63] Bodansky, *supra* n.15, p.509.

Land-use, Land-use Change and Forestry

The issue of the extent to which forestry projects can be utilised under the Protocol has always been a particularly controversial one. Forests planted in certain latitudes can undoubtedly act as "carbon sinks" or stores reducing carbon dioxide in the atmosphere, and emissions can be reduced by restricting deforestation. Scientists are however unsure as to the extent to which afforestation/reforestation is universally successful, and it is very difficult to determine with certainty the extent to which emissions are actually reduced. Additionally, environmentalists have criticised national policies which seek to plant forests rather than to take the tougher political decisions to curb public consumption of fossil fuels.

The EC and many developing states initially took the view that carbon sinks should not be taken into account, but this was not a view held by USA, Australia, Canada or New Zealand. As a result, in addition to emission reductions initiated by action in the energy, industrial, agricultural and waste sectors, reductions in greenhouse gases attributable to the land-use, land-use change and forestry (LULUCF) sector can be used to offset reduction commitments. More specifically, the Protocol notes that emissions and removals from afforestation, reforestation and deforestation activities that started on or after 1 January 1990 can be used to meet individual state's emission targets. Furthermore, the Marrakesh Accords allow a State Party to elect to choose all or any of four additional activities to meet targets in the first commitment period: revegetation, forest management, cropland management, and grazing land management.[64] Countries can generate Removal Units (RMUs) to meet emissions reduction targets where emissions are removed by "sink" activity. Any such removal must however be validated by expert review teams, must have occurred since 1990, and be human-induced.

Assessment and Review

Annex I Parties must submit an annual inventory of emissions to the Convention Secretariat enabling expert review teams to provide a full assessment of their compliance with the Protocol.[65] These expert assessments will be reviewed by the

---

[64] In a situation where emissions from afforestation, reforestation and deforestation activities actually increase a State Party's overall emissions rather than decrease them, these emissions can be compensated for through removals due to forest management activities up to, but not further than, a total of 9 megatons of carbon per year for the 2008-2012 commitment period. In this first commitment period, the extent to which emission targets can be offset by forest management activity reductions beyond 9 megatons per year is subject to country-specific limits. Canada, Japan and especially the Russian Federation negotiated considerably larger individual caps than the majority of other Annex I Parties in this respect; their ability to do so can be put down to the urgency to reach agreement at Marrakesh. Whilst the Community would no doubt have not wished these countries to make use of reductions from forest management activity to the extent finally agreed, the finalised arrangement must be seen as part of the inevitable compromise deal at Marrakesh designed to facilitate agreement on the "rulebook" for the Protocol.

[65] See Articles 7(1) and 8(1) of the Protocol. The obligation to submit an annual inventory is actionable once the Protocol enters into force.

Conference of the Parties which will adopt decisions on implementation.[66] Bearing in mind the importance of the review of Articles 4(2)a and 4(2)b of the Climate Change Convention which led to the adoption of the Berlin Mandate and the Protocol itself, it is significant that the Protocol includes a review clause which requires the Conference of the Parties to the Protocol to undertake a general review of the Protocol at its second annual session and subsequently to review obligations at regular intervals.[67] Specifically on the issue of emissions, the Conference of the Parties to the Protocol must begin to give consideration to the adoption of further reductions by the end of 2005.[68] The Protocol makes reference to the period 2008 - 2012 as being the first commitment period, Article 3(9) indicating that further commitments to emission reductions by industrialised countries "shall be established".[69]

Commitments by All Parties to the Protocol

It is important to stress that the Protocol introduces no new commitments for developing states and is therefore in line with the Berlin Mandate. However, Article 10 of the Protocol reaffirms existing commitments in the Climate Change Convention on the part of both Annex I and non-Annex I Parties.[70] As such it includes the obligation periodically to update national inventories of greenhouse gases, to formulate and implement national programmes to reduce the effects of climate change, to cooperate on scientific and technical research, and to develop education and training programmes. In addition the Protocol reaffirms the existing commitment on Parties to cooperate in the transfer of environmentally friendly technology to developing states.[71] Many developing countries had stressed the critical importance of the transfer of environmentally sound technology from Annex I Parties on preferential terms to the Third World.[72]

Several Annex I Parties (including Australia, Canada, Japan and the USA) strongly supported a proposal by New Zealand that reference to a process to establish new commitments in the form of emission limitation objectives on the part of the

---

[66] Article 8(6) of the Protocol.
[67] Article 9(2) of the Protocol.
[68] Article 3(9) of the Protocol.
[69] *Ibid.*
[70] Article 4(1) of the Climate Change Convention.
[71] Articles 4(1)c and 4(5) of the Climate Change Convention; Article 10(c)of the Protocol.
[72] Earth Negotiations Bulletin (13 December 1997) vol. 12 no 76, p.10. Article 11 of the Climate Change Convention provides for a financial mechanism. The Global Environmental Facility operates this mechanism on an interim basis under a Memorandum of Understanding with the Conference of the Parties. The Global Environmental Facility has provided for the transfer of technology in projects such as an "efficient industrial boilers project in China, the solar thermal-electric project in India, and the renewable energy small power project in Indonesia"; see UN Document FCCC/CP/1996/8. The Protocol reaffirms Annex II States' commitment to funding such technology transfer and the cost incurred by developing countries in providing updated national inventories of greenhouse gases (Article 11 of the Protocol).

wealthier developing states should be included in the Protocol. The proposal noted that any emission limitation objectives adopted in this process would not have been applicable in the 2008-2012 commitment period. This proposal was rejected by developing countries as being contrary to the spirit of the Berlin Mandate and capable of hindering social and economic development in the Third World. Developing countries continue to take the view that they should not be made to either take on commitments to reduce emissions to a specified level within a given time frame, or to begin a process which could lead to the adoption of such commitments, until the developed world has taken effective action to reduce greenhouse gas emissions. The New Zealand proposal was dropped and, as such, no new commitments on the part of non-Annex I Parties were included in the Protocol.[73]

It is submitted that it is surely correct that the developed world should take the initial lead to reduce emissions as per the Protocol. It is however equally clear that, once leadership has been shown by Annex I countries in this way, the richer developing countries will need to commit themselves to specific emission reduction timetables in the future. This is a view shared by the EC which is of the opinion that there is a great deal of variation in the economic capability of developing countries to reduce greenhouse emissions, but that it is important that the wealthier developing countries take on more responsibilities when circumstances allow. In the meantime, it is the responsibility of Annex I Parties to encourage countries such as China and India to agree to specific emission targets when economic and social circumstances allow by fulfilling their own obligations including the transfer of environmentally friendly technology to the developing world.

Flexible Mechanisms

A key to the success of the negotiations in Kyoto was the flexibility offered in the Protocol to Annex I Parties in achieving their respective emission targets. By endorsing the three flexible mechanisms of joint implementation by Annex I parties, the Clean Development Mechanism, and emissions trading within the Protocol, Annex I countries need not only take action at a domestic level to fulfil their emission reduction obligations. The flexible mechanisms introduce a degree of flexibility in reaching reduction targets without which certain developed states, such as Canada, Japan, and particularly the USA, would have been very unlikely to agree to make commitments to reduce emissions. Although the flexible mechanisms were not "an integral part of the [Community's] approach at Kyoto",[74] the Community and its Member States have indicated a willingness to utilise these flexible

---

73 See Earth Negotiations Bulletin, *supra* n.72, pp.34-35.
74 European Commission, "Climate Change - Towards an EU Post-Kyoto Strategy" COM (98) 353.

mechanisms in its implementation programme. In effect, the Community accepted the flexible mechanisms as part of the compromise deal which established timetabled reductions.

A major concern has been the extent to which developed countries could utilise the flexible mechanisms to offset their emission targets. Whilst the Protocol indicated that use of the mechanisms had to be supplemental to domestic action to reduce emissions, the Community advocated the adoption of a "concrete ceiling" on the use of flexible mechanisms. In this respect, the EC, concerned that unlimited use of the flexible mechanisms to meet reduction commitments would provide a cost-effective alternative to making domestic reductions, proposed that industrialised countries (including the fifteen Member States) be allowed to meet no more than 50 per cent of their greenhouse gas reductions through use of the flexible mechanisms. The Marrakesh Accords do not however introduce any such ceiling but rather refer to the fact that use of the mechanisms shall be "supplemental to domestic action" and that action at home "shall thus constitute a significant element" of efforts made by a given state to meet its emission target. A compromise had been reached which can be criticised for its ambiguous nature, but which was necessary to ensure agreement amongst the States Parties. In particular, the USA (prior to its withdrawal from the Kyoto Protocol) and Australia had not wished to see any sort of concrete ceiling introduced, preferring to be allowed maximum flexibility in the manner in which obligations were to be reached. It is of importance to appreciate that any country wishing to benefit from use of the flexible mechanisms must have ratified the Protocol, and be in compliance with the Protocol's methodological and reporting provisions.[75]

Joint implementation by industrialised countries (JI) Annex I countries are able to acquire "emission reduction units" (ERUs) from participation in joint projects with other Annex I Parties which reduce emissions or enhance natural carbon sinks.[76] These reduction units can be used to contribute to the sponsor nation's emission reduction targets under the Protocol, while the country playing host to the initiative attracts investment to meet not only its environmental but also economic objectives. The USA was a strong advocate of this system as it introduces greater flexibility into the process of making emission cuts allowing the wealthier industrialised states to achieve emission reductions more cheaply by sponsoring projects in the least efficient industrialised economies (for instance in Central and Eastern European

---

[75] These methodological and reporting requirements relate to the obligation on states to have in place a national system for the estimation of greenhouse gas emissions no later than the beginning of 2007, and the obligation to include information in its annual inventory of emissions which will enable a determination to be made as to whether a state is in compliance with its reduction commitments (see more particularly Articles 5(1)and (2), and 7(1) and (4) of the Protocol which note the requirements in question).

[76] Article 6 of the Protocol.

states undergoing a period of economic transition). Joint implementation therefore involves a transfer of credits for demonstrated reductions from a given joint initiative – ERUs pass from the host nation to the sponsor nation to offset the latter's emission reduction commitments.

In 1995 the first Conference of the Parties to the Climate Change Convention initiated a pilot phase for activities implemented jointly. The United States' Initiative on Joint Implementation gave approval for 25 pilot projects between 1992-97, and since 1998 Japan has announced 20 such projects with the Russian Federation. The Community's Member States have also endorsed the notion of project-based joint implementation and those countries participating in the pilot phase include the Netherlands, Germany, France and Sweden. Most pilot projects to date focus on improving energy efficiency and promoting renewable energy, although afforestation and fuel switching initiatives have also been introduced. Many projects in the pilot phase have been between EC Member States and countries in Central and Eastern Europe (many of which are Accession applicants to the Community).This trend is likely to continue.

If joint implementation is to prove effective in the long term, it is acknowledged that projects need to attract financial sponsorship not only from national governments, but also from the private sector. But why would a company based, for instance, in the EC be motivated to invest in a project abroad which leads to emission reductions? An option open to a country to meet its Kyoto emission reduction obligation would be to oblige specific companies to reduce their emissions to a given level. In this scenario private industry could be encouraged to invest in jointly implemented projects based abroad if they can use emission reduction units gained abroad towards their own domestic reduction obligations.

It is important to stress that any joint implementation must supplement domestic action to reduce greenhouse gases, and that therefore an Annex I country would not be able to depend solely on joint action taken in another industrialised country.[77] A JI project must also have the approval of all States Parties involved and must lead to reductions of removals of gases in addition to any which would have taken place without the project. ERUs must only be issued after 2008, but projects which start in 2000 and meet the criteria can be listed as JI projects.[78]

---

[77] Article 6(1)d of the Protocol.

[78] Where host States Parties meet the eligibility requirements to use the flexible mechanisms (see *supra* n.75), they may verify reductions in emissions as being additional to those which would otherwise have occurred, issue ERUs themselves and transfer them to sponsoring states. Where a host State Party fails to comply with the eligibility requirements, verification must be made by the "supervisory committee". This verification process would render a JI project to a system of management similar to that relating to a CDM project; see discussion *infra* nn.79-84 and accompanying text as to the operation of the CDM.

The Clean Development Mechanism (CDM)   The concept of project-based joint implementation by a developed country and a developing country (rather than joint implementation between only industrialised countries or "JI") is endorsed through this new mechanism. The CDM has a dual purpose in that it enables developing countries to operate projects which result in emissions reductions and thus to contribute to the overall objective of the convention. It also allows Annex I countries who finance jointly implemented projects through the CDM to use certified emission reductions (CERs) attributable to such projects to contribute to their own emissions reduction targets under the Protocol.[79]

As with the other project-based flexible mechanism (the previously addressed joint implementation between industrialised countries), the private sector will be encouraged to participate in such projects.[80] Only those projects in which all Parties participate voluntarily, which produce real, measurable, long-term benefits to mitigate climate changes, and which result in reduction of emissions over and above that which would otherwise occur, will be deemed to be projects capable of verification under the CDM. Companies can apply for accreditation to verify a proposed CDM project as of August 2002.

The introduction of the CDM was supported by the G-77 group of developing states,[81] despite long-standing fears that this type of joint implementation between Annex I Parties and developing states would allow rich developed states to finance projects in the Third World, gain credit for doing so, and reduce the need on the part of Annex I Parties involved in such projects to take action at a domestic level. The Protocol seeks to allay any fears in this regard by stressing that Annex I Parties may gain credit through CDM projects, but that such projects will only contribute to "part" of their emission reduction targets.[82] The European Commission has endorsed the concept of the CDM, and the notion of Member States and private industry becoming involved in projects in the Third World under the CDM's direction. It sees the introduction of the CDM as a way in which financial investment from the North can bring about the transfer of environmentally sound technology to developing countries, and as a means to encourage both private and public sector investment in emission reductions in such countries.

An "Executive Board" supervises the CDM. All CDM projects must be validated by "operational entities" (independent organisations accredited by the Executive Board). In making the decision as to whether a project should be validated, an

---

[79]   Article 12(3) of the Protocol.
[80]   Article 12(9) of the Protocol.
[81]   Earth Negotiations Bulletin, *supra* n.72, p.13.
[82]   Article 12(3)b of the Protocol.

operational entity must assess a project design document prepared by the project participants and allow for public consultation. All projects must have in place a monitoring plan allowing for the collection of accurate emissions data. If an operational entity takes the view that a project should be validated, it will forward it to the Executive Board which will formally register the project.[83] The operational entity is responsible for the certification of emission reductions. Restrictions have been imposed on the extent to which LULUCF projects are eligible under the CDM.[84]

Emissions trading The third and perhaps most controversial flexible mechanism endorsed in the Protocol is an emissions trading system which will allow Annex I countries to buy and sell "assigned amount units" (AAUs) from each other.[85] If for instance Canada was in danger of exceeding its emission quota under the Protocol, it would have the option of purchasing some or all of the unused quota of another industrialised country. Canada would then be able to use this emission credit to increase its total allowable emissions under the Protocol.[86] Emissions trading can start as of 2008 under the Protocol. The Commission's plans to bring in a Community-wide trading system will be addressed later.

There is a real fear that even within an international emissions trading system limited to developed countries, some states, such as the Ukraine and the Russian Federation which are highly unlikely to use their full quota due to the collapse of their heavy industry, will be tempted to sell their unused quotas ("hot air") to richer developed countries. This would reduce the need for the latter to overhaul domestic economies excessively reliant on fossil fuels. It has been estimated that both the Ukraine and the Russian Federation will in fact emit approximately 30 per cent less than their 1990 emission levels by 2008-12. As they are both only committed to

---

[83] Registration by the Executive Board will be deemed final eight weeks after it has received the request for registration unless a project participant or three members of the ten-member Executive Board request a review of the proposed CDM project.

[84] With regard to LULUCF projects, it was determined in the Marrakesh Accords that only afforestation and reforestation projects would be eligible under the CDM, and that greenhouse gas removals accredited to a State Party from such projects "shall not exceed one per cent of base year emissions of that Party times five" for the first commitment period. Put more simply, Annex I Parties can only use CERs from eligible LULUCF CDM projects up to one per cent of their base year emissions for each of the five-year commitment period (2008-12). Typically a State Party's base year is 1990 (but see *supra* n.49). Prior to the Marrakesh Accords, the EC had favoured the adoption of a list of CDM-eligible projects which were mainly energy-related. On the other hand, the USA, Australia, New Zealand, Canada and Japan had favoured more wide-ranging eligibility including sinks-related projects like afforestation.

[85] Article 16 *bis* of the Protocol notes that "[t]he Parties included in Annex B may participate in emissions trading for the purposes of fulfilling their commitment under Article 3 of the Protocol". In the Marrakesh Accords, it was determined that Annex I Parties could also acquire CERs and ERUs from other Annex I Parties in addition to AAUs. In addition, RMUs from LULUCF forestry management and agriculture projects can be similarly acquired.

[86] Article 3(10) of the Protocol.

stabilise at 1990 levels under the agreement, they will presumably be in positions to sell their "hot air" reductions to the highest bidder.[87]

Studies in recent years have advocated the introduction of some sort of tradeable permit system for all parties to the Climate Change Convention which would allow the purchasing of permits by those states in excess of their emission quotas.[88] It is to be stressed that the system of emissions trading established by the Protocol does not endorse such an approach as it is limited to the buying and selling of credits among industrialised countries which are party to the Protocol and, as such, have bound themselves to limiting emissions of greenhouse gases with a view to ensuring emissions are collectively reduced by at least five per cent by 2008-2012. Many developing states, including India and China, had expressed strong reservations to an emissions trading system which would allow developed states to purchase credits from Third World countries, fearing that developed countries would rely on this procedure rather than take action at a domestic level to reduce emissions.[89] The introduction of any emissions trading system applicable to both developing and developed states would have necessitated the adoption of general emission quotas for all countries and not just for industrialised countries; this proved unacceptable to developing countries.

Compliance Regime

The Marrakesh Accords established a compliance regime which seeks to facilitate and enforce implementation of the Protocol's obligations. The Compliance Committee operates through two branches, the Facilitative Branch and the Enforcement Branch. It will also function through a plenary and is assisted by a Bureau consisting of the Chair and Vice-Chair of both of the two aforementioned branches. The Facilitative Branch will give advice to States Parties on implementation, and promote compliance with commitments. The Enforcement Branch will determine whether or not a State Party has failed to comply with obligations including reduction commitments, and monitoring and reporting obligations. It can also determine eligibility to utilise the flexible mechanisms.

Issues relating to compliance in a particular country can be raised by the state in question (where it wants the assistance of the Facilitative Branch), by another country

---

[87]   The Marrakesh Accords introduced measures to limit the over-selling of ERUs, CERs, AAUs and RMUs by adopting the "commitment period reserve", but this fails specifically to address the "hot air" issue as noted above.

[88]   See United Nations, *Controlling Carbon Dioxide Emissions: the Tradeable Permit System* (1995) which indicates such purchasing and selling of permits "is the basis on which any international commodity market works. Those who have more than they want sell to those with deficits, at a profit"; p.17. On tradeable permits see also Bohm, *An Analytical Approach to Evaluating the National Net Costs of a Global System of Tradeable Carbon Emission Entitlements: with Special Emphasis on the Effects on Different Country Categories* (1994).

[89]   Earth Negotiations Bulletin, *supra* n.72, pp.15-17.

concerned about non-compliance in the state in question, or by expert review teams. The Bureau will then allocate the particular issue to one of the two branches. The plenary will report on the activities of the two branches to the Conference of the Parties (COP), develop any further rules of procedure which may be needed, and also submit proposals on administrative and budgetary issues to the COP.

The Facilitative Branch has the ability to apply certain consequences such as the provision of advice and assistance, the facilitation of financial and technical assistance, and the making of recommendations. Consequences that can be applied by the Enforcement Branch include a declaration of non-compliance. It also has the power to require the state in question to develop a plan which must indicate those measures which it intends to implement to remedy its non-compliance, and a timetable for the implementation of such measures (within a time frame not exceeding twelve months). Regular progress reports must be made by the non-complying country to the Enforcement Branch as to implementation of any such plan. Where a state does not meet eligibility requirements for the flexible mechanisms, the Enforcement Branch can suspend the ability of that country to utilise such mechanisms. Where a country fails to abide by its reduction commitment, the Enforcement Branch shall determine that it makes up the reduction shortfall in the next commitment period together with a penalty of 30 per cent of the excess emissions. It would also be suspended from trading in emissions and made to develop a plan of action to attain full compliance.

Some Conclusions on the Kyoto Protocol

In general terms, the adoption of the Kyoto Protocol must be regarded as a highly significant step in the elaboration of an effective legal regime to combat global warming, as the Protocol has succeeded in introducing legally binding emission targets for developed states. The Marrakesh Accords have added the necessary detail to the operation of the Protocol's regime to allow for more widespread State Party ratification. Indeed, the EC gave its formal approval to be bound by the Kyoto Protocol in May 2002 at which time all 15 Member States also became bound by separately ratifying or approving of the Protocol.[90]

However, Kyoto represents but a first step. Further reduction timetables in commitment periods subsequent to the 2008-12 period must be adopted in the future. Despite the progress made in the Protocol, it is a sobering thought to note that

[e]nsuring ... further temperature increases are at no more than 0.1 per cent per decade, and that sea levels rise by no more than 2cm per decade ... would require industrialised countries to reduce emissions of greenhouse gases by at least 30-55 per cent by 2010 from 1990 levels.[91]

---

[90] OJ 2002 L130/1. Status of Ratification can be checked on http://unfccc.int/resource/convkp.html.

[91] European Environment Agency, *Europe's Environment: the Second Assessment* (1998), p.37.

Whilst the Protocol can still enter into force without ratification by the USA, the biggest threat to the effectiveness of the regime is the possibility that the United States will never ratify the Protocol. Ratification by the USA looks a very remote possibility at present. Without the world's larger polluter re-engaging with the process, even more of a responsibility has been placed on the Community and its Member States to live up to the leadership role they have assumed in international negotiations by fulfilling their own reduction commitments. The EC proved to be a powerful driving force behind moves to establish meaningful emission reductions by Annex I countries, ex-Commissioner Ritt Bjerregaard noting that the EC had

> *managed to pull the US and Japan up from very low targets for reductions in greenhouse gas emissions ... to more credible targets with safeguards to help to ensure that reported reductions in emissions are genuine.*[92]

However, effective action must now be taken by the Community itself to implement its own reduction commitments. It is only in this way that it can hope to retain its credibility internationally as a party which has continually lobbied for timetabled emissions for developed countries and for the introduction of meaningful greenhouse gas reduction programmes.

The Community's Internal Strategy to Reduce Greenhouse Gas Emissions

In seeking to assess the effectiveness of the Community's internal policy to meet its political commitment to stabilise carbon dioxide emissions by the year 2000 at 1990 levels and its Kyoto obligations, it is important to stress that action at Community level is intended to complement Member States' national programmes to reduce greenhouse gas emissions. The Commission has noted that

> *[i]n line with the subsidiarity principle action to address climate change should be taken at the appropriate level. Member States have a major role since they are individually responsible for their own targets within the agreed burden sharing ... However, the fact that the Community has a target, the integration of the European economy and the need to ensure a level playing field requires that actions are also taken at the Community level.*[93]

The success or otherwise of the Community's policy is dependent on the cooperation of Member States who are obliged as parties to the Framework Convention on Climate Change, and under Decision 93/389/EEC for a Monitoring Mechanism of Community Carbon Dioxide and other Greenhouse Gas Emissions to

---

[92]   European Commission, *supra* n.5.
[93]   European Commission, *supra* n.74 at p.7.

devise and implement their own national policies.[94] It is in this context that the Community's overall strategy should ultimately be scrutinised. The focus of the remainder of this chapter is however to introduce the reader to some of the key measures proposed or adopted at the Community level to date.[95]

Despite being perceived in international negotiations as an influential voice which has provided leadership in successfully lobbying for the establishing of emission reduction targets for industrialised countries, the Community runs a real risk of failing to meet its own Kyoto target. As such, the practical difficulties of integrating environmental concerns into other policy areas in accordance with the integration principle have been underlined, and a credibility gap is clearly opening between the Community's stance on the international stage and its actual practice in implementing its international obligations at home.[96]

Mindful of the need for further action, the Commission launched the European Climate Change Programme (ECCP) in March 2000 establishing a consultative process involving key stakeholders.[97] Designed to develop ideas and proposals to ensure Kyoto obligations are met, a variety of working groups were set up comprising experts from industry, national governments, environmental pressure groups and also Commission representatives. Seven working groups were established concentrating on energy supply, energy consumption, transport, industry, the Kyoto flexible mechanisms, research and agriculture respectively. Their common task was to identify the most cost and environmentally effective additional measures to ensure the Community's compliance with Kyoto obligations. The implications of a wide variety of measures were investigated and policy recommendations subsequently made to the Commission. There is little doubt that the ECCP has provided momentum to the policy process by providing the

---

[94] See Decision 93/389/EEC for a Monitoring Mechanism of Community Carbon Dioxide and other Greenhouse Gas Emissions (OJ 1993 L167/31) as amended by Council Decision 99/296/EC (OJ 1999 L117/35). Article 2(1) of the original decision obliges Member States to "devise, publish and implement national programmes" to contribute to the Community's international obligations under the Climate Change Convention, and to the Community's political commitment to stabilise carbon dioxide emissions by 2000 at 1990 levels. Importantly a monitoring mechanism is established (Article 1) and Member States are obliged to report annually to the Commission on their level of emissions (Article 3). The 1999 amendment to the original decision now obliges Member States to monitor all six greenhouse gases included in the Kyoto Protocol and to implement national strategies to fulfil Kyoto commitments. On the Commission's 2001 report on the monitoring mechanism, see COM (2001) 708. See also the proposal to replace the 1993 Decision as amended; COM (2003) 51.

[95] However, it is certainly acknowledged that, in relation to such Community action, reference to and assessment of every measure and approach would not be practicable in the confines of this chapter. The reader is however referred to the more comprehensive Community's communications under the Framework Convention on Climate Change in this regard. See for example European Commission, "Third Communication from the EC Under the UN Framework Convention on Climate Change" SEC (2001) 2053 (20/12/2001) available on http://unfccc.int/resource/docs/natc/.

[96] European Commission, "Preparing for Implementation of the Kyoto Protocol" COM (99) 230, p.1.

[97] European Commission, "EU Policies and Measures to Reduce Greenhouse Gas Emissions: Towards a European Climate Change Programme" COM(2000) 88. The programme envisages the establishing of an internal EC greenhouse gas emissions trading scheme; see *infra* nn.134-136 with accompanying text.

Commission with information on a range of potential measures, some of which the Commission intends to develop in the short to medium term.[98]

Energy Sector

The Commission's Green Paper on the Security of Energy Supply attempts to outline the basic elements of the Community's long-term energy strategy and gives the task of tackling climate change a high priority.[99] In particular, it underlines the need to increase energy efficiency, and to develop new and renewable energies. Bearing in mind that the EC's energy sector is responsible for the production of 80 per cent of the Community's carbon dioxide and 26 per cent of it methane emissions,[100] it is indeed no surprise that many of the Community's initiatives to date have promoted the more rational use of energy.

Fiscal measures The objective of the proposed staged introduction of an EC-wide "carbon/energy tax" was to "improve energy efficiency and favour fuel substitution towards products emitting less or no carbon dioxide".[101] This tax was to have been the lynchpin of the Commission's strategy in the first half of the 1990s,[102] but the failure to reach agreement in Council on its introduction severely undermined the Community's early policy. This failure was due partly to the reluctance of the UK to agree to the imposition of any type of EC-wide environmental taxation, arguing that matters of taxation in this area fall within the remit of individual Member States rather than that of the Community. Without UK approval the proposed tax was doomed to failure bearing in mind that there was, and still is, a need for unanimity in Council for the adoption of fiscal measures of this type. The Commission's original proposal in 1992 had envisaged the introduction of a tax on all energy products apart from renewables.[103] Concerns as to the effect the measure may have had on the competitiveness of European industry in comparison with industry in third countries proved important factors in the failure of the Commission's proposal.

---

[98]   See Communication on the implementation of the first phase of the ECCP, COM (2001) 580. This document outlines a package of measures which the Commission intends to make progress on during the course of 2002/2003. The package covers cross-cutting measures as well as those specifically relating to the energy sector, transport and industry.

[99]   COM (2000) 769.

[100]   European Commission, "Climate Change: Facts and Figures", p.3.

[101]   European Commission, "Second Communication from the European Community Under the UN Framework Convention on Climate Change" (26 June 1998), p.32.

[102]   See European Commission "A Community Strategy to Limit Carbon Dioxide Emissions and to Improve Energy Efficiency", COM (92) 246 final.

[103]   COM (92) 226 final. The original proposal was amended in 1995; see COM (95) 172 final. On the proposals, see Scott, *EC Environmental Law* (1998), pp.45-49.

The Commission has however subsequently encouraged Member States to take their own domestic action to introduce carbon taxes.[104]

The Council, following the failure to reach agreement on the "carbon/energy tax" proposal, requested that the Commission propose new fiscal measures on energy products to reduce greenhouse gases. In March 1997 the Commission put forward a proposal to restructure the Community excise duty system on energy products.[105] The proposal builds on the Community's existing system of minimum levels of taxation (duty rates) applicable to mineral oils (petrol and diesel)[106] by introducing minimum duty rates for all other sources of energy including coal, coke, lignite, bitumen, natural gas and electricity used both domestically and industrially. Existing minimum duty rates on mineral oils would be increased, and rebates would be available for firms whose energy costs represent a particularly high percentage of their overall production costs. Renewable energy sources would enjoy preferential treatment in the form of exemptions or reduced rates. Incentives would additionally be put in place to encourage more widespread use of public transport which utilises natural gas or LPG, and transportation by rail and inland waterways. To date slow progress has been made in adopting this proposal which lacks the required unanimity in Council.[107]

Promotion of the use of renewable energy The Community began the ALTENER I programme in 1993 making available funding to develop and promote the use of renewable energy as part of its strategy to reduce carbon dioxide emissions.[108] Under ALTENER I Member States were encouraged to give due consideration in the formulation of their national energy strategies to increasing the use of renewable energy, bearing in mind the Community's objective to increase the share of renewables to the overall supply of energy in the Community in the period 1991-2005 from under four per cent to eight per cent ALTENER I ran for a five-year period to the end of 1997 with an overall budget of 40 million ECUs. The programme supported general studies and technical evaluations which *inter alia*

---

[104] See ENDS Report No. 244, p.39. On the use of environmental taxes and charges by Member States in such a way as to ensure their compatibility with EC law within the framework of the single market, see European Commission, "Environmental Taxes and Charges in the Single Market" COM (97) 9 final. As of October 1996 this document notes that Denmark, Finland, the Netherlands, Norway and Sweden had introduced domestic carbon/energy taxes on motor fuels and other energy products; Austria had not introduced a tax on motor fuels but had on other energy products (see *ibid*, Appendix 1). In March 1999 the British Government announced the introduction of an energy tax for industry which is intended to reduce carbon dioxide consumption by 1.5 million tons annually; see *The Independent* 10 March 1999, p.9.

[105] Proposal for a Council Directive Restructuring the Community Framework for the Taxation of Energy Products COM(97) 30 final.

[106] Council Directive 92/81/EEC on the Harmonisation of the Structures of Excise Duties on Mineral Oils OJ 1992 L 316/12, and Council Directive 92/82/EEC on the Approximation of the Rates of Excise Duties on Mineral Oils OJ 1992 L 316/19.

[107] See ENDS Environment Daily, "Prospects for EU Energy Tax 'hopeless'", issue 1270 (19 August 2002)

[108] Decision 93/500/EEC Concerning the Promotion of Renewable Energy Sources in the Community OJ 1993 L235/41.

identified barriers to renewable energy sources, set technical standards for solar panels and wind turbines, and engaged in training and information programmes. Other projects established networks to exchange information on liquid biofuels, energy from waste, and agricultural and forestry biomass.[109]

The share of the Community's energy requirements attributed to renewable energy sources rose from under four per cent in 1991 to six per cent by the end of 2001,[110] although it is uncertain to what extent the ALTENER programme has played a part. Much of the "increase" can in fact be put down to the accession of Austria, Finland and Sweden in 1995 as these countries all use renewables to a far greater extent than other Member States.[111] The Community's current objective is to ensure that 12 per cent of the Community's overall energy consumption is met by renewable energy by 2010.[112] With this in mind the Community adopted ALTENER II to run for a two-year period from January 1998.[113] The ALTENER programme has since been extended and modified to run for a further two years until 2002.[114] Provision was made in ALTENER II for the funding of projects to develop *inter alia* the potential use of renewables by improving awareness through education and training programmes, and to facilitate market access of renewables (market strategies, harmonisation of standards and certification of products, and tax incentives). In addition, projects were eligible for funding which were involved in the monitoring and evaluation of Member States, activities in developing renewable energy sources.

The Community's strategy on renewables, while acknowledging that significant technological progress has been made in recent years due partly to EC-funded demonstration programmes for energy saving technology,[115] notes that high initial

---

[109] See European Commission, "The Results of the ALTENER Programme" COM (97) 122 final.

[110] European Commission, *supra* n.6, p.32.

[111] See European Commission's White Paper, "Energy for the Future: Renewable Sources of Energy", COM (97) 599 final, Table 1. Renewable energy sources accounted for over 20 per cent of overall energy consumption in all three countries in 1995. At the same time, in Germany the share of energy consumption attributable to renewables was just 1.8 per cent, and in the UK 0.7 per cent.

[112] *Ibid.* There is real doubt as to whether this target will be met; see European Commission, "Communication on the Implementation of the Community Strategy and Action Plan on Renewable Energy Sources" COM (2001) 69.

[113] Council Decision Concerning a Multiannual Programme for the Promotion of Renewable Energy Sources in the Community (ALTENER II) OJ 1998 L159/53. The ALTENER programmes are non-technological in nature. They are complemented by the technological CARNOT Programme which seeks to promote the clean and efficient use of solid fuels; see Council Decision 1999/24 Adopting a Multiannual Programme of Technological Actions Promoting the Clean and Efficient use of Solid Fuels (OJ 1999 L7/28).

[114] Decision 646/2000/EC, OJ 2000 L79/1.

[115] Such as Regulation 2008/90 establishing the THERMIE programme (OJ 1990 L 185) which ran from 1990-1994. THERMIE II (1995-98) continued the programme commenced by its predecessor by offering financial support for demonstration projects which utilised innovative energy technologies. See also Decision 182/1999/EC concerning the Fifth Framework Programme of the European Community for Research, Technological Development and Demonstrative Activities (1998-2002), OJ 1999 L26/1; this programme continued support to the development of renewable energy sources by promoting research and demonstration activities.

capital investment costs and lack of confidence in unfamiliar energy sources has limited the market penetration of renewables to date.[116] Member States must therefore play a key role in adopting national strategies and objectives. Greater emphasis should be placed on ensuring the dissemination of consumer information on renewable energies to industry and the general public. In addition, the Commission stresses the importance of providing access for renewables to electricity networks at fair prices within the single market in electricity to be established under Directive 96/92/EC.[117] The latter measure permits Member States to give certain preferences to renewable sources.[118]

As part of the process in adding definition to the Community's strategy, a working paper was issued by the Commission in April 1999 outlining policy options to establish a competitive renewable energy market in the Community.[119] It endeavoured to "test the water" as to the suitability of options, including the adoption of Community harmonisation measures, to support the generation of energy from renewables. The need for support was recognised in three particular respects:[120]

1. Cost of renewables

The cost of renewable generated energy exceeds that from more traditional sources, and necessitates a stable price support system allowing producers to establish themselves on the market and make a profit.

2. Infrastructure

Grid connection can be expensive, and problems have been encountered in the often lengthy procedures to obtain planning permission for generating plants which are far more likely to be located closer to communities than traditional plants.

3. Research and technological development

Work in this area must continue to contribute to the further decreasing of the cost of renewable generated energy, and to the remedying of problems relating to grid connection.

---

[116] European Commission, *supra* n.111, pp.4-5.

[117] Directive 96/92/EC concerning Common Rules for the Internal Market in Electricity (OJ 1997 L27/20). The measure provides for a staged opening of the electricity market to competition. The Commission notes that 26.48 per cent of each Member State's market will be open to competition by 19 February 1999, a further 28 per cent by 19 February 2000, and 33 per cent more by 19 February 2003; European Commission, "Guide to the Electricity Directive", p.5. In relation to the 1996 directive, note Common Position 5/2003 with a view to adopting a directive concerning common rules for the internal market in electricity and repealing Directive 96/92; OJ 2003 C50/15.

[118] See Article 8(3) which allows Member States to ensure the sale of electricity generated from renewable sources even where the cost of electricity of this type is higher than electricity generated from more conventional sources.

[119] European Commission, "Electricity from Renewable Energy Sources and the Internal Electricity Market", issued on 13 April 1999.

[120] *Ibid*, pp.10-11.

A number of schemes have been established by individual Member States to provide support to the generation of renewable energy. For instance in the UK a levy on all domestic consumption of electricity supports the desired level of electricity supplied by renewables. In Germany and Spain a system of guaranteed prices and a purchase obligation on utilities is in operation, and certain Member States subsidise capital investment in renewables.[121] However, the Commission took the view that, although the application of these and other rules by Member States would eventually lead to increased trade and competition in renewable generated electricity, there was a need for a harmonising measure to further promote electricity produced from renewable energy sources. In October 2001 a directive on the promotion of electricity from such sources came into effect ("Renewables Directive").[122] The measure creates a framework for desired increases in electricity supplied from renewables, and also intends to facilitate market access for renewables. Member States are obliged to take steps to encourage greater consumption of electricity from renewable sources in conformity with national indicative targets. If all indicative targets are reached, just over 22 per cent of the Community's electricity will be met by renewable energy in 2010. Steps also have to be taken to facilitate access to national grids: action must be taken at the national level to ensure the proper certification of electricity produced from renewable sources, and to guarantee the transmission and distribution of renewable energy.

The issue of whether or not to move at an early stage towards a harmonised financial support scheme for renewables proved contentious in debate leading to the adoption of the Renewables Directive. The advantage of such an approach would have been the introduction of a level playing field throughout the Community. However, certain Member States (especially Germany) felt that the introduction of a harmonised support regime would have severely undermined the effectiveness of their own existing national support regimes, and hence have had a detrimental impact on existing investor confidence in renewables. Although the directive in its finalised form does not aim to harmonise renewables price support schemes, it is important to appreciate that this is certainly not ruled out in the future. The Commission will monitor the situation and, following the production of an interim report by late October 2005 on experience gained on the application of the various national support mechanisms, may put forward a proposal for a Community framework directive in relation to support schemes for electricity produced from renewables.

---

[121] *Ibid*, pp.11-12.

[122] Directive 2001/77/EC on the Promotion of Electricity Produced from Renewable Energy Sources in the Internal Electricity Market (OJ 2001 L283/33). To obtain the necessary information on a possible future Community price support scheme, the Commission would be obliged under the terms of the proposal to monitor the effectiveness of national support schemes. Any future proposal to harmonise price support structures would be adopted if appropriate, and in the light of a Commission report.

Promotion of energy efficiency   Under the Community's Specific Actions for Vigorous Energy Efficiency (SAVE) programmes,[123] Member States have been obliged to improve energy efficiency by drawing up and implementing programmes which include energy certification of buildings, the thermal insulation of new buildings, and the introduction of energy auditing for undertakings with high energy consumption. Community legislation has also been adopted establishing minimum efficiency requirements for fridges and freezers, and hot water boilers,[124] and the SAVE II programme allowed for the provision of Community funding for energy efficiency projects which *inter alia* accelerated energy efficiency investment, disseminated information, monitored progress to date, and promoted energy efficiency management.

The Community has additionally enacted legislation promoting the rational use of energy through a labelling and product information programme for household appliances;[125] manufacturers of items such as fridges, freezers, washing machines and ovens are obliged to provide labels and product fiches supplying information relating to energy consumption on the assumption that the consumer's choice of product will be influenced by the provision of accurate and comparable information of this nature. In this way consumers will be encouraged to make informed choices in their consumption patterns. An energy efficiency labelling programme has also been enacted for office equipment.[126]

The Commission has underlined the importance of further developing the Community's strategy for energy efficiency which it believes can potentially lead to an 18 per cent saving of the Community's total energy consumption in 1995 by the year 2010.[127] While such an ambitious vision is laudable, there is much room for improvement in the Community's record to date. The Council has noted that, despite certain measures being adopted, "the profile of energy efficiency must be raised significantly".[128] In particular the Council acknowledges that increased emphasis

---

[123] SAVE I (Council Decision 91/565/EEC OJ 1991 L307/34) ran from 1 January 1991 to 31 December 1995 and was followed by SAVE II (Council Decision 96/737/EC OJ 1996 L335/50) which ran to 31 December 2000. The SAVE II programme was extended to 2002 (Decision 647/2000/EC OJ 2000 L79/6).

[124] Council Directive 96/57/EC on Efficiency Requirements for Household Electric Refrigerators, Freezers and Combinations thereof OJ 1996 L236/36, and Council Directive 92/42 on Efficiency Requirements for New Hot Water Boilers Fired with Liquid or Gaseous Fuels OJ 1992 L167/17.

[125] Council Directive 92/75/EEC on the Indication by Labelling and Standard Product Information of the Consumption of Energy and other Resources by Household Appliances, OJ 1992 L297/16. This directive envisages the adoption of implementing directives such as Commission Directive 97/17/EC on Energy Labelling of Dishwashers OJ 1997 L118/1 [as amended by Directive 1999/9/EC OJ 1999 L56/46].

[126] Regulation 2422/2001 on a Community Energy Efficiency Labelling Programme for Office Equipment, OJ 2001 L332/1.

[127] European Commission, "Energy Efficiency in the EC: Towards a Strategy for the Rational use of Energy" COM (98) 246.

[128] Council Resolution on Energy Efficiency in the European Community, OJ 1999 C394/1. As for other policy strategies see European Commission, "Action Plan to Improve Energy Efficiency in the European Community" COM (2000) 247; the Action Plan envisages the strengthening of the SAVE programme and also the introduction of new policies such as energy audits in industry, and "technology procurement" under which energy-efficient technology is developed in a competitive tendering process.

should be placed on energy use in the building sector,[129] the revision of existing legislation and development of new policies, and also on the need to take energy efficiency into account in public procurement practices. Clearly, as the Community expands eastwards, there will be opportunities to improve energy efficiency patterns in the industries of those Central and Eastern European states which have applied for accession (as has been acknowledged in the Sixth Environmental Action Programme).

Particular emphasis has been placed by the Commission on the role that the increased use of combined heat and power (CHP) can play in reducing greenhouse gas emissions.[130] A CHP operation produces heat and power in one and the same process, and saves at least ten per cent of the fuel which would otherwise have been used in separate heat and power production. The promotion of CHP will continue through existing Community programmes such as SAVE and ALTENER, and the Commission also envisages the negotiating of voluntary agreements with those sectors in industry where energy savings can be made utilising CHP-produced energy. However whilst the Community can help to coordinate an overall EC strategy to promote CHP, the Commission has placed the major responsibility on Member States themselves to develop effective national strategies. Member States have been encouraged to develop national strategies to eradicate barriers to the production of energy by CHP. These barriers include the restricted access of CHP-produced energy to the electricity network, and fluctuations in the price of energy which have proved to be a disincentive for long-term investment in CHP production.[131] The onus placed on Member States was acknowledged by the Council,[132] and indeed the Netherlands, Finland and Denmark have pursued successful policies on CHP to date.

It soon became clear however that there was a need for the Community to take action to complement national action if a rise in CHP-produced electricity from 9 per cent in 1994 to the Community's goal of 18 per cent in 2010 is to be realised. With this in mind, the Commission adopted a proposal in July 2002 which is intended to set up a framework within which the introduction and operation of the CHP technique can be supported.[133] The measure seeks to establish a guarantee of origin for electricity from CHP, and to introduce procedures to analyse potential for and barriers to cogeneration. It also attempts to guarantee the transmission and distribution of electricity produced by CHP, facilitate the evaluation of national support schemes for

---

[129] See Directive 2002/91 on the Energy Performance of Buildings OJ 2003 L1/65.

[130] See European Commission, "A Community Strategy to Promote Combined Heat and Power (CHP) and to Dismantle Barriers to its Development" COM (97) 514.

[131] *Ibid*, p.4.

[132] See Council Resolution on a Combined Strategy to Promote Combined Heat and Power OJ 1999 C4/1.

[133] COM (2002) 415.

cogeneration, and to set up a methodology to establish energy savings from CHP processes.

Industrial Sector

The potential use of the Kyoto Protocol's flexible mechanisms, and implementation of the Integrated Pollution Prevention and Control (IPPC) Directive merit particular attention. Acknowledging that the flexible mechanisms are market-based economic measures which are new to the Community's environmental strategy and policy, the Commission called for a constructive discussion on their utilisation in a Community context. In March 2000 the Commission published a Green Paper on greenhouse gas emission trading within the Community with a view to stimulating debate on the establishment of a market-based EC-wide emissions trading scheme by 2005. This Green Paper envisaged a limited trading system which would initially involve trading in carbon dioxide emissions between large fixed-point sources (such as large combustion plants, iron and steel production plants, and industry in the refining sector). It envisaged the allocation of emissions allowances to companies, and subsequent trading between those companies which reduce emissions below their allocated quota and those that run the risk of exceeding their allowances.[134]

The feedback received on the Green Paper was largely favourable and a proposal for a Directive on Emissions Trading was subsequently put forward in late 2001.[135] The Commission proposes that the scheme would come into effect in 2005 for carbon dioxide emissions from major industry and energy-generating installations only (although an extension of the scheme could be made to other sectors and greenhouse gases at a later date). Under the proposal, installations will apply to the relevant competent authority for a greenhouse gas emissions permit. Each installation will be allocated annual emissions allowances and any unused allowance can be traded. In relation to the other flexible mechanisms, the Commission advocates private sector involvement in JI and the CDM, and encourages Member States to recognise credits gained under these flexible mechanisms in the fulfilment of national reduction obligations.[136]

Member States' implementation of the IPPC Directive[137] will in principle lead to the more efficient use of energy by heavy industry. The measure is the most important in relation to the operation of industrial plants, and adopts an integrated approach to reduce pollution by preventing or minimising emissions to air, water and soil. New

---

[134] European Commission, "Green Paper on Greenhouse Gas Emissions Trading Within the European Union" COM(2000) 87.

[135] COM (2001) 581. The Council reached political agreement on a common position on the Commission's proposal in December 2002.

[136] European Commission, *supra* n.6, pp.70-71.

[137] Council Directive 96/61/EC concerning Integrated Pollution Prevention and Control OJ 1996 L257/26.

heavy industrial installations which operate in a diverse number of fields – such as in the production of energy, metals and chemicals, and the management of waste – require an IPPC permit to be operational from 30 October 1999. Existing plants – those already in operation on 30 October 1999 – are required to comply with the directive's obligations from 30 October 2007. The necessary permit will contain conditions to ensure that industrial plants operate in such a manner that a high level of protection for the environment as a whole is achieved. Member States are therefore obliged to adopt the necessary measures to ensure that emissions of greenhouse gases are prevented or minimised, and installations function in such a way that *inter alia* "energy is used efficiently".[138] Clearly the introduction of technologies which already exist would significantly improve industrial energy efficiency throughout the Community – research has estimated that potential savings of 25 per cent or over in refineries, and of 15 per cent in the steel industry could be made with the incorporation of energy management and process technologies, as well as CHP.[139] It appears too early at this stage to assess the impact of the IPPC Directive in relation to the promotion of energy efficiency, but the ECCP has underlined the potential importance of the IPPC Directive in this respect.

Transport Sector

Growth in the volume of road transport has been apparent throughout the Community's Member States (particularly in Ireland, Spain, Portugal and Greece).[140] In May 1999 the Commission acknowledged that greenhouse gas emissions generated by the transport sector are likely to rise unless effective action is taken: "[t]he transport sector is expected to increase its carbon dioxide emissions by ... 39 per cent in 2010 from the 1999 level".[141] The Commission has therefore drawn up a strategy to reduce by half the growth in emissions, suggesting *inter alia* the promotion of public transport and improved management practice in the freight industry.[142] The White Paper on a Common Transport Policy has underlined the need to integrate sustainable development and environmental aspects into transport policies.[143] It advocates a shifting of transport from road/rail to more

---

[138] Article 3(d).

[139] AEA Technology plc, "Study on Energy Management and Optimisation in Industry", a report prepared for the European Commission (July 2000).

[140] European Commission, *supra* n.6 p.57.

[141] European Commission, *supra* n.96, p.3.

[142] See European Commission, "Transport and Carbon Dioxide: Developing a Community Approach" COM (98) 204, and "The Common Transport Policy: Sustainable Mobility - Perspectives for the Future" COM (98) 716.

[143] COM (2001) 370.

environmentally friendly methods, the continued introduction of new technology to improve efficiency and the promotion of alternative energy for the transport sector. The Commission has also been an advocate of the promotion of the use of agricultural biofuels for transport.[144]

Potentially of great importance, the Commission has seen fit to enter into voluntary agreements with the automobile manufacturers. The first of these agreements was concluded with the European Automobile Manufacturers' Association (ACEA),[145] and seeks to reduce carbon dioxide emissions from new cars sold in the Community in 2008 by 25 per cent compared to 1995 levels.[146] This commitment will be monitored jointly by the Commission and ACEA.[147] The latter envisages that the decrease in emissions will for the main part be met by improving automobile technology, although at this stage the precise nature of such technology remains uncertain. For this reason, and the fact that the passing of an appropriate directive would have taken several years, a voluntary agreement seemed to the Commission to be the most appropriate measure rather than binding legislation.[148]

The ACEA agreement is one of the most important elements in the Commission's overall objective to reduce carbon dioxide emissions from new passenger cars to 120g/km by 2005, and at the latest by 2010. If successful, the strategy will contribute approximately 15 per cent of the Community's reduction commitment under the Kyoto Protocol.[149] Consumers are also targeted under the strategy in that legislation was adopted in December 1999 which seeks to ensure that information on the fuel-economy of new cars is made available in promotional literature and at the point of sale.[150] Implementation of this measure was required by mid-January 2001.

---

[144] Proposal for a Directive on the Promotion of the Use of Biofuels for Transport COM (2001) 547. The adoption of the proposal may well be delayed seeing as the Council would wish to see optional rather than mandatory targets; this is unlikely to meet with the approval of the European Parliament [see ENDS Environment Daily issue 1239 (19 June 2002)].

[145] COM (98) 495. ACEA represents BMW, Daimler-Benz, Fiat, Ford of Europe, General Motors, Peugeot-Citroen, Renault, VW and Volvo.

[146] See Commission Recommendation on the Decrease of Carbon Dioxide from Passenger Cars (OJ 1999 L40/49) and COM (98) 495. Also see the European Commission's Second Report on the Strategy to Reduce Carbon Dioxide Emissions from Cars; COM (2001) 643.

[147] See Council and Parliament Decision 1753/2000 Establishing a Scheme to Monitor the Average Specific Emissions of Carbon Dioxide from New Passenger Cars (OJ 2000 L202/1) which sets up a scheme to monitor carbon dioxide emissions from new passenger cars registered in the Community. Article 8 notes that the "data collected under the monitoring system from the year 2003 onward shall serve as the basis for monitoring voluntary obligations to reduce emissions of carbon dioxide from motor vehicles agreed between the Commission and the automobile industry, and where necessary, for their revision".

[148] See generally Bongaerts, "Carbon Dioxide Emissions and Cars: An Environmental Agreement at EU Level" (1999) 8(4) EELR 101, at p.103.

[149] European Commission, "Carbon Dioxide Emissions from Cars: the EU Implementing the Kyoto Protocol" (1998).

[150] Directive 1999/94/EC Relating to the Availability of Consumer Information on Fuel Economy and Carbon Dioxide Emissions in Respect of the Marketing of New Passenger Cars OJ 2000 L12/16.

The ACEA agreement was signed in July 1998 and assumed that similar agreements would be made with non-European manufacturers. Agreements of this nature were indeed reached with the Japanese Automobile Manufacturers Association (JAMA) and the Korean Automobile Manufacturers Association (KAMA) in 1999.[151] The conclusion of these voluntary market-based agreements is symptomatic of the approach instigated in the Fifth Environmental Action Programme of widening the type of instrument beyond traditional command-and-control measures.[152] It is encouraging to note that in the period 1995-1999 ACEA, JAMA and KAMA all managed to reduce the average carbon dioxide emissions of cars which were sold in the Community. Taking into account these figures, the Commission in late 2000 stipulated that it had "no particular reason to believe that any of the associations would not live up to its commitment".[153] Indeed, ACEA has indicated that new cars made by European manufacturers in 2001 emitted 2.5 per cent less carbon dioxide compared to the year 2000, and has expressed confidence that the target set in the ACEA voluntary agreement will indeed be met.[154]

Agriculture Sector

In relation to agriculture, the main sources of greenhouse gases are methane emissions (from enteric fermentation and manure management) and nitrous oxide emissions (from soils as a result of crop fertilisation, and manure management). No policy in this sector can be said specifically to target the reduction of greenhouse gas emissions, although the Commission takes the view that general policy approach has led to such reductions.[155] For example, the 1992 Common Agricultural Policy (CAP) reforms are believed to have contributed to a four per cent drop in emissions from 1990 to 1999.[156] These reforms *inter alia* brought about increases in livestock productivity and changes in livestock types which contributed to the reduction in emissions.[157] Although a number of the measures linked to the more recent CAP reforms may lead to further reductions in emissions,[158] the ECCP has underlined that

---

[151] COM (1999) 446 final. JAMA comprises Daihatsu, Honda, Isuzu, Mazda, Nissan, Mitsubishi, Subaru, Suzuki and Toyota. KAMA is made up of Daewoo, Hyundai and the Kia Motor Corporation.

[152] On the use of voluntary agreements, see Khalastchi and Ward, "New Instruments for Sustainability: an Assessment of Environmental Agreements under Community Law" (1998) 10(2) JEL 257.

[153] European Commission, "Implementing the Community Strategy to Reduce Carbon Dioxide Emissions from Cars: First Annual Report on the Effectiveness of the Strategy" COM (2000) 615, p.7.

[154] ENDS Environment Daily, "Further fall in European new car carbon dioxide levels", issue 1254 (10 July 2002).

[155] European Commission, *supra* n.6, pp.111-112. In addition to CAP reforms, note should be made that any action which curbs forest fires will assist in reducing the greenhouse effect. In this respect, see Council Regulation 2158/92 on the Protection of Community's Forests Against Fire (OJ 1992 L217/3), and Regulation 804/94 on the Application of Forest Fire Information Systems (OJ 1994 L93/11). Note also the proposal for a Regulation concerning Monitoring of Forests and Environmental Interactions in the Community (COM (2002) 404).

[156] European Commission, *supra* n.6, p.112.

[157] *Ibid.*

[158] *Ibid.*, p.113.

climate change concerns should be more fully integrated into the CAP in the future. Reducing livestock numbers by changing consumer behaviour (eating less meat and consuming less dairy products) has, for instance, been earmarked by the ECCP as providing potential for "significant reduction" in the level of emissions.[159]

Waste Management

The Community has endeavoured to reduce emissions of greenhouse gases from the waste sector. The most significant action to date relates to those obligations placed on Member States under the Landfill Directive to reduce significantly the amount of biodegradable municipal waste disposed of by landfill.[160] The decay of biodegradable waste in landfill operations is responsible for approximately one third of the Community's methane emissions. The Landfill Directive obliges Member States to reduce the total amount of biodegradable municipal waste disposed of by landfill by 2016 to 35 per cent of the total amount of such waste produced in 1995. Additionally, the measure requires the vast majority of landfill sites dealing with biodegradable waste to have gas control mechanisms fitted by 2007. Alternatives to landfill include the composting of biodegradable waste by private households and by relevant waste management authorities, the recycling of paper and cardboard, and incineration with possible energy recovery. Implementation of other directives will also contribute to emission reduction.[161] The End-of-Life Vehicles Directive will for example lead to increased recycling and recovery rates for used cars, and the improved treatment of fluids containing greenhouse gases.[162]

Some Conclusions

The Community is responsible for 16 per cent of the world's energy-related carbon dioxide emissions and yet its population represents just six per cent of global population.[163] The Community's political pledge made in 1992 to stabilise carbon dioxide emissions in 2000 at 1990 levels has been met but largely due to reductions in just two Member States, Germany (due to efficiency increases and the restructuring of the economies in the five "new" Länder since reunification), and the UK (resulting from market liberalisation and the consequent move from the use of coal to gas in electricity production).[164] Despite action to date, the Community is in

---

[159] *Ibid.*, p.115.

[160] OJ 1999 L182/1. This measure is discussed in greater depth in chapter 7.

[161] European Commission, *supra* n.6, p.124.

[162] OJ 2000 L269/34.

[163] See European Commission, "The Energy Dimension of Climate Change" COM (97) 196, at p.3

[164] Sixth Environmental Action Programme, "Environment 2010: Our Future, Our Choice" COM (2001) 31, at p.25.

real danger of failing its Kyoto Protocol emissions reduction commitment. Taking into account existing policies and measures, the Commission indicated in 2001 that emissions by 2010 may fall by just 1.4 per cent at best when compared to the 1990 level.[165] This contrasts poorly with the reduction of eight per cent required under the Kyoto Protocol. The Commission has stressed the importance of adopting effective policies in this area, placing particular emphasis on Member States' responsibilities to develop and implement their own domestic strategies. However, it is clear that a lack of political will to introduce certain measures at a Community level (such as the carbon/energy tax) has certainly undermined progress. Member States have not placed an effective priority on the need to reduce emissions. The Commission has indeed acknowledged that the Community

> *has always been very ambitious in the climate change negotiations. Ambition, however, has to be complemented by concrete action and tangible results. When assessing the current situation, the conclusions are not very positive.*[166]

There is no doubt that, while some encouragement can be taken from some initiatives such as the voluntary agreements with ACEA, JAMA and KAMA, the Community will lose credibility in international negotiations if it fails to meet its own international commitments. In doing so, it would lend support to those states which oppose the Community's international stance and leadership. Decisive action is required both at the Community level and by national governments if such a state of affairs is to be avoided.

The Sixth Environmental Action Programme draws special attention to the issue of climate change by identifying it as one of four priority areas for action.[167] The giving of priority in this way is appropriate bearing in mind that between 1990 and 1998 only three Member States (Germany, Luxembourg and the UK) reduced their greenhouse emissions.[168]

Internationally, the richer developing countries must be encouraged to accept new commitments in the longer term. The European Commission has noted that

> *in view of their huge expected emission increase, participation from developing countries in climate change mitigation is indispensable for any effective action against climate change.*[169]

However the Community remains firm in its belief that the industrialised world must show the lead in reducing emissions.[170] Only then can political pressure be placed

165 *Ibid.* A later Commission projection suggests emissions may have decreased by 4.7 per cent; but the Commission adds a word of caution in noting that "projections are subject to considerable uncertainties"; COM (2002) 702.

166 European Commission, *supra* n.96, p.1.

167 Sixth Environmental Action Programme, *supra* n. 164, at pp.24-29.

168 European Commission, Report under Council Decision 1999/296/EC for a Monitoring Mechanism of Community Greenhouse Gas Emissions [COM (2000) 749], at p.18.

169 European Commission, *supra* n.96, p.19.

170 *Ibid.*

on the more advanced countries in the developing world to take similar steps with financial and technological backing from Annex I States. Pressure must equally be brought to bear on Annex I Parties to take on further emission reduction commitments for the period after 2008-12.

Select Bibliography

Bodansky, "The United Nations Framework Convention on Climate Change: A Commentary" (1993) 18 Yale Journal of International Law, pp.451-558.

Bongaerts, "Carbon Dioxide Emissions and Cars: An Environmental Agreement at EU Level" (1999) 8(4) EELR 101.

European Commission, "Climate Change - Towards an EU Post-Kyoto Strategy" COM(98) 353.

European Commission, "Preparing for Implementation of the Kyoto Protocol" COM (99) 230.

European Commission, "EU Policies and Measures to Reduce Greenhouse Gas Emissions: Towards a European Climate Change Programme" COM(2000) 88.

European Commission, "Communication on the Implementation of the First Phase of the ECCP" COM (2001) 580.

European Commission, "Third Communication from the EC under the UN Framework Convention on Climate Change" SEC (2001) 2053.

French, "1997 Kyoto Protocol to the 1992 UN Framework Convention on Climate Change" (1998) 10(2) JEL 227.

Grubb, Vrolijk and Brack, *The Kyoto Protocol: A Guide and Assessment* (1999).

Haigh, *Manual of Environmental Policy: the EC and Britain* (looseleaf), chapter 14.

Oberthur and Ott, *The Kyoto Protocol: International Climate Policy for the 21st Century* (1999).

Index